THE SECRET LIFE OF PROGRAMS

THE SECRET LIFE OF PROGRAMS

Understand Computers — Craft Better Code

by Jonathan E. Steinhart

no starch press

San Francisco

Printed in USA

First printing

23 22 21 20 19   1 2 3 4 5 6 7 8 9

ISBN-10: 1-59327-970-1
ISBN-13: 978-1-59327-970-7

Publisher: William Pollock
Production Editor: Janelle Ludowise
Cover Illustration: Josh Ellingson
Interior Design: Octopod Studios
Developmental Editors: Corbin Collins and Annie Choi
Technical Reviewer: Aubrey Anderson
Copyeditor: Rachel Monaghan
Compositor: Happenstance Type-O-Rama
Proofreader: Paula L. Fleming
Indexer: JoAnne Burek

The following images are attributed as follows: Composition in Figure 6-36 courtesy of Hanalei Steinhart. Brick wall in Figures 11-3, 11-4, 11-7 and 11-8 from *www.cadhatch.com*. Figure 14-25 from *The Rocky Horror Picture Show* (1975).

For information on distribution, translations, or bulk sales, please contact No Starch Press, Inc. directly:
No Starch Press, Inc.
245 8th Street, San Francisco, CA 94103
phone: 1.415.863.9900; info@nostarch.com
www.nostarch.com

Library of Congress Cataloging-in-Publication Data

```
Names: Steinhart, Jonathan E., author.
Title: The Secret Life of Programs / Jonathan E. Steinhart.
Description: San Francisco : No Starch Press,Inc., [2019]
Identifiers: LCCN 2019018295 (print) | LCCN 2019021631 (ebook) | ISBN
   9781593279714 (epub) | ISBN 159327971X (epub) | ISBN 9781593279707 (print)
   | ISBN 1593279701 (print)
Subjects: LCSH: Computer programming. | Programming languages (Electronic
   computers) | Browsers (Computer programs)
Classification: LCC QA76.6 (ebook) | LCC QA76.6 .S735 2019 (print) | DDC
   005.1--dc23
LC record available at https://lccn.loc.gov/2019018295
```

To Julie and Hanalei for making
me learn how to explain complex
technologies to laypeople.

To the amazing place that was Bell
Telephone Laboratories and all the
people who worked there, especially to
Carl for making a place for me there
when I was a teenager.

About the Author

Jonathan E. Steinhart has been involved in engineering since the 1960s. He started designing hardware in middle school and software in high school, which led to summer jobs at Bell Telephone Laboratories. He received his BSEE in Electrical Engineering and Computer Science from Clarkson University in 1977. After graduation, he worked for Tektronix before trying his hand at startup companies. He became a consultant in 1987, focused on safety-critical systems engineering. He cut back a bit starting in the 1990s to start Four Winds Vineyard.

About the Technical Reviewer

Aubrey Anderson has a BSEE in Electrical Engineering and Computer Science from Tufts University. While there, he was a Teaching Fellow and helped to improve curricula for introductory computer science courses. He started programming at 14 and since then has worked on a variety of robotics, system design, and web programming projects. Aubrey currently works as a Software Engineer at Google.

BRIEF CONTENTS

CONTENTS IN DETAIL

2
COMBINATORIAL LOGIC   33

3
SEQUENTIAL LOGIC   69

15
REAL-WORLD CONSIDERATIONS   413

ACKNOWLEDGMENTS

There are a lot of influences that contributed to making this book possible. That starts with my parents Robert and Rosalyn Steinhart for making me possible and then encouraging my interest in science, at least up to the point at which it started to scare them. Many awesome teachers took it from there including Beatrice Seagal, William Mulvahill, and Miller Bugliari. Much thanks to Paul Rubenfield for telling me about both Civil Defense and the Bell Labs Explorer Scout post.

It's impossible to give enough credit to my Explorer Scout advisors Carl Christiansen and Heinz Lycklama. They changed my life. Through them I met many amazing people at Bell Telephone Laboratories including Joe Condon, Sandy Fraser, Dave Hagelbarger, Dick Hause, Jim Kaiser, Hank McDonald, Max Mathews, Dennis Ritchie, Ken Thompson, and Dave Weller. I learned a lot from each of them.

Thanks to Aubrey Anderson, Clem Cole, Lee Jalovec, A.C. Mendiones, Ed Post, and Betsy Zeller for making it through the whole thing at least once. And especially to Aubrey for technical editing.

Thanks also to Matt Blaze, Adam Cecchetti, Sandy Clark, Tom Duff, Natalie Freed, Frank Heidt, DV Henkel-Wallace (a.k.a Gumby), Lou Katz, Sara-Jaye Terp, Talin, and Paul Vixie for providing feedback on particular chapters.

And thanks to all of the people who answered the phone when I called with general questions including Ward Cunningham, John Gilmore, Evelyn Mast, Mike Perry, Alex Polvi, Alan Wirfs-Brock, and Mike Zuhl. And of course, Rakel Hellberg, the girl on the ski lift, for providing one of the nudges that motivated me finish this project.

This book would not have been possible without the support and encouragement of people in various geek communities including AMW, Hackers, and TUHS.

Thanks to Hanalei Steinhart for the composition in Figure 6-36 and to Julie Donnelly for the scarf in Figure 11-41.

Thanks to Tony Cat for allowing me to use his image and for keeping my keyboard full of fur.

PREFACE

I was born a geek. According to my father, I used an imaginary switch to turn on the swings before using them, and I would turn them off when I was done. Machinery just spoke to me about its inner workings. I resembled C-3PO understanding "the binary language of moisture vaporators." I was fortunate to grow up in a time in which one could examine the workings of most things without a microscope.

In hindsight, I had a very surreal childhood growing up in New Jersey. I tinkered with everything, often to the detriment of my mom's nervous system. My parents gave me lots of "50-in-one" project kits but became uncomfortable when I started hooking them together for projects that weren't in the books. This culminated with the Pillow Burglar Alarm, which caught the tooth fairy in action—a poor economic choice that was nevertheless emotionally satisfying. I collected broken televisions and other appliances that people would leave out on garbage day so that I could take them apart, learn how they worked, and build things out of the parts. One of my favorite toys was my dad's 1929 Erector Set. The space program made it a great time to be interested technology; I remember standing in our front yard with my father one night watching Echo 1 fly over.

Most kids had paper routes; I repaired televisions and stereos. My father worked for IBM, and I occasionally went with him to work and was awed by the big computers. He took me with him to the Electro Show in Atlantic City when I was eight, and I remember playing with an IBM 1620. I also remember being fascinated by the equipment at the Tektronix booth, which may have influenced my later choice to work for them. A year later I went to the World's Fair in New York and was awed by the Bell System exhibit; by chance I later worked with one of its designers.

I received an amazing post-Sputnik public school education, the likes of which no longer exists in America. We passed around the jug of mercury in fifth grade. I blew up the chemistry lab in sixth grade and learned from the experience instead of being locked away. (I can still quote the recipe for making nitrogen triiodide.) I remember my eighth-grade science teacher marching us out of the classroom and taking us into New York City to see the movie *2001: A Space Odyssey* because he thought that it was important. He did this with no parental notes or permissions slips; a teacher who did that today would likely lose their job, or worse. We made gunpowder in high school chemistry, shot rockets at each other on the football field in physics class, lanced our own fingers to do blood typing in biology. A far cry from today when so many millions are drowning in five-gallon buckets that warnings are required, wet floors strike fear into the hearts of man, and government officials are dismissive of science and unable to distinguish tinkering from terrorism.

Outside of school, my parents signed me up for the Boy Scouts, which I loved, and Little League, which I hated. Scouting taught me a lot about the physical world from horseback riding to safely playing with fire to outdoor survival. Little League taught me that I didn't like team sports.

Ham radio was big in those days; it was where tinkering happened. I volunteered for the local Civil Defense emergency radio communications group just so I could play with the equipment. They had a primitive radio-teletype system, which I redesigned and ended up building units for other municipalities. I loved the three-dimensional mechanical contraption that was a Teletype.

When I was in high school, a friend told me about an Explorer Scout post that met every Monday evening at Bell Telephone Laboratories in nearby Murray Hill. I joined and got to play with computers back when they were the size of large houses. I was hooked. It wasn't long before I was leaving school early, hitchhiking up to the Labs, and talking people into letting me in. This turned into a series of amazing summer jobs working with incredible people that changed my life. I learned a lot just by poking my head into people's labs and asking them what they were doing. I ended up writing software for them even though I planned to study electrical engineering, because hardware projects just couldn't be finished in a summer.

I felt that the best way to honor my scout advisors was to follow in their footsteps by trying to help newer generations of budding young technologists along their path once I was in a position to do so. This turned out to be difficult, as the heyday of American research has given way to increasing shareholder value; products themselves are not valued as highly as the profits they generate, which makes research hard to justify. Companies rarely let kids run wild on their premises anymore, for liability reasons. I had originally thought I would work through scouting, but realized I couldn't because scouting had adopted some polices that I couldn't support, as I had never gotten my sexual discrimination merit badge. Instead, I volunteered in my local school system.

I started writing this book to supplement a class that I volunteered to teach. I did this before the internet was as readily accessible as it is today. I currently live in a fairly poor rural farming community, so the original draft of this book tried to be all-inclusive under the assumption that students wouldn't be able to afford supplementary materials. That turned out to be an impossible task.

Lots of material about different programming languages and concepts is now available online, and most people have internet access at home or at their school or library. I've rewritten the material with the expectation that readers can now much more easily find additional information online. So, if something isn't clear or you want more information, look it up.

Recently, a number of students I know have expressed frustration with the way they're being taught programming. Although they can find information online, they keep asking where they can find everything they need in one place. This book is written to be that resource.

I was lucky to grow up contemporaneously with computers. We developed together. I have a hard time imagining what it must be like to jump into the mature field that computing is today without having the background. The most challenging parts of writing this book were deciding how far to reach back into the past for examples and choosing elements of modern technology to discuss. I settled on sort of a retro feel, as one can learn most of what's necessary from older, simpler technology that's easier to understand. Newer, more complex technologies are built using the same building blocks as the older ones; knowing those blocks makes understanding new technologies much easier.

It's a different age now. Gadgets are much harder to take apart, repair, and modify. Companies are abusing laws such as the Digital Millennium Copyright Act (DMCA) to prevent people from repairing devices they own, which is fortunately resulting in "right to repair" laws in some places. As Americans, we get mixed messages from our government; on the one hand we're encouraged to go into STEM careers, while on the other hand we see science denigrated and STEM jobs outsourced. It's not clear that the US would have ever become a technology powerhouse if this environment had existed a half-century ago.

Then again, there are bright spots. Maker spaces are proliferating. Some kids are being allowed to build things and are discovering that it's fun. Electronic parts are cheaper than they've ever been, as long as you don't want ones with wires on them. Smartphones have more processing power than all the computers in the world combined when I was a kid. Computers are cheaper than anybody ever imagined; small computers such as the Raspberry Pi and Arduino cost less than a pizza and have a huge variety of available toppings.

With such power available, it's tempting to just play with the high-level functionality. It's like playing with LEGO. My parents gave me one of the first LEGO sets made; it pretty much just had rectangular blocks. But I had my imagination and I could build anything I wanted. Today, you can get a *Star Wars* LEGO set and deploy a prefabricated Yoda. It's much harder to invent new characters. The fancy pieces hamper the imagination.

There's a great scene in the classic 1939 movie *The Wizard of Oz* in which the wizard is exposed and bellows, "Pay no attention to that man behind the curtain." This book is for those of you who aren't going to listen to that and want to know what's behind the curtain. My intent is to shine light on the fundamental building blocks on which high-level functionality is built. This book is for those whose imagination isn't satisfied by high-level functionality alone; it's for those who are drawn to creating *new* high-level functionality. If you're interested in becoming a wizard in addition to being a mere wielder of magic items, then this book is for you.

INTRODUCTION

A few years ago, I was riding on a ski lift with our Swedish exchange student. I asked her if she had thought about what she was going to do after high school. She said that she was considering engineering and had taken a programming class the previous year. I asked her what they taught. She replied, "Java." I instinctively responded with "That's too bad."

Why did I say that? Took me a while to figure it out. It's not that Java is a bad programming language; it's actually pretty decent. I said it because of the way in which Java (and other languages) are typically used to teach programming today—*without teaching anything about computers*. If this strikes you as a bit odd, then this book is for you.

The Java programming language was invented by James Gosling, Mike Sheridan, and Patrick Naughton in the 1990s at Sun Microsystems. It was modeled in part after the C programming language, which was widely used at the time. C doesn't include automatic management of memory, and memory management errors were a common headache at the time. Java eliminated that class of programming errors by design; it hid the underlying memory management from the programmer. That's part of what makes it such a good programming language for beginners. But it takes much more than a good programming language to produce good programmers and programs. And it turned out that Java introduced a whole new class of harder-to-debug programming problems, including poor performance resulting from the hidden memory management system.

As you'll see in this book, understanding memory is a key skill for programmers. When you're learning to program, it's easy to develop habits that become hard to break. Studies have shown that children who grew up playing at so-called "safe" playgrounds have a higher rate of injuries later in life than those who didn't, presumably because they didn't learn that falling hurts. Programming is an analogous situation. Safe programming environments make getting started less scary, but you also need to prepare for the outside world. This book helps you make that transition.

Why Good Programming is Important

To understand why it's problematic to teach computer programming without also teaching about computers, first consider how ubiquitous computers have become. The price of computers has fallen so dramatically that using them is now the cheapest way to build many things. For example, using a computer to display an image of an old-fashioned analog clock on a car dashboard costs much less than a mechanical clock. This is a result of how computer chips are manufactured; they're more or less printed. It's no longer a big deal to stamp out a chip that contains billions of components. Note that I'm talking about the price of computers themselves, not the price of things that contain computers. In general, a computer chip today costs less than the packaging in which it's shipped. Computer chips are available that cost pennies. There will likely come a time when it will be difficult to find anything that doesn't contain a computer.

Lots of computers doing lots of things means lots of computer programs. Because computers are so ubiquitous, the field of computer programming is incredibly diverse. As in medicine, many programmers become specialists. You can specialize in areas such as vision, animation, web pages, phone apps, industrial control, medical devices, and more.

But the strange thing about computer programming is that unlike in medicine, in programming you can become a specialist without ever being a generalist. You probably wouldn't want a heart surgeon who never learned anatomy, but the equivalent has become normal for many programmers today. Is this really a problem? In fact, there's plenty of evidence that this isn't working very well, with almost daily reports of security breaches and product recalls. There have been court cases in which people convicted of drunk driving by breathalyzer have won the right to have the breathalyzer code reviewed. It turned out that the code was full of bugs, which resulted in overturned convictions. Recently, a piece of antivirus software crashed a piece of medical equipment in the middle of a heart surgery. Lives were lost due to design issues in the Boeing 737 MAX airplane. The large number of incidents like these don't inspire a lot of confidence.

Learning to Code is Only a Starting Place

Part of the reason for this state of affairs is that it's not all that difficult to write computer programs that *appear* to work, or work much of the time. Let's use the changes in music (not disco!) in the 1980s as an analogy. People used to have to develop a foundation in order to make music. This included learning music theory, composition, and how to play an instrument; ear training; and lots of practicing. Then the Musical Instrument Digital Interface (MIDI) standard, originally proposed by Ikutaro Kakehashi of Roland, came along, which let anyone make "music" from their computer without ever having to develop calluses. It's my opinion that only a small percentage of computer-generated "music" is actually music; it's mostly noise. *Music* is produced by actual musicians—who may or may not use MIDI to build on their foundation. Programming these days has become a lot like using MIDI. You no longer have to sweat much or spend years practicing or even learn theory in order to write programs. But that doesn't mean these are good or reliable programs.

This situation is likely to get worse, at least in the United States. Wealthy people with vested interests, like those who own software companies, have been lobbying for legislation mandating that everybody learn to code in school. This sounds great in theory, but it's not a great idea in practice because not everybody has the aptitude to become a good programmer. We don't mandate that everybody learn to play football because we know that it's not for everybody. The likely goal of this initiative is not to produce great programmers but rather to increase software company profits by flooding the market with large numbers of poor programmers, which will drive down wages. The people behind this push don't care very much about code quality—they also push for legislation that limits their liability for defective products. Of course, you can program for fun just like you can play football for fun. Just don't expect to be drafted for the Super Bowl.

In 2014, President Obama said that he had learned to code. He did drag a few things around in the excellent visual programming tool Blockly, and he even typed in one line of code in JavaScript (a programming language unrelated to Java, which was invented at Netscape, the predecessor to the Mozilla Foundation that maintains numerous software packages, including the *Firefox* web browser.) Now, do you think that he actually learned to code? Here's a hint: if you do, you should probably work on honing your critical thinking skills in addition to reading this book. Sure, he may have learned a teensy bit about programming, but *no, he didn't learn to code*. If he could learn to code in an hour, then it follows that coding is so trivial that there wouldn't be a need to teach it in schools.

Importance of Low-Level Knowledge

An interesting and somewhat contrary view about how to teach programming was expressed in a blog post titled "How to Teach Computational Thinking" by Stephen Wolfram, the creator of Mathematica and the Wolfram language. Wolfram defines computational thinking as "formulating things with enough clarity, and in a systematic enough way, that one can tell a computer how to do them." I completely agree with this definition. In fact, it's in large part my motivation for writing this book.

But I strongly disagree with Wolfram's position that those learning to program should develop computational thinking skills using powerful high-level tools, such as those that he's developed, instead of learning the underlying foundational technologies. For example, it's clear from the rising interest in statistics over calculus that "data wrangling" is a growing field. But what happens when people just feed giant piles of data into fancy programs that those same people don't intimately understand?

One possibility is that they generate interesting-looking but meaningless or incorrect results. For example, a recent study ("Gene Name Errors Are Widespread in the Scientific Literature" by Mark Ziemann, Yotam Eren, and Assam El-Osta) showed that one-fifth of published genetics papers have errors due to improper spreadsheet usage. Just think of the kinds of errors and ramifications that more powerful tools in the hands of more people could produce! Getting it right is crucial when people's lives are affected.

Understanding underlying technologies helps you develop a sense of what can go wrong. Knowing just high-level tools makes it easy to ask the wrong questions. It's worth learning to use a hammer before graduating to a nail gun. Another reason for learning underlying systems and tools is that it gives you the power to build new tools, which is important because there will always be a need for tool builders, even if tool users are more common. Learning about computers so that the behavior of programs isn't a mystery enables you to craft better code.

Who Should Read This Book?

This book is for people who want to become good programmers. What makes a good programmer? First and foremost, a good programmer has good critical thinking and analysis skills. To solve complex problems, a programmer needs the ability to evaluate whether or not programs actually solve the right problem correctly. This is more difficult than it sounds. It's not uncommon for an experienced programmer to look at someone else's program and snarkily comment, "Why, that's a complex nonsolution to a simple nonproblem."

You may be familiar with a classic fantasy trope of wizards acquiring power over things by learning their true names. And woe be to the wizard who forgets a detail. Good programmers are like these wizards who can hold the essence of things in their minds without dropping details.

Good programmers also have some degree of artistry, like skilled craftspeople. It's not uncommon to find code that is completely incomprehensible, just like many English speakers are baffled by James Joyce's novel *Finnegans Wake*. Good programmers write code that not only works but is also easy for others to understand and maintain.

Finally, good programmers need a deep understanding of how computers work. You can't solve complex problems well using a shallow base of knowledge. This book is for people who are learning programming but are unsatisfied with the lack of depth. It's also for people who are already programming but want more.

What Are Computers?

A common answer is that computers are appliances that people use for tasks such as checking email, shopping online, writing papers, organizing photos, and playing games. This definition is partly the result of sloppy terminology that became commonplace as consumer products began to incorporate computers. Another common answer is that computers are the brains that make our high-tech toys, such as cell phones and music players, work. This is closer to the mark.

Sending email and playing games are made possible by programs running on computers. The computer itself is like a newborn baby. It doesn't really know how to do much. We hardly ever think about the basic machinery of human beings, because we mostly interact with the personalities that are running on that basic machinery, just like programs running on computers. For example, when you're on a web page, you're not reading it using just the computer itself; you're reading it using programs someone else wrote that are running on your computer, the computer hosting the web page, and all of the computers in between that make the internet function.

What Is Computer Programming?

Teachers are people who train the basic human machinery to perform certain tasks. Similarly, programming is about becoming a teacher of computers. Programmers teach computers to do what the programmers want them to do.

Knowing how to teach computers is useful, especially when you want a computer to do something that it doesn't know how to do and you can't just go buy a program for it because nobody has created one yet. For example, you probably take the World Wide Web for granted, but it was invented not long ago, when Sir Tim Berners-Lee needed a better way for scientists at the European Organization for Nuclear Research (Conseil Européen pour la Recherche Nucléaire, or CERN) to share information. And he got knighted for it. How cool is that?

Teaching computers is complicated, but it's easier than teaching people. We know a lot more about how computers work. And computers are a lot less likely to throw up on you.

Computer programming is a two-step process:

1. Understand the universe.
2. Explain it to a three-year-old.

What does this mean? Well, you can't write computer programs to do things that you yourself don't understand. For example, you can't write a spellchecker if you don't know the rules for spelling, and you can't write a good action video game if you don't know physics. So, the first step in becoming a good computer programmer is to learn as much as you can about everything else. Solutions to problems often come from unexpected places, so don't ignore something just because it doesn't seem immediately relevant.

The second step of the process requires explaining what you know to a machine that has a very rigid view of the world, like young children do. This rigidity in children is really obvious when they're about three years old. Let's say you're trying to get out the door. You ask your child, "Where are your shoes?" The response: "There." She *did* answer your question. The problem is, she doesn't understand that you're really asking her to put her shoes on so that you both can go somewhere. Flexibility and the ability to make inferences are skills that children learn as they grow up. But computers are like Peter Pan: they never grow up.

Computers are also like young children in that they don't know how to generalize. They're still useful because once you figure out how to explain something to them, they're very fast and tireless about doing it, though they don't have any common sense. A computer will tirelessly do what you ask without evaluating whether it's the wrong task, much like the enchanted broomsticks in "The Sorcerer's Apprentice" segment of the 1940 movie *Fantasia*. Asking a computer to do something is like asking the genie from a magic lantern (not the FBI version) to grant a wish. You have to be really careful how you phrase it!

You may doubt what I'm saying here because computers seem more capable than they are. When you use a computer, for example, it knows how to draw pictures, correct your spelling, understand what you're saying, play music, and so on. But keep in mind, that's not the computer—it's a complicated set of computer programs that someone else wrote that allows the computer to do all of those tasks. Computers are separate from the programs that run on them.

It's like watching a car on the road. It seems pretty good at stopping and starting at the right times, avoiding obstacles, getting where it's going, eating when it gets hungry, and so on. But it's not just the car. It's the car and the driver packaged together. Computers are like the cars, and programs are like the drivers. Without knowledge, you can't tell what's done by the car and what's done by the driver. (See "Southbound on the Freeway" by May Swenson. You might change your answer to the question posed at the end of the poem during your lifetime.)

In sum, computer programming involves learning what you need to know to solve a problem and then explaining it to a young child. Because there are lots of ways to solve a problem, programming is just as much an art as it is a science. It involves finding elegant solutions as opposed to using brute force. Yes, you *can* get out of a house by bashing a hole in the wall, but it's probably a lot easier to go out the door. Many can write something like *HealthCare.gov* in millions of lines of code, but it takes skill to do it in thousands of lines.

Before you can instruct a three-year-old, though, you need to learn about three-year-olds and what they understand. And this isn't any ordinary three-year-old—it's an alien life form. A computer doesn't play by the same rules that we do. You may have heard of artificial intelligence (AI), which tries to get computers to act more like people. Progress in that field has moved much slower than originally anticipated. That's mainly because we don't really understand the problem; we don't know enough about how humans think. As you can imagine, it's pretty hard to teach an alien to think as we do when we ourselves don't know how exactly it's done.

The human brain lets you do things without consciously thinking about them. Your brain started out as just a piece of hardware, which then got programmed. For example, you learned to move your fingers and then you learned to grab things. After practice, you can just grab things without thinking about all the steps that make it possible. Philosophers such as Jean Piaget (French psychologist, 1898–1980) and Noam Chomsky (American linguist born in 1928) have developed different theories about how this process of learning works. Is the brain just a general piece of equipment, or does it have special hardware for functions like language? This issue is still being studied.

Our incredible ability to perform tasks unconsciously makes learning how to program difficult, because programming requires breaking down tasks into smaller steps that a computer can follow. For example, you probably know how to play tic-tac-toe. Get a group of people together and have each of you independently list the steps a player should take in order to make a good move for any configuration of the board. (I'm sure you can find this online, but don't look it up.) After everybody has made their lists, hold a playoff. Find out whose rules rule! How good were your rules? What sort of things did you miss? Do you actually know what you're doing when you play the game? Chances are, there were a number of factors that you didn't think to spell out because you understand them intuitively.

In case it's not obvious, the first step, understanding the universe, is much more important than the second, explaining it to a three-year-old. Think about it: what good is it to know how to talk if you don't know what to say? Despite this, current education focuses on the second step. This is because it's much easier to teach and grade the mechanical aspects of the task than the creative elements. And in general, teachers have little training in the field and are working from curricula developed elsewhere that they were given to use. This book, however, focuses on the first step. While it can't cover the universe in general, it examines problems and their solutions in the computer universe instead of dwelling on the exact programming syntax needed to implement those solutions.

Coding, Programming, Engineering, and Computer Science

A number of different terms are used to describe working with software. These terms have no exact definitions, although they have acquired some rough meanings.

Coding, a fairly recent term popularized as part of "learning to code," can be viewed as the somewhat mechanical work of translation. Let's compare it to the job of medical coding. When you visit a doctor, getting a diagnosis is the easy part. The hard part is translating that diagnosis into one of the over 100,000 codes in the ICD standards, ICD-10 at the time of writing. A Certified Professional Coder who has learned these codes knows that, when a doctor comes up with a diagnosis of "struck by cow," it should be assigned code W55.2XA. This is actually harder than many coding jobs in the programming space due to the sheer number of codes. But the process is similar to what a coder would do if directed to "make that text bold" on a web page; a coder knows which code to use to make that happen.

The ICD-10 standard is so complicated that few coders know it all. Instead, medical coders get certified in specialty areas such as "Diseases of the nervous system" or "Mental and behavioral disorders." This is analogous to a coder being proficient in a language such as HTML or JavaScript.

But *programming*—that is, being a programmer—means knowing more than a specialty area or two. The doctor in this scenario is analogous to a programmer. The doctor determines a diagnosis by evaluating the patient. This can be pretty complex. For example, if a patient has burns and is soaking wet, is it a "bizarre personal appearance" (R46.1) or a "burn due to water skis on fire, initial encounter" (V91.07XA)? Once the doctor has a diagnosis, a treatment plan can be devised. The treatment plan must be effective; the doctor probably doesn't want to see the same patient suffering from a bad case of "parental overprotection" (Z62.1).

Just like the doctor, a programmer evaluates a problem and determines a solution. For example, maybe there's a need for a website that allows people to rank ICD-10 codes in terms of silliness. A programmer would determine the best algorithms for storing and manipulating the data, the structure of the communication between the web client and server, the user interface, and so on. It's not a simple "plug in the code" sort of thing.

Engineering is the next step up in complexity. In general, engineering is the art of taking knowledge and using it to accomplish something. You could consider the creation of the ICD standards to be engineering; it took the large field of medical diagnoses and reduced them to a set of codes that could be more easily tracked and analyzed than doctor's notes. It's a matter of opinion as to whether or not such a complex system represents *good* engineering. As an example of computer engineering, many years ago I worked on a project to build a low-cost medical monitor such as those that you see in hospitals. The charge I was given was to make a system that a doctor or nurse could figure out how to use in less than 5 minutes without any documentation. As you might imagine, this required much more than just knowledge of programming. And I beat the goal—my solution ended up taking about 30 seconds to learn to use.

Programming is often confused with computer science. While many computer scientists program, most programmers aren't computer scientists. *Computer science* is the study of computing. Computer science discoveries are used by engineers and programmers.

Coding, programming, engineering, and computer science are independent but related disciplines that differ in the type and amount of knowledge required. Being a computer scientist, engineer, or coder doesn't automatically make someone a good programmer. While this book gives you a taste of how engineers and computer scientists think, it's not going to make you one; that typically requires a college education combined with some hard-earned relevant experience. Engineering and programming are similar to music or painting—they're part skill and part art. The exposition of both aspects in this book should help you to improve your skills as a programmer.

The Landscape

Computer design and programming is a huge field of study, which I won't be able to cover here. You can visualize it in layers, as shown in Figure 1.

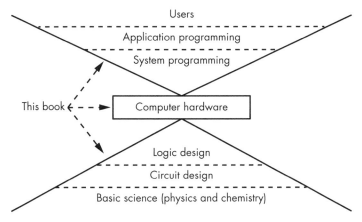

Figure 1: Computer landscape

Keep in mind that Figure 1 is a simplification and that the lines dividing the various layers are not as clean in reality.

The majority of people are *users* of computer systems. You're probably in that camp right now. There are specialized sorts of users called *system administrators* whose job is to keep computer systems working. They install software, manage user accounts, do backups, and so on. They typically have special powers not granted to normal users.

The people who write programs like web pages, phone apps, and music players are called *application programmers*. They write the software that users use to interact with the computers, using blocks that others have created. Application programming is being taught in most "learn to code" classes as if all programmers have to learn is how to import these other blocks and glue them together. Although you can get away with that a lot of the time, it's much better to actually understand both those blocks and the glue.

Application programs don't talk to the computer hardware directly; that's where *system programming* comes into play. System programmers make the building blocks used by application programmers. System programmers need to know about hardware because their code interacts with it. One of the goals of this book is to teach you things you need to know in order to be a good system programmer.

Computer hardware includes not only the part that does the actual computing but also how that part connects to the world outside. Computer hardware is expressed as *logic*. It's the same logic used to write computer programs, and it's key to understanding the workings of the computer. The logic is constructed from various types of electronic *circuits*. Circuit design is beyond the scope of this book, but you can learn more about it by studying electrical engineering. Consider a double major in electrical engineering and computer science if you want to rule the world.

Of course, basic science underpins it all, providing everything from our understanding of electricity to the chemistry needed to create chips.

As shown in Figure 1, each level builds on the one beneath it. This means that poor design choices or errors at lower levels affect everything above. For example, a design error in Intel Pentium processors circa 1994 caused some division operations to produce incorrect results. This affected all software that used floating-point division in these processors.

As you can see, system programming is at the bottom of the software hierarchy. It's similar to infrastructure, like roads, electricity, and water. Being a good programmer always matters, but it matters more if you're a system programmer, because others rely on your infrastructure. You can also see that system programming is sandwiched between application programming and computer hardware, which means you need to learn something about both of those. The Sanskrit word *yoga* translates to "union," and just as yoga practitioners seek to unify their mind and body, system programmers are techno-yogis who unify the hardware and software.

You don't have to learn system programming in order to work at one of the other levels. But if you don't, you'll have to find someone else to help you deal with issues out of your domain rather than being able to figure them out for yourself. An understanding of the core technology also leads to better solutions at higher levels. This isn't just my opinion; check out the 2014 blog post "The Resource Leak Bug of Our Civilization" by Ville-Matias Heikkilä for a similar view.

This book also aims to cover a lot of retro history. Most programmers aren't learning the history of their craft because there is so much material to cover. The result is that a lot of people are making mistakes that have already been made. Knowing some of the history allows you to at least make new and better mistakes rather than repeat past ones. Bear in mind that the hot new technology you're using today will quickly become retro tomorrow.

Speaking of history, this book is jam-packed with interesting technologies and the names of their inventors. Take some time to learn more about both the technologies and the people. Most of the people mentioned solved at least one interesting problem, and it's worth learning about how they perceived their world and the way in which they approached and solved problems. There's a great exchange in Neal Stephenson's 2008 novel *Anathem*:

> "Our opponent is an alien starship packed with atomic bombs. We have a protractor."
>
> "Okay, I'll go home and see if I can scrounge up a ruler and a piece of string."

Note the reliance on fundamentals. It's not "Let's look up what to do on Wikipedia" or "I'll post a question on Stack Overflow" or "I'll find some package on GitHub." Learning to solve problems that nobody else has solved is a crucial skill.

Many of the examples in this book are based on old technology such as 16-bit computers. That's because you can learn almost everything you need to know from them and they're easier to fit on a page.

What's in This Book

The book is conceptually divided into three parts. The first part explores computer hardware, both what it is and how it's built. The second part examines the behavior of software running on hardware. The last part covers the art of programming—working with others to produce good programs.

Chapter 1: The Internal Language of Computers
This chapter starts exploring the three-year-old mentality. Computers are bit players; they herd bits for a living. You'll learn what they are and what can be done with them. We'll play make-believe to ascribe meaning to bits and to collections of bits.

Chapter 2: Combinatorial Logic
This chapter examines the rationale for using bits instead of digits and explores the justification for digital computers. This includes a discussion of some of the older technologies that paved the way for what we have today. It covers the basics of combinatorial logic. You'll learn how to build more complicated functionality from bits and logic.

Chapter 3: Sequential Logic
Here you'll learn how to use logic to build memory. This includes learning how to generate time, because memory is nothing but state that persists over time. This chapter covers the basics of sequential logic and discusses various memory technologies.

Chapter 4: Computer Anatomy
This chapter shows how computers are constructed from the logic and memory elements discussed in the earlier chapters. A number of different implementation methodologies are examined.

Chapter 5: Computer Architecture

In this chapter, we'll explore some of the add-ons to the basic computer that we saw in Chapter 4. You'll learn how they provide essential functionality and efficiency.

Chapter 6: Communications Breakdown

Computers need to interact with the outside world. This chapter covers input and output. It also revisits the difference between digital and analog and how we get digital computers to work in an analog world.

Chapter 7: Organizing Data

Now that you've seen how computers work, we'll look at how to use them effectively. Computer programs manipulate data in memory, and it's important to map the way memory is used to the problem being solved.

Chapter 8: Language Processing

Languages have been invented to make programming computers easier for people. This chapter looks at the process of converting languages into something that actually runs on computers.

Chapter 9: The Web Browser

A lot of programming is done for web browsers. This chapter looks at how a web browser works and teases out its main components.

Chapter 10: Application and System Programming

In this chapter, we'll write two versions of a program that runs at two of the different levels from Figure 1. The chapter exposes many of the differences between application- and system-level programming.

Chapter 11: Shortcuts and Approximations

Making programs efficient is important. This chapter explores some of the ways in which we can make programs more efficient by having them avoid unnecessary work.

Chapter 12: Deadlocks and Race Conditions

Many systems include more than one computer. This chapter examines some of the problems that can occur when we're trying to get computers to cooperate.

Chapter 13: Security

Computer security is an advanced topic. This chapter covers the basics while punting on the heavy math.

Chapter 14: Machine Intelligence

This chapter also covers an advanced topic. New applications result from the combination of big data, artificial intelligence, and machine learning—from driving your car to driving you nuts with advertisements.

Chapter 15: Real-World Considerations

Programming is a very methodical and logical process. But humans are involved in the determination of what and how to program, and humans are often lacking in logic. This chapter discusses some of the issues of programming in the real world.

When reading this book, bear in mind that many of the explanations are simplified and therefore not correct down to the smallest detail. Making the explanations perfect would require too much distracting detail. Don't be surprised if you discover this as you learn more. You can consider this book to be a glossy travel brochure for a trip to computer-land. It can't cover everything in detail, and when you go visit, you'll find plenty of subtle differences.

1

THE INTERNAL LANGUAGE
OF COMPUTERS

The whole point of language is to be able to communicate information. Your job as a programmer is to give instructions to computers. They don't understand our language, so you have to learn theirs.

Human language is the product of thousands of years of evolution. We don't know a lot about how it evolved, since early language development wasn't advanced to the point that history could be recorded. (Apparently nobody wrote ballads about language development.) Computer languages are a different story, as they're a fairly recent invention that occurred long after the development of human language, which enables us to write about them.

Human and computer languages share many of the same elements, such as written symbols and rules for their proper arrangement and usage. One thing that they don't share is nonwritten language forms; computers have written language only.

In this chapter, you'll start to learn the language of computers. This process happens in stages just like with human language. We have to start with letters before building up to words and sentences. Fortunately, computer languages are much simpler than their human counterparts.

What Is Language?

Language is a convenient shortcut. It allows us to communicate complex concepts without having to demonstrate them. It also allows concepts to be conveyed at a distance, even via intermediaries.

Every language—whether written, spoken, or expressed in a series of gestures or by banging two rocks together—is meaning *encoded* as a set of symbols. Encoding meaning as symbols isn't enough, though. Language only works if all communicating parties have the same *context*, so they can assign the same meaning to the same symbols. For example, the word *Toto* might suggest the dog from *The Wizard of Oz* to many people, while others might think of the Japanese manufacturer of heated toilet seats. I recently encountered much confusion while discussing clothing with my French exchange student. It turns out that the common interpretation of the word *camisole* in America is undershirt, but in France it's straitjacket! In both of these examples, the same symbols can be distinguished only by context, and that context is not always readily discernible. Computer languages have this issue too.

Written Language

Written language is a sequence of symbols. We form words by placing symbols in a particular order. For example, in English we can form the word *yum* by placing three symbols (that is, letters) in order from left to right as follows: *y u m.*

There are many possible symbols and combinations. There are 26 basic symbols (A–Z) in English—if we ignore things like upper- and lowercase, punctuation, ligatures, and so on—which native English speakers learn as toddlers. Other languages have different types and numbers of symbols. Some languages, such as Chinese and Japanese as written in kanji, have a very large number of symbols where each symbol is a word unto itself.

Languages also use different ordering, such as reading right to left in Hebrew and vertically in Chinese. Symbol order is important: *d o g* is not the same as *g o d.*

Although style can in some ways be considered a language unto itself, we don't distinguish symbols based on typeface: a, *a*, and **a** are all the same symbol.

Three components frame the technology of written language, including computer language:

- The containers that hold symbols
- The symbols that are allowed in the containers
- The ordering of the containers

Some languages include more complicated rules that constrain the permitted symbols in containers based on the symbols in other containers. For example, some symbols can't occupy adjacent containers.

The Bit

We'll begin with the container. This might be called a *character* in a human language and a *bit* for computers. The term *bit* is an awkward marriage between *binary* and *digit*. It's awkward because *binary* is a word for something with two parts, whereas *digit* is a word for one of the 10 symbols (0–9) that make up our everyday number system. You'll learn why we use bits in the next chapter; for now, it's enough to know that they're cheap and easy to build.

A bit is binary, which means a bit container can hold only one of two symbols, kind of like the dot and dash from Morse code. Morse code uses just two symbols to represent complex information by stringing those symbols together in different combinations. The letter *A* is dot-dash, for example. *B* is dash-dot-dot-dot, *C* is dash-dot-dash-dot, and so on. The order of the symbols is important just like in a human language: dash-dot means *N*, not *A*.

The concept of symbols is abstract. It really doesn't matter what they stand for; they could be off and on, day and night, or duck and goose. But remember, language doesn't work without context. Things would get weird fast if a sender thought they were saying *U* (dot-dot-dash), but the recipient heard *duck-duck-goose*.

In the remainder of this chapter, you'll learn about some of the common ways in which meaning is assigned to bits for computing. Keep in mind that there is a lot of make-believe involved—for example, you may run into things like, "Let's pretend that this bit means blue." Programming actually works that way, so even though you'll be learning some standard bit uses, don't be afraid to invent your own when appropriate.

Logic Operations

One use of bits is to represent the answers to yes/no questions such as "Is it cold?" or "Do you like my hat?" We use the terms *true* for yes and *false* for no. Questions like "Where's the dog party?" don't have a yes/no answer and can't be represented by a single bit.

In human language, we often combine several yes/no clauses into a single sentence. We might say, "Wear a coat if it is cold or if it is raining" or "Go skiing if it is snowing and it's not a school day." Another way of saying those things might be "Wear coat is true if cold is true or raining is true" and "Skiing is true if snowing is true and school day is not true." These are *logic operations* that each produce a new bit based on the contents of other bits.

Boolean Algebra

Just as algebra is a set of rules for operating on numbers, *Boolean algebra*, invented in the 1800s by English mathematician George Boole, is a set of rules that we use to operate on bits. As with regular algebra, the associative, commutative, and distributive rules also apply.

There are three basic Boolean operations, *NOT*, *AND*, and *OR*, as well as one composite operation, *XOR* (short for "exclusive-or"), as described here:

NOT This operation means "the opposite." For example, if a bit is false, *NOT* that bit would be true. If a bit is true, *NOT* that bit would be false.

AND This operation involves 2 or more bits. In a 2-bit operation, the result is true only if both the first *AND* second bit are true. When more than 2 bits are involved, the result is true only if *all* bits are true.

OR This operation also involves 2 or more bits. In a 2-bit operation, the result is true if the first *OR* second bit is true; otherwise, the result is false. With more than 2 bits, the result is true if any bit is true.

XOR The result of an *exclusive-or* operation is true if the first and second bits have different values. It's either but not both. Because "exclusive-or" is a mouthful, we often use the abbreviation XOR (pronounced "ex-or").

Figure 1-1 summarizes these Boolean operations graphically in what are known as *truth tables*. The *inputs* are outside of the boxes and the *outputs* are inside. In these tables, T stands for True and F stands for False.

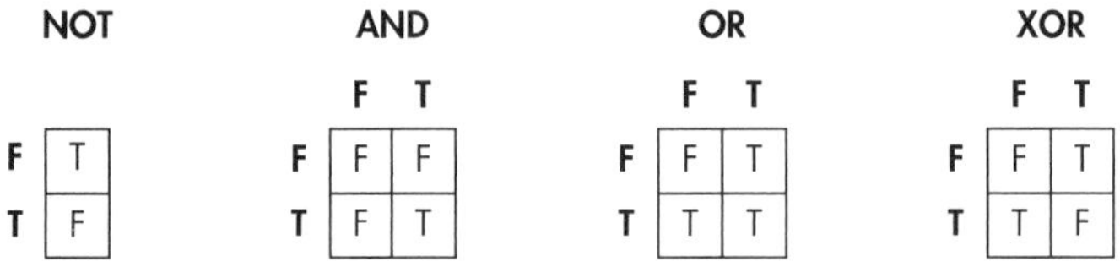

NOT			AND				OR				XOR		
				F	T			F	T			F	T
F	T		F	F	F		F	F	T		F	F	T
T	F		T	F	T		T	T	T		T	T	F

Figure 1-1: Truth tables for Boolean operations

Figure 1-2 shows how this works for the NOT and AND operations. We can find the output by tracing a path from the input or inputs.

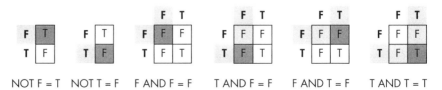

NOT F = T   NOT T = F   F AND F = F   T AND F = F   F AND T = F   T AND T = T

Figure 1-2: Using truth tables

As you can see, the NOT operation simply reverses the state of the input. On the other hand, the AND operation returns true only when both inputs are true.

The XOR operation is built from other operations. For example, the XOR of 2 bits, a and b, *is the same thing as* (a OR b) AND NOT (a AND b). *This shows that basic Boolean operations can be combined in different ways to yield the same result.*

De Morgan's Law

In the 1800s, British mathematician Augustus De Morgan added a law that applies only to Boolean algebra, the eponymous *De Morgan's law*. This law states that the operation *a AND b* is equivalent to the operation *NOT(NOT a OR NOT b)*, as shown in Figure 1-3.

a	b	a AND b	NOT a	NOT b	NOT a OR NOT b	NOT (NOT a OR NOT b)
F	F	F	T	T	T	F
F	T	F	T	F	T	F
T	F	F	F	T	T	F
T	T	T	F	F	F	T

Figure 1-3: The truth table for De Morgan's law

Notice that the results of *a AND b* in the second column are identical to the results listed in the final *NOT(NOT a OR NOT b)* column. This means that with enough NOT operations, we can replace AND operations with OR operations (and vice versa). This is useful because computers operate on real-world input that's not under their control. While it would be nice if inputs were of the form *cold* or *raining*, they're often *NOT cold* or *NOT raining*. Similar to double negatives in languages such as English ("We didn't not go skiing"), De Morgan's law is a tool that lets us operate on these *negative logic* propositions in addition to the *positive logic* that we've already seen. Figure 1-4 illustrates the coat-wearing decision for both positive and negative logic forms.

cold	raining	wear-coat	not-cold	not-raining	not-wear-coat
F	F	F	F	F	F
F	T	T	F	T	F
T	F	T	T	F	F
T	T	T	T	T	T

Figure 1-4: Positive and negative logic

On the left (positive logic) side, we can make our decision using a single OR operation. On the right (negative logic) side, De Morgan's law allows us to make our decision using a single AND operation. Without De Morgan's law, we'd have to implement the negative logic case as *NOT*

not-cold *OR NOT* not-raining. Although that works, there is a cost in price and performance to each operation, so minimizing operations minimizes costs. The hardware that performs the NOT operation costs real money and, as you'll learn in the next chapter, cascading operations slows things down.

De Morgan tells us that this is equivalent to "cold and raining," which is much simpler.

Representing Integers Using Bits

Let's move up the food chain and learn how to use bits to represent numbers. Numbers are more complicated than logic but much simpler than words.

Representing Positive Numbers

We commonly use the *decimal* number system because it corresponds to our anatomy. Ten different symbols called *digits* can go into the containers: 0123456789. Containers are stacked right to left. Each container has a name that is separate from its contents; we call the rightmost container the ones, next is the tens, then the hundreds, thousands, and so on. These names are aliases for powers of 10; 10^0 is one, 10^1 is ten, 10^2 is one hundred, 10^3 is one thousand. This system is called *base-10* since 10 is the base holding up the exponents. The value of a number is derived from the sum of the product of each container value and the value of its contents. For example, the number 5,028 is the sum of 5 thousands, 0 hundreds, 2 tens, and 8 ones, or $5 \times 10^3 + 0 \times 10^2 + 2 \times 10^1 + 8 \times 10^0$, as shown in Figure 1-5.

10^3	10^2	10^1	10^0
5	0	2	8

Figure 1-5: The number 5,028 in decimal notation

We can use a similar approach to make numbers using bits. Since we're using bits instead of digits, we only have two symbols: 0 and 1. But that's not a problem. In decimal, we add a container whenever we run out of room; we can fit a 9 in a single container but need two containers for 10. That works in binary too; we just need a new container for anything greater than a 1. The rightmost container would still be the ones, but what's the next one? It's the *twos*. The value of a container in decimal where there are 10 symbols is 10 times that of the one on the right. Thus, in binary where there are two symbols, the container value is two times that of the one on the right. That's all there is to it! The container values are powers of 2, which means it's a *base-2* system instead of base-10.

Table 1-1 lists some of the powers of 2. We can use it as a reference to understand the binary representation of the number 5,028.

Table 1-1: Powers of 2

Expansion	Power	Decimal
$2 \div 2$	2^0	1
2	2^1	2
2×2	2^2	4
$2 \times 2 \times 2$	2^3	8
$2 \times 2 \times 2 \times 2$	2^4	16
$2 \times 2 \times 2 \times 2 \times 2$	2^5	32
$2 \times 2 \times 2 \times 2 \times 2 \times 2$	2^6	64
$2 \times 2 \times 2 \times 2 \times 2 \times 2 \times 2$	2^7	128
$2 \times 2 \times 2 \times 2 \times 2 \times 2 \times 2 \times 2$	2^8	256
$2 \times 2 \times 2 \times 2 \times 2 \times 2 \times 2 \times 2 \times 2$	2^9	512
$2 \times 2 \times 2 \times 2 \times 2 \times 2 \times 2 \times 2 \times 2 \times 2$	2^{10}	1,024
$2 \times 2 \times 2 \times 2 \times 2 \times 2 \times 2 \times 2 \times 2 \times 2 \times 2$	2^{11}	2,048
$2 \times 2 \times 2 \times 2 \times 2 \times 2 \times 2 \times 2 \times 2 \times 2 \times 2 \times 2$	2^{12}	4,096
$2 \times 2 \times 2 \times 2 \times 2 \times 2 \times 2 \times 2 \times 2 \times 2 \times 2 \times 2 \times 2$	2^{13}	8,192
$2 \times 2 \times 2 \times 2 \times 2 \times 2 \times 2 \times 2 \times 2 \times 2 \times 2 \times 2 \times 2 \times 2$	2^{14}	16,384
$2 \times 2 \times 2 \times 2 \times 2 \times 2 \times 2 \times 2 \times 2 \times 2 \times 2 \times 2 \times 2 \times 2 \times 2$	2^{15}	32,768

Each number in the far-right column of Table 1-1 represents the value of a binary container. Figure 1-6 shows how the number 5,028 can be written in binary, using essentially the same process that we used earlier for decimal notation.

2^{12}	2^{11}	2^{10}	2^9	2^8	2^7	2^6	2^5	2^4	2^3	2^2	2^1	2^0
1	0	0	1	1	1	0	1	0	0	1	0	0

Figure 1-6: The number 5,028 in binary

The result of the conversion to binary is:

$$1 \times 2^{12} + 0 \times 2^{11} + 0 \times 2^{10} + 1 \times 2^9 + 1 \times 2^8 + 1 \times 2^7 + 0 \times 2^6 + 1 \times 2^5 + 0 \times 2^4 + 0 \times 2^3 + 1 \times 2^2 + 0 \times 2^1 + 0 \times 2^0 = 5{,}028$$

As you can see, the number 5,028 in binary has one 4,096 (2^{12}), zero 2,048s (2^{11}), zero 1,024s (2^{10}), one 512 (2^9), one 256 (2^8), and so on to make up 1001110100100. Performing the same sort of calculation that we do for decimal numbers, we write $1 \times 2^{12} + 0 \times 2^{11} + 0 \times 2^{10} + 1 \times 2^9 + 1 \times 2^8 + 1 \times 2^7 + 0 \times 2^6 + 1 \times 2^5 + 0 \times 2^4 + 0 \times 2^3 + 1 \times 2^2 + 0 \times 2^1 + 0 \times 2^0$. Substituting the decimal numbers from Table 1-1, we get 4,096 + 512 + 256 + 128 + 32 + 4, which is equal to 5,028.

We would say that 5,028 is a four-digit number in decimal. In binary it's a 13-bit number.

The number of digits determines the range of values that we can represent in decimal. For example, 100 different values in the range 0–99 can be represented by two digits. Likewise, the number of bits determines the range of values we can represent in binary. For example, 2 bits can represent four values in the range 0–3. Table 1-2 summarizes both the number and range of values that we can represent with different numbers of bits.

Table 1-2: Ranges of Binary Number Values

Number of bits	Number of values	Range of values
4	16	0...15
8	256	0...255
12	4,096	0...4,095
16	65,536	0...65,535
20	1,048,576	0...1,058,575
24	16,777,216	0...16,777,215
32	4,294,967,296	0...4,294,967,295
64	18,446,744,073,709,551,616	0...18,446,744,073,709,551,615

The rightmost bit in a binary number is called the *least significant bit* and the leftmost bit is called the *most significant bit*, because changing the value of the rightmost bit has the smallest effect on the value of the number and changing the value of the leftmost bit has the greatest effect. Computer people are fond of three-letter acronyms, or TLAs as we call them, so these are commonly referred to as the *LSB* and *MSB*. Figure 1-7 shows an example of the number 5,028 held in 16 bits.

MSB → | 0 | 0 | 0 | 1 | 0 | 0 | 1 | 1 | 1 | 0 | 1 | 0 | 0 | 1 | 0 | 0 | ← LSB

15 14 13 12 11 10 9 8 7 6 5 4 3 2 1 0

Figure 1-7: MSB and LSB

You'll notice that while the binary representation of 5,028 takes 13 bits, Figure 1-7 shows it in 16 bits. Just like in decimal, we can always use more containers than the minimum required by adding *leading zeros* on the left. In decimal, 05,028 has the same value as 5,028. Binary numbers are often represented this way because computers are built around blocks of bits.

Binary Addition

Now that you know how to represent numbers using binary, let's look at how to do simple arithmetic with binary numbers. In decimal addition, we add up each digit from right (least significant digit) to left (most significant digit), and if the result is greater than 9, we carry the 1. Similarly, we add together each bit in a binary number, going from the least significant to the most significant bit, and if the result is greater than 1, we carry the 1.

Addition is actually a bit easier in binary because there are only 4 possible combinations of 2 bits compared to 100 combinations of 2 digits. For example, Figure 1-8 shows how to add 1 and 5 using binary numbers, showing the number being carried above each column.

```
 1        ⁰0  ¹0  ⁰1
 5         1   0   1
───       ──────────
 6         1   1   0
```

Figure 1-8: Binary addition

The number 1 is 001 in binary, while the number 5 is 101 because $(1 \times 4) + (0 \times 2) + (1 \times 1) = 5$. To add the binary numbers 001 and 101 together, we start with the least significant bit in the rightmost column. Adding the binary numbers 1 and 1 in that column gives us 2, but we don't have a symbol for 2 in binary. But we know that 2 is actually 10 in binary $([1 \times 2] + [0 \times 1] = 2)$, so we put 0 as the sum and carry the 1 to the next digit. Because the middle bits are zeros, we only have 1, which we carried over from before, as the sum. Then we add the digits in the leftmost column: 0 plus 1 is simply 1 in binary. The final result is the binary 110, or 6 in decimal notation, which is what you would get by adding 1 and 5.

You might notice that the rules for binary addition can be expressed in terms of the logical operations that we discussed previously, as Figure 1-9 illustrates. We'll see in Chapter 2 that this is in fact how computer hardware does binary addition.

A	B	A AND B	A + B	A XOR B	A	B
0	0	0 ----➤	00 ◀----	0	0	0
0	1	0 ----➤	01 ◀----	1	0	1
1	0	0 ----➤	01 ◀----	1	1	0
1	1	1 ----➤	10 ◀----	0	1	1

Figure 1-9: Binary addition using logical operations

When we add 2 bits together, the value of the result is the XOR of the 2 bits, and the value of the carry is the AND of the 2 bits. You can see that this is true in Figure 1-9, where adding 1 and 1 in binary results in 10. This means that the carry value is 1, which is what you get by performing the expression (1 *AND* 1). Likewise, the expression (1 *XOR* 1) yields 0, which is the value that we assign to the bit position itself.

Adding 2 bits is an operation that rarely happens in isolation. Referring back to Figure 1-8, it appears that we're adding 2 bits together in each column, but we're really adding 3 because of the carry. Fortunately, we don't need to learn anything new to add 3 bits together (because A + B + C is the same as (A + B) + C, according to the associative rule), so we can add 3 bits together using a pair of 2-bit adds.

What happens when the result of addition doesn't fit in the number of bits that we have? This results in *overflow*, which happens whenever we have a carry from the most significant bit. For example, if we have 4-bit numbers, and add 1001 (9_{10}) to 1000 (8_{10}), the result should be 10001 (17_{10}), but it will end up being 0001 (1_{10}) because there's no place for the most significant bit. As we'll see in more detail later, computers have a *condition code register*, which is a place that holds odd pieces of information. One of these is an *overflow bit*, which holds the carry value from the most significant bit. We can look at this value to determine whether or not overflow occurred.

You're probably aware that you can subtract one number from another by adding the negative of that number. We'll learn how to represent negative numbers in the next section. Borrowing beyond the most significant bit is called *underflow*. Computers have a condition code for this too.

Representing Negative Numbers

All of the numbers we represented using binary in the last section were positive. But lots of real-world problems involve both positive and negative numbers. Let's see how we can use bits to represent negative numbers. For example, let's assume that we have 4 bits to play with. As you learned in the last section, 4 bits can represent 16 numbers in the range of 0 through 15. Just because we can hold 16 numbers in 4 bits doesn't mean that those numbers have to be 0 through 15. Remember, language works through meaning and context. That means that we can devise new contexts in which we can interpret bits.

Sign and Magnitude

A *sign* is commonly used to distinguish negative numbers from positive ones. The sign has two values, plus and minus, so it can be represented using a bit. We'll arbitrarily use the leftmost bit (MSB) for the sign, leaving us 3 bits that can represent a number between 0 and 7. If the sign bit is 0, we treat that number as positive. If it's 1, we treat it as negative. This lets us represent 15 different positive and negative numbers in total, not 16, because there is both a positive 0 and a negative 0. Table 1-3 shows how this allows us to represent the numbers between –7 and +7.

This is called *sign and magnitude* representation because there's a bit that represents a sign and bits that represent the magnitude, or how far the value is from zero.

Sign and magnitude representation is not used much for two reasons. First, bits cost money to build, so we don't want to waste them by having two different representations for zero; we'd much rather use that bit combination to represent another number. Second, arithmetic using XOR and AND doesn't work using this representation.

Table 1-3: Sign and Magnitude Binary Numbers

Sign	2^2	2^1	2^0	Decimal
0	1	1	1	+7
0	1	1	0	+6
0	1	0	1	+5
0	1	0	0	+4
0	0	1	1	+3
0	0	1	0	+2
0	0	0	1	+1
0	0	0	0	+0
1	0	0	0	−0
1	0	0	1	−1
1	0	1	0	−2
1	0	1	1	−3
1	1	0	0	−4
1	1	0	1	−5
1	1	1	0	−6
1	1	1	1	−7

Let's say that we want to add +1 to −1. We'd expect to get 0, but using sign and magnitude representation we get a different result, as shown in Figure 1-10.

```
    0   0   0   1 | +1
+   1   0   0   1 | −1
    1   0   1   0 | −2
```

Figure 1-10: Sign and magnitude addition

As you can see, 0001 represents positive 1 in binary, because its sign bit is 0. The 1001 represents −1 in binary, because the sign bit is 1. Adding these together using XOR and AND arithmetic gives us 1010. This evaluates to −2 in decimal notation, which is not the sum of +1 and −1.

We could make sign and magnitude arithmetic work by using more complicated logic, but there's value in keeping things as simple as possible. Let's explore a few other ways of representing numbers to find a better approach.

One's Complement

Another way to get negative numbers is to take positive numbers and flip all the bits, which is called *one's complement* representation. We partition the bits in a manner similar to sign and magnitude. In this context, we get a complement using the NOT operation. Table 1-4 shows −7 through 7 using one's complement.

Table 1-4: One's Complement Binary Numbers

Sign	2^2	2^1	2^0	Decimal
0	1	1	1	+7
0	1	1	0	+6
0	1	0	1	+5
0	1	0	0	+4
0	0	1	1	+3
0	0	1	0	+2
0	0	0	1	+1
0	0	0	0	+0
1	1	1	1	−0
1	1	1	0	−1
1	1	0	1	−2
1	1	0	0	−3
1	0	1	1	−4
1	0	1	0	−5
1	0	0	1	−6
1	0	0	0	−7

As you can see, flipping each bit of 0111 (+7) yields 1000 (−7).

One's complement representation still has the problem of two different representations for zero. It still doesn't let us perform addition easily, either. To get around this, we use *end-around carry* to add 1 to the LSB if there is a carry out of the most significant position in order to get the correct result. Figure 1-11 illustrates how this works.

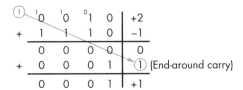

Figure 1-11: One's complement addition

To add +2 and −1 using one's complement, we perform binary addition of 0010 and 1110 as we would normally. Because adding the digits in the most significant bit (sign bit) results in 10, we bring down 0 and carry the 1 as the end-around carry for each digit. But we only have 4 bits to work with, so when we get to the MSB, we bring the carry back to the first bit to give us 0001, or +1, which is the correct sum of +2 and −1. As you can see, making this work adds a significant amount of complexity.

While this works, it still isn't a great solution because we need additional hardware to add the end-around carry bit.

Neither sign and magnitude nor one's complement representation is used in modern computers. Arithmetic using these methods doesn't work without extra hardware, and extra hardware costs money. Let's see if we can come up with a representation that solves this problem.

Two's Complement

What would happen if we didn't add any special hardware and just stuck with the XOR and AND operations? Let's figure out what bit pattern, when added to +1, would result in 0 and call that –1. If we stick with 4-bit numbers, +1 is 0001. Adding 1111 to it results in 0000, as shown in Figure 1-12, so we'll use that bit pattern to represent –1.

```
+1      ¹0  ¹0  ¹0  ⁰1
–1        1   1   1   0
──      ──────────────
 0        0   0   0   0
```

Figure 1-12: Finding –1

This is called *two's complement* representation, and it's the most commonly used binary representation for signed integers. We can obtain the negative of a number by complementing the number (that is, doing a NOT of each bit) and then adding 1, throwing away any carry from the MSB. The complement of +1, 0001, is 1110, and adding 1 gives us 1111 for –1. Likewise, +2 is 0010, its complement is 1101, and adding 1 gives us 1110 to represent –2. Table 1-5 shows –8 through 7 using two's complement representation.

Table 1-5: Two's Complement Binary Numbers

Sign	2^2	2^1	2^0	Decimal
0	1	1	1	+7
0	1	1	0	+6
0	1	0	1	+5
0	1	0	0	+4
0	0	1	1	+3
0	0	1	0	+2
0	0	0	1	+1
0	0	0	0	+0
1	1	1	1	–1
1	1	1	0	–2
1	1	0	1	–3
1	1	0	0	–4
1	0	1	1	–5
1	0	1	0	–6
1	0	0	1	–7
1	0	0	0	–8

Let's try this using 0 to see if two's complement fixes the issue of duplicate representations for zero. If we take 0000 and flip every bit, we get 1111 as its complement. Adding 1 to 1111 gives us [1]0000, but because this is a 5-bit number that exceeds the number of bits available to us, we can disregard the 1 in the carry bit. This leaves us with 0000, which is what we started with, so zero has only one representation in two's complement.

Programmers need to know how many bits are required to hold the numbers they need. This will eventually become second nature. In the meantime, you can refer to Table 1-6, which shows the range of values that we can represent using two's complement numbers of various sizes.

Table 1-6: Ranges of Two's Complement Binary Number Values

Number of bits	Number of values	Range of values
4	16	–8...7
8	256	–128...127
12	4,096	2,048...2,047
16	65,536	–32,768...32,767
20	1,048,576	–524,288...524,287
24	16,777,216	–8,388,608...8,388,607
32	4,294,967,296	–2,147,483,648...2,137,483,647
64	18,446,744,073,709,551,616	–9,223,372,036,854,775,808 ...9,223,372,036,854,775,807

As you can see from Table 1-6, as the number of bits increases, the range of values that can be represented increases exponentially. It's important to keep in mind that we always need context to determine whether a 4-bit number that we're looking at is a 15 instead of a –1 using two's complement, a –7 using sign and magnitude, or a –0 using one's complement. You have to know which representation you're using.

Representing Real Numbers

So far, we've managed to represent whole numbers using binary. But what about real numbers? Real numbers include a decimal point in base 10. We need some way to represent the equivalent binary point in base 2. Once again, this can be accomplished by interpreting bits in different contexts.

Fixed-Point Representation

One way to represent fractions using binary is by choosing an arbitrary place for a binary point, the binary equivalent of the decimal point. If we have 4 bits, for example, we can pretend that two of them are to the right of the binary point, representing four fractional values, and two are to the left, representing four whole values. This is called a *fixed-point* representation, because the location of the binary point is fixed. Table 1-7 shows how this would work.

Table 1-7: Fixed-Point Binary Numbers

Whole			Fraction		Value
0	0	.	0	0	0
0	0	.	0	1	¼
0	0	.	1	0	½
0	0	.	1	1	¾
0	1	.	0	0	1
0	1	.	0	1	1¼
0	1	.	1	0	1½
0	1	.	1	1	1¾
1	0	.	0	0	2
1	0	.	0	1	2¼
1	0	.	1	0	2½
1	0	.	1	1	2¾
1	1	.	0	0	3
1	1	.	0	1	3¼
1	1	.	1	0	3½
1	1	.	1	1	3¾

The whole numbers to the left of the point should look familiar from binary notation. Similar to what we saw with integers, we have four values from the 2 bits to the right of the point; they represent fourths instead of the familiar tenths from decimal.

While this approach works pretty well, it's not often used in general-purpose computers because it takes way too many bits to represent a useful range of numbers. Certain special-purpose computers, called *digital signal processors (DSP)*, still use fixed-point numbers. And, as you'll see in Chapter 11, fixed-point numbers are useful in certain applications.

General-purpose computers are built to solve general-purpose problems, which involve a wide range of numbers. You can get an idea of this range by skimming a physics textbook. For example, there are tiny numbers such as Planck's constant (6.63×10^{-34} joule-seconds) and huge numbers such as Avogadro's constant (6.02×10^{23} molecules/mole). This is a range of 10^{57}, which comes out to about 2^{191}. That's almost 200 bits! Bits just aren't cheap enough to use a few hundred of them to represent every number, so we need a different approach.

Floating-Point Representation

We solve this using a binary version of the scientific notation used to represent the wide range of numbers that includes Planck's and Avogadro's constants. Scientific notation represents a large range of numbers by (how else?) creating a new context for interpretation. It uses a number with a single digit to the left of the decimal point, called the *mantissa*, multiplied by 10 raised to some power, called the *exponent*. Computers use the same system, except that the mantissa and exponent are binary numbers and 2 is used instead of 10.

This is called *floating-point* representation, which is confusing because the binary (or decimal) point is always in the same place: between the ones and halves (tenths in decimal). The "float" is just another way of saying "scientific notation," which allows us to write 1.2×10^{-3} instead of 0.0012.

Note that we don't need any bits to indicate that the base is 2, because the floating-point definition says that it's there by default. By separating the significant digits from the exponents, the floating-point system allows us to represent very small or very large numbers without having to store all those zeros.

Table 1-8 shows a 4-bit floating-point representation with 2 bits of mantissa and 2 bits of exponent.

Table 1-8: Floating-Point Binary Numbers

Mantissa			Exponent		Value
0	0	.	0	0	0 (0×2^0)
0	0	.	0	1	0 (0×2^1)
0	0	.	1	0	0 (0×2^1)
0	0	.	1	1	0 (0×2^3)
0	1	.	0	0	0.5 ($\frac{1}{2} \times 2^0$)
0	1	.	0	1	1.0 ($\frac{1}{2} \times 2^1$)
0	1	.	1	0	2.0 ($\frac{1}{2} \times 2^2$)
0	1	.	1	1	4.0 ($\frac{1}{2} \times 2^3$)
1	0	.	0	0	1.0 (1×2^0)
1	0	.	0	1	2.0 (1×2^1)
1	0	.	1	0	4.0 (1×2^2)
1	0	.	1	1	8.0 (1×2^3)
1	1	.	0	0	1.5 ($1\frac{1}{2} \times 2^0$)
1	1	.	0	1	3.0 ($1\frac{1}{2} \times 2^1$)
1	1	.	1	0	6.0 ($1\frac{1}{2} \times 2^2$)
1	1	.	1	1	12.0 ($1\frac{1}{2} \times 2^3$)

While this example uses only a few bits, it reveals some inefficiencies present in this floating-point system. First, you'll notice that there are a lot of wasted bit combinations. For example, there are four ways to represent 0 and two ways to represent 1.0, 2.0, and 4.0. Second, there aren't bit patterns for every possible number; the exponent makes numbers farther apart as they get bigger. One of the side effects is that, while we can add 0.5 and 0.5 to get 1.0, we can't add 0.5 and 6.0 because there's no bit pattern that represents 6.5. (There is a whole subbranch of mathematics, called *numerical analysis*, that involves keeping track of how inaccurate calculations are.)

The IEEE Floating-Point Standard

Strange as it is, the floating-point system is the standard way to represent real numbers in computing. More bits are used than in Table 1-8, and there are two signs, one for the mantissa and a hidden one that is part of the exponent. There are also a lot of tricks to make sure that things like rounding work as well as possible and to minimize the number of wasted bit combinations. A standard called *IEEE 754* spells all of this out. IEEE stands for the Institute of Electrical and Electronic Engineers, which is a professional organization whose activities include producing standards.

We want to maximize our precision given the available bits. One clever trick is called *normalization*, which adjusts the mantissa so that there are no leading (that is, on the left) zeros. Every left adjustment of the mantissa requires a corresponding adjustment of the exponent. A second trick, from Digital Equipment Corporation (DEC), doubles the accuracy by throwing away the leftmost bit of the mantissa since we know that it will always be 1, which makes room for one more bit.

You don't need to know all of the gory details of IEEE 754 (yet). But you should know about two types of floating-point numbers that you'll run into a lot: single precision and double precision. Single-precision numbers use 32 bits and can represent numbers approximately in the range $\pm 10^{\pm 38}$ with about 7 digits of accuracy. Double-precision numbers use 64 bits and can represent a wider range of numbers, approximately $\pm 10^{\pm 308}$, with about 15 digits of accuracy. Figure 1-13 shows how they're laid out.

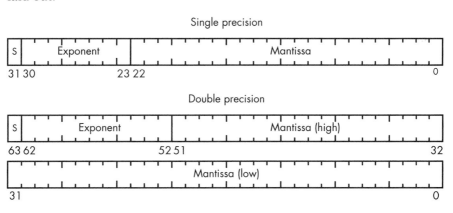

Figure 1-13: IEEE floating-point number formats

Both formats have a sign bit for the mantissa—the *S* in Figure 1-13. You can see that double-precision numbers have three more exponent bits than single precision, giving eight times the range. Double-precision numbers also have 29 more mantissa bits than single-precision ones, yielding greater accuracy. This all comes at the cost of taking twice as many bits as single-precision numbers, however.

You might have noticed that there is no explicit sign bit for the exponent. The designers of IEEE 754 decided that the exponent values of all 0s and all 1s would have special meaning so the actual exponent had to be crammed into the remaining bit patterns. They did this by using a *biased* (offset) exponent value. For single-precision numbers, the bias is 127, which means that the bit pattern for 127 (01111111) represents an exponent of 0. The bit pattern for 1 (00000001) represents an exponent of –126, and 254 (11111110) represents +127. Double precision is similar except that the bias is 1023.

One other handy part of IEEE 754 is that it has special bit patterns to represent things like division by zero, which evaluates to positive or negative infinity. It also specifies a special value called *NaN*, which stands for "not a number"—so if you find yourself in the NaNny state, it probably means that you did some illegal arithmetic operation. These special bit patterns use the reserved exponent values discussed previously.

Binary-Coded Decimal System

You've just seen some of the more common ways to represent numbers in binary, but there are many alternative systems. One is *binary-coded decimal (BCD)*, in which we use 4 bits to represent each decimal digit. For example, the number 12 in binary is 1100. But in BCD, it's 0001 0010, where 0001 represents 1 in the tens digit and 0010 represents 2 in the ones digit. This is a much more familiar and comfortable representation for people who are used to working in decimal.

Computers used to know how to operate on BCD numbers, but that system is no longer mainstream. However, it does crop up in many places, so it's worth knowing about. In particular, many devices with which computers interact, such as displays and accelerometers, use BCD.

The main reason the BCD system has fallen out of favor is that it doesn't use bits as efficiently as binary. You can see that BCD needs more bits than binary to represent a number. While bits are much cheaper than they used to be, they're not so cheap that we want to throw away 6 out of every 16 bit combinations, as that would be equivalent to wasting a whopping 37.5 percent of available bits.

Easier Ways to Work with Binary Numbers

It's a well-known fact that manipulating binary numbers leads to blindness; it can be visually exhausting! People have come up with a few ways to make binary numbers easier to read. We'll look at a few of them here.

Octal Representation

One eyeball-friendly approach is *octal representation. Octal* means base-8, and the idea behind octal representation is to group bits in threes. As you should know by now, 3 bits can be used to represent 2^3, or eight values from 0 through 7. Let's say that we have some monster binary number like 100101110001010100. This hurts my eyeballs. Figure 1-14 shows how to transform it into octal representation.

100	101	110	001	010	100
4	5	6	1	2	4

Figure 1-14: Octal representation of binary numbers

As you can see, we divide the bits into groups of three, and we assign the octal value to each group to get 456124, which is a lot easier to read. To get the octal value of 100, for example, we simply treat it as a binary number: $(1 \times 2^2) + (0 \times 2^1) + (0 \times 2^0) = 4$.

Hexadecimal Representation

Octal representation is still in use, but not as widely as in the past. *Hexadecimal representation* (meaning base-16) has pretty much taken over because the insides of computers are built in multiples of 8 bits these days, which is evenly divisible by 4 but not by 3.

It was easy to repurpose some of the symbols from our familiar digits for binary because we needed only two of them, the 0 and 1. We needed only 8 of the 10 for octal. But we need 16 for hexadecimal, which is more than we have. We need a symbol to represent 10, another for 11, all the way up through 15. We *make believe* (I told you that we'd be doing that) that the symbols abcdef (or ABCDEF) represent the values 10 through 16. For example, let's say we have another scary binary number like 1101001111111000001. Figure 1-15 shows how to convert it into hexadecimal.

1101	0011	1111	1100	0001
d	3	f	c	1

Figure 1-15: Hexadecimal representation of binary numbers

In this example, we divide the bits into groups of four. Then we assign one of the 16 symbol values (0123456789abcdef) to each group. For example, 1101 (the first group of 4 bits) would be d because it evaluates to $1(2^3) + 1(2^2) + 0(2^1) + 1(2^0) = 13$ in decimal notation and d represents the number 13. We map the next group of 4 bits (0011) to another symbol, and so on. For example, 1101001111111000001 converts to d3fc1 in hexadecimal. Table 1-9 shows a handy list of hexadecimal values that you can refer to until they become second nature.

Table 1-9: Binary-to-Hexadecimal Conversion

Binary	Hexadecimal	Binary	Hexadecimal
0000	0	1000	8
0001	1	1001	9
0010	2	1010	a
0011	3	1011	b
0100	4	1100	c
0101	5	1101	d
0110	6	1110	e
0111	7	1111	f

Representing the Context

How do you know how to interpret a number? For example, the number 10 is 2 if it's a binary number, 8 if it's octal, 10 if it's decimal, and 16 if it's hexadecimal. Math books use subscripts, so we can use those to distinguish between them like this: 10_2, 10_8, 10_{10}, or 10_{16}. But subscripts are inconvenient to type on a computer keyboard. It would be nice if we could use a consistent notation, but unfortunately lots of people think they have a better way and keep inventing new ones. The following notations are used by many computer programming languages:

- A number that begins with a 0 is an octal number—for example, 017.
- A number that begins with one of the digits 1 through 9 is a decimal number—for example, 123.
- A number that's prefixed with 0x is a hexadecimal number—for example, 0x12f.

Note that we can't tell the difference between octal and decimal 0, but that's not important because they have the same value. And few programing languages have a notation for binary because it really isn't used very much anymore and can usually be determined by context. Some languages, such as C++, use a 0b prefix to represent binary numbers.

Naming Groups of Bits

Computers are not just unorganized buckets of bits. The people who design them have to make decisions about the number of bits and their organization for cost reasons. Just as with number representations, many ideas have been tried, and only some have survived.

Bits are too small a unit to be very useful, so they're organized into larger chunks. For example, the Honeywell 6000 series of computers used 36-bit chunks as its basic organization and allowed those to be partitioned into 18-, 9-, or 6-bit chunks or combined into 72-bit chunks. The

DEC PDP-8, the first commercial minicomputer (introduced in 1965), used 12-bit chunks. Over time the world has settled on 8-bit chunks as a fundamental unit, which we call a *byte*.

Chunks of different sizes have names to make them easier to reference. Table 1-10 summarizes the names and sizes of some of the common units in use today.

Table 1-10: Names for Bit Collections

Name	Number of bits
Nibble	4
Byte	8
Half word	16
Long word	32
Double word	64

You might be wondering why we have half, long, and double words but no plain words. *Word* is used to describe the natural size of things in a particular computer design. The natural size refers to the largest chunk that can be operated on quickly. For example, although you could access bytes, half words, and long words on the DEC PDP-11, it had a 16-bit internal organization, making the natural size 16 bits. Programming languages such as C and C++ allow variables to be declared as int (short for *integer*), which makes them the natural size. You can also declare variables using a set of supported specific sizes.

There are some standard terms that make it easy to refer to big numbers. Well, there was a standard, and now it's been replaced with a new one. Engineers have a habit of finding words that mean something close to what they want, and then using them as if they mean what they want. For example, in the metric system *kilo* means thousand, *mega* means million, *giga* means billion, and *tera* means trillion. These terms have been borrowed but changed a little because we use base-2 in computing instead of base-10. When we talk about a *kilobit* or *kilobyte* (*K* or *KB*) in computing, however, we don't actually mean a thousand. We mean the closest thing to a thousand in base-2, which would be 1,024, or 2^{10}. The same goes for *megabyte* (*M* or *MB*), which is 2^{20}; *giga* (*G* or *GB*), which is 2^{30}; and *tera* (*T* or *TB*), which is 2^{40}.

But sometimes we do mean the base-10 version. You need to know the context in order to know which interpretation to apply. Traditionally, the base-10 version was used to refer to the size of disk drives. An American lawyer feigned ignorance about this and sued *(Safier v. WDC)*, claiming that a disk drive was smaller than advertised. (In my opinion, this was just as dumb as the lawsuits claiming that 2 × 4 lumber doesn't actually measure 2 inches by 4 inches, despite the fact that those have always been the dimensions of the unplaned, unfinished lumber.) This led to the creation of new IEC standard prefixes: *kibi (KiB)* for 2^{10}, *mebi (MiB)* for 2^{20}, *gibi (GiB)* for 2^{30}, and *tebi (TiB)* for 2^{40}. These are slowly catching on, although "kibis" sounds like dog food to me.

The term *character* is often used interchangeably with *byte* because, as we'll see in the next section, characters' codes have typically been designed to fit in bytes. Now, with better support for non-English languages, there's often a need to talk about multibyte characters.

Representing Text

At this point, you've learned that bits are all we have to work with in computers and that we can use bits to represent other things, such as numbers. It's time to take it to the next level and use numbers to represent other things, such as the letters and other symbols on your keyboard.

The American Standard Code for Information Interchange

There were several competing ideas for representing text, just like we saw for number representations. The winner, from back in 1963, is called the *American Standard Code for Information Interchange (ASCII)*, which assigns 7-bit numeric values to all of the symbols on the keyboard. For example, 65 means capital A, 66 means capital B, and so on. The losing idea was IBM's *Extended Binary-Coded Decimal Interchange Code (EBCDIC)*, which was based on the encoding used for punched cards. And, yes, the "BCD" part of EBCDIC stands for the same binary-coded decimal that we saw earlier. Table 1-11 shows the ASCII code chart.

Table 1-11: ASCII Code Chart

Dec	Hex	Char	Dec	Hex	Char	Dec	Hex	Char	Dec	Hex	Char
0	00	NUL	32	20	SP	64	40	@	96	60	`
1	01	SOH	33	21	!	65	41	A	97	61	a
2	02	STX	34	22	"	66	42	B	98	62	b
3	03	ETX	35	23	#	67	43	C	99	63	c
4	04	EOT	36	24	$	68	44	D	100	64	d
5	05	ENQ	37	25	%	69	45	E	101	65	e
6	06	ACK	38	26	&	70	46	F	102	66	f
7	07	BEL	39	27	'	71	47	G	103	67	g
8	08	BS	40	28	(	72	48	H	104	68	h
9	09	HT	41	29	)	73	49	I	105	69	i
10	0A	NL	42	2A	*	74	4A	J	106	6A	j
11	0B	VT	43	2B	+	75	4B	K	107	6B	k
12	0C	FF	44	2C	,	76	4C	L	108	6C	l
13	0D	CR	45	2D	-	77	4D	M	109	6D	m
14	0E	SO	46	2E	.	78	4E	N	110	6E	n
15	0F	SI	47	2F	/	79	4F	O	111	6F	o
16	10	DLE	48	30	0	80	5	P	112	70	p
17	11	DC1	49	31	1	81	51	Q	113	71	q
18	12	DC2	50	32	2	82	52	R	114	72	r

Dec	Hex	Char	Dec	Hex	Char	Dec	Hex	Char	Dec	Hex	Char
19	13	DC3	51	33	3	83	53	S	115	73	s
20	14	DC4	52	34	4	84	54	T	116	74	t
21	15	NAK	53	35	5	85	55	U	117	75	u
22	16	SYN	54	36	6	86	56	V	118	76	v
23	17	ETB	55	37	7	87	57	W	119	77	w
24	18	CAN	56	38	8	88	58	X	120	78	x
25	19	EM	57	39	9	89	59	Y	121	79	y
26	1A	SUB	58	3A	:	90	5A	Z	122	7A	z
27	1B	ESC	59	3B	;	91	5B	[	123	7B	{
28	1C	FS	60	3C	<	92	5C	\	124	7C		
29	1D	GS	61	3D	=	93	5D	]	125	7D	}
30	1E	RS	62	3E	>	94	5E	^	126	7E	~
31	1F	US	63	3F	?	95	5F	_	127	7F	DEL

Let's find the letter *A* in this table. You can see that it has a decimal value of 65, which is 0x41 in hexadecimal—that's also 0101 in octal. As it turns out, ASCII character codes are one place where octal is still used a lot, for historical reasons.

You'll notice a lot of funny codes in the ASCII table. They're called *control characters* because they control things as opposed to printing. Table 1-12 shows what they stand for.

Table 1-12: ASCII Control Characters

NUL	null	SOH	start of heading
STX	start of text	ETX	end of text
EOT	end of transmission	ENQ	enquiry
ACK	acknowledge	BEL	bell
BS	backspace	HT	horizontal tab
NL	new line	VT	vertical tab
FF	form feed	CR	carriage return
SO	shift out	SI	shift in
DLE	data link escape	DC1	device control #1
DC2	device control #2	DC3	device control #3
DC4	device control #4	NAK	negative acknowledgment
SYN	synchronous idle	ETB	end of transmission block
CAN	cancel	EM	end of medium
SUB	substitute	ESC	escape
FS	file separator	GS	group separator
RS	record separator	US	unit separator
SP	space	DEL	delete

Many of these were intended for communications control. For example, ACK (acknowledgment) means "I got the message," and NAK (negative acknowledgment) means "I didn't get the message."

The Evolution of Other Standards

ASCII worked for a while because it contained the characters necessary for the English language. Most of the early computers were American, and the ones that weren't were British. The need to support other languages grew as computers became more widely available. The *International Standards Organization (ISO)* adopted ISO-646 and ISO-8859, which are basically ASCII with some extensions for the accent symbols and other diacritical marks used in European languages. The *Japanese Industrial Standards (JIS)* committee came up with JIS X 0201 for Japanese characters. There are also Chinese standards, Arabic standards, and more.

One reason for all of the different standards is that they were created at a time when bits were a lot more expensive than they are today, so characters were packed into 7 or 8 bits. As the price of bits began to fall, a newer standard called *Unicode* was crafted that assigned 16-bit codes to characters. At the time, it was believed that 16 bits would be enough to hold all of the characters in all languages on Earth with room to spare. Unicode has since been extended to 21 bits (of which 1,112,064 values are valid), which we think will do the job, but even that might not last given our propensity to create new cat emojis.

Unicode Transformation Format 8-bit

Computers use 8 bits to store an ASCII character because they're not designed to handle 7-bit quantities. Again, while bits are a whole lot cheaper than they used to be, they're not so cheap that we want to use 16 of them to store a single letter when we can get by with using just 8. Unicode addresses this problem by having different encodings for the character codes. An *encoding* is a bit pattern that represents another bit pattern. That's right—we're using abstractions like bits to create numbers that represent characters and then using other numbers to represent those numbers! You see what I meant by make-believe? There's one encoding in particular called *Unicode Transformation Format–8 bit* (*UTF-8*), invented by American computer scientist Ken Thompson and Canadian programmer Rob Pike, that we use most commonly for its efficiency and backward compatibility. UTF-8 uses 8 bits for each ASCII character so that it doesn't consume any additional space for ASCII data. It encodes non-ASCII characters in a way that doesn't break programs that expect ASCII.

UTF-8 encodes characters as a sequence of 8-bit chunks, often called *octets*. A clever aspect of UTF-8 is that the number of most significant ones in the first chunk yields the length of the sequence, and it's easy to recognize the first chunk. This is useful because it allows programs to easily find character boundaries. The ASCII characters all fit in 7 bits, so they take one chunk apiece, which is pretty convenient for us English speakers because it's more compact than for other languages that need non-ASCII symbols. Figure 1-16 illustrates how UTF-8 encodes characters compared to Unicode.

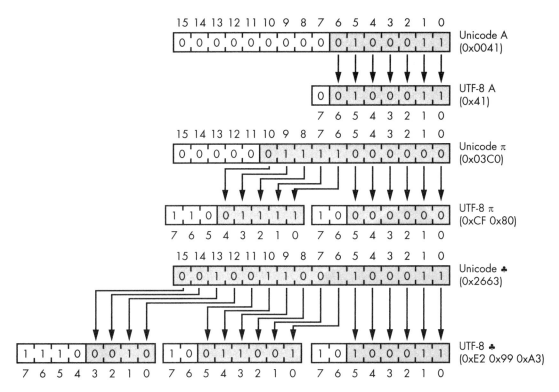

Figure 1-16: Examples of UTF-8 encoding

In Figure 1-16, we can see that the numeric code for the letter *A* is identical in ASCII and Unicode. To encode *A* in UTF-8, we say that whatever codes that fit in 7 bits get a single UTF-8 chunk with the MSB set to 0. This is why there's a leading 0 in the UTF-8 for the letter *A*. Next we see the Unicode for the π symbol, which does not fit in 7 bits but does fit into 11. To encode π in UTF-8, we use two 8-bit chunks with the first chunk starting with 110 and the second with 10, which leaves 5 and 6 bits left over in each chunk respectively to hold the remaining code. Finally, we see the Unicode for ♣, which fits in 16 bits and so takes three UTF-8 chunks.

Using Characters to Represent Numbers

UTF-8 uses numbers to represent numbers that represented numbers made from bits that represented characters. But we're not done yet! Now we're going to use characters to represent some of those numbers. People wanted to send more than text between computers in the early days of computer-to-computer communication; they wanted to send binary data. But doing this wasn't straightforward because, as we saw earlier, many of the ASCII values were reserved for control characters, and they weren't handled consistently between systems. Also, some systems supported transmission of only 7-bit characters.

Quoted-Printable Encoding

Quoted-Printable encoding, also known as QP encoding, is a mechanism that allows 8-bit data to be communicated over a path that only supports 7-bit data. It was created for email attachments. This encoding allows any 8-bit byte value to be represented by three characters: the character = followed by a pair of hexadecimal numbers, one for each nibble of the byte. Of course, in doing this, the = now has special meaning and so must be represented using =3D, its value from Table 1-11.

Quoted-Printable encoding has a few extra rules. The tab and space characters must be represented as =09 and =20, respectively, if they occur at the end of a line. Lines of encoded data can't be more than 76 characters in length. An = at the end of a line is a soft line break that is removed when the data is decoded by the recipient.

Base64 Encoding

While Quoted-Printable encoding works, it's not very efficient because it takes three characters to represent a byte. *Base64* encoding is more efficient, which was really important when computer-to-computer communication was much slower than it is today. Base64 encoding packs 3 bytes of data into 4 characters. The 24 bits of data in the three bytes is partitioned into four 6-bit chunks, each of which is assigned a printing character, as shown in Table 1-13.

Table 1-13: Base64 Character Encoding

Number	Character	Number	Character	Number	Character	Number	Character
0	A	16	Q	32	g	48	w
1	B	17	R	33	h	49	x
2	C	18	S	34	i	50	y
3	D	19	T	35	j	51	z
4	E	20	U	36	k	52	0
5	F	21	V	37	l	53	1
6	G	22	W	38	m	54	2
7	H	23	X	39	n	55	3
8	I	24	Y	40	o	56	4
9	J	25	Z	41	p	57	5
10	K	26	a	42	q	58	6
11	L	27	b	43	r	59	7
12	M	28	c	44	s	60	8
13	N	29	d	45	t	61	9
14	O	30	e	46	u	62	+
15	P	31	f	47	v	63	/

The bytes 0, 1, 2 would be encoded as AAEC. Figure 1-17 shows how this is accomplished.

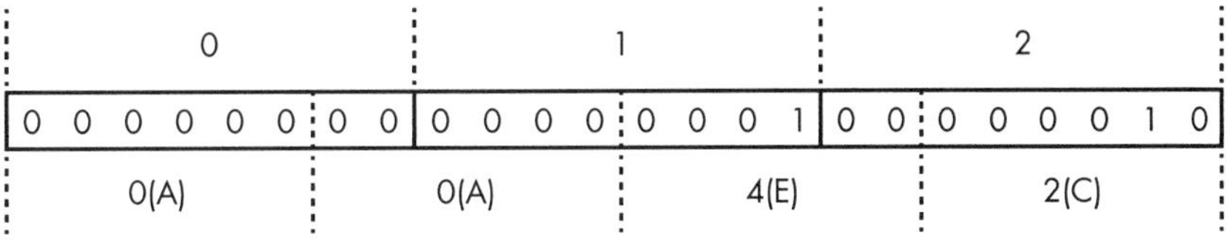

0	1	2
0 0 0 0 0 0 : 0 0	0 0 0 0 : 0 0 0 1	0 0 : 0 0 0 0 1 0
0(A) 0(A)	4(E)	2(C)

Figure 1-17: Base64 encoding

This encoding converts every set of 3 bytes to four characters. But there's no guarantee that the data will be a multiple of 3 bytes in length. This is solved with *padding* characters; a = would be tacked on to the end if there were only 2 bytes at the end and == if there were only 1 byte.

This encoding is still commonly used for email attachments.

URL Encoding

You saw above that the Quoted-Printable encoding gave special power to the = character, and that the encoding included a mechanism for representing the = without its special powers. An almost identical scheme is used in web page URLs.

If you've ever examined a web page URL, you may have noticed character sequences such as *%26* and *%2F*. These exist because certain characters have special meaning in the context of a URL. But sometimes we need to use those characters as *literals*—in other words, without those special meanings.

As we saw in the last section, characters are represented as a sequence of 8-bit chunks. Each chunk can be represented by two hexadecimal characters, as Figure 1-16 demonstrated. *URL encoding*, also known as *percent-encoding*, replaces a character with a % followed by its hexadecimal representation.

For example, the forward slash character (/) has special meaning in a URL. It has an ASCII value of 47, which is 2F in hex. If we need to use a / in a URL without triggering its special meaning, we replace it with %2F. (And because we've just given a special meaning to the % character, it needs to be replaced by %25 if we literally mean %.)

Representing Colors

Another common use of numbers is to represent colors. You already know that numbers can be used to represent coordinates on a graph. Computer graphics involves making pictures by plotting blobs of color on the equivalent of electronic graph paper. The blob plotted at each coordinate pair is called a *picture element* or, more commonly, *pixel*.

Computer monitors generate color by mixing red, green, and blue lights using the aptly named *RGB color model*. The colors can be represented by a *color cube*, in which each axis represents a *primary* color, as shown in Figure 1-18. A value of 0 means that a particular light is off, and 1 means that it's as bright as it can get.

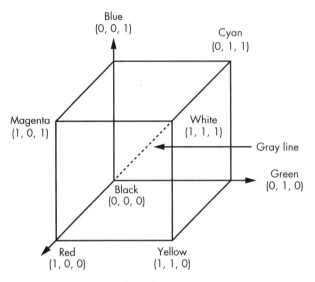

Figure 1-18: An RGB color cube

You can see that the color is black if no lights are on and white if all of the lights are fully up, meaning they're at maximum brightness. A shade of red results if only the red light is on. Mixing red and green creates yellow. Gray results from setting all three lights to the same level. This way of mixing colors is called an *additive* color system, as adding the primaries produces different colors. Figure 1-19 shows the coordinates of a few colors in the color cube.

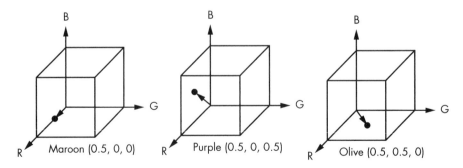

Figure 1-19: RGB color cube examples

If you've tried your hand at painting, you're probably more familiar with a *subtractive* color system, in which the primaries are cyan, magenta, and yellow. A subtractive color system produces colors by removing wavelengths from white light rather than by adding colored light as in the additive system. While neither color system can produce all of the colors that your eye can see, the subtractive system can produce more than the additive system. A whole set of *prepress* technologies exists to make it possible for artists to work on computer monitors and still have their designs look correct when printed in magazines. If you're really interested in color, read *A Field Guide to Digital Color* by Maureen Stone.

The human eye is a very messy piece of machinery that evolved for survival, not computing. It can distinguish around 10 million colors, but it's not linear; doubling the light level doesn't necessarily translate to doubling perceived brightness. Even worse, the eye's response changes slowly over time in response to overall light level. This is called *dark adaptation*. And the response is different for different colors; the eye is very sensitive to changes in green but relatively insensitive to changes in blue, a phenomenon that was exploited in the National Television System Committee (NTSC) standard. Modern computers have settled on rounding up 10 million to the nearest power of 2 and using 24 bits to represent color. These 24 bits are divided up into three 8-bit fields, one for each of the color primaries.

You might have noticed that there is no name for 24 bits in Table 1-10. That's because modern computers aren't designed to operate on 24-bit units (although there were a few 24-bit machines, such as the Honeywell DDP-224). As a result, colors get packed into the nearest standard size, which is 32 bits (*long word*), as shown in Figure 1-20.

Figure 1-20: RGB color packing

You can see that this scheme leaves 8 unused bits for every color. That's a lot, considering that computer monitors today have in excess of 8 million pixels. We can't just let those bits go to waste, so what can we do with them? The answer is that we can use them for something that's missing from our discussion of color above: *transparency*, meaning how much you can "see through" the color. So far, we've only discussed opaque colors, but those can't be used for rose-colored glasses, for example.

Adding Transparency

In early animated movies, each frame was drawn by hand. Not only was this very labor-intensive, but there was also a lot of visual "jitter," because it was impossible to exactly reproduce the background on each frame. American animators John Bray (1879–1978) and Earl Hurd (1880–1940) solved this problem with their invention of *cel animation* in 1915. In cel animation, moving characters were drawn on transparent sheets of celluloid, which could then be moved over a static background image.

Although computer animation traces its roots back to the 1940s, it really took off in the 1970s and 1980s. Computers weren't fast enough back then to do everything that movie directors wanted (and likely never will be because, well, directors). And a mechanism was needed to combine objects generated by different algorithms. Like cel animation, transparency allows for *compositing*, or combining together images from different sources. You're probably familiar with this concept if you've ever played with an image editor like GIMP or Photoshop.

In 1984, Tom Duff and Thomas Porter at Lucasfilm invented a way to implement transparency and compositing that has since become standard. They added a transparency value called *alpha* (α) to each pixel. The α is a mathematical value between 0 and 1, where 0 means that a color is completely transparent and 1 means that a color is completely opaque. A set of *compositing algebra* equations define how colors with different alphas combine to produce new colors.

Duff and Porter's implementation is clever. Since they're not using a floating-point system, they represent an α value of 1 using 255, taking advantage of those extra 8 bits in Figure 1-20. Rather than storing red, green, and blue, Duff and Porter store the color values multiplied by α. For example, if the color were medium red, it would have a value of 200 for red and 0 for green and blue. The red value would be 200 if it were opaque because the α would be 1 (with an α value represented by 255). But the α of a medium red color that was half transparent would be 0.5, so the stored value for red would be $200 \times 0.5 = 100$ and the stored α would be 127 ($255 \times 0.5 = 127$). Figure 1-21 shows the storage arrangement for pixels with α.

Figure 1-21: RGBα color packing

Compositing images, therefore, involves multiplying the color values by α. Storing colors in premultiplied form means we don't have to do these multiplications every time a pixel is used.

Encoding Colors

Because web pages are primarily *text* documents, meaning they're a sequence of human-readable characters often in UTF-8, we need a way of representing colors using text.

We do this in a manner similar to URL encoding, specifying colors using *hex triplets*. A hex triplet is a # followed by six hexadecimal values formatted as #rrggbb where rr is the red value, gg is the green value, and bb is the blue value. For example, #ffff00 would be yellow, #000000 would be black, and #ffffff would be white. Each of the three 8-bit color values is converted to a two-character hexadecimal representation.

Although α is also available in web pages, there is no concise format for its representation. It uses yet another set of schemes entirely.

Summary

In this chapter, you learned that although bits are conceptually simple, they can be used to represent complex things like very large numbers, characters, and even colors. You learned how to represent decimal numbers in binary, perform simple arithmetic using binary numbers, and represent negative numbers and fractions. You also learned different standards for encoding letters and characters using bits.

There's a geek joke that goes, "There are 10 types of people in the world—those who understand binary and those who don't." You should now be in the first of those categories.

In Chapter 2, you'll learn some hardware basics that will help you understand the physical components of a computer and why computers use bits in the first place.

2

COMBINATORIAL LOGIC

In the 1967 *Star Trek* episode "The City on the Edge of Forever," Mr. Spock says, "I am endeavoring, ma'am, to construct a mnemonic memory circuit using stone knives and bearskins." Like Mr. Spock, people have come up with all sorts of ingenious ways to build computing devices using the resources available to them. Few fundamental technologies were invented explicitly for computing; most were invented for other purposes and then *adapted* for computing. This chapter covers some of this evolution, leading up to the convenient but fairly recent innovation of electricity.

In Chapter 1, you learned that modern computers use binary containers called *bits* for their internal language. You may wonder why computers use bits when decimal numbers work fine for people. In this chapter, we'll start by looking at some early computing devices that *didn't* use bits to learn why bits are the right choice for the technology available today. Bits aren't found naturally in a useful form for computing, so we'll talk about what's needed to make them. We'll work through some older, simpler technologies like relays and vacuum tubes, then compare them to the modern implementation of bits in hardware using electricity and integrated circuits.

The discussion of bits in Chapter 1 was pretty abstract. Here we'll be getting down to the nitty-gritty. Physical devices, including those that operate on bits, are called *hardware*. We'll talk about hardware that implements *combinatorial logic*, another name for the Boolean algebra discussed in Chapter 1. And just as you did in that chapter, here you'll learn about the simple building blocks first and then we'll combine them to yield more complex functionality.

The Case for Digital Computers

Let's begin by looking at some gear-based mechanical computing devices that predate the modern era. When two gears are meshed together, the ratio of the number of teeth on each gear determines their relative speed, making them useful for multiplication, division, and other calculations. One gear-based mechanical device is the Antikythera mechanism, the oldest known example of a computer, found off a Greek island and dating back to around 100 BCE. It performed astronomical calculations whereby the user entered a date by turning a dial and then turned a crank to get the positions of the sun and the moon on that date. Another example is World War II–era artillery fire control computers, which performed trigonometry and calculus using lots of strangely shaped gears with a complex design that made them works of art as well.

An example of a mechanical computer that doesn't use gears is the *slide rule*, invented by English minister and mathematician William Oughtred (1574–1660). It's a clever application of logarithms that were discovered by Scottish physicist, astronomer, and mathematician John Napier (1550–1617). The basic function of a slide rule is to perform multiplication by exploiting the fact that $\log(x \times y) = \log(x) + \log(y)$.

A slide rule has fixed and moving scales marked in logarithms. It computes the product of two numbers by lining up the fixed x scale with the moving y scale, as shown in Figure 2-1.

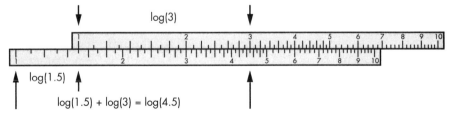

Figure 2-1: Slide rule addition

Considered by many to be the first mass-produced computing device, the slide rule is a great example of how people solved a problem using the technology available to them at the time. Today, airplane pilots still use a circular version of the slide rule called a *flight computer* that performs navigation-related calculations as a backup device.

Counting is a historically important application of computing devices. Because of our limited supply of fingers—and the fact that we need them for other things—notched bones and sticks called *tally sticks* were used as computing aids as early as 18,000 BCE. There is even a theory that the Egyptian Eye of Horus was used to represent binary fractions.

English polymath Charles Babbage (1791–1871) convinced the British government to fund the construction of a complex decimal mechanical calculator called a *difference engine*, which was originally conceived by Hessian army engineer Johann Helfrich von Müller (1746–1830). Popularized by the William Gibson and Bruce Sterling novel named after it, the difference engine was ahead of its time because the metalworking technologies of the period were not up to the task of making parts with the required precision.

Simple decimal mechanical calculators could be built, however, as they didn't require the same level of metalworking sophistication. For example, adding machines that could add decimal numbers were created in the mid-1600s for bookkeeping and accounting. Many different models were mass-produced, and later versions of adding machines replaced hand-operated levers with electric motors that made them easier to operate. In fact, the iconic old-fashioned cash register was an adding machine combined with a money drawer.

All of these historical examples fall into two distinct categories, as we'll discuss next.

The Difference Between Analog and Digital

There's an important difference between devices such as the slide rule versus tally sticks or adding machines. Figure 2-2 illustrates one of the slide rule scales from Figure 2-1 compared to a set of numbered fingers.

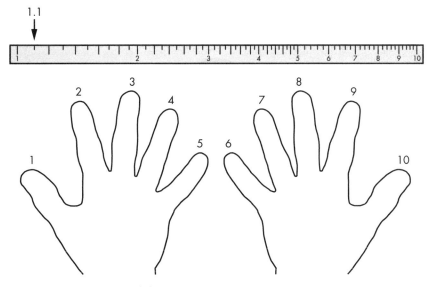

Figure 2-2: Continuous and discrete measures

Both the slide rule scale and the fingers go from 1 to 10. We can represent values such as 1.1 on the scale, which is pretty handy, but we can't do that using fingers without some fancy prestidigitation (sleight of hand or maybe doing the hand jive). That's because the scale is what mathematicians call *continuous*, meaning that it can represent real numbers. The fingers, on the other hand, are what mathematicians call *discrete* and can only represent integers. There are no values between integers. They jump from one whole number value to another, like our fingers.

When we're talking about electronics, we use the word *analog* to mean continuous and *digital* to mean discrete (it's easy to remember that fingers are digital because the Latin word for finger is *digitus*). You've probably heard the terms analog and digital before. You've been learning to program using digital computers, of course, but you may not have been aware that analog computers such as slide rules also exist.

On one hand, analog appears to be the better choice for computing because it can represent real numbers. But there are problems with precision. For example, we can pick out the number 1.1 on the slide rule scale in Figure 2-2 because that part of the scale is spacious and there's a mark for it. But it's much harder to find 9.1 because that part of the scale is more crowded and the number is somewhere between the tick marks for 9.0 and 9.2. The difference between 9.1 and 9.105 would be difficult to discern even with a microscope.

Of course, we could make the scales larger. For example, we could get a lot more accurate if the scale were the length of a football field. But it would be hard to make a portable computer with 120-yard-long scales, not to mention the huge amount of energy it would take to manipulate such large objects. We want computers that are small, fast, and low in power consumption. We'll learn another reason why size is important in the next section.

Why Size Matters in Hardware

Imagine you have to drive your kids to and from school, which is 10 miles away, at an average speed of 40 miles per hour. The combination of distance and speed means that only two round trips per hour are possible. You can't complete the trip more quickly without either driving faster or moving closer to school.

Modern computers drive electrons around instead of kids. Electricity travels at the speed of light, which is about 300 million meters per second (except in the US, where it goes about a billion feet per second). Because we haven't yet discovered a way around this physical limitation, the only way we can minimize travel time in computers is to have the parts close together.

Computers today can have clock speeds around 4 GHz, which means they can do four billion things per second. Electricity only travels about 75 millimeters in a four-billionth of a second.

Figure 2-3 shows a typical CPU that measures about 18 millimeters on each side. There's just enough time to make two complete round trips across this CPU in four-billionths of a second. It follows that making things small permits higher performance.

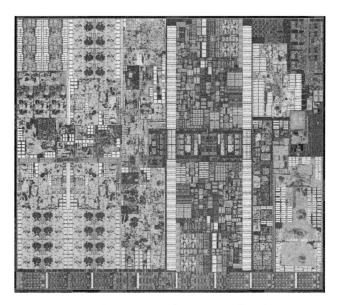

Figure 2-3: CPU photomicrograph (Courtesy of Intel Corporation)

Also, just like driving kids to and from school, it takes energy to travel, and coffee alone is insufficient. Making things small reduces the amount of travel needed, which reduces the amount of energy needed. That translates into lower power consumption and less heat generation, which keeps your phone from burning a hole in your pocket. This is one of the reasons why the history of computing devices has been characterized by efforts to make hardware smaller. But making things very small introduces other problems.

Digital Makes for More Stable Devices

Although making things small allows for speed and efficiency, it's pretty easy to interfere with things that are very small. German physicist Werner Heisenberg (1901–1976) was absolutely certain about that.

Picture a glass measuring cup with lines marked for 1 through 10 ounces. If you put some water in the cup and hold it up, it may be hard to tell how many ounces are in the cup because your hand shakes a little. Now imagine that the measuring cup was a billion times smaller. Nobody would be able to hold it still enough to get an accurate reading. In fact, even if you put that tiny cup on a table, it still wouldn't work because at that size, atomic motion would keep it from holding still. At very small scales, the universe is a noisy place.

Both the measuring cup and the slide rule are analog (continuous) devices that don't take much jiggling to produce incorrect readings. Disturbances like stray cosmic radiation are enough to make waves in microscopic measuring cups, but they're less likely to affect discrete devices such as fingers, tally sticks, or mechanical calculators. That's because discrete devices employ *decision criteria*. There are no "between" values when you're counting on your fingers. We could modify a slide rule to include decision criteria by adding *detents* (some sort of mechanical sticky spots) at the integer positions. But as soon as we do that, we've made it a discrete device and eliminated its ability to represent real numbers. In effect, decision criteria prevent certain ranges of values from being represented. Mathematically, this is similar to rounding numbers to the nearest integer.

So far, we've talked about interference as if it comes from outside, so you might think we could minimize it by using some sort of shielding. After all, lead protected Superman from kryptonite. But there is another, more insidious source of interference. Electricity affects things at a distance, just like gravity—which is good, or we wouldn't have radio. But that also means that a signal traveling down a wire on a chip can affect signals on other wires, especially when they're so close together. The wires on a modern computer chip are a few nanometers (10^{-9} meters) apart. For comparison, a human hair is about 100,000 nanometers in diameter. This interference is a bit like the wind you feel when two cars pass each other on the road. Because there's no simple way to protect against this *crosstalk* effect, using digital circuitry that has higher *noise immunity* from the decision criteria is essential. We could, of course, decrease the impact of interference by making things bigger so that wires are farther apart, but that would run counter to our other goals. The extra energy it takes to jump over the hurdle of a decision criterion gives us a degree of immunity from the noise that we don't get by using continuous devices.

In fact, the stability that comes from using decision criteria is the primary reason we build digital (discrete) computers. But, as you may have noticed, the world is an analog (continuous) place, as long as we stay away from things that are so small that quantum physics applies. In the next section, you'll learn how we manipulate the analog world to get the digital behavior necessary for building stable computing devices.

Digital in an Analog World

A lot of engineering involves clever applications of naturally occurring *transfer functions* discovered by scientists. These are just like the functions you learn about in math class, except they represent phenomena in the real world. For example, Figure 2-4 shows a graph of the transfer function for a digital camera sensor (or the film in an old-style analog camera, for that matter).

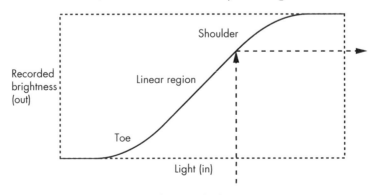

Figure 2-4: Camera sensor or film transfer function

The x-axis shows the amount of light coming in (input), and the y-axis represents the amount of recorded brightness, or the light registered by the sensor (output). The curve represents the relationship between them.

Let's play transfer function pool by bouncing an input ball off of the curve to get an output. You can see that the transfer function produces different values of recorded brightness for different values of light. Notice that the curve isn't a straight line. If too much of the light hits the *shoulder* of the curve, then the image will be overexposed, since the recorded brightness values will be closer together than in the actual scene. Likewise, if we hit the *toe* of the curve, the shot is going to be underexposed. The goal (unless you're trying for a special effect) is to adjust your exposure to hit the *linear region*, which will yield the most faithful representation of reality.

Engineers have developed all manner of tricks to take advantage of transfer functions, such as adjusting the shutter speed and aperture on a camera so that the light hits the linear region. Amplifier circuits, such as those that drive the speakers or earbuds in your music player, are another example.

Figure 2-5 shows the effect that changing the volume has on an amplifier transfer function.

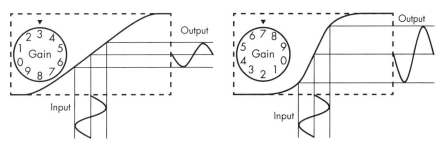

Figure 2-5: Effect of gain on amplifier transfer function

The volume control adjusts the *gain*, or steepness of the curve. As you can see, the higher the gain, the steeper the curve and the louder the output. But what if we have one of those special amplifiers from the 1984 movie *This Is Spinal Tap* on which the gain can be cranked up to 11? Then the signal is no longer confined to the linear region. This results in *distortion* because the output is no longer a faithful reproduction of the input, which makes it sound bad. You can see in Figure 2-6 that the output doesn't look like the input because the input extends outside the linear region of the transfer function.

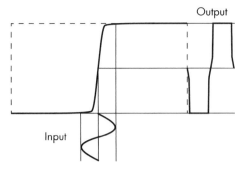

Figure 2-6: Amplifier clipping

A small change in the input causes a jump in the output at the steep part of the curve. It's like jumping from one finger to another—the sought-after decision criterion, called a *threshold*. This distortion is a useful phenomenon because the output values fall on one side of the threshold or the other; it's difficult to hit those in between. This partitions the continuous space into discrete regions, which is what we want for stability and noise immunity—the ability to function in the presence of interference. You can think of analog as aiming for a big linear region and digital as wanting a small one.

You may have intuitively discovered this phenomenon while playing on a seesaw as a child (if you had the good fortune to grow up in an era before educational playground equipment was deemed dangerous, that is). It's much more stable to be in the toe region (all the way down) or the shoulder region (all the way up) than it is to try to balance somewhere in between.

Why Bits Are Used Instead of Digits

We've talked about why digital technology is a better choice for computers than analog. But why do computers use bits instead of digits? After all, people use digits, and we're really good at counting to 10 because we have 10 fingers.

The obvious reason is that computers don't have fingers. That would be creepy. On one hand, counting on your fingers may be intuitive, but it's not a very efficient use of your fingers because you use one finger per digit. On the other hand, if you use each finger to represent a value as you did with bits, you can count to more than 1,000. This is not a new idea; in fact, the Chinese used 6-bit numbers to reference hexagrams in the *I Ching* as early as 9 BCE. Using bits instead of fingers improves efficiency by a factor of more than 100. Even using groups of four fingers to represent decimal numbers using the binary-coded decimal (BCD) representation we saw in Chapter 1 beats our normal counting method in the efficiency department.

Another reason why bits are better than digits for hardware is that with digits, there's no simple way to tweak a transfer function to get 10 distinct thresholds. We could build hardware that implements the left side of Figure 2-7, but it would be much more complicated and expensive than 10 copies of the one that implements the right side of the figure.

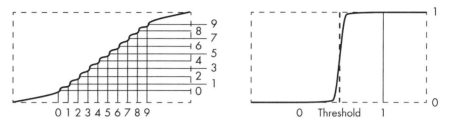

Figure 2-7: Decimal versus binary thresholds

Of course, if we *could* build 10 thresholds in the same space as one, we'd do that. But, as we've seen, we'd be better off with 10 bits instead of one digit. This is how modern hardware works. We take advantage of the transfer function's toe and shoulder regions, called *cutoff* and *saturation*, respectively, in electrical engineering language. There's plenty of wiggle room; getting the wrong output would take a lot of interference. The transfer function curve is so steep that the output snaps from one value to another.

A Short Primer on Electricity

Modern computers function by manipulating electricity. Electricity makes computers faster and easier to build than other current technologies would. This section will help you learn enough about electricity that you can understand how it's used in computer hardware.

Using Plumbing to Understand Electricity

Electricity is invisible, which makes it hard to visualize, so let's imagine that it's water. Electricity comes from an energy source such as a battery just like water comes from a tank. Batteries run out of energy and need recharging, just like water tanks go dry and need refilling. The sun is the only major source of energy we have; in the case of water, heat from the sun causes evaporation, which turns into rain that refills the tank.

Let's start with a simple water valve, something like Figure 2-8.

Figure 2-8: A water valve

As you can see, there's a handle that opens and closes the valve. Figure 2-9 shows a real-life gate valve, which gets its name after the gate that is opened and closed by the handle. Water can get through when the valve is open. We'll make believe that 0 means closed and 1 means open.

Figure 2-9: Closed and open gate valve

We can use two valves and some pipe to illustrate the AND operation, as shown in Figure 2-10.

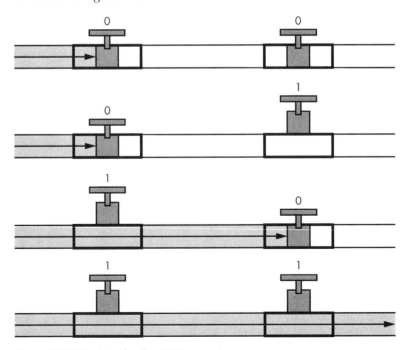

Figure 2-10: Plumbing for the AND operation

As you can see, water flows only when both valves are open, or equal to 1, which as you learned in Chapter 1 is the definition of the AND operation. When the output of one valve is hooked to the input of another, as in Figure 2-10, it's called a *series connection*, which implements the AND operation. A *parallel connection*, as shown in Figure 2-11, results from connecting the inputs of valves and the outputs of valves together, which implements the OR operation.

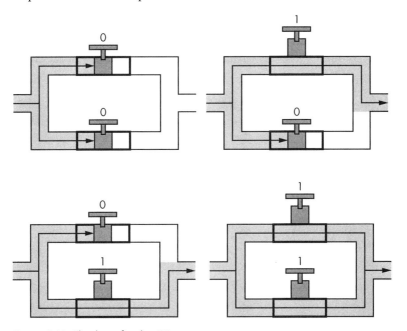

Figure 2-11: Plumbing for the OR operation

Just as it takes time for electricity to make its way across a computer chip, it takes time for water to flow or propagate through a pipe. You've probably experienced this when waiting for the water temperature to change in the shower after you've turned the knobs. This effect is called *propagation delay*, and we'll talk more about it soon. The delay is not a constant; with water, the temperature causes the pipes to expand or contract, which changes the flow rate and thus the delay time.

Electricity travels through a wire like water travels through a pipe. It's a flow of electrons. There are two parts to a piece of wire: the metal inside, like the space inside a pipe, is the *conductor*, and the covering on the outside, like the water pipe itself, is the *insulator*. The flow can be turned on and off with valves. In the world of electricity, valves are called *switches*. They're so similar that a mostly obsolete device called a vacuum tube was also known as a thermionic valve.

Water doesn't just trickle passively through plumbing pipes; it's pushed by *pressure*, which can vary in strength. The electrical equivalent of water pressure is *voltage*, measured in *volts (V)*, named after Italian physicist

Alessandro Volta (1745–1827). The amount of flow is called the *current (I)*, and that's measured in *amperes*, named after French mathematician André-Marie Ampère (1775–1836).

Water can course through wide pipes or narrow ones, but the narrower the pipe, the more that resistance limits the amount of water that can flow through. Even if you have a lot of voltage (water pressure), you can't get very much current (flow) if there's a lot of resistance from using too narrow a conductor (pipe). *Resistance (R)* is measured in *ohms (Ω)*, named after German mathematician and physicist Georg Simon Ohm (1789–1854).

These three variables—voltage, current, and resistance—are all related by *Ohm's law*, which says $I = V/R$, read as "current equals voltage divided by resistance (ohms)." So, as with water pipes, more resistance means less current. Resistance also turns electricity into heat, which is how everything from toasters to electric blankets works. Figure 2-12 illustrates how resistance makes it harder for voltage to push current.

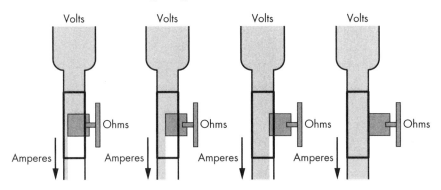

Figure 2-12: Ohm's law

An easy way to understand Ohm's law is to suck a milkshake through a straw.

Electrical Switches

Making a switch (valve) for electricity is just a matter of inserting or removing an insulator from between conductors. Think of manually operated light switches. They contain two pieces of metal that either touch or are pushed apart by the handle that operates the switch. It turns out that air is a pretty good insulator; electricity can't flow if the two pieces of metal aren't touching. (Notice I said air is a "pretty good" insulator; at a high enough voltage, air ionizes and turns into a conductor. Think lightning.)

The plumbing system in a building can be shown on a blueprint. Electrical systems called *circuits* are documented using *schematic diagrams*, which use symbols for each of the components. Figure 2-13 shows the symbol for a simple switch.

Figure 2-13: Single-pole, single-throw switch schematic

This kind of switch is like a drawbridge: electricity (cars) can't get from one side to the other when the arrow on the diagram (the bridge) is up. This is easy to see on the old-fashioned *knife switches*, shown in Figure 2-14 and often featured in cheesy science fiction movies. Knife switches are still used for things like electrical disconnect boxes, but these days they're usually hidden inside protective containers to make it harder for you to fry yourself.

Figure 2-14: Single-pole, single-throw knife switch

Figures 2-13 and 2-14 both show *single-pole, single-throw (SPST)* switches. A *pole* is the number of switches connected together that move together. Our water valves in the preceding section were single pole; we could make a *double-pole* valve by welding a bar between the handles on a pair of valves so that they both move together when you move the bar. Switches and valves can have any number of poles. *Single-throw* means that there's only one point of contact: something can be either turned on or off, but not one thing off and another on at the same time. To do that, we'd need a *single-pole, double-throw (SPDT)* device. Figure 2-15 shows the symbol for such a beast.

Figure 2-15: SPDT switch schematic

This is like a railroad switch that directs a train onto one track or another, or a pipe that splits into two pipes, as shown in Figure 2-16.

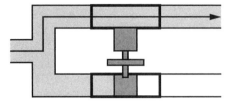

Figure 2-16: SPDT water valve

As you can see, when the handle is pushed down, water flows through the top valve. Water would flow through the bottom valve if the handle were pushed up.

Switch terminology can be extended to describe any number of poles and throws. For example, a *double-pole, double-throw (DPDT)* switch would be drawn as shown in Figure 2-17, with the dashed line indicating that the poles are *ganged*, meaning they move together.

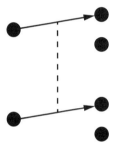

Figure 2-17: DPDT switch schematic

Figure 2-18 shows what a DPDT knife switch looks like in real life.

Figure 2-18: DPDT knife switch

I left out a few details about our waterworks earlier: the system won't work unless the water has somewhere to go. Water can't go in if the drain is clogged. And there has to be some way to get the water from the drain back to the water tank, or the system will run dry.

Electrical systems are similar. Electricity from the energy source passes through the components and returns to the source. That's why it's called an electrical *circuit*. Or think about it like this: a person running track has to make it back to the starting line in order to do another lap.

Look at the simple electrical circuit in Figure 2-19. It introduces two new symbols, one for a voltage source (on the left) and one for a light bulb (on the right). If you built such a circuit, you could turn the light on and off using the switch.

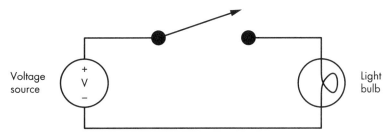

Figure 2-19: A simple electrical circuit

Electricity can't flow when the switch is open. When the switch is closed, current flows from the voltage source through the switch, through the light bulb, and back to the voltage source. Series and parallel switch arrangements work just like their water valve counterparts.

Now you've learned a little about electricity and some basic circuit elements. Although they can be used to implement some simple logic functionality, they're not powerful enough by themselves to do much else. In the next section, you'll learn about an additional device that made early electrically powered computers possible.

Building Hardware for Bits

Now that you've seen why we use bits for hardware, you're ready to learn how they're built. Diving straight into modern-day electronic implementation technologies can be daunting, so instead I'll build up the discussion from other historical technologies that are easier to understand. Although some of these examples aren't used in today's computers, you may still encounter them in systems that work alongside computers, so they're worth knowing about.

Relays

Electricity was used to power computers long before the invention of electronics. There's a convenient relationship between electricity and magnetism, discovered by Danish physicist Hans Christian Ørsted (1777–1851) in 1820. If you coil up a bunch of wire and run some electricity through it, it becomes an *electromagnet*. Electromagnets can be turned on and off and can be used to move things. They can also be used to control water valves, which is how most automatic sprinkler systems work. There are clever ways to make motors using electromagnetism. And waving a magnet around a coil of wire produces electricity, which is how a generator works; that's how we get most of our electricity, in fact. Just in case you're inclined to play with these things, turning off the electricity to an electromagnet is equivalent to waving a magnet near the coil very fast. It can be a very shocking experience, but this effect, called *back-EMF*, is handy; it's how a car ignition coil makes the spark for the spark plugs. It's also how electric fences work.

A *relay* is a device that uses an electromagnet to move a switch. Figure 2-20 shows the symbol for a single-pole, double-throw relay, which you can see looks a lot like the symbol for a switch grafted to a coil.

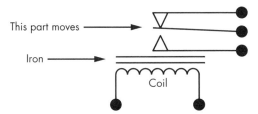

Figure 2-20: SPDT relay schematic

Figure 2-21 shows a real-life example of a single-pole, single-throw relay. The switch part is open when there is no power on the coil, so it's called a *normally open* relay. It would be a *normally closed* relay if the switch were closed without power.

Figure 2-21: Normally open SPST relay

The connections on the bottom go to the coil of wire; the rest looks pretty much like a variation on a switch. The contact in the middle moves depending on whether or not the coil is energized. We can implement logic functions using relays, as shown in Figure 2-22.

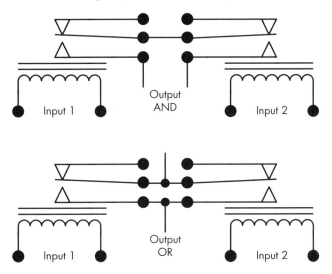

Figure 2-22: Relay circuits for AND and OR functions

On the top of Figure 2-22, you can see that the two output wires are connected together only if *both* relays are activated, which is our definition of the AND function. Likewise, on the bottom, the wires are connected together if *either* relay is activated, which is the OR function. Notice the small black dots in this figure. These indicate connections between wires in schematics; wires that cross without a dot aren't connected.

Relays allow us to do things that are impossible with switches. For example, we can build *inverters*, which implement the NOT function, without which our Boolean algebra options are very limited. We could use the output from the AND circuit on the top to drive one of the inputs on the OR circuit on the bottom. It's this ability to make switches control other switches that lets us build the complex logic needed for computers.

People have done amazing things with relays. For example, there is a single-pole, 10-throw *stepper relay* that has two coils. One coil moves the contact to the next position every time it's energized, and the other resets the relay by moving the contact back to the first position. Huge buildings full of stepper relays used to count out the digits of telephone numbers as they were dialed to connect calls. Telephone exchanges were very noisy places. Stepper relays are also what give old pinball machines their charm.

Another interesting fact about relays is that the transfer function threshold is vertical; no matter how slowly you increase the voltage on the coil, the switch always snaps from one position to the other. This mystified me as a kid; it was only when studying Lagrange-Hamilton equations as a junior in college that I learned that the value of the transfer function is undefined at the threshold, which causes the snap.

The big problems with relays are that they're slow, take a lot of electricity, and stop working if dirt (or bugs) get onto the switch contacts. In fact, the term *bug* was popularized by American computer scientist Grace Hopper in 1947 when an error in the Harvard Mark II computer was traced to a moth trapped in a relay. Another interesting problem comes from using the switch contacts to control other relays. Remember that suddenly turning off the power to a coil generates very high voltage for an instant and that air becomes conductive at high voltages. This phenomenon often results in sparks across the switch contacts, which makes them wear out. Because of these drawbacks, people began looking for something that would do the same work as relays but without moving parts.

Vacuum Tubes

British physicist and electrical engineer Sir John Ambrose Fleming (1849–1945) invented the vacuum tube. He based it on a principle called *thermionic emission*, which says that if you heat something up enough, the electrons want to jump off. Vacuum tubes have a *heater* that heats a *cathode*, which acts like a pitcher in baseball. In a vacuum, electrons (baseballs) flow from the cathode to the *anode* (catcher). Some examples of vacuum tubes are shown in Figure 2-23.

Figure 2-23: Vacuum tubes

Electrons have some properties in common with magnets, including the one where opposite charges attract and like charges repel. A vacuum tube can contain an additional "batter" element, called a *grid*, that can repel the electrons coming from the cathode to prevent them from getting to the anode. A vacuum tube that contains three elements (cathode, grid, and anode) is called a *triode*. Figure 2-24 shows the schematic symbol for a triode.

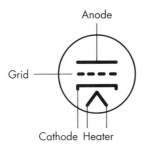

Figure 2-24: Triode schematic

Here, the heater heats up the cathode, making electrons jump off. They land on the anode unless the grid swats them back. You can think of the grid, then, as the handle on a switch.

The advantage of vacuum tubes is that they have no moving parts and are therefore much faster than relays. Disadvantages are that they get very hot and are fragile, just like light bulbs. The heaters burn out like the filaments in light bulbs. But vacuum tubes were still an improvement over relays and allowed the construction of faster and more reliable computers.

Transistors

These days transistors rule. A contraction of *transfer resistor*, a *transistor* is similar to a vacuum tube but uses a special type of material, called a *semiconductor*, that can change between being a conductor and being an insulator. In fact, this property is just what's needed to make valves for electricity that require no heater and have no moving parts. But, of course, transistors aren't perfect. We can make them really, really small, which is good, but skinny conductors have more resistance, which generates heat. Getting rid of the heat in a transistor is a real problem, because semiconductors melt easily.

You don't need to know everything about the guts of transistors. The important thing to know is that a transistor is made on a *substrate*, or slab, of some semiconducting material, usually silicon. Unlike other technologies such as gears, valves, relays, and vacuum tubes, transistors aren't individually manufactured objects. They're made through a process called *photolithography*, which involves projecting a picture of a transistor onto a silicon wafer and developing it. This process is suitable for mass production because large numbers of transistors can be projected onto a single silicon wafer substrate, developed, and then sliced up into individual components.

There are many different types of transistors, but the two main types are the *bipolar junction transistor (BJT)* and the *field effect transistor (FET)*. The manufacturing process involves *doping*, which infuses the substrate material with nasty chemicals like arsenic to change its characteristics. Doping creates regions of p and n type material. Transistor construction involves making p and n sandwiches. Figure 2-25 shows the schematic symbols that are used for some transistor types.

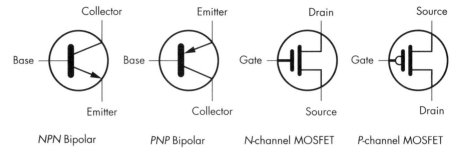

Figure 2-25: Transistor schematic symbols

The terms *NPN*, *PNP*, *N*-channel, and *P*-channel refer to the sandwich construction. You can think of the transistor as a valve or switch; the *gate* (or *base*) is the handle, and electricity flows from the top to the bottom when the handle is raised, similar to how the coil in a relay moves the contacts. But unlike the switches and valves we've seen so far, electricity can flow only in one direction with bipolar transistors.

You can see that there's a gap between the gate and the rest of the transistor in the symbols for the FETs. This gap symbolizes that FETs work using static electricity; it's like using static cling to move a switch.

The *metal-oxide semiconductor field effect transistor*, or *MOSFET*, is a variation on the FET that's very commonly used in modern computer chips because of its low power consumption. The *N*-channel and *P*-channel variants are often used in complementary pairs, which is where the term *CMOS* (complementary metal oxide semiconductor) originates.

Integrated Circuits

Transistors enabled smaller, faster, and more reliable logic circuitry that took less power. But building even a simple circuit, such as the one that implemented the AND function, still took a lot of components.

This changed in 1958, when Jack Kilby (1923–2005), an American electrical engineer, and Robert Noyce (1927–1990), an American mathematician, physicist, and cofounder of both Fairchild Semiconductor and Intel, invented the *integrated circuit*. With integrated circuits, complicated systems could be built for about the same cost as building a single transistor. Integrated circuits came to be called *chips* because of how they look.

As you've seen, many of the same types of circuits can be built using relays, vacuum tubes, transistors, or integrated circuits. And with each new technology, these circuits became smaller, cheaper, and more power-efficient. The next section talks about integrated circuits designed for combinatorial logic.

Logic Gates

In the mid-1960s, Jack Kilby's employer, Texas Instruments, introduced the 5400 and 7400 families of integrated circuits. These chips contained ready-made circuits that performed logic operations. These particular circuits, called *logic gates*, or simply *gates*, are hardware implementations of Boolean functions we call combinatorial logic. Texas Instruments sold gazillions of these. They're still available today.

Logic gates were a huge boon for hardware designers: they no longer had to design everything from scratch and could build complicated logic circuits with the same ease as complicated plumbing. Just like plumbers can find bins of pipe tees, elbows, and unions in a hardware store, logic designers could find "bins" of AND gates, OR gates, XOR gates, and *inverters* (things that do the NOT operation). Figure 2-26 shows the symbols for these gates.

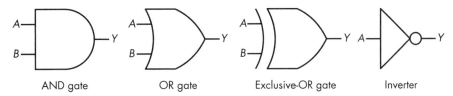

Figure 2-26: Gate schematics

As you would expect, the *Y* output of the AND gate is true if both the *A* and *B* inputs are true. (You can get the operation of the other gates from the truth tables shown back in Figure 1-1.)

The key part of the symbol for an inverter in Figure 2-26 is the ○ (circle), not the triangle it's attached to. A triangle without the circle is called a *buffer*, and it just passes its input to the output. The inverter symbol is pretty much used only where an inverter isn't being used in combination with anything else.

It's not efficient to build AND and OR gates using the *transistor-transistor logic (TTL)* technology of the 5400 and 7400 series parts, because the output from a simple gate circuit is naturally inverted, so it takes an inverter to make it come out right side up. This would make them more expensive, slower, and more power-hungry. So, the basic gates were *NAND* (not and) and *NOR* (not or), which use the inverting circle and look like Figure 2-27.

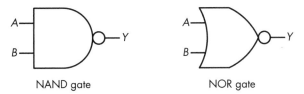

Figure 2-27: NAND and NOR gates

Fortunately, this extra inversion doesn't affect our ability to design logic circuits because we have De Morgan's law. Figure 2-28 applies De Morgan's law to show that a NAND gate is equivalent to an OR gate with inverted inputs.

Figure 2-28: Redrawing a NAND gate using De Morgan's law

All the gates we've seen so far have had two inputs, not counting the inverter, but in fact gates can have more than two inputs. For example, a three-input AND gate would have an output of true if each of the three inputs was true. Now that you know how gates work, let's look at some of the complications that arise when using them.

Improving Noise Immunity with Hysteresis

You saw earlier that we get better noise immunity using digital (discrete) devices because of the decision criteria. But there are situations where that's not enough. It's easy to assume that logic signals transition instantaneously from 0 to 1 and vice versa. That's a good assumption most of the time, especially when we're connecting gates to each other. But many real-world signals change more slowly.

Let's see what happens when we have a slowly changing signal. Figure 2-29 shows two signals that ramp slowly from 0 to 1.

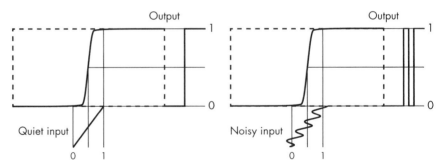

Figure 2-29: Noise glitch

The input on the left is quiet and has no noise, but there's some noise on the signal on the right. You can see that the noisy signal causes a *glitch* in the output because the noise makes the signal cross the threshold more than once.

We can get around this using *hysteresis*, in which the decision criterion is affected by history. As you can see in Figure 2-30, the transfer function is not symmetrical; in effect, there are different transfer functions for rising signals (those going from 0 to 1) and falling signals (those going from 1 to 0) as indicated by the arrows. When the output is 0, the curve on the right is applied, and vice versa.

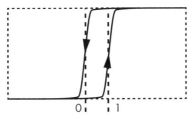

Falling threshold   Rising threshold

Figure 2-30: Hysteresis transfer function

This gives us two different thresholds: one for rising signals and one for falling signals. This means that when a signal crosses one of the thresholds, it has a lot farther to go before crossing the other, and that translates into higher noise immunity.

Gates that include hysteresis are available. They're called *Schmitt triggers* after the American scientist Otto H. Schmitt (1913–1998), who invented the circuit. Because they're more complicated and expensive than normal gates, they're used only where they're really needed. Their schematic symbol depicts the addition of hysteresis, as shown for the inverter in Figure 2-31.

Figure 2-31: Schmitt trigger gate schematic symbol

Differential Signaling

Sometimes there's so much noise that even hysteresis isn't enough. Think about walking down a sidewalk. Let's call the right edge of the sidewalk the *positive-going threshold* and the left edge the *negative-going threshold*. You might be minding your own business when someone pushing a double-wide stroller knocks you off the right-hand edge of the sidewalk and then a pack of joggers forces you back off the left side. We need protection in this case, too.

So far, we've measured our signal against an absolute threshold, or pair of thresholds in the case of a Schmitt trigger. But there are situations in which there is so much noise that both Schmitt trigger thresholds are crossed, making them ineffective.

Let's try the buddy system instead. Now imagine you're walking down that sidewalk with a friend. If your friend is on your left, we'll call it a 0; if your friend is on your right, we'll call it a 1. Now when that stroller and those joggers come by, both you and your friend get pushed off to the side. But you haven't changed positions, so if that's what we're measuring, then the noise had no effect. Of course, if the two of you are just wandering around near each other, one of you could get pushed around without the other. That's why holding hands is better, or having your arms around each other's waists. Yes, snuggling yields greater noise immunity! This is called *differential signaling*, because what we're measuring is the *difference* between a pair of *complementary* signals. Figure 2-32 shows a differential signaling circuit.

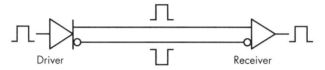

Figure 2-32: Differential signaling

You can see that there's a *driver* that converts the input signal into *complementary outputs*, and a *receiver* that converts complementary inputs back into a *single-ended* output. It's common for the receiver to include a Schmitt trigger for additional noise immunity.

Of course, there are limitations. Too much noise can push electronic components out of their specified operating range—imagine there's a building next to the sidewalk and you and your friend both get pushed into the wall. A *common-mode rejection ratio (CMRR)* is part of a component specification and indicates the amount of noise that can be handled. It's called "common-mode" because it refers specifically to noise that is common to both signals in a pair.

Differential signaling is used in many places, such as telephone lines. This application became necessary in the 1880s when electric streetcars made their debut, because they generated a lot of electrical noise that interfered with telephone signals. Scottish inventor Alexander Graham Bell (1847–1922) invented *twisted-pair* cabling, in which pairs of wires were twisted together for the electrical equivalent of snuggling (see Figure 2-33). He also patented the telephone. Today, twisted pair is ubiquitous; you'll find it in USB, SATA (disk drive), and Ethernet cables.

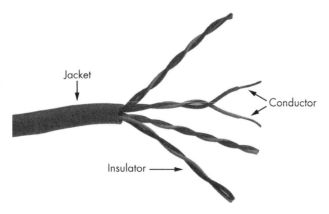

Figure 2-33: Twisted-pair Ethernet cable

An interesting application of differential signaling can be found in the Wall of Sound concert audio system used by the American band The Grateful Dead (1965–1995). It addressed the problem of vocal microphone feedback by using microphones in pairs wired so that the output from one microphone was subtracted from the output of the other. That way, any sound hitting both mics was common-mode and canceled out. Vocalists would sing into one of the mics in the pair so their voice would come through. An artifact of this system, which can be heard in the band's live recordings, is that audience noise sounds tinny. That's because lower-frequency sounds have longer wavelengths than higher-frequency sounds; lower-frequency noise is more likely to be common-mode than higher-frequency noise.

Propagation Delay

I touched on propagation delay back in "Using Plumbing to Understand Electricity" on page 41. *Propagation delay* is the amount of time it takes for a change in input to be reflected in the output. It is a statistical measure due to variances in manufacturing processes and temperature, plus the number and type of components connected to the output of a gate. Gates have both a minimum and maximum delay; the actual delay is somewhere in between. Propagation delay is one of the factors that limits the maximum speed that can be achieved in logic circuits. Designers have to use the *worst-case* values if they want their circuits to work. That means they have to design assuming the shortest and longest possible delays.

In Figure 2-34, gray areas indicate where we can't rely on the outputs because of propagation delay.

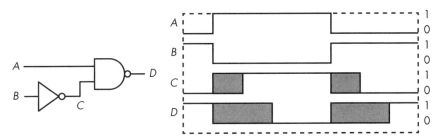

Figure 2-34: Propagation delay example

The outputs could change as early as the left edge of the gray regions, but they're not guaranteed to change until the right edge. And the length of the gray areas increases as more gates are strung together.

There is a huge range of propagation delay times that depends on process technology. Individual components, such as 7400 series parts, can have delays in the 10-nanosecond range (that is, 10 billionths of a second). The gate delays inside modern large components, such as microprocessors, can be in picoseconds (trillionths of a second). If you're reading the specifications for a component, the propagation delays are usually specified as t_{PLH} and t_{PHL} for the propagation time from low to high and high to low, respectively.

Now that we've discussed the inputs and what happens on the way to the outputs, it's time to look at the outputs.

Output Variations

We've talked some about gate inputs, but we haven't said much about outputs. There are a few different types of outputs designed for different applications.

Totem-Pole Output

A normal gate output is called a *totem pole* because the way in which one transistor is stacked on top of another resembles a totem pole. We can model this type of output using switches, as shown in Figure 2-35.

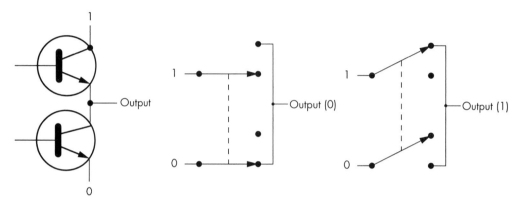

Figure 2-35: Totem-pole output

The schematic on the left illustrates how totem-pole outputs get their name. The top switch in the figure is called an *active pull-up* because it connects the output to the high logic level to get a 1 on the output. Totem-pole outputs can't be connected together. As you can see in Figure 2-35, if you connected one with a 0 output to one with a 1 output, you would have connected the positive and negative power supplies together—which would be as bad as crossing the streams from the 1984 movie *Ghostbusters* and could melt the components.

Open-Collector Output

Another type of output is called *open-collector* or *open-drain*, depending on the type of transistor used. The schematic and switch model for this output are shown in Figure 2-36.

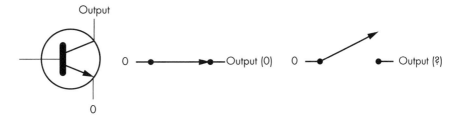

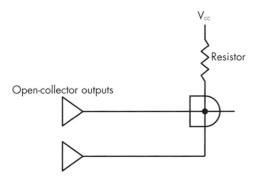

Figure 2-36: Open-collector/open-drain output

This seems odd at first glance. It's fine if we want a 0 output, but when it's not, 0 the output just *floats*, so we don't know what its value is.

Because the open-collector and open-drain versions don't have active pull-ups, we can connect their outputs together without harm. We can use a *passive pull-up*, which is just a *pull-up resistor* connecting the output to the supply voltage, which is the source of 1s. This is called V_{CC} for bipolar transistors and V_{DD} for MOS (metal-oxide-semiconductor) transistors. A passive pull-up has the effect of creating a *wired-AND*, shown in Figure 2-37.

Figure 2-37: Wired-AND

What's happening here is that when neither open-collector output is low, the resistor pulls the signal up to a 1. The resistor limits the current so that things don't catch fire. The output is 0 when any of the open-collector outputs is low. You can wire a large number of things together this way, eliminating the need for an AND gate with lots of inputs.

Another use of open-collector and open-drain outputs is to drive devices like LEDs (light-emitting diodes). Open-collector and open-drain devices are often designed to support this use and can handle higher current than totem-pole devices. Some versions allow the output to be pulled up to a voltage level that is higher than the logic 1 level, which allows us to interface to other types of circuitry. This is important because although the threshold is consistent within a family of gates such as the 7400 series, other families have different thresholds.

Tri-State Output

Although open-collector circuits allow outputs to be connected together, they're just not as fast as active pull-ups. So let's move away from the two-state solution and introduce *tri-state* outputs. The third state is off. There is an extra *enable* input that turns the output on and off, as shown in Figure 2-38.

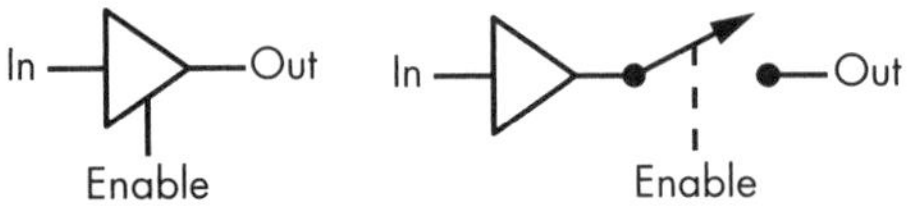

Figure 2-38: Tri-state output

Off is known as the *hi-Z*, or high-impedance, state. *Z* is the symbol for *impedance*, the mathematically complex version of resistance. You can imagine a tri-state output as the circuit from Figure 2-35. Controlling the bases separately gives us four combinations: 0, 1, hi-Z, and meltdown. Obviously, circuit designers must make sure that the meltdown combination cannot be selected.

Tri-state outputs allow a large number of devices to be hooked together. The caveat is that only one device can be enabled at a time.

Building More Complicated Circuits

The introduction of gates greatly simplified the hardware design process. People no longer had to design everything from discrete components. For example, where it took around 10 components to build a two-input NAND gate, the 7400 included four of them in a single package, called a *small-scale integration (SSI)* part, so that one package could replace 40.

Hardware designers could build anything from SSI gates just as they could using discrete components, which made things cheaper and more compact. And because certain combinations of gates are used a lot, *medium-scale integration (MSI)* parts were introduced that contained these combinations, further reducing the number of parts needed. Later came *large-scale integration (LSI)*, *very large-scale integration (VLSI)*, and so on.

You'll learn about some of the gate combinations in the following sections, but this isn't the end of the line. We use these higher-level functional building blocks themselves to make even higher-level components, similar to the way in which complex computer programs are constructed from smaller programs.

Building an Adder

Let's build a two's-complement adder. You may never need to design one of these, but this example will demonstrate how clever manipulation of logic can improve performance—which is true for both hardware and software.

We saw back in Chapter 1 that the sum of 2 bits is the XOR of those bits and the carry is the AND of those bits. Figure 2-39 shows the gate implementation.

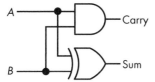

Figure 2-39: Half adder

You can see that the XOR gate provides the sum and the AND gate provides the carry. Figure 2-39 is called a *half adder* because something is missing. It's fine for adding two bits, but there needs to be a third input so that we can carry. This means that two adders are needed to get the sum for each bit. We carry when at least two of the inputs are 1. Table 2-1 shows the truth table for this *full adder*.

Table 2-1: Truth Table for Full Adder

A	B	C	Sum	Carry
0	0	0	0	0
0	0	1	1	0
0	1	0	1	0
0	1	1	0	1
1	0	0	1	0
1	0	1	0	1
1	1	0	0	1
1	1	1	1	1

A full adder is a bit more complicated to build and looks like Figure 2-40.

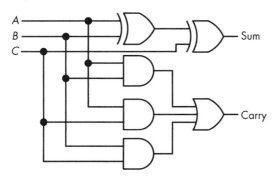

Figure 2-40: Full adder

As you can see, this takes many more gates. But now that we have the full adder, we can use it to build an adder for more than one bit. Figure 2-41 shows a configuration called a *ripple-carry adder.*

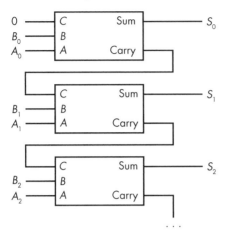

Figure 2-41: Ripple-carry adder

This *ripple-carry adder* gets its name from the way that the carry ripples from one bit to the next. It's like doing the wave. This works fine, but you can see that there are two gate delays per bit, which adds up fast if we're building a 32- or 64-bit adder. We can eliminate these delays with a *carry look-ahead adder,* which we can figure out how to make work using some basic arithmetic.

We can see in Figure 2-40 that the full-adder carry-out for bit i that is fed into the carry-in for bit $i + 1$:

$$C_{i+1} = \left(A_i \mathrm{AND} B_i\right) \mathrm{OR} \left(A_i \mathrm{AND} C_i\right) \mathrm{OR} \left(B_i \mathrm{AND} C_i\right)$$

The big sticking point here is that we need C_i in order to get C_{i+1}, which causes the ripple. You can see this in the following equation for C_{i+2}:

$$C_{i+2} = \left(A_{i+1} \mathrm{AND} B_{i+1}\right) \mathrm{OR} \left(A_{i+1} \mathrm{AND} C_{i+1}\right) \mathrm{OR} \left(B_{i+1} \mathrm{AND} C_{i+1}\right)$$

We can eliminate this dependency by substituting the first equation into the second, as follows:

$$\begin{aligned}
C_{i+2} = {} & \left(A_{i+1} \mathrm{AND} B_{i+1}\right) \\
& \mathrm{OR}\left(A_{i+1} \mathrm{AND}\left(\left(A_i \mathrm{AND} B_i\right) \mathrm{OR}\left(A_i \mathrm{AND} C_i\right) \mathrm{OR}\left(B_i \mathrm{AND} C_i\right)\right)\right) \\
& \mathrm{OR}\left(B_{i+1} \mathrm{AND}\left(\left(A_i \mathrm{AND} B_i\right) \mathrm{OR}\left(A_i \mathrm{AND} C_i\right) \mathrm{OR}\left(B_i \mathrm{AND} C_i\right)\right)\right)
\end{aligned}$$

Note that although there are a lot more ANDs and ORs, there's still only two gates' worth of propagation delay. C_n is dependent only on the A and B inputs, so the carry time, and hence the addition time, doesn't depend on the number of bits. C_n can always be generated from C_{n-1}, which uses an increasingly large number of gates as n increases. Although gates are cheap, they do consume power, so there is a trade-off between speed and power consumption.

Building Decoders

In "Representing Integers Using Bits" on page 6, we built or *encoded* numbers from bits. A *decoder* does the opposite by turning an encoded number back into a set of individual bits. One application of decoders is to drive displays. You may have seen *nixie tubes* (shown in Figure 2-42) in old science fiction movies; they're a really cool retro display for numbers. They're essentially a set of neon signs, one for each digit. Each glowing wire has its own connection, requiring us to turn a 4-bit number into 10 separate outputs.

Figure 2-42: A nixie tube

Recall that octal representation takes eight distinct values and encodes them into 3 bits. Figure 2-43 shows a 3:8 decoder that converts an octal value back into a set of single bits.

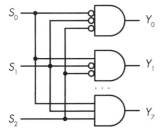

Figure 2-43: A 3:8 decoder

When the input is 000, the Y_0 input is true; when the input is 001, Y_1 is true; and so on. Decoders are principally named by the number of inputs and outputs. The example in Figure 2-43 has three inputs and eight outputs, so it's a 3:8 decoder. This decoder would commonly be drawn as shown in Figure 2-44.

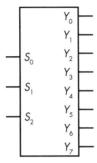

Figure 2-44: The 3:8 decoder schematic symbol

Building Demultiplexers

You can use a decoder to build a *demultiplexer*, commonly abbreviated as *dmux*, which allows an input to be directed to one of several outputs, as you would do if sorting Hogwarts students into houses. A demultiplexer combines a decoder with some additional gates, as shown in Figure 2-45.

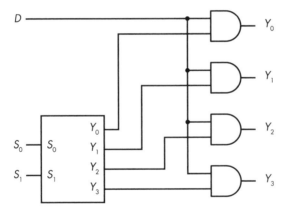

Figure 2-45: A 1:4 demultiplexer

The demultiplexer directs the input signal D to one of the four outputs Y_{0-3} based on the decoder inputs S_{0-1}. The symbol in Figure 2-46 is used in schematics for demultiplexers.

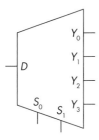

Figure 2-46: The demultiplexer
schematic symbol

Building Selectors

Choosing one input from a number of inputs is another commonly performed function. For example, we might have several operand sources for an adder and need to choose one. Using gates, we can create another functional block called a *selector* or *multiplexer (mux)*.

A selector combines a decoder with some additional gates, as shown in Figure 2-47.

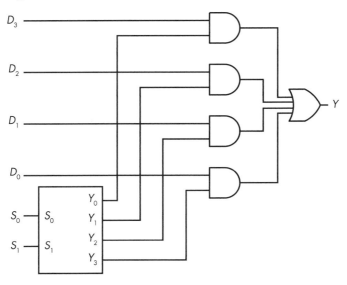

Figure 2-47: A 4:1 selector

Selectors are also used a lot and have their own schematic symbol. Figure 2-48 shows the symbol for a 4:1 selector, which is pretty much the reverse of the symbol for a decoder.

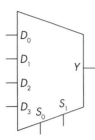

Figure 2-48: The 4:1 selector schematic symbol

You're probably familiar with selectors but don't know it. You might have a toaster oven that has a dial with positions labeled Off, Toast, Bake, and Broil. That's a *selector switch* with four positions. A toaster oven has two heating elements, one on top and another on the bottom. Toaster oven logic works as shown in Table 2-2.

Table 2-2: Toaster Oven Logic

Setting	Top element	Bottom element
Off	Off	Off
Bake	Off	On
Toast	On	On
Broil	On	Off

We can implement this logic using a pair of 4:1 selectors ganged together, as shown in Figure 2-49.

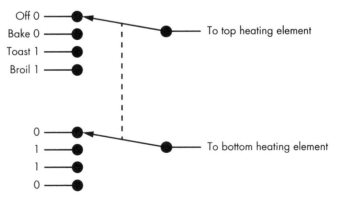

Figure 2-49: Toaster oven selector switch

Summary

In this chapter, you learned why we use bits instead of digits to build hardware. You also saw some of the developments in technology that have allowed us to implement bits and combinatorial digital logic. You learned about modern logic design symbols and how simple logic elements can be combined to make more complex devices. We looked at how the outputs of combinatorial devices are a function of their inputs, but because the outputs change in response to the inputs, there's no way to remember anything. Remembering requires the ability to "freeze" an output so that it doesn't change in response to inputs. Chapter 3 discusses sequential logic, which enables us to remember things over time.

3

SEQUENTIAL LOGIC

The combinatorial logic you learned about in the last chapter "goes with the flow." In other words, the outputs change in response to the inputs. But we can't build computers out of combinatorial logic alone, because it doesn't give us any way to remove something from the flow and remember it. You can't add up all the numbers from 1 to 100, for example, unless you can keep track of where you are.

You'll learn about *sequential logic* in this chapter. The term comes from the word *sequence*, which means "one thing after another in time." As a human, you have intuitive knowledge about time, just as you do about counting on your fingers, but that doesn't mean that time is natural for digital circuitry. We have to create it somehow.

Combinatorial logic deals only with the present state of inputs. Sequential logic, however, deals with both the present and the past. In this chapter, you'll learn about circuitry both for generating time and for remembering things. We'll trace some of the various technologies that have been used for these purposes from their early roots through the present day.

Representing Time

We measure time using some sort of *periodic* function, such as the rotation of the Earth. We call one full rotation a day, which we subdivide into smaller units such as hours, minutes, and seconds. We could define a second as 1/86,400th of an Earth rotation, since there are 86,400 seconds in a day.

In addition to using an external event like the rotation of the Earth, we can also generate our own periodic functions by applying certain elements of physics, such as the time that it takes for a pendulum to swing. This technique produced the "tick tock" sound in old grandfather clocks. Of course, to be useful, the pendulum has to be calibrated to the measured length of a second.

With computers, we're working with electronics, so we need a periodic electrical signal. We could generate one by placing a switch so that it's whacked by a pendulum. But unless you're a serious steampunk geek, you probably don't want a pendulum-powered computer. We'll learn about more modern approaches in the next section.

Oscillators

Let's look at a trick we can do with an inverter: we can connect the output to the input, as shown in Figure 3-1.

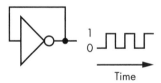

Figure 3-1: An oscillator

This produces *feedback,* just like what you get when a microphone is too close to a loudspeaker. The output of the inverter bounces back and forth, or *oscillates*, between 0 and 1. The speed at which it oscillates is a function of the propagation delay (see "Propagation Delay" on page 57), and that tends to vary with temperature. It would be useful to have an oscillator with a stable frequency so that we could generate an accurate time reference.

A cost-effective way to do this is with a crystal. Yes, very new age. Crystals, like magnets, have a relationship with electricity. If you attach *electrodes* (wires) to a crystal and give it a squeeze, it'll generate electricity. And if you put some electricity on those wires, the crystal will bend. This is called the *piezoelectric* effect, and it was discovered by brothers Paul-Jacques (1855–1941) and Pierre (1859–1906) Curie in the late 1800s. The piezoelectric effect has all sorts of applications. A crystal can pick up sound vibrations, making a microphone. Sound vibrations generated by applying electricity to crystals are responsible for the annoying beeps made by many appliances. You can spot a crystal in a circuit diagram by the symbol shown in Figure 3-2.

Figure 3-2: The crystal schematic symbol

A crystal oscillator alternately applies electricity to a crystal and receives electricity back, using electronic single-pole, double-throw switches. The time it takes a crystal to do this is predictable and very accurate. Quartz is one of the best crystal materials to use. That's why you see advertisements for accurate quartz timepieces. Keep in mind when you see the price tag on a fancy watch that a really good crystal retails for only about 25 cents.

Clocks

Oscillators give us a way to measure time, as you've seen. Computers need to keep time for obvious reasons, like being able to play a video at a consistent speed. But there's another, lower-level reason why time is important. In Chapter 2, we discussed how propagation delay affects the time that it takes circuitry to do things. Time gives us a way to wait, for example, for the worst-case delay in an adder before looking at the result so that we know it's stable and correct.

Oscillators supply clocks to computers. A computer's clock is like the drummer in a marching band; it sets the pace for the circuitry. The maximum clock speed or fastest tempo is determined by the propagation delays.

Component manufacturing involves a lot of statistics because there's a lot of variance from part to part. The *binning* process puts components into different bins, or piles, depending on their measured characteristics. The fastest parts that fetch the highest price go into one bin; slower, less expensive parts go into another; and so on. It's not practical to have an infinite number of bins, so there's variance within the parts in a bin, although it's less than the variance for the whole lot of parts. This is one reason why propagation delays are specified as a range; manufacturers provide minimum and maximum values in addition to a typical value. A common logic circuit design error is to use the typical values instead of the minimums and maximums. When you hear about people *overclocking* their computers, it means they're gambling that their part was statistically in the middle of its bin and that its clock can be increased by some amount without causing the part to fail.

Latches

Now that we have a source of time, let's try to remember a single bit of information. We can do that with feedback, such as tying the output of an OR gate back to an input, as shown in Figure 3-3. This doesn't create an oscillator such as we saw in Figure 3-1, since there's no inversion. Assume that *out* starts off at 0 in the circuit in Figure 3-3. Now, if *in* goes to 1, *out* does too, and because it's connected to another input it stays that way, even if *in* goes back to 0. In other words, it remembers.

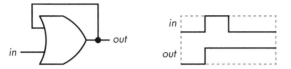

Figure 3-3: An OR gate latch

Of course, this scheme needs some work because there's no way to make *out* be 0 again. We need a way to reset it by disconnecting the feedback, as shown in Figure 3-4.

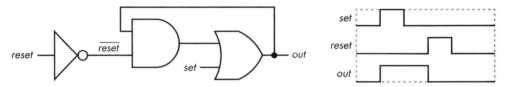

Figure 3-4: An AND-OR gate latch

Note that we've labeled the output of the inverter $\overline{reset}$. Putting a line over a symbol is hardware-speak meaning "the opposite." It means that something is true when it's a 0 and false when it's a 1. Sometimes this is referred to as *active low* instead of *active high*, meaning that it does its thing when it's 0 instead of 1. The line is pronounced "bar," so in speech the signal would be referred to as "reset bar."

When *reset* is low, $\overline{reset}$ is high, so the output from the OR gate is fed back into the input. When *reset* goes high, $\overline{reset}$ goes low, breaking that feedback so that *out* goes to 0.

Figure 3-5 shows an *S-R latch*, a slightly cleverer way of building a bit of memory. *S-R* stands for *set-reset*. It has active low inputs and *complementary* outputs, meaning one is active low and one is active high. You could build a version of this that has active high inputs by using NOR gates, but NOR gates are often more power-hungry than NAND gates, in addition to being more complicated and expensive to build.

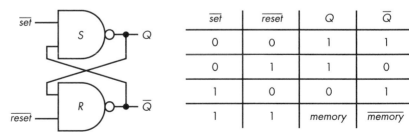

$\overline{set}$	$\overline{reset}$	Q	$\overline{Q}$
0	0	1	1
0	1	1	0
1	0	0	1
1	1	memory	$\overline{memory}$

Figure 3-5: An S-R latch

The case where both $\overline{set}$ and $\overline{reset}$ are active is weird and not intended for use, because both outputs are true. Also, if both inputs become inactive (that is, transition from 0 to 1) at the same time, the state of the outputs is not predictable because it's dependent on the propagation delays.

The circuit in Figure 3-5 has a nice property that the circuit in Figure 3-4 does not, which is that its design is symmetrical. That means the propagation delays are similar for both the *set* and *reset* signals.

Gated Latches

Now that we have some way of remembering information, let's look at what it takes to remember something at a point in time. The circuit in Figure 3-6 has an extra pair of gates added to the inputs.

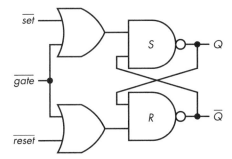

Figure 3-6: A gated S-R latch

As you can see, when the $\overline{gate}$ input is inactive (high), it doesn't matter what $\overline{set}$ and $\overline{reset}$ are doing; the outputs won't change because the inputs to the S and R gates will both be 1.

Because we want to remember one bit of information, the next improvement we can make is to add an inverter between the $\overline{set}$ and $\overline{reset}$ inputs so that we need only a single data input, which we'll abbreviate as *D*. This modification is shown in Figure 3-7.

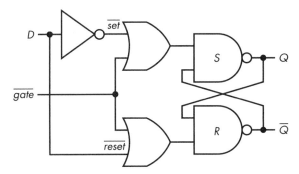

Figure 3-7: A gated D latch

Now, if *D* is a 1 when the $\overline{gate}$ is low, the *Q* output will be set to 1. Likewise, if *D* is a 0 when the $\overline{gate}$ is low, the *Q* output will be set to 0. Changes on *D* when $\overline{gate}$ is high have no effect. That means we can remember the state of D. You can see this in the timing diagram shown in Figure 3-8.

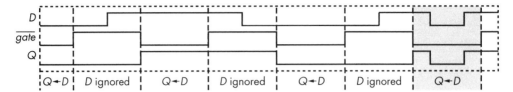

Figure 3-8: A gated D latch timing diagram

The problem with this circuit is that changes in *D* pass through whenever the $\overline{gate}$ is low, as you can see in the shaded section. This means we have to count on *D* being "well-behaved" and not changing when the "gate" is "open." It would be better if we could make the opening instantaneous. We'll see how to do that in the next section.

Flip-Flops

As we discussed in the last section, we want to minimize the chances of getting incorrect results due to changing data. The way that's commonly done is to use the transition between logic levels to grab the data instead of grabbing it when the logic level has a particular value. These transitions are called *edges*. You can think of an edge as a decision criterion for time. Back in Figure 3-8, you can see the almost-instantaneous transition between logic levels. Edge-triggered latches are called *flip-flops*.

Latches are a building block used to make flip-flops. We can construct a positive edge-triggered flip-flop called a *D flip-flop* by cleverly combining three S-R latches, as shown in Figure 3-9. *Positive edge-triggered* means that the flip-flop operates on the transition from a logic 0 to a logic 1; a *negative edge-triggered* flip-flop would operate on the transition from a logic 1 to a logic 0.

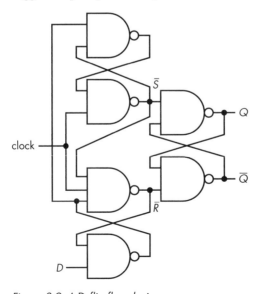

Figure 3-9: A D flip-flop design

This circuit can be somewhat mind-boggling. The two gates on the right form an S-R latch. We know from Figure 3-5 that those outputs won't change unless either $\overline{S}$ or $\overline{R}$ goes low.

Figure 3-10 shows how the circuit behaves for various values of D and *clock*. The thin lines show logic 0s; the thick lines are logic 1s.

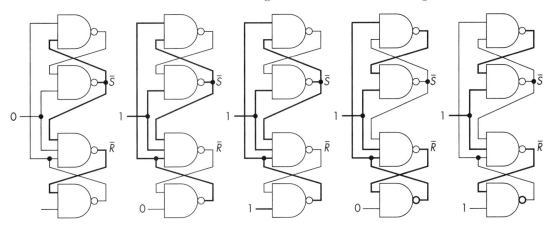

Figure 3-10: A D flip-flop operation

Starting at the left, you can see that when the clock is 0, the value of D doesn't matter because both $\overline{S}$ and $\overline{R}$ are high, so the state of the latch on the right-hand side of Figure 3-9 is unchanged. Moving toward the right, you can see in the next two diagrams that if $\overline{R}$ is low, changing the value of D has no effect. Likewise, the two rightmost diagrams show that if $\overline{S}$ is low, changing the value of D has no effect. The upshot is that changes to D have no effect when the clock is either high or low.

Now, let's look at what happens when the clock changes from low to high, as shown in Figure 3-11.

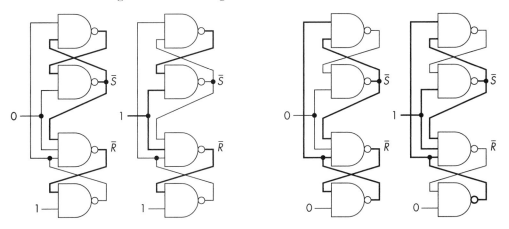

Figure 3-11: A D flip-flop positive edge operation

You can see on the left that when the clock is low and *D* is high, $\overline{S}$ and $\overline{R}$ are high, so nothing changes. But when the clock changes to 1, $\overline{S}$ goes low, which changes the state of the flip-flop. On the right, you can see similar behavior when *D* is low and the clock goes high, causing $\overline{R}$ to go low and changing the flip-flop state. You saw in Figure 3-10 that no other changes matter.

In 1918 British physicists William Eccles and Frank Jordan invented the first electronic version of a flip-flop, which used vacuum tubes. Figure 3-12 shows the diagram for a slightly less antique *D flip-flop* called the 7474.

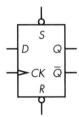

Figure 3-12: A D flip-flop

The D flip-flop has complementary *Q* and $\overline{Q}$ (outputs and $\overline{S}$ (set) and $\overline{R}$ (reset) inputs. It's a little confusing, as the diagram shows *S* and *R*; it's the combination of those with the ○ that make them $\overline{S}$ and $\overline{R}$. So, except for the mysterious things on the left-hand side, it's just like our S-R latch. The mysterious things are two extra inputs, *D* for data and *CK* for clock, which is represented by the triangle. It's positive edge-triggered, so the value of the *D* input is stored whenever the signal on the *CK* goes from a 0 to a 1.

Edge-triggered devices have other timing considerations in addition to propagation delay. There is the *setup time*, which is the amount of time before the clock edge that the signal must be stable, and the *hold time*, which is the amount of time after the clock edge that the signal must be stable. These are shown in Figure 3-13.

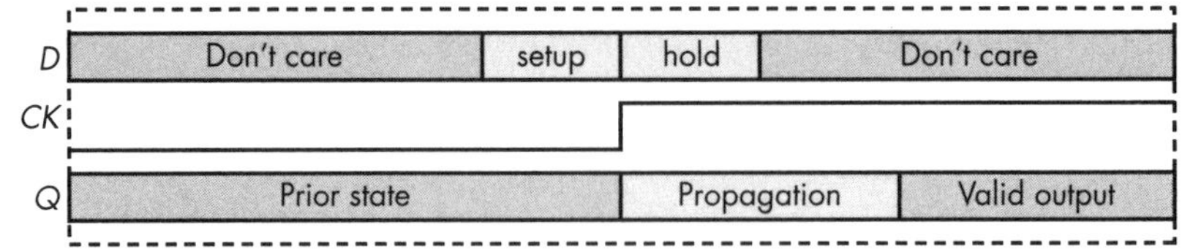

D	Don't care	setup	hold	Don't care
CK				
Q	Prior state		Propagation	Valid output

Figure 3-13: Setup and hold times

As you can see, we don't have to care what's happening on the *D* input except during the setup and hold times surrounding the clock edge. And, as with all other logic, the output is stable after the propagation delay time and stays stable independent of the *D* input. Setup and hold times are typically denoted by t_{setup} and t_{hold}.

The edge behavior of flip-flops works well with clocks. We'll see an example in the next section.

Counters

Counting is a common application of flip-flops. For example, we could count time from an oscillator and drive a display with a decoder to make a digital clock. Figure 3-14 shows a circuit that produces a 3-bit number (C_2, C_1, C_0) that is the count of the number of times the *signal* changes from 0 to 1. The $\overline{reset}$ signal can be used to set the counter to 0.

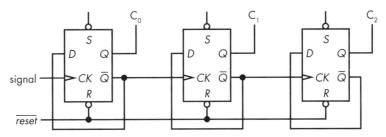

Figure 3-14: A 3-bit ripple counter

This counter is called a *ripple counter* because the result ripples from left to right, not because it's useful for counting bottles of cheap wine. C_0 changes C_1, C_1 changes C_2, and so on if there are more bits. Since the D input of each flip-flop is connected to its $\overline{Q}$ output, it will change state on every positive transition of the CK signal.

This is also called an *asynchronous* counter because everything just happens when it gets around to it. The problem with asynchronous systems is that it's hard to know when to look at the result. The outputs (C_2, C_1, C_0) are invalid during rippling. You can see how it takes longer to get a result for each successive bit in Figure 3-15, where the gray areas represent undefined values due to propagation delay.

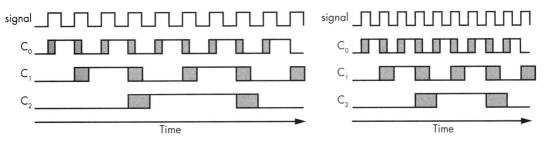

Figure 3-15: Ripple counter timing

The *timing diagram* on the left shows that we get a valid 3-bit number after the propagation delays settle out. But on the right, you can see that we're trying to count faster than the propagation delays permit, so there are times where no valid number is produced.

This is a variation of the problem we saw with the ripple-carry adder back in Figure 2-41. Just as we were able to solve that problem with the carry look-ahead design, we can address the ripple problem with a *synchronous* counter design.

Unlike the ripple counter, the synchronous counter outputs all change at the same time (in sync). This implies that all the flip-flops are clocked in parallel. A 3-bit synchronous counter is shown in Figure 3-16.

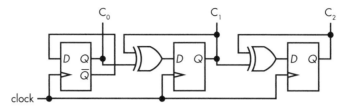

Figure 3-16: A 3-bit synchronous counter

You can see that all the flip-flops in the counter change state at the same time because they're all clocked at the same time. Although propagation delay is still a factor in knowing when the outputs are valid, the cascade effect has been eliminated.

Counters are yet another functional building block, which means they have their own schematic symbol. In this case it's yet another rectangular box, as you can see in Figure 3-17.

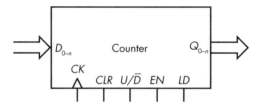

Figure 3-17: A counter schematic symbol

The figure includes a number of inputs we haven't seen before. Counters are available that have some or all of these inputs. Most counters have a *CLR* input that clears the counter, setting it to 0. Also common is an *EN* input that enables the counter—the counter doesn't count unless enabled. Some counters can count in either direction; the $U/\overline{D}$ input selects up or down. Finally, some counters have data inputs D_{0-n} and a load signal *LD* that allows the counter to be set to a specific value.

Now that we have counters, we can use them to keep track of time. But that's not the only thing we can do with flip-flops. We'll start learning how to remember large amounts of information in the next section.

Registers

D flip-flops are good for remembering things. It's a common enough application that you can get *registers*, which are a bunch of D flip-flops in a single package that share a common clock. Figure 3-18 shows an example of a register holding the result of addition using the adder circuit discussed earlier.

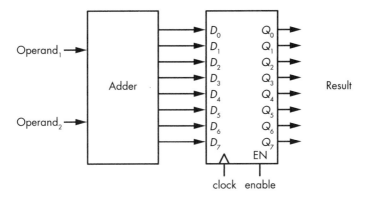

Figure 3-18: A register holding an adder result

Once the output of the adder has been clocked into the register, the operands can change without changing the result. Note that registers often have *enable* inputs similar to those we saw for counters.

Memory Organization and Addressing

We've seen that flip-flops are useful when we need to remember a bit and that registers are handy when we need to remember a collection of bits. What do we do when we need to remember a lot more information, though? For example, what if we want to be able to store several different addition results?

Well, we can start with a big pile of registers. But now we have a new problem: how to specify the register we want to use. This situation looks like Figure 3-19.

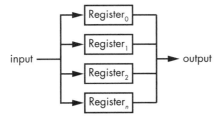

Figure 3-19: Multiple registers

One way to solve this problem is to assign each register a number, as in the figure. We can have this number or *address* specify the register using one of our standard building blocks, the decoder from "Building Decoders" on page 63. The decoder outputs are connected to the enable inputs on the registers.

Next we need to be able to select the output from the addressed register. Fortunately, we learned how to build selectors in "Building Selectors" on page 65, and they're just what we need.

Systems often have multiple memory components that need to be hooked together. Time for yet another of our standard building blocks: the *tri-state* output.

Putting it all together, a memory component looks like Figure 3-20.

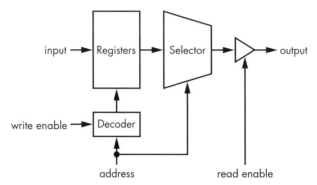

Figure 3-20: A memory component

Memory components have a lot of electrical connections. If we want to do something with 32-bit numbers, we would need 32 connections each for the inputs and the outputs, plus connections for the address, control signals, and power. Programmers don't have to worry about how to fit circuitry into packages or how to route wires, but hardware designers do. We can cut down on the number of connections by realizing that memory rarely needs to be read and written at the same time. We can get by with one set of data connections plus a *read/write* control. Figure 3-21 shows a schematic of a simplified memory chip. The *enable* control turns the whole thing on and off so that multiple memory chips can be connected together.

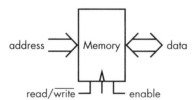

Figure 3-21: A simplified memory chip

You'll notice that the figure uses big fat arrows for the address and data instead of showing the individual signals. We call groups of related signals *buses*, so the memory chip has an *address bus* and a *data bus*. Yup, it's mass transit for bits.

The next challenge in memory chip packaging comes when the memory size increases and lots of address bits need connections. Referring back to Table 1-2 in Chapter 1, we'd need 32 address connections for a 4-GiB memory component.

Memory designers and road planners deal with similar traffic-management issues. Many cities are organized into grids, and that's also how memory chips are laid out internally. You can see several rectangular regions that are chunks of memory in the CPU photomicrograph shown back in Figure 2-3. The address is partitioned into two chunks: a *row* address and a *column* address. A memory location is addressed internally using the intersection of the row and column, as shown in Figure 3-22.

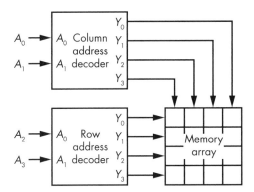

Figure 3-22: Row and column addressing

Obviously we don't need to worry about the number of address lines in the 16-location memory shown in this figure. But what if there were a lot more? We could halve the number of address lines by *multiplexing* the row and column addresses. All we would need is registers on the memory chip to save them, as shown in Figure 3-23.

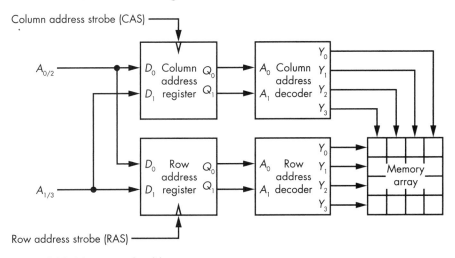

Figure 3-23: Memory with address registers

Since the address comes in two parts, it follows that performance would be better if we only had to change one part, such as by setting the row address and then varying the column address. This is what we find in today's large memory chips.

Memory chips are described by their size in depth × width format. For example, a 256 × 8 chip would have 256 8-bit wide memory locations; a 64 Mib × 1 chip would have 64 mebibits.

Random-Access Memory

The memory we've talked about so far is called *random-access memory*, or *RAM*. With RAM, the entire width of any memory location can be read or written in any order.

Static RAM, or *SRAM*, is expensive but fast. It takes six transistors for each bit. Because transistors take up space, SRAM isn't a great choice for storing billions or trillions of bits.

Dynamic memory (DRAM) is a clever hack. Electrons are stored in microscopic buckets called *capacitors*, using only one transistor for the lids. The problem is, these buckets leak, so it's necessary to *refresh* the memory every once in a while, which means regularly topping off the buckets. You have to be careful that the topping off doesn't occur at a critical time that would conflict with accessing the memory; this was a problem with one of the first DRAM-based computers, the DEC LSI-11. One of the interesting side effects of DRAM is that the buckets leak more when light shines on them. This enables them to be used as digital cameras.

DRAM is used for large memory chips because of its high density (number of bits per area). Large memory chips mean lots of addresses, which means that DRAM chips use the multiplexed addressing scheme discussed in the previous section. Because of other internal design considerations, it's only faster to save the row address using the row address strobe and then to vary the column address via the column address strobe. It's an overused term, but rows are sometimes called *pages*. It's comparable to reading a book like this one; it's much easier to scan a page than it is to flip pages. Or, as stated by the great performance pioneer Jimmy Durante, best performance is a-ras-a-ma-cas. This is a very important consideration in programming: keeping things that are used together in the same row greatly improves performance.

Both SRAM and DRAM are *volatile* memory, which means that data can be lost when the power is interrupted. *Core* memory is an antique *nonvolatile* type of RAM that stores bits in *toroidal* (doughnut-shaped) pieces of iron, which you can see in Figure 3-24. Toroids were magnetized in one direction for a 0 and the other for a 1. The physics of toroids is cool because they're very resistant to electromagnetic interference from outside the doughnut. In this type of memory, cores were arranged in a grid called a *plane* with row and column wires through them. There was also a third wire, called the *sense* wire, because the only way to read the state of a bit was to try to change it and then sense what happened. Of course, if you sensed that it changed, you had to change it back or the data would be lost, making the bit useless. That required a lot of circuitry in addition to all the stitching. Core was actually three-dimensional memory, as planes were assembled into bricks.

While core is antique technology, the nonvolatile characteristic is still prized, and research continues making commercially practical *magnetoresistive* memory that combines the best of core memory and RAM.

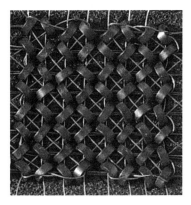

Figure 3-24: Core memory

Read-Only Memory

Read-only memory, or *ROM*, is not a very accurate name. Memory that could only be read but never written wouldn't be useful. Even though the name has stuck, it's more accurate to say that ROM is write-once memory. ROM can be written once and then read multiple times. ROM is important for devices that need to have a program built in, such as a microwave oven; you wouldn't want to have to program your microwave every time you needed popcorn.

One of the early forms of ROM was the Hollerith card, which later became known as the *IBM card*, shown in Figure 3-25. Bits were punched into pieces of paper. Really! They were pretty cheap because American inventor Herman Hollerith (1860–1929) was big into cutting corners. Hollerith invented the card in the late 1800s, although it might be more accurate to say that he appropriated the idea from the Jacquard loom, which was invented by Joseph Marie Jacquard in 1801. The Jacquard loom used punched cards to control the weaving pattern. Of course, Jacquard borrowed the idea from Basile Bouchon, who had invented a punched paper tape–controlled loom in 1725. Sometimes it's hard to distinguish between invention and appropriation, because the future is built on the past. Keep this in mind when you hear people arguing for longer and more restrictive patent and copyright laws; progress slows if we can't build on the past.

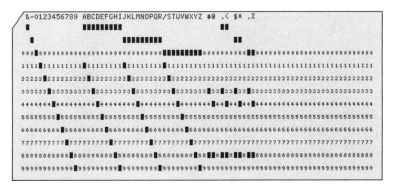

Figure 3-25: An IBM card

Early IBM card readers used switches to read the bits. Cards would be slid under a row of springy wires that poked through the holes and made contact with a piece of metal on the other side. Later versions, which worked by shining light through the holes onto a row of *photodetectors* on the other side, were considerably faster.

Punched paper tape is a related ROM technology; rolls of paper tape with holes punched in it were used to represent bits (see Figure 3-26). Tape had an advantage over cards in that dropping a deck of cards would scramble the data. Then again, tape could tear and was difficult to repair; many a masking tape repair job clogged up the works.

Figure 3-26: Punched paper tape

Cards and tape were very slow because they had to be physically moved in order to be read.

A ROM variation called *core rope memory* was used in the Apollo flight computer (see Figure 3-27). Because it could be written only by sewing, it was impervious to interference—which is important in the harsh environment of space.

Figure 3-27: Core rope memory from the Apollo guidance computer

IBM cards and paper tape were *sequential* memory; that is, the data was read in order. Card readers couldn't go backward, so they were really only good for long-term storage of data. The contents had to be read into some sort of RAM in order to be used. The first commercial availability of a single-chip microprocessor, the Intel 4004 in 1971, created demand for better program storage technology. These first microprocessors were used for devices like calculators that ran a fixed program. Along came *mask-programmable* ROM. A *mask* is a stencil used as part of the integrated circuit–manufacturing process. You'd write a program and send the bit pattern off to a semiconductor manufacturer along with a really big check. They'd turn it into a mask, and you'd get back a chip containing your program. It was read-only because there was no way to change it without writing another big check and having a different mask made. Mask-programmable ROM could be read in a random-access manner.

Masks were so expensive that they could be justified only for high-volume applications. Along came *programmable read-only memory (PROM)*, ROM chips that you could program yourself, but only once. The original mechanism for PROM involved melting nichrome (a nickel-chromium alloy) fuses on the chip. Nichrome is the same stuff that makes the glowing wires in your toaster.

People would go through a big pile of PROM chips quickly when developing a program. Engineers are pain-adverse, so next came *erasable programmable read-only memory (EPROM)*. These chips were like PROMs, except that they had a quartz window on top and you could erase them by putting them under a special ultraviolet light.

Life got better with the introduction of *electrically erasable programmable read-only memory* (what a mouthful!), or *EEPROM*. This is an EPROM chip that can be erased electrically—no light, no quartz window. Erasing EEPROM is comparatively very slow, though, so it's not something you want to do a lot. EEPROMs are technically RAM, since it's possible to read and write the contents in any order. But because they're slow to write and more expensive than RAM, they're used as a substitute for ROMs.

Block Devices

It takes time to talk to memory. Imagine you had to go to the store every time you needed a cup of flour. It's much more practical to go to the store once and bring home a whole sack of flour. Larger memory devices use this principle. Think warehouse shopping for bits.

Disk drives, also known as *mass storage*, are great for storing immense amounts of data. An 8-TB drive cost less than $200 when this book was written. They're often referred to as *mass storage*. Some religious institutions use mass storage for their ceremonies in between use. Disk drives store bits on rotating magnetic platters, sort of like a lazy Susan. Bits periodically come around to where you're sitting, and you use your hand to pluck them off or put them on. In a disk drive, your hand is replaced by the *disk head*.

Disk drives are relatively slow compared to other types of memory. If you want something that just passed by the head, you have to wait almost an entire rotation for it to come around again. Modern disks spin at 7,200 rotations per minute (RPM), which means a rotation takes slightly longer than 8 milliseconds. The big problem with disk drives is that they're mechanical and wear out. Bearing wear is one of the big causes of disk failure. The difference between commercial and consumer-grade devices is primarily the amount of grease in the bearing—manufacturers are able to charge hundreds of dollars for something that costs less than a penny. Disk drives store data by magnetizing areas on the disk, which makes them nonvolatile just like core memory.

Disk drives are a trade-off between speed and density. They're slow because of the time it takes for the bits you want to show up under the head, but because the data is being brought to the head, no space is required for address and data connections, unlike, for example, in a DRAM. Figure 3-28 shows the insides of a disk drive. They're built in sealed containers because dust and dirt would cause them to fail.

Figure 3-28: A disk drive

Disks are block-addressable rather than byte-addressable. A *block* (historically called a *sector*) is the smallest unit that can be accessed. Disks have historically had 512-byte sectors, although newer devices have 4,096-byte sectors. That means in order to change a byte on a disk, you have to read an entire block, change the byte, and then write back the entire block. Disks contain one or more *platters* that are laid out as shown in Figure 3-29.

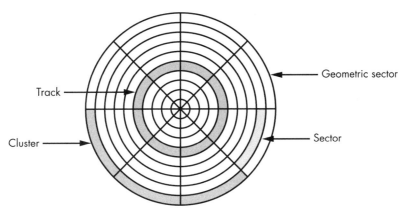

Figure 3-29: Disk layout

Since all of the sectors contain the same number of bits, the *bit density* (bits/mm^2) is greater at the center of each platter than it is at the outer edge. This is wasteful because there's clearly room to cram more bits onto the outer tracks. Newer disks address this problem by dividing the disk into a set of *radial zones*, effectively having more sectors in the outer zones than in the inner ones.

There are a couple of numbers that describe the performance of disk drives. Modern disks have a head on an actuator arm that moves radially across the disk; the position of the head divides the disks into tracks. The *seek time* is the amount of time that it takes to move the head from one track to another. It would, of course, be much faster to have one head per track so that seeking wasn't necessary; you could get that on very old disk drives, but the tracks are too close together on modern disks to make that practical. In addition to the seek time, there's the time it takes for the part of the disk you're interested in to rotate so that it's under the head, called *rotational latency*, which as we saw above is in the millisecond range.

Disk drives are often called *hard drives*. Originally, all disk drives were hard drives. The distinction arose when cheap removable storage devices called *floppy disks* appeared on the scene. Floppy disks were bendable, so calling the other type "hard" made them easy to differentiate.

An antiquated variation on disk drives is *magnetic drum* storage, which was just what it sounds like: a rotating magnetic drum with stripes of heads on it.

Magnetic tape is another nonvolatile storage technology that uses reels of magnetized tape. It is way slower than a disk drive, and it can take a long time to wind the tape to the requested position. Early Apple computers used consumer-grade audio cassettes for magnetic tape storage.

Optical disks are similar to magnetic disks except that they use light instead of magnetism. You know these as CDs and DVDs. A big advantage of optical disks is that they can be mass-produced via printing. Preprinted disks are ROMs. PROM-equivalent versions that can be written once (CD-R, DVD-R) are also available, as are versions that can be erased and rewritten (CD-RW). Figure 3-30 shows a close-up of a portion of an optical disk.

Figure 3-30: Optical disk data

Flash Memory and Solid State Disks

Flash memory is the most recent incarnation of EEPROM. It's good solution for some applications, like music players and digital cameras. It works by storing electrons in buckets just like DRAM. In this case, the buckets are bigger and better built so they don't leak. But the lid hinges on the buckets eventually wear out if they're opened and closed too many times. Flash memory can be erased more quickly than EEPROM and is cheaper to make. It works like RAM for reading and also for writing a blank device filled with 0s. But although 0s can be turned into 1s, they can't be turned back without being erased first. Flash memory is internally divided into blocks, and only blocks can be erased, not individual locations. Flash memory devices are random-access for reads, and block-access for writes.

Disk drives are slowly being replaced by *solid-state disk drives*, which are pretty much just flash memory packaged up to look like a disk drive. Right now their price per bit is much higher than spinning disks, but that's expected to change. Because flash memory wears out, solid-state drives include a processor that keeps track of the usages in different blocks and tries to even it out so that all blocks wear out at the same rate.

Error Detection and Correction

You never know when a stray cosmic ray is going to hit a piece of memory and corrupt the data. It would be nice to know when this happens and even nicer to be able to repair the damage. Of course, such improvements cost money and are not typically found in consumer-grade devices.

We'd like to be able to detect errors without having to store a complete second copy of the data. And that wouldn't work anyway, because we wouldn't know which copy was correct. We could store two extra copies and assume that the matching pair (if any) is the right one. Computers designed for very harsh environments do this. They also use a more expensive circuit design that doesn't burn up when hit by a proton. For example, the space shuttle had redundant computers and a voting system in the event that an error was detected.

We can test for a 1-bit error using a method called *parity*. The idea is to add up the number of bits that are set to 1 and use an extra bit to store whether that sum is an odd or even number. We can do this by taking the XOR of the bits. There are two forms of this: in *even parity* the sum of the bits is used, and in *odd parity* the complement of the sum of the bits is used. This choice may seem, well, odd, but the nomenclature comes from the number of 1s or 0s including the parity bit.

The left half of Figure 3-31 shows the calculation of even parity; there are four 1s, so the parity is 0. The right half shows the checking of the parity; a 0 out means that the data is good, or at least as good as we can tell with parity. The big problem with parity is that it's one place where two wrongs sure look like a right; it only catches odd numbers of errors.

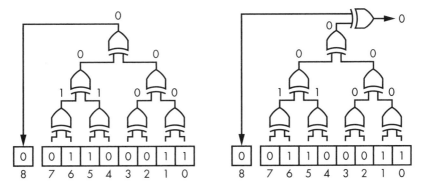

Figure 3-31: Even parity generation and checking

There are more complicated methods, such as Hamming codes, invented by American mathematician Richard Hamming (1915–1998), which take more bits and allow for more errors to be detected and for some to be corrected. *Error checking and correcting (ECC)* memory chips are available that include this circuitry. They're typically used in big data centers, not in consumer devices.

Methods like parity are good for data that is constantly changing. There are less expensive methods that allow for verification of static block data, such as a computer program. The simplest of these is the *checksum*, where the contents of every data location are summed into some n-bit value and the overflow bits are thrown away. The checksum can be compared against the program, usually just before it is run. The larger the checksum value (that is, larger n), the lower the chance of getting a false positive.

Cyclic redundancy checks, or *CRCs*, are a mathematically better replacement for checksums. Hash codes are another. The goal is to calculate a verification number that is unique enough for the data so that for most changes, the check will no longer be correct.

Hardware vs. Software

The techniques used to make PROMs, EEPROMs, and flash aren't just limited to memory. We'll soon see how computer hardware is constructed from logic circuits. And since you're learning programming, you know that programs include logic in their code, and you may know that computers expose logic to programs via their instruction sets. What's the difference between doing that in hardware versus software? It's a blurry line. To a large degree, there is little distinction except that it's much easier to build software since there are no additional costs other than design time.

You've probably heard the term *firmware*, which originally just referred to software in a ROM. But most firmware now lives in flash memory or even RAM, so the difference is minimal. And it's even more complicated than that. It used to be that chips were designed by geeks who laid out circuits by sticking colored masking tape on big sheets of clear Mylar. In 1979 American scientists and engineers Carver Mead and Lynn Conway changed the world with their publication of *Introduction to VLSI Systems*, which helped kick-start the electronic design automation (EDA) industry. Chip design became software. Chips today are designed using specialized programming languages such as Verilog, VHDL, and SystemC.

Much of the time, a computer programmer is simply given a piece of hardware to use. But you might get the opportunity to participate in the design of a system that includes both hardware and software. The design of the interface between hardware and software is critical. There are countless examples of chips with unusable, unprogrammable, and unnecessary features.

Integrated circuits are expensive to make. In the early days, all chips were *full custom* designs. Chips are built up in layers, with the actual components on the bottom and metal layers on top to wire them together. *Gate arrays* were an attempt to lower the cost for some applications; a set of predesigned components was available, and only the metal layers were custom. Just like with memory, these were supplanted by PROM-equivalent versions that you could program yourself. And there was an EPROM equivalent that could be erased and reprogrammed.

Modern *field-programmable gate arrays (FPGAs)* are the flash memory equivalent; they can be reprogrammed in software. In many cases, using an FPGA is cheaper than using other components. FPGAs are very rich in features; for example, you can get a large FPGA that contains a couple of ARM processor cores. Intel recently purchased Altera and may include FPGAs on its processor chips. There's a good chance you'll work on a project containing one of these devices, so be prepared to turn your software into hardware.

Summary

In this chapter, you've learned where computers get their sense of time. You were introduced to sequential logic, which, along with combinatorial logic from Chapter 2, provides us with all of the fundamental hardware building blocks. And you've learned something about how memory is built. We'll put all of this knowledge together to make a computer in Chapter 4.

4

COMPUTER ANATOMY

You learned about the properties of bits and ways of using them to represent things in Chapter 1. In Chapters 2 and 3, you learned why we use bits and how they're implemented in hardware. You also learned about a number of basic building blocks and how they could be combined into more complex configurations. In this chapter, you'll learn how those building blocks can be combined into a circuit that can manipulate bits. That circuit is called a *computer*.

There are many ways of constructing a computer. The one we'll build in this chapter was chosen for ease of explanation, not because it's the best possible design. And although simple computers work, a lot of additional complexity is required to make them work *well*. This chapter sticks to the simple computer; the next two chapters cover some of the extra complications.

There are three big pieces in a modern computer. These are the *memory*, the *input and output (I/O)*, and the *central processing unit (CPU)*. This section covers how these pieces relate to each other. Chapter 3 introduced memory, and Chapter 5 covers computers and memory in more detail. I/O is the subject of Chapter 6. The CPU lives in what I'm calling "City Center" in this chapter.

Memory

Computers need someplace to keep the bits that they're manipulating. That place is memory, as you learned in Chapter 3. Now it's time to find out how computers use it.

Memory is like a long street full of houses. Each house is exactly the same size and has room for a certain number of bits. Building codes have pretty much settled on 1 byte per house. And just like on a real street, each house has an *address*, which is just a number. If you have 64 MiB of memory in your computer, that's $64 \times 1,024 \times 1,024 = 67,108,864$ bytes (or 536,870,912 bits). The bytes have addresses from 0 to 67,108,863. This numbering makes sense, unlike the numbering on many real streets.

It's pretty common to refer to a memory *location*, which is just memory at a particular address, such as 3 Memory Lane (see Figure 4-1).

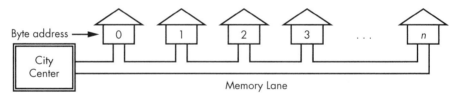

Figure 4-1: Memory Lane

Just because the basic unit of memory is a byte doesn't mean we always look at it that way. For example, 32-bit computers usually organize their memory in 4-byte chunks, while 64-bit computers usually organize their memory in 8-byte chunks. Why does that matter? It's like having a four- or eight-lane highway instead of a one-lane road. More lanes can handle more traffic because more bits can get on the data bus. When we address memory, we need to know what we're addressing. Addressing long words is different from addressing bytes because there are 4 bytes to a long word on a 32-bit computer, and 8 bytes to a long word on a 64-bit computer. In Figure 4-2, for example, long-word address 1 contains byte addresses 4, 5, 6, and 7.

Another way to look at it is that the street in a 32-bit computer contains fourplexes, not single houses, and each fourplex contains two duplexes. That means we can address an individual unit, a duplex, or a whole building.

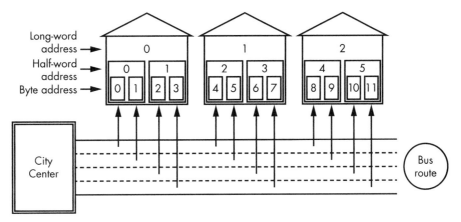

Figure 4-2: Memory highway

You may have noticed that each building straddles the highway such that each byte has its own assigned lane, and a long word takes up the whole road. Bits commute to and from City Center on a bus that has four seats, one for each byte. The doors are set up so that there's one seat for each lane. On most modern computers, the bus stops only at one building on each trip from City Center. This means we can't do things like form a long word from bytes 5, 6, 7, and 8, because that would mean that the bus would have to make two trips: one to building 0 and one to building 1. Older computers contained a complicated loading dock that allowed this, but planners noticed that it wasn't all that useful and so they cut it out of the budget on newer models. Trying to get into two buildings at the same time, as shown in Figure 4-3, is called a *nonaligned access*.

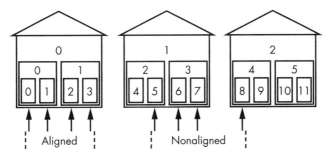

Figure 4-3: Aligned and nonaligned accesses

There are lots of different kinds of memory, as we saw in the previous chapter. Each has a different *price/performance ratio*. For example, SRAM is fast and expensive, like the highways near where the politicians live. Disk is cheap and slow—the dirt road of memory.

Who gets to sit in which seat when commuting on the bus? Does byte 0 or byte 3 get to sit in the leftmost seat when a long word heads into town? It depends on the processor you're using, because designers have made them both ways. Both work, so it's pretty much a theological debate. In fact, the term *endian*—based on the royal edicts in Lilliput and Blefuscu in Jonathan Swift's *Gulliver's Travels* regarding which was the proper end on which to crack open a soft-boiled egg—is used to describe the difference.

Byte 0 goes into the rightmost seat in little-endian machines like Intel processors. Byte 0 goes into the leftmost seat in big-endian machines like Motorola processors. Figure 4-4 compares the two arrangements.

Figure 4-4: Big- and little-endian arrangements

Endianness is something to keep in mind when you're transferring information from one device to another, because you don't want to inadvertently shuffle the data. A notable instance of this occurred when the UNIX operating system was ported from the PDP-11 to an IBM Series/1 computer. A program that was supposed to print out "Unix" printed out "nUxi" instead, as the bytes in the 16-bit words got swapped. This was sufficiently humorous that the term *nuxi syndrome* was coined to refer to byte-ordering problems.

Input and Output

A computer that couldn't communicate with the outside world wouldn't be very useful. We need some way to get things in and out of the computer. This is called *I/O* for *input/output*. Things that connect to the I/O are called *I/O devices*. Since they're on the periphery of the computer, they're also often called *peripheral devices* or just *peripherals*.

Computers used to have a separate I/O avenue, as shown in Figure 4-5, that was similar to Memory Lane. This made sense when computers were physically huge, because they weren't squeezed into small packages with a limited number of electrical connections. Also, Memory Lane wasn't very long, so it didn't make sense to limit the number of addresses just to support I/O.

Figure 4-5: Separate memory and I/O buses

Memory Lane is much longer now that 32- and 64-bit computers are common. It's so long that there aren't houses at every address; many empty lots are available. In other words, there are addresses that have no memory associated with them. As a result, it now makes more sense to set aside a portion of Memory Lane for I/O devices. It's like the industrial district on the edge of town. Also, as more circuitry is crammed into a package that has a limited number of connections, it just makes sense for I/O to be on the same bus as memory.

Many computers are designed with standard input/output *slots* so that I/O devices can be connected in a uniform manner. This is done sort of like how property was distributed in the Old West; the unincorporated territory is partitioned into a set of land grants, as shown in Figure 4-6. Each slot holder gets the use of all addresses up to its borders. Often there is a specific address in each slot that contains some sort of identifier so that City Center can conduct a census to determine who's living in each slot.

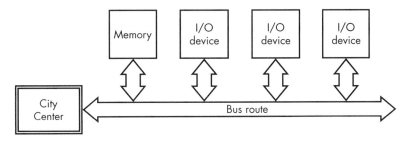

Figure 4-6: Shared memory and I/O bus

We often use a shipping metaphor and say that things are hooked up to *I/O ports*.

The Central Processing Unit

The *central processing unit (CPU)* is the part of the computer that does the actual computing. It lives at City Center in our analogy. Everything else is the supporting cast. The CPU is made up of many distinct pieces that we'll learn about in this section.

Arithmetic and Logic Unit

The *arithmetic logic unit (ALU)* is one of the main pieces of a CPU. It's the part that knows how to do arithmetic, Boolean algebra, and other operations. Figure 4-7 shows a simple diagram of an ALU.

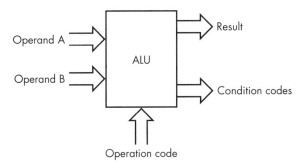

Figure 4-7: A sample ALU

The *operands* are just bits that may represent numbers. The operation code, or *opcode*, is a number that tells the ALU what *operator* to apply to the operands. The *result*, of course, is what we get when we apply the operator to the operands.

The *condition codes* contain extra information about the result. They are usually stored in a *condition code register*. A register, which we saw back in Chapter 3, is just a special piece of memory that's on a different street from the rest of the memory—the street with the expensive, custom homes. A typical condition code register is shown in Figure 4-8. The numbers on top of the boxes are the bit numbers, which is a convenient way to refer to them. Note that some of the bits are not used; this is not unusual.

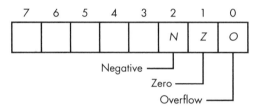

Figure 4-8: A condition code register

The N is set to 1 if the result of the last operation is a negative number. The Z bit is set to 1 if the result of the last operation is 0. The O bit is set to 1 if the result of the last operation created an overflow or underflow.

Table 4-1 shows what an ALU might do.

Table 4-1: Sample ALU Opcodes

Opcode	Mnemonic	Description
0000	clr	Ignore the operands; make each bit of the result 0 (clear).
0001	set	Ignore the operands; make each bit of the result 1.
0010	not	Ignore B; turn 0s from A to 1s and vice versa.
0011	neg	Ignore B; the result is the two's complement of A, −A.
0100	shl	Shift A left by the low 4 bits of B (see next section).
0101	shr	Shift A right by the low 4 bits of B (see next section).
0110		Unused.
0111		Unused.
1000	load	Pass operand B to the result.
1001	and	The result is A AND B for each bit in the operands.
1010	or	The result is A OR B for each bit in the operands.
1011	xor	The result is A XOR B for each bit in the operands.
1100	add	The result is A + B.
1101	sub	The result is A − B.
1110	cmp	Set condition codes based on B − A (compare).
1111		Unused.

The ALU may appear mysterious, but it's really just some logic gates feeding a selector, which you've seen before. Figure 4-9 shows the general design of an ALU, omitting some of the more complicated functions for the sake of simplicity.

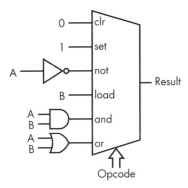

Figure 4-9: ALU partial internals

Shiftiness

You may have noticed the shift operations in Table 4-1. A left shift moves every bit left one position, throwing away the leftmost bit and moving a 0 into the vacated rightmost position. If we left-shift 01101001 (105_{10}) by 1, we'll get 11010010 (210_{10}). This is pretty handy because left-shifting a number one position multiplies it by 2.

A right shift moves every bit right one position, throwing away the rightmost bit and moving a 0 into the vacated leftmost position. If we right-shift 01101001 (105_{10}) by 1, we'll get 00110100 (52_{10}). This divides a number by 2, throwing away the remainder.

The value of the MSB (most significant bit) lost when left-shifting or the LSB (least significant bit) when right-shifting is often needed, so it's saved in the condition code register. Let's make believe that our CPU saves it in the *O* bit.

You might have noticed that everything in the ALU looks like it can be implemented in combinatorial logic except these shift instructions. You can build *shift registers* out of flip-flops where the contents are shifted one bit position per clock.

A sequential shift register (shown in Figure 4-10) is slow because it takes one clock per bit in the worst case.

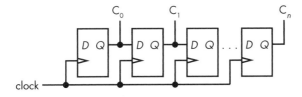

Figure 4-10: A sequential shift register

We can solve this by constructing a *barrel shifter* entirely out of combinatorial logic using one of our logic building blocks, the selector (refer back to Figure 2-47). To build an 8-bit shifter, we would need eight of the 8:1 selectors.

There is one selector for each bit, as shown in Figure 4-11.

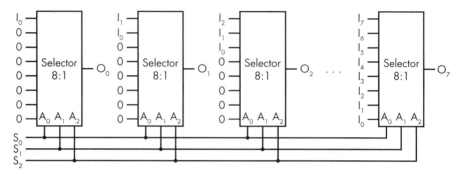

Figure 4-11: A combinatorial barrel shifter

The amount of right shift is provided on S_{0-2}. You can see that with no shift (000 for S), input bit 0 (I_0) gets passed to output bit 0 (O_0), I_1 to O_1, and so on. When S is 001, the outputs are shifted right by one because that's the way the inputs are wired up to the selector. When S is 010, the outputs are shifted right by two, and so on. In other words, we have all eight possibilities wired and just select the one we want.

You may wonder why I keep showing these logic diagrams as if they're built out of old 7400 series parts. Functions such as gates, multiplexors, demultiplexors, adders, latches, and so on are available as predefined components in integrated circuit design systems. They're used just like the old components, except instead of sticking lots of the 7400 series parts I mentioned in Chapter 2 onto a circuit board, we now assemble similar components into a single chip using design software.

You may have noticed the absence of multiplication and division operations in our simple ALU. That's because they're much more complicated and don't really show us anything we haven't already seen. You know that multiplication can be performed by repeated addition; that's the sequential version. You can also build a combinatorial multiplier by cascading barrel shifters and adders, keeping in mind that a left shift multiplies a number by 2.

Shifters are a key element for the implementation of floating-point arithmetic; the exponents are used to shift the mantissas to line up the binary points so that they can be added together, subtracted, and so on.

Execution Unit

The *execution unit* of a computer, also known as the *control unit*, is the boss. The ALU isn't much use by itself, after all—something has to tell it what to do. The execution unit grabs opcodes and operands from the right places in memory, tells the ALU what operations to perform, and puts the results back in memory. Hopefully, it does all that in an order that serves some useful purpose. (By the way, we're using the "to perform" definition of *execute*. No bits are actually killed.)

How might the execution unit do this? We give it a list of instructions, things like "add the number in location 10 to the number in location 12 and put the result in location 14." Where does the execution unit find these instructions? In memory! The technical name for what we have here is a *stored-program computer*. It has its genesis in work by English wizard Alan Turing (1912–1954).

That's right, we have yet another way of looking at bits and interpreting them. *Instructions* are bit patterns that tell the computer what to do. The bit patterns are part of the design of a particular CPU. They're not some general standard, like numbers, so an Intel Core i7 CPU would likely have a different bit pattern for the inc A instruction than an ARM Cortex-A CPU.

How does the execution unit know where to look for an instruction in memory? It uses a *program counter* (often abbreviated *PC*), which is sort of like a mail carrier, or like a big arrow labeled "You are here." Shown in Figure 4-12, the program counter is another register, one of those pieces of memory on the special side street. It's constructed from a counter (see "Counters" on page 77) instead of a vanilla register (see "Registers" on page 78). You can view the counter as a register with additional counting functionality.

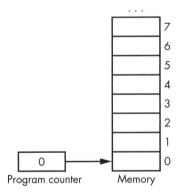

Figure 4-12: A program counter

The program counter contains a memory address. In other words, it points at, or *references*, a location in memory. The execution unit fetches an instruction from the location referenced by the program counter. There are special instructions that change the value of the program counter, which we'll see shortly. Unless we're executing one of these, the program counter is *incremented* (that is, the size of one instruction is added to it) after the instruction is executed so that the next instruction will come from the next memory location. Note that CPUs have some initial program counter value, usually 0, when the power is turned on. The counter we saw in Figure 3-17 has inputs to support all these functions.

It all works kind of like a treasure hunt. The computer goes to a certain place in memory and finds a note. It reads that note, which tells it to do something, and then goes someplace else to get the next note, and so on.

Instruction Set

The notes that computers find in memory during their treasure hunt are called *instructions*. This section goes into what those instructions contain.

Instructions

To see what sort of instructions might we find in a CPU, and how we choose bit patterns for them, our example assumes a computer with 16-bit-wide instructions.

Let's try dividing our instruction into four fields—the opcode plus addresses for two operands and result—as shown in Figure 4-13.

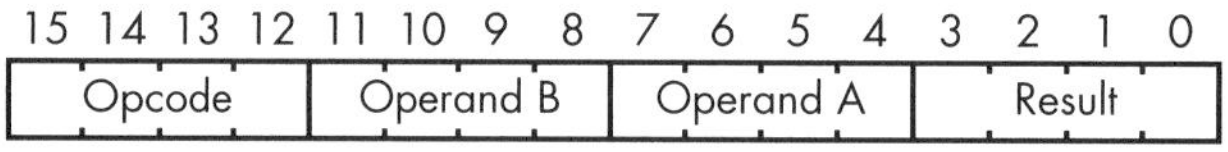

```
15 14 13 12 11 10 9  8  7  6  5  4  3  2  1  0
┌──────────────┬─────────────┬─────────────┬─────────────┐
│   Opcode     │  Operand B  │  Operand A  │   Result    │
└──────────────┴─────────────┴─────────────┴─────────────┘
```

Figure 4-13: Three-address instruction layout

This may seem like a good idea, but it doesn't work very well. Why? Because we only have room for 4 bits of address for each of the operands and the result. It's kind of hard to address a useful amount of memory when you have only 16 addresses. We could make the instruction bigger, but even if we went to 64-bit-wide instructions, we'd have only 20 bits of address, which would reach only a mebibyte of memory. Modern machines have gibibytes of memory.

Another approach would be to duplicate the DRAM addressing trick we saw in Figure 3-23. We could have an *address extension register* and load it with the high-order address bits using a separate instruction. This technique was used by Intel to allow its 32-bit machines to access more than 4-GiB of memory. Intel called it PAE, for *physical address extension*. Of course, it takes extra time to load this register, and lots of register loads are required if we need memory on both sides of the boundary created by this approach.

There's an even more important reason why the three-address format doesn't work well, though: it counts on some magic, nonexistent form of memory that allows three different locations to be addressed at the same time. All three memory blocks in Figure 4-14 are the same memory device; there aren't three address buses and three data buses.

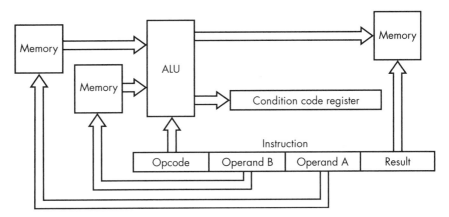

Figure 4-14: Unworkable computer architecture

We could make this work by having one register hold the contents of operand A and another hold the contents of operand B. The hardware would need to do the following:

1. Load the instruction from memory using the address in the program counter.
2. Load the operand A register using the address from the operand A portion of the instruction.
3. Load the operand B register using the address from the operand B portion of the instruction.
4. Store the result in memory using the address from the result portion of the instruction.

That's a lot of complicated hardware. If each of these steps took a clock cycle, then it would take four cycles just to get something done. We should take a hint from the fact that we can access only one memory location at a time and design our instruction set accordingly. More address bits would be available if we tried to address only one thing at a time.

We can do that by adding another house to the register street. We'll call this register the *accumulator*, or *A* register for short, and it will hold the result from the ALU. Rather than doing an operation between two memory locations, we'll do it between one memory location and the accumulator. Of course, we'll have to add a *store* instruction that stores the contents of the accumulator in a memory location. So now we can lay out our instructions as shown in Figure 4-15.

15 14 13 12	11 10 9 8 7 6 5 4 3 2 1 0
Opcode	Address

Figure 4-15: Single-address instruction layout

This gets us more address bits, but it takes more instructions to get things done. We used to be able to have an instruction that said:

$$C = A + B$$

But now we need three instructions:

Accumulator = A
Accumulator = Accumulator + B
C = Accumulator

You might notice that we just replaced one instruction with three, effectively making the instruction bigger and contradicting ourselves. That's true for this simple case, but it's not true in general. Let's say we needed to calculate this:

$$D = A + B + C$$

We couldn't do that in a single instruction even if it could access three addresses because now we need four. We'd have to do it like this:

Intermediate = $A + B$
D = Intermediate + C

Sticking with 12 bits of address, we'd need 40-bit instructions to handle three address plus the opcode. And we'd need two of these instructions for a total of 80 bits to calculate D. Using the single-address version of the instructions requires four instructions for a total of 64 bits.

Accumulator = A
Accumulator = Accumulator + B
Accumulator = Accumulator + C
D = Accumulator

Addressing Modes

Using an accumulator managed to get us 12 address bits, and although being able to address 4,096 bytes is much better than 16, it's still not enough. This way of addressing memory is known as *direct addressing*, which just means that the address is the one given in the instruction.

We can address more memory by adding *indirect addressing*. With indirect addressing, we get the address from the memory location contained in the instruction, rather than directly from the instruction itself. For example, let's say memory location 12 contains the value 4,321, and memory location 4,321 contains 345. If we used direct addressing, loading from location 12 would get 4,321, while indirect addressing would get 345, the contents of location 4,321.

This is all fine for dealing with memory, but sometimes we just need to get constant numbers. For example, if we need to count to 10, we need some way of loading that number. We can do this with yet another addressing mode, called *immediate mode addressing*. Here the address is just treated as a number, so, using the previous example, loading 12 in immediate mode would get 12. Figure 4-16 compares these addressing modes.

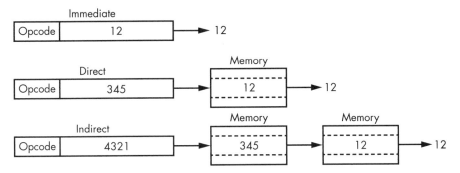

Figure 4-16: Addressing modes

Clearly, direct addressing is slower than immediate addressing as it takes a second memory access. Indirect is slower still as it takes a third memory access.

Condition Code Instructions

There are still a few things missing from our CPU, such as instructions that work with the condition codes. We've seen that these codes are set by addition, subtraction, and comparison. But we need some way of setting them to known values and some way of looking at the values. We can do that by adding a cca instruction that copies the contents of the condition code register to the accumulator and an acc instruction that copies the contents of the accumulator to the condition code register.

Branching

Now we have instructions that can do all sorts of things, but all we can do is execute a list of them from start to finish. That's not all that useful. We'd really like to have programs that can make decisions and select portions of code to execute. Those would take instructions that let us change the value of the program counter. These are called *branch* instructions, and they cause the program counter to be loaded with a new address. By itself, that's not any more useful than just being able to execute a list of instructions. But branch instructions don't always branch; they look at the condition codes and branch only if the conditions are met. Otherwise, the program counter is incremented normally, and the instruction following the branch instruction is executed next. Branch instructions need a few bits to hold the condition, as shown in Table 4-2.

Table 4-2: Branch Instruction Conditions

Code	Mnemonic	Description
000	bra	Branch always.
001	bov	Branch if the O (overflow) condition code bit is set.
010	beq	Branch if the Z (zero) condition code bit is set.
011	bne	Branch if the Z condition code bit is not set.
100	blt	Branch if N (negative) is set and Z is clear.
101	ble	Branch if N or Z is set.
110	bgt	Branch if N is clear and Z is clear.
111	bge	Branch if N is clear or Z is set.

Sometimes we need to explicitly change the contents of the program counter. We have two special instructions to help with this: pca, which copies the current program counter value to the accumulator, and apc, which copies the contents of the accumulator to the program counter.

Final Instruction Set

Let's integrate all these features into our instruction set, as shown in Figure 4-17.

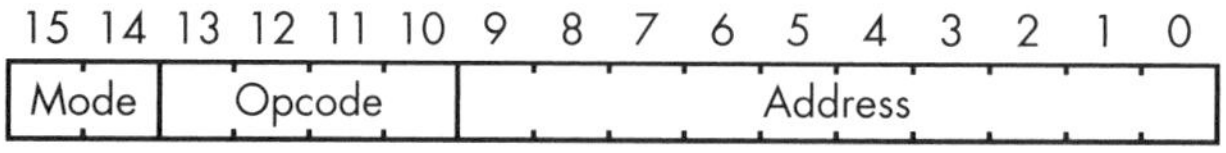

Figure 4-17: The final instruction layout

We have three *addressing modes*, which means that we need 2 bits in order to select the mode. The unused fourth-bit combination is used for operations that don't involve memory.

The addressing mode and opcode decode into instructions, as you can see in Table 4-3. Note that the branch conditions are merged into the opcodes. The opcodes for addressing mode 3 are used for operations that involve only the accumulator. A side effect of the complete implementation is that the opcodes don't exactly match the ALU that we saw in Table 4-1. This is not unusual and requires some additional logic.

Table 4-3: Addressing Modes and Opcodes

Opcode	Addressing mode			
	Direct (00)	Indirect (01)	Immediate (10)	None (11)
0000	load	load	load	
0001	and	and	and	set
0010	or	or	ore	not
0011	xor	xor	xor	neg
0100	add	add	add	shl
0101	sub	sub	sub	shr
0110	cmp	cmp	cmp	acc
0111	store	store		cca
1000	bra	bra	bra	apc
1001	bov	bov	bov	pca
1010	beq	beq	beq	
1011	bne	bne	bne	
1100	blt	blt	blt	
1101	ble	bge	ble	
1110	bgt	bgt	bgt	
1111	bge	bge	bge	

The shift-left and shift-right instructions put some of the otherwise unused bits to use as a count of the number of positions to shift, as shown in Figure 4-18.

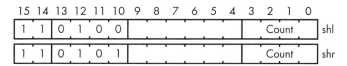

Figure 4-18: Shift instruction layout

Now we can actually instruct the computer to do something by writing a *program*, which is just a list of instructions that carry out some task. We'll compute all Fibonacci (Italian mathematician, 1175–1250) numbers up to 200. Fibonacci numbers are pretty cool; the number of petals on flowers, for example, are Fibonacci numbers. The first two Fibonacci numbers are 0 and 1. We get the next one by adding them together. We keep adding the new number to the previous one to get the sequence, which is 0, 1, 1, 2, 3, 5, 8, 13, and so on. The process looks like Figure 4-19.

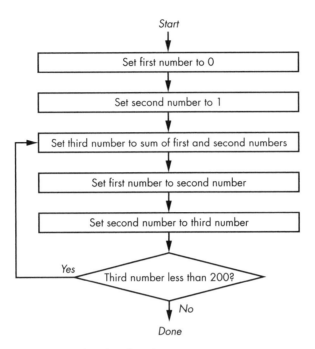

Start

Set first number to 0

Set second number to 1

Set third number to sum of first and second numbers

Set first number to second number

Set second number to third number

Third number less than 200?

Yes

No

Done

Figure 4-19: Flowchart for Fibonacci sequence program

The short program shown in Table 4-4 implements this process. The Instruction column is divided into fields as per Figure 4-17. The addresses in the comments are decimal numbers.

Table 4-4: Machine Language Program to Compute Fibonacci Sequence

Address	Instruction	Description
0000	10 0000 0000000000	Clear the accumulator (load 0 immediate).
0001	00 0111 0001100100	Store the accumulator (0) in memory location 100.
0010	10 0000 0000000001	Load 1 into the accumulator (load 1 immediate).
0011	00 0111 0001100101	Store the accumulator (1) in memory location 101.
0100	00 0000 0001100100	Load the accumulator from memory location 100.
0101	10 0100 0001100101	Add the contents of memory location 101 to the accumulator.
0110	00 0111 0001100110	Store the accumulator in memory location 102.
0111	00 0000 0001100101	Load the accumulator from memory location 101.
1000	00 0111 0001100100	Store it in memory location 100.
1001	00 0000 0001100110	Load the accumulator from memory location 102.
1010	00 0111 0001100101	Store it in memory location 101.
1011	10 0110 0011001000	Compare the contents of the accumulator to the number 200.
1100	00 0111 0000000100	Do another number if the last one was less than 200 by branching to address 4 (0100).

The Final Design

Let's put all the pieces that we've seen so far together into an actual computer. We'll need a few pieces of "glue" to make it all work.

The Instruction Register

You might be fooled into thinking that the computer just executes the Fibonacci program one instruction at a time. But more is happening behind the scenes. What does it take to execute an instruction? There's a *state machine* doing the two-step, shown in Figure 4-20.

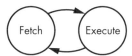

Figure 4-20: The fetch-execute cycle

The first thing that we have to do is to fetch an instruction from memory. Once we have that instruction, then we can worry about executing it.

Executing instructions usually involves accessing memory. That means we need someplace to keep the instruction handy while we're using memory for some other task. In Figure 4-21, we add an *instruction register* to our CPU to hold the current instruction.

Figure 4-21: Adding an instruction register

Data Paths and Control Signals

Here comes the complicated part. We need a way to feed the contents of the program counter to the memory address bus and a way to feed the memory data into the instruction register. We can do a similar exercise to determine all the different connections required to implement everything in our instruction set as detailed in Table 4-4. We end up with Figure 4-22, which probably seems confusing. But it's really just things we've seen before: some registers, some selectors, the ALU, and a tri-state buffer.

Although this looks pretty complicated, it's just like a road map. And it's way simpler than a real city map. The address selector is just a three-way intersection, and the data selector is a four-way. There are connections hanging off of the address bus and data bus for things like the I/O devices that we'll discuss in Chapter 6.

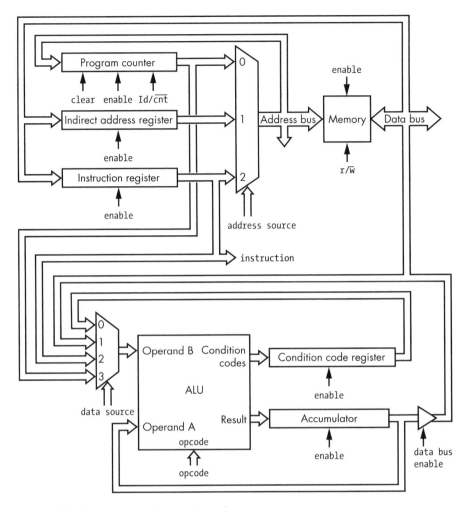

Figure 4-22: Data paths and control signals

The only new part is the *indirect address register*. We need that because we need somewhere to hold indirect addresses fetched from memory, similar to how the instruction register holds instructions fetched from memory.

For simplicity, Figure 4-22 omits the system clock that goes to all of the registers and memory. In the simple register case, just assume the register is loaded on the next clock if enabled. Likewise, the program counter and memory do what their control signals tell them to do on each clock. All the other components, such as the selectors, are purely combinatorial and don't use the clock.

Traffic Control

Now that you're familiar with all the inputs and outputs, it's time to build our traffic control unit. Let's look at a couple of examples of how it needs to behave.

Fetching is common to all instructions. The following signals are involved:

- The address source must be set to select the program counter.
- The memory must be enabled, and the read-write signal r/w̄ must be set to read (1).
- The instruction register must be enabled.

For our next example, we'll store the contents of the accumulator at the memory address pointed to by the address contained in the instruction—in other words, using indirect addressing. Fetching works as before.

Get the indirect address from memory:

- The address source must be set to select the instruction register, which gets us the address portion of the instruction.
- Memory is enabled, and r/w̄ is set to read (1).
- The indirect address register is enabled.

Store the accumulator in that address:

- The address source must be set to select the indirect address register.
- The data bus enable must be set.
- Memory is enabled and r/w̄ is set to write (0).
- The program counter is incremented.

Since multiple steps are involved in fetching and executing instructions, we need a counter to track them. The counter contents plus the opcode and mode portions of the instruction are all we need to generate all the control signals. We need 2 bits of counter because three states are needed to execute our most complicated instructions, as illustrated in Figure 4-23.

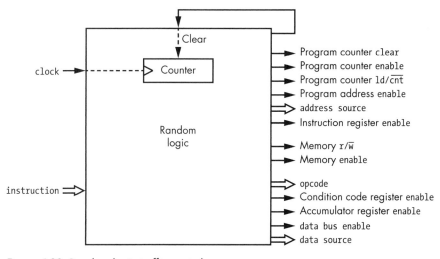

Figure 4-23: Random logic traffic control

This is a big box full of what's called *random logic*. All the logic diagrams we've seen so far follow some regular pattern. Functional blocks, such as selectors and registers, are assembled from simpler blocks in a clear manner. Sometimes, such as when we're implementing our traffic control unit, we have a set of inputs that must be mapped to a set of outputs to accomplish a task that has no regularity. The schematic looks like a rat's nest of connections—hence the descriptor "random."

But there's another way we could implement our traffic control unit. Instead of random logic, we could use a hunk of memory. The address would be formed from the counter outputs plus the opcode and mode portions of the instruction, as shown in Figure 4-24.

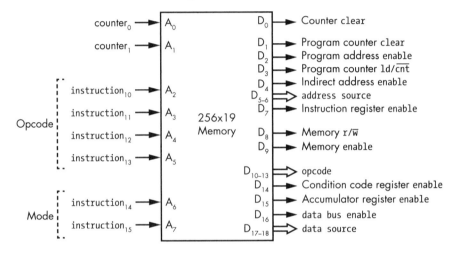

Figure 4-24: Memory-based traffic control

Each 19-bit memory word is laid out as shown in Figure 4-25.

DS$_1$	DS$_0$	DBE	ARE	CCRE	OP$_3$	OP$_2$	OP$_1$	OP$_0$	ME	R/$\overline{W}$	IRE	LD/$\overline{CNT}$	AS$_1$	AS$_0$	IAE	PCE	PCC	CC
18	17	16	15	14	13	12	11	10	9	8	7	6	5	4	3	2	1	0

Figure 4-25: The layout of a microcode word

This might strike you as somewhat strange. On the one hand, it's just another state machine implemented using memory instead of random logic. On the other, it sure looks like a simple computer. Both interpretations are correct. It is a state machine because computers are state machines. But it is also a computer because it's programmable.

This type of implementation is called *microcoded*, and the contents of memory are called *microcode*. Yes, we're using a small computer as part of the implementation of our larger one.

Let's look at the portion of the *microinstructions*, shown in Figure 4-26, that implement the examples we've discussed.

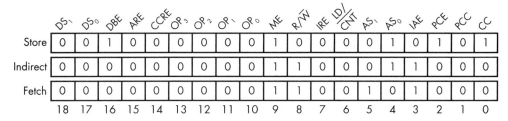

	DS₁	DS₀	DBE	ARE	CCRE	OP₃	OP₂	OP₁	OP₀	ME	R/W̄	IRE	LD/CNT	AS₁	AS₀	IAE	PCE	PCC	CC
Store	0	0	1	0	0	0	0	0	0	1	0	0	0	0	1	0	1	0	1
Indirect	0	0	0	0	0	0	0	0	0	1	1	0	0	0	1	1	0	0	0
Fetch	0	0	0	0	0	0	0	0	0	1	1	0	0	1	0	1	0	0	0
	18	17	16	15	14	13	12	11	10	9	8	7	6	5	4	3	2	1	0

Figure 4-26: Microcode example

As you might expect, it's hard to avoid abusing a good idea. There are machines that have a *nanocoded* block that implements a *microcoded* block that implements the instruction set.

Using ROM for the microcode memory makes a certain amount of sense, because otherwise we'd need to keep a copy of the microcode somewhere else and we'd require additional hardware to load the microcode. However, there are situations where RAM, or a mix of ROM and RAM, is justified. Some Intel CPUs have writable microcode that can be patched to fix bugs. A few machines, such as the HP-2100 series, had a *writable control store*, which was microcode RAM that could be used to extend the basic instruction set.

Machines that have writable microcode today rarely permit users to modify it for several reasons. Manufacturers don't want users to rely on microcode they themselves write for their applications because once users become dependent on it, manufacturers have difficulty making changes. Also, buggy microcode can damage the machine—for example, it could turn on both the memory *enable* and data bus *enable* at the same time in our CPU, connecting together totem-pole outputs in a way that might burn out the transistors.

RISC vs. CISC Instruction Sets

Designers used to create instructions for computers that seemed to be useful but that resulted in some pretty complicated machines. In the 1980s, American computer scientists David Patterson at Berkeley and John Hennessey at Stanford did statistical analyses of programs and discovered that many of the complicated instructions were rarely used. They pioneered the design of machines that contained only the instructions that accounted for most of a program's time; less used instructions were eliminated and replaced by combinations of other instructions. These were called *RISC* machines, for *reduced instruction set computers*. Older designs were called *CISC* machines, for *complicated instruction set computers*.

One of the hallmarks of RISC machines is that they have a *load-store architecture*. This means there are two categories of instructions: one for accessing memory and one for everything else.

Of course, computer use has changed over time. Patterson and Hennessey's original statistics were done before computers were commonly used for things like audio and video. Statistics on newer programs are prompting designers to add new instructions to RISC machines. Today's RISC machines are actually more complicated than the CISC machines of yore.

One of the CISC machines that had a big impact was the PDP-11 from Digital Equipment Corporation. This machine had eight general-purpose registers instead of the single accumulator we used in our example. These registers could be used for indirect addressing. In addition, *auto-increment* and *autodecrement* modes were supported. These modes enabled the values in the registers to be incremented or decremented before or after use. This allowed for some very efficient programs. For example, let's say we want to copy *n* bytes of memory starting at a source address to memory starting at a destination address. We can put the source address in register 0, the destination in register 1, and the count in register 2. We'll skip the actual bits here because there's no real need to learn the PDP-11 instruction set. Table 4-5 shows what these instructions do.

Table 4-5: PDP-11 Copy Memory Program

Address	Description
0	Copy the contents of the memory location whose address is in register 0 to the memory location whose address is in register 1, then add 1 to each register.
1	Subtract 1 from the contents of register 2 and then compare the result to 0.
2	Branch to location 0 if the result was not 0.

Why should we care about this? The C programming language, a follow-on to B (which was a follow-on to BCPL), was developed on the PDP-11. C's use of *pointers*, a higher-level abstraction of indirect addressing, combined with features from B such as the autoincrement and autodecrement operators, mapped well to the PDP-11 architecture. C became very influential and has affected the design of many other languages, including C++, Java, and JavaScript.

Graphics Processing Units

You've probably heard about *graphics processing units*, or GPUs. These are mostly outside the scope of this book but are worth a quick mention.

Graphics is a massive paint-by-numbers exercise. It's not uncommon to have 8 million color spots to paint and need to paint them 60 times per second if you want video to work well. That works out to around a half-billion memory accesses per second.

Graphics is specialized work and doesn't require all the features of a general-purpose CPU. And it's something that parallelizes nicely: painting multiple spots at a time can improve performance.

Two features distinguish GPUs. First, they have large numbers of simple processors. Second, they have much wider memory buses than CPUs, which means they can access memory much faster. GPUs have a fire hose instead of a garden hose.

GPUs have acquired more general-purpose features over time. Work has been done to make them programmable using variants of standard programming languages, and they are now used for certain classes of applications that can take advantage of their architectures. GPUs were in short supply when this book was written because they were all being snapped up for Bitcoin mining.

Summary

In this chapter, we've created an actual computer using the building blocks introduced in previous chapters. Though simple, the machine we designed in this chapter could actually be built and programmed. It's missing some elements found in real computers, however, such as stacks and memory management hardware. We'll learn about those in Chapter 5.

5

COMPUTER ARCHITECTURE

Chapter 4 walked through the design of a simple computer system and discussed how the CPU communicates with memory and I/O devices over the address and data buses. That's not the end of the story, however. Many improvements over the years have made computers run faster while requiring less power and being easier to program. These improvements have added a lot of complexity to the designs.

Computer architecture refers to the arrangement of the various components into a computer—not to whether the box has Doric or Ionic columns or a custom shade of beige like the one American entrepreneur Steve Jobs (1955–2011) created for the original Macintosh computer. Many different architectures have been tried over the years. What's worked and what hasn't makes for fascinating reading, and many books have been published on the subject.

This chapter focuses primarily on architectural improvements involving memory. A photomicrograph of a modern microprocessor shows that the vast majority of the chip area is dedicated to memory handling. It's so important that it deserves a chapter of its own. We'll also touch on a few other differences in architectures, such as instruction set design, additional registers, power control, and fancier execution units. And we'll discuss support for *multitasking,* the ability to run multiple programs simultaneously, or at least to provide the illusion of doing so. Running multiple programs implies the existence of some sort of supervisory program called an *operating system (OS)* that controls their execution.

Basic Architectural Elements

The two most common architectures are the *von Neumann* (named after Hungarian-American wizard John von Neumann, 1903–1957) and the *Harvard* (named after the Harvard Mark I computer, which was, of course, a Harvard architecture machine). We've already seen the parts; Figure 5-1 shows how they're organized.

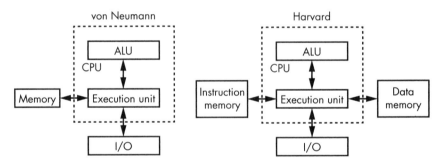

Figure 5-1: The von Neumann and Harvard architectures

Notice that the only difference between them is the way the memory is arranged. All else being equal, the von Neumann architecture is slightly slower because it can't access instructions and data at the same time, since there's only one memory bus. The Harvard architecture gets around that but requires additional hardware for the second memory bus.

Processor Cores

Both architectures in Figure 5-1 have a single CPU, which, as we saw in Chapter 4, is the combination of the ALU, registers, and execution unit. *Multiprocessor* systems with multiple CPUs debuted in the 1980s as a way to get higher performance than could be achieved with a single CPU. As it turns out, though, it's not that easy. Dividing up a single program so that it can be *parallelized* to make use of multiple CPUs is an unsolved problem in the general case, although it works well for some things such as particular types of heavy math. However, it's useful when you're running more than one program at the same time and was a lifesaver in the early days of graphical workstations, as the X Window System was such a resource hog that it helped to have a separate processor to run it.

Decreasing fabrication geometries lowers costs. That's because chips are made on silicon wafers, and making things smaller means more chips fit on one wafer. Higher performance used to be achieved by making the CPU faster, which meant increasing the clock speed. But faster machines required more power, which, combined with smaller geometries, produced more heat-generating power per unit of area. Processors hit the *power wall* around 2000 because the power density couldn't be increased without exceeding the melting point.

Salvation of sorts was found in the smaller fabrication geometries. The definition of CPU has changed; what we used to call a CPU is now called a *processor core. Multicore* processors are now commonplace. There are even systems, found primarily in data centers, with multiple multicore processors.

Microprocessors and Microcomputers

Another orthogonal architectural distinction is based on mechanical packaging. Figure 5-1 shows CPUs connected to memory and I/O. When the memory and I/O are not in the same physical package as the processor cores, we call it a *microprocessor*, whereas when everything is on a single chip, we use the term *microcomputer*. These are not really well-defined terms, and there is a lot of fuzziness around their usage. Some consider a microcomputer to be a computer system built around a microprocessor and use the term *microcontroller* to refer to what I've just defined as a microcomputer.

Microcomputers tend to be less powerful machines than microprocessors because things like on-chip memory take a lot of space. We're not going to focus on microcomputers much in this chapter because they don't have the same complexity of memory issues. However, once you learn to program, it is worthwhile to pick up something like an Arduino, which is a small Harvard architecture computer based on an Atmel AVR microcomputer chip. Arduinos are great for building all sorts of toys and blinky stuff.

To summarize: microprocessors are usually components of larger systems, while microcomputers are what you find in things like your dishwasher.

There's another variation called a *system on a chip (SoC)*. A passable but again fuzzy definition is that a SoC is a more complex microcomputer. Rather than having relatively simple on-chip I/O, a SoC can include things like Wi-Fi circuitry. SoCs are found in devices such as cell phones. There are even SoCs that include field-programmable gate arrays (FPGAs), which permit additional customization.

Procedures, Subroutines, and Functions

Many engineers are afflicted with a peculiar variation of laziness. If there's something they don't want to do, they'll put their energy into creating something that does it for them, even if that involves more work than the original task. One thing programmers want to avoid is writing the same piece of code more than once. There are good reasons for that besides laziness. Among them is that it makes the code take less space and, if there is a bug in the code, it only has to be fixed in one place.

The *function* (or *procedure* or *subroutine*) is a mainstay of code reuse. Those terms all mean the same thing as far as you're concerned; they're just regional differences in language. We'll use *function* because it's the most similar to what you may have learned in math class.

Most programming languages have similar constructs. For example, in JavaScript we could write the code shown in Listing 5-1.

```
function
cube(x)
{
        return (x * x * x);
}
```

Listing 5-1: A sample JavaScript function

This code creates a function named cube that takes a single parameter named x and returns its cube. Keyboards don't include the multiplication (×) symbol, so many programming languages use * for multiplication instead. Now we can write a program fragment like Listing 5-2.

```
y = cube(3);
```

Listing 5-2: A sample JavaScript function call

The nice thing here is that we can invoke, or *call*, the cube function multiple times without having to write it again. We can find cube(4) + cube(6) without having to write the cubing code twice. This is a trivial example, but think about how convenient this capability would be for more complicated chunks of code.

How does this work? We need a way to run the function code and then get back to where we were. To get back, we need to know where we came from, which is the contents of the program counter (which you saw back in Figure 4-12 on page 101). Table 5-1 shows how to make a function call using the example instruction set we looked at in "Instruction Set" on page 102.

Table 5-1: Making a Function Call

Address	Instruction	Operand	Comments
100	pca		Program counter → accumulator
101	add	5 (immediate)	Address for return (100 + 5 = 105)
102	store	200 (direct)	Store return address in memory
103	load	3 (immediate)	Put number to cube (3) in accumulator
104	bra	300 (direct)	Call the cube function
105			Continues here after function
...			
200			Reserved memory location
...			
300	...	...	The cube function
...			Remainder of cube function
310	bra	200 (indirect)	Branch to stored return address

What's happening here? We first calculate the address of where we want execution to continue after returning from the cube function. It takes us a few instructions to do that; plus, we need to load the number that must be cubed. That's five instructions later, so we store that address in memory location 200. We branch off to the function, and when the function is done, we branch indirect through 200, so we end up at location 105. This process plays out as shown in Figure 5-2.

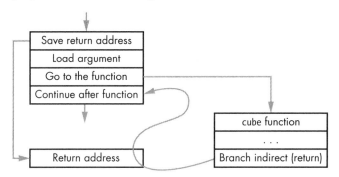

Figure 5-2: A function call flow

This is a lot of work for something that is done a lot, so many machines add helper instructions. For example, ARM processors have a *Branch with Link (BL)* instruction that combines the branch to the function with saving the address of the following instruction.

Stacks

Functions aren't limited to simple pieces of code such as the example we just saw. It's common for functions to call other functions and for them to call themselves.

Wait, what was that? A function calling itself? That's called *recursion*, and it's really useful. Let's look at an example. Your phone probably uses *JPEG (Joint Photographic Experts Group) compression* to reduce the file size of photos. To see how compression works, let's start with a square black-and-white image, shown in Figure 5-3.

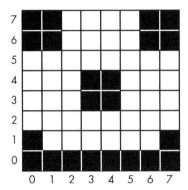

Figure 5-3: A crude smiley face

We can attack the compression problem using *recursive subdivision*: we look at the image, and if it's not all one color, we divide it into four pieces, then check again, and so on until the pieces are one pixel in size.

Listing 5-3 shows a subdivide function that processes a portion of the image. It's written in *pseudocode*, an English-like programming language made up for examples. It *takes* the x- and y-coordinates of the lower-left corner of a square along with the *size* (we don't need both the width and the height, since the image is a square). "Takes" is just shorthand for what's called the *arguments to a function* in math.

```
function
subdivide(x, y, size)
{
    IF (size ≠ 1 AND the pixels in the square are not all the same color) {
        half = size ÷ 2
        subdivide(x, y, half) lower          left quadrant
        subdivide(x, y + half, half)         upper left quadrant
        subdivide(x + half, y + half, half)  upper right quadrant
        subdivide(x + half, y, half)         lower right quadrant
    }
    ELSE {
        save the information about the square
    }
}
```

Listing 5-3: A subdivision function

The subdivide function partitions the image into same-colored chunks starting with the lower-left quadrant, then the upper left, upper right, and finally the lower right. Figure 5-4 shows things that need subdividing in gray and things that are solidly one color in black or white.

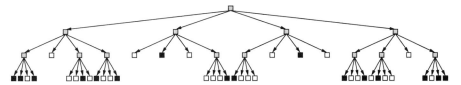

Figure 5-4: Subdividing the image

What we have here looks like what computer geeks call a *tree* and what math geeks call a *directed acyclic graph (DAG)*. You follow the arrows. In this structure, arrows don't go up, so there can't be loops. Things with no arrows going out of them are called *leaf nodes*, and they're the end of the line, like leaves are the end of the line on a tree branch. If you squint enough and count them in Figure 5-4, you can see that there are 40 solid squares, which is fewer than the 64 squares in the original image, meaning there's less information to store. That's compression.

For some reason, probably because it's easier to draw (or maybe because they rarely go outside), computer geeks always put the root of the tree at the top and grow it downward. This particular variant is called a *quadtree* because each node is divided into four parts. Quadtrees are *spatial data structures*. Hanan Samet has made these his life's work and has written several excellent books on the subject.

There's a problem with implementing functions as shown in the previous section. Because there's only one place to store the return value, functions like this can't call themselves because that value would get overwritten and we'd lose our way back.

We need to be able to store multiple return addresses in order to make recursion work. We also need a way to associate the return addresses with their corresponding function calls. Let's see if we can find a pattern in how we subdivided the image. We went down the tree whenever possible and only went across when we ran out of downward options. This is called a *depth-first traversal*, as opposed to going across first and then down, which is a *breadth-first traversal*. Every time we go down a level, we need to remember our place so that we can go back. Once we go back, we no longer need to remember that place.

What we need is something like those gadgets that hold piles of plates in a cafeteria. When we call a function, we stick the return address on a plate and put it on top of the pile. When we return from the call, we remove that plate. In other words, it's a *stack*. You can sound important by calling it a *LIFO* ("last in, first out") structure. We *push* things onto the stack, and *pop* them off. When we try to push things onto a stack that doesn't have room, that's called a *stack overflow*. Trying to pop things from an empty stack is a *stack underflow*.

We can do this in software. In our earlier function call example in Table 5-1, every function could take its stored return address and push it onto a stack for later retrieval. Fortunately, most computers have hardware support for stacks because they're so important. This support includes *limit registers* so that the software doesn't have to constantly check for possible overflow. We'll talk about how processors handle *exceptions*, such as exceeding limits, in the next section.

Stacks aren't just used for return addresses. Our subdivide function included a *local variable* where we calculated half the size once and then used it eight times to make the program faster. We can't just overwrite this every time we call the function. Instead, we store local variables on the stack too. That makes every function call independent of other function calls. The collection of things stored on the stack for each call is a *stack frame*. Figure 5-5 illustrates an example from our function in Listing 5-3.

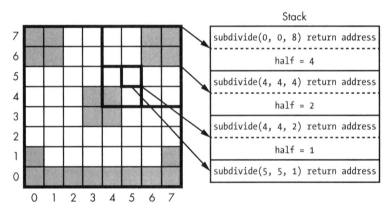

Figure 5-5: Stack frames

We follow the path shown by the heavy black squares. You can see that each call generates a new stack frame that includes both the return address and the local variable.

Several computer languages, such as *forth* and *PostScript*, are stack-based (see "Different Equation Notations"), as are several classic HP calculators.

Stacks aren't restricted to just computer languages, either. Japanese is stack-based: nouns get pushed onto the stack and verbs operate on them. Yoda's cryptic utterances also follow this pattern.

Interrupts

Imagine that you're in the kitchen whipping up a batch of chocolate chip cookies. You're following a recipe, which is just a program for cooks. You're the only one home, so you need to know if someone comes to the door. We'll represent your activity using a *flowchart*, which is a type of diagram used to express how things work, as shown in Figure 5-6.

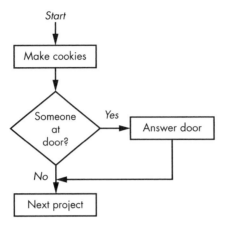

Figure 5-6: Home alone making cookies #1

This might work if someone really patient comes to the door. But let's say that a package is being delivered that needs your signature. The delivery person isn't going to wait 45 minutes, unless they can smell the cookies and are hoping to get some. Let's try something different, like Figure 5-7.

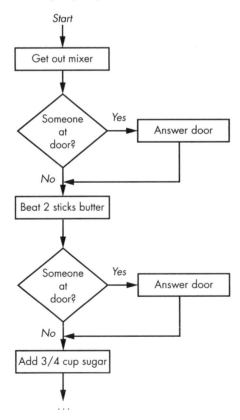

Figure 5-7: Home alone making cookies #2

This technique is called *polling*. It works, but not very well. You're less likely to miss your delivery, but you're spending a lot of time checking the door.

We could divide up each of the cookie-making tasks into smaller subtasks and check the door in between them. That would improve your chances of receiving the delivery, but at some point you'd be spending more time checking the door than making cookies.

This is a common and important problem for which there is really no software solution. It's not possible to make this work well by rearranging the structure of a program. What's needed is some way to *interrupt* a running program so that it can respond to something external that needs attention. It's time to add some hardware features to the execution unit.

Pretty much every processor made today includes an *interrupt* unit. Usually it has pins or electrical connections that generate an interrupt when wiggled appropriately. *Pin* is a colloquial term for an electrical connection to a chip. Chips used to have parts that looked like pins, but as devices and tools have gotten smaller, many other variants have emerged. Many processor chips, especially microcomputers, have *integrated peripherals* (on-chip I/O devices) that are connected to the interrupt system internally.

Here's how it works. A peripheral needing attention generates an *interrupt request*. The processor (usually) finishes up with the currently executing instruction. It then puts the currently executing program on hold and veers off to execute a completely different program called an *interrupt handler*. The interrupt handler does whatever it needs to do, and the main program continues from where it left off. Interrupt handlers are functions.

The equivalent mechanism for the cookie project is a doorbell. You can happily make cookies until you're interrupted by the doorbell, although it can be annoying to be interrupted by pollsters. There are a few things to consider. First is your *response time* to the interrupt. If you spend a long time gabbing with the delivery person, your cookies may burn; you need to make sure that you can service interrupts in a timely manner. Second, you need some way to save your *state* when responding to an interrupt so that you can go back to whatever you were doing after *servicing* it. For example, if the interrupted program had something in a register, the interrupt handler must save the contents of that register if it needs to use it and then restore it before returning to the main program.

The interrupt system uses a stack to save the place in the interrupted program. It is the interrupt handler's job to save anything that it might need to use. This way, the handler can save the absolute minimum necessary so that it works fast.

How does the computer know where to find the interrupt handler? Usually, there's a set of reserved memory addresses for interrupt vectors, one for each supported interrupt. An *interrupt vector* is just a pointer, the address of a memory location. It's similar to a vector in math or physics—an arrow that says, "Go there from here." When an interrupt occurs, the computer looks up that address and transfers control there.

Many machines include interrupt vectors for exceptions including stack overflow and using an invalid address such as one beyond the bounds of physical memory. Diverting exceptions to an interrupt handler often allows the interrupt handler to fix problems so that the program can continue running.

Typically, there are all sorts of other special interrupt controls, such as ways to turn specific interrupts on and off. There is often a *mask* so that you can say things like "hold my interrupts while the oven door is open." On machines with multiple interrupts, there is often some sort of *priority* ordering so that the most important things get handled first. That means that the handlers for lower-priority interrupts may themselves be interrupted. Most machines have one or more built-in *timers* that can be configured to generate interrupts.

Operating systems, discussed in the next section, often keep access to the *physical* (hardware) interrupts out of reach from most programs. They substitute some sort of *virtual* or software interrupt system. For example, the UNIX operating system has a *signal* mechanism. More recently developed systems call these *events*.

Relative Addressing

What would it take to have multiple programs running at the same time? For starters, we'd have to have some sort of supervisor program that knew how to switch between them. We'll call this program an operating system or operating system *kernel*. We'll make a distinction between the OS and the programs it supervises by calling the OS a *system* program and everything else *user* programs, or *processes*. A simple OS might work something like Figure 5-8.

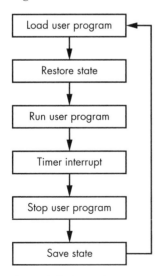

Figure 5-8: A simple operating system

The OS here is using a timer to tell it when to switch between user programs. This scheduling technique is called *time slicing* because it gives each program a slice of time in which to run. The user program *state* or *context* refers to the contents of the registers and any memory that the program is using, including the stack.

This works, but it's pretty slow. It takes time to load a program. It would be much faster if you could load the programs into memory as space allows and keep them there, as shown in Figure 5-9.

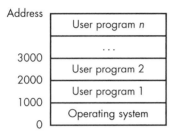

Figure 5-9: Multiple programs in memory

In this example, user programs are loaded into memory one after another. But wait, how can this work? As explained back in "Addressing Modes" on page 104, our sample computer used *absolute addressing*, which means that the addresses in the instructions referred to specific memory locations. It's not going to work to run a program that expects to be at address 1000 at a different address, such as 2000.

Some computers solve this problem by adding an *index register* (Figure 5-10). This is a register whose contents are added to addresses to form *effective addresses*. If a user program expects to be run at address 1000, the OS could set the index register to 2000 before running it at address 3000.

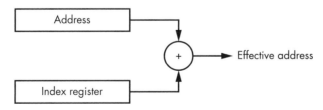

Figure 5-10: An index register

Another way to fix this is with *relative addressing*—which is not about sending a birthday card to your auntie. Instead of the addresses in instructions being relative to 0 (the beginning of memory in most machines), they can be relative to the address of their instruction. Go back and review Table 4-4 on page 108. You can see that the second instruction contains the address 100 (110100 in binary). With relative addressing, that would become +99, since the instruction is at address 1 and address 100 is 99 away. Likewise, the last instruction is a branch to address 4, which would become a branch to −8 with relative addressing. This sort of stuff is a nightmare to do in binary, but modern language tools do all the arithmetic for us. Relative addressing allows us to *relocate* a program anywhere in memory.

Memory Management Units

Multitasking has evolved from being a luxury to being a basic requirement now that everything is connected to the internet, because communications tasks are constantly running in the *background*—that is, in addition to what the user is doing. Index registers and relative addressing help, but they're not enough. What happens if one of these programs contains bugs? For example, what if a bug in user program 2 (Figure 5-9) causes it to overwrite something in user program 1—or even worse, in the OS? What if someone deliberately wrote a program to spy on or change other programs running on the system? We'd really like to isolate each program to make those scenarios impossible. To that end, most microprocessors now include *memory management unit (MMU)* hardware that provides this capability. MMUs are very complicated pieces of hardware.

Systems with MMUs make a distinction between *virtual addresses* and *physical addresses*. The MMU translates the virtual addresses used by programs into physical addresses used by memory, as shown in Figure 5-11.

Figure 5-11: MMU address translation

How is this different from an index register? Well, there's not just one. And the MMUs aren't the full width of the address. What's happening here is that we're splitting the virtual address into two parts. The lower part is identical to the physical address. The upper part undergoes *translation* via a piece of RAM called the *page table*, an example of which you can see in Figure 5-12.

Memory is partitioned into 256-byte *pages* in this example. The page table contents control the actual location of each page in physical memory. This allows us to take a program that expects to start at address 1000 and put it at 2000, or anywhere else as long as it's aligned on a *page boundary*. And although the virtual address space appears continuous to the program, it does not have to be mapped to contiguous physical memory pages. We could even move a program to a different place in physical memory while it's running. We can provide one or more cooperating programs with *shared memory* by mapping portions of their virtual address space to the same physical memory. Note that the page table contents become part of a program's context.

Virutal address

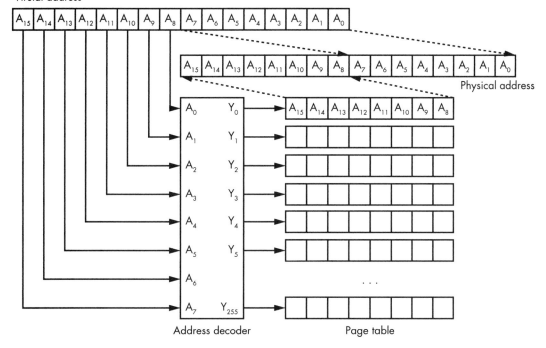

Figure 5-12: Simple page table for a 16-bit machine

Now, if you've been paying attention, you might notice that the page table just looks like a piece of memory. And you'd be correct. And you'd expect me to tell you that it's not that simple. Right again.

Our example uses 16-bit addresses. What happens if we have a modern machine with 64-bit addresses? If we split the address in half, we need 4 GiB of page table, and the page size would also be 4 GiB—not very useful since that's more memory than many systems have. We could make the page size smaller, but that would increase the page table size. We need a solution.

The MMU in a modern processor has a limited page table size. The complete set of *page table entries* is kept in main memory, or on disk if memory runs out. The MMU loads a subset of the page table entries into its page table as needed.

Some MMU designs add further control bits to their page tables—for example, a *no-execute bit*. When this bit is set on a page, the CPU won't execute instructions from that page. This prevents programs from executing their own data, which is a security risk. Another common control bit makes pages *read only*.

MMUs generate a *page fault* exception when a program tries to access an address that isn't mapped to physical memory. This is useful, for example, in the case of stack overflow. Rather than having to abort the running program, the OS can have the MMU map some additional memory to grow the stack space and then resume the execution of the user program.

MMUs make the distinction between von Neumann and Harvard architectures somewhat moot. Such systems have the single bus of the von Neumann architecture but can provide separate instruction and data memory.

Virtual Memory

Operating systems manage the allocation of scarce hardware resources among competing programs. For example, we saw an OS manage access to the CPU itself in Figure 5-8. Memory is also a managed resource. Operating systems use MMUs to provide *virtual memory* to user programs.

We saw earlier that the MMU can map a program's virtual addresses to physical memory. But virtual memory is more than that. The page fault mechanism allows programs to think that they can have as much memory as they want, even if that exceeds the amount of physical memory. What happens when the requested memory exceeds the amount available? The OS moves the contents of memory pages that aren't currently needed out to larger but slower mass storage, usually a disk. When a program tries to access memory that has been *swapped out*, the OS does whatever it needs to in order to make space and then copies the requested page back in. This is known as *demand paging*. Figure 5-13 shows a virtual memory system with one page swapped out.

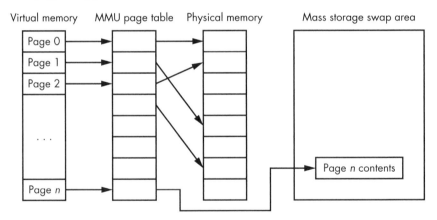

Figure 5-13: Virtual memory

System performance takes a big hit when swapping occurs, but it's still better than not being able to run a program at all because of insufficient memory. Virtual memory systems use a number of tricks to minimize the performance hit. One of these is a *least recently used (LRU)* algorithm that tracks accesses to pages. The most frequently used pages are kept in physical memory; the least recently used are swapped out.

System and User Space

Multitasking systems give each process the illusion that it's the only program running on the computer. MMUs help to foster this illusion by giving each process its own address space. But this illusion is difficult to maintain when it comes to I/O devices. For example, the OS uses a timer device to tell it when to switch between programs in Figure 5-8. The OS decides to set the timer to generate an interrupt once per second, but if one of the user programs changes it to interrupt once per hour, things won't work as expected. Likewise, the MMU wouldn't provide any serious isolation between programs if any user program could modify its configuration.

Many CPUs include additional hardware that addresses this problem. There is a bit in a register that indicates whether the computer is in *system* or *user* mode. Certain instructions, such as those that deal with I/O, are *privileged* and can be executed only in system mode. Special instructions called *traps* or *system calls* allow user mode programs to make requests of system mode programs, which means the operating system.

This arrangement has several advantages. First, it protects the OS from user programs and user programs from each other. Second, since user programs can't touch certain things like the MMU, the OS can control resource allocation to programs. System space is where hardware exceptions are handled.

Any programs that you write for your phone, laptop, or desktop will run in user space. You need to get really good before you touch programs running in system space.

Memory Hierarchy and Performance

Once upon a time, CPUs and memory worked at the same speed, and there was peace in the land. However, CPUs got faster and faster, and although memory got faster too, it couldn't keep up. Computer architects have come up with all sorts of tricks to make sure that those fast CPUs aren't sitting around waiting for memory.

Virtual memory and swapping introduce the notion of *memory hierarchy*. Although all memory looks the same to a user program, what happens behind the scenes greatly affects the system performance. Or, to paraphrase George Orwell, all memory accesses are equal, but some memory accesses are more equal than others.

Computers are fast. They can execute billions of instructions per second. But not much would get done if the CPU had to wait around for those instructions to arrive, or for data to be retrieved or stored.

We've seen that processors include some very fast, expensive memory called registers. Early computers had only a handful of registers, whereas some modern machines contain hundreds. But overall, the ratio of registers to memory has gotten smaller. Processors communicate with *main memory*, usually DRAM, which is less than a tenth as fast as the processor. Mass storage devices such as disk drives may be a *millionth* as fast the processor.

Time for a food analogy courtesy of my friend Clem. Registers are like a refrigerator: there's not a lot of space in there, but you can get to its contents quickly. Main memory is like a grocery store: it has a lot more space for stuff, but it takes a while to get there. Mass storage is like a warehouse: there's even more space for stuff, but it's much farther away.

Let's milk this analogy some more. You often hit the fridge for one thing. When you make the trip to the store, you fill a few grocery bags. The warehouse supplies the store by the truckload. Computers are the same way. Small blocks of stuff are moved between the CPU and main memory. Larger blocks of stuff are moved between main memory and the disk. Check out *The Paging Game* by Jeff Berryman for a humorous explanation of how all this works.

Skipping a lot of gory details, let's assume the CPU runs about 10 times the speed of main memory. That translates to a lot of time spent waiting for memory, so additional hardware (faster on-chip memory) was added for a pantry or *cache*. It's much smaller than the grocery store, but much faster when running at full processor speed.

How do we fill the pantry from the grocery store? Way back in "Random-Access Memory" on page 82, we saw that DRAM performs best when accessing columns out of a row. When you examine the way programs work, you notice that they access sequential memory locations unless they hit a branch. And a fair amount of the data used by a program tends to clump together. This phenomenon is exploited to improve system performance. The CPU *memory controller* hardware fills the cache from consecutive columns in a row because, more often than not, data is needed from sequential locations. Rather than getting one box of cereal, we put several in sacks and bring them home. By using the highest-speed memory-access mode available, CPUs are usually ahead of the game even when there is a cache miss caused by a nonsequential access. A *cache miss* is not a contestant in a Miss Cache pageant; it's when the CPU looks for something in the cache that isn't there and has to fetch it from memory. Likewise, a *cache hit* is when the CPU finds what it's looking for in the cache. You can't have too much of a good thing.

There are several levels of cache memory, and they get bigger and slower as they get farther away from the CPU (even when they're on the same chip). These are called the *L1*, *L2*, and *L3* caches, where the *L* stands for *level*. Yup, there's the spare freezer in the garage plus the storeroom. And there's a dispatcher that puts air traffic control to shame. There's a whole army of logic circuitry whose job it is to pack and unpack grocery bags, boxes, and trucks of different sizes to make all this work. It actually takes up a good chunk of the chip real estate. The memory hierarchy is outlined in Figure 5-14.

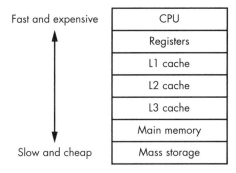

Fast and expensive

| CPU |
| Registers |
| L1 cache |
| L2 cache |
| L3 cache |
| Main memory |
| Mass storage |

Slow and cheap

Figure 5-14: Memory hierarchy

Additional complicated tweaks have improved performance even further. Machines include *branch prediction* circuitry that guesses the outcome of conditional branch instructions so that the correct data can be *prefetched* from memory and in the cache ready to go. There is even circuitry to handle *out-of-order execution*. This allows the CPU to execute instructions in the most efficient order even if it's not the order in which they occur in a program.

Maintaining *cache coherency* is a particularly gnarly problem. Imagine a system that contains two processor chips, each with four cores. One of those cores writes data to a memory location—well, really to a cache, where it will eventually get into memory. How does another core or processor know that it's getting the right version of the data from that memory location? The simplest approach is called *write through*, which means that writes go directly to memory and are not cached. But that eliminates many of the benefits of caching, so there's a lot of additional cache-management hardware for this that is outside of the scope of this book.

Coprocessors

A processor core is a pretty complicated piece of circuitry. You can free up processor cores for general computation by offloading common operations to simpler pieces of hardware called *coprocessors*. It used to be that coprocessors existed because there wasn't room to fit everything on a single chip. For example, there were floating-point coprocessors for when there wasn't space for floating-point instruction hardware on the processor itself. Today there are on-chip coprocessors for many things, including specialized graphics processing.

In this chapter we've talked about loading programs into memory to be run, which usually means that the programs are coming from some slow and cheap memory, such as a disk drive. And we've seen that virtual memory systems may be reading from and writing to disks as part of swapping. And we saw in "Block Devices" on page 85 that disks aren't byte-addressable—they transfer blocks of 512 or 4,096 bytes. This means there's a lot of copying between main memory and disk that's straightforward, because no other computation is needed. Copying data from one place to another is one of the biggest consumers of CPU time. Some coprocessors do nothing but move data around. These are called *direct memory access (DMA)* units. They can be configured to do operations like "move this much stuff from here to there and let me know when you're done." CPUs offload a lot of grunt work onto DMA units, leaving the CPU free to do more useful operations.

Arranging Data in Memory

We learned from the program in Table 4-4 that memory is used not only for the instructions but for data as well. In this case, it's *static* data, meaning that the amount of memory needed is known when the program is written. We saw earlier in this chapter that programs also use memory for stacks. These data areas need to be arranged in memory so that they don't collide.

Figure 5-15 illustrates the typical arrangement for both von Neumann and Harvard architecture machines without MMUs. You can see that the only difference is that instructions reside in separate memory on Harvard architecture machines.

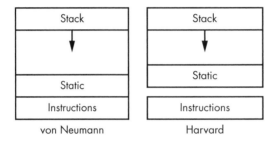

Figure 5-15: Memory arrangement

There's one more way in which programs use memory. Most programs have to deal with *dynamic* data, which has a size that is unknown until the program is running. For example, an instant messaging system doesn't know in advance how many messages it needs to store or how much storage will be needed for each message. Dynamic data is customarily piled into memory above the static area, called the *heap*, as shown in Figure 5-16. The heap grows upward as more space is needed for dynamic data, while the stack grows downward. It's important to make sure they don't collide. There are a few minor variations on this theme; some processors reserve memory addresses at the beginning or end of memory for interrupt vectors and registers that control on-chip I/O devices.

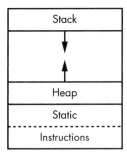

Figure 5-16: Memory arrangement with the heap

You'll find this memory layout when using microcomputers, as they typically don't have MMUs. When MMUs are involved, the instructions, data, and stack are mapped to different physical memory pages whose size can be adjusted as needed. But the same memory layout is used for the virtual memory presented to programs.

Running Programs

You've seen that computer programs have a lot of pieces. In this section, you'll learn how they all come together.

Earlier I said that programmers use functions for code reuse. That's not the end of the story. There are many functions that are useful for more than one program—for example, comparing two text strings. It would be nice if we could just use these third-party functions rather than having to write our own every time. One way to do that is by grouping related functions into *libraries*. There are a large number of libraries available for everything from string handling to hairy math to MP3 decoding.

In addition to libraries, nontrivial programs are usually built in pieces. Though you could put the entirety of a program into a single file, there are several good reasons to break it up. Chief among these is that it makes it easier for several people to work on the same program at the same time.

But breaking programs up means we need some way to hook or *link* all the different pieces together. The way we accomplish this is by processing each program piece into an intermediate format designed for this purpose and then running a special *linker* program that makes all the connections. Many intermediate file formats have been developed over the years. *Executable and Linkable Format (ELF)* is currently the most popular flavor. This format includes sections similar to want ads. There might be something in the For Sale section that says, "I have a function named cube." Likewise, we might see "I'm looking for a variable named date" in the Wanted section.

A linker is a program that *resolves* all the ads, resulting in a program that can actually be run. But of course, there are complications in the name of performance. It used to be that you treated libraries just like one of your files full of functions and linked them in with the rest of your program. This was called *static linking*. Sometime in the 1980s, however, people noticed that lots of programs were using the same libraries. This was a great testament to the value of those libraries. But they added to the size of every program that used them, and there were many copies of the libraries using up valuable memory. Enter *shared libraries*. The MMU can be used to allow the same copy of a library to be shared by multiple programs, as illustrated in Figure 5-17.

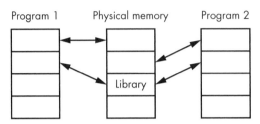

Figure 5-17: A shared library

Keep in mind that the instructions from the shared library are common to the programs that use it. The library functions must be designed so that they use the heap and stack of the calling programs.

Programs have an *entry point*, which is the address of the first instruction in the program. Though it's counterintuitive, that instruction is not the first one executed when a program is run. When all the pieces of a program are linked to form an *executable*, an additional *runtime library* is included. Code in this library runs before hitting the entry point.

The runtime library is responsible for setting up memory. That means establishing a stack and a heap. It also sets the initial values for items in the static data area. These values are stored in the executable and must be copied to the static data after acquiring that memory from the system.

The runtime library performs many more functions, especially for complicated languages. Fortunately, you don't need to know any more about it right now.

Memory Power

We've approached memory from a performance perspective so far. But there's another consideration. Moving data around in memory takes *power*. That's not a big deal for desktop computers. But it's a huge issue for mobile devices. And although battery life isn't an issue in data centers such as those used by large internet companies, using extra power on thousands of machines adds up.

Balancing power consumption and performance is challenging. Keep both in mind when writing code.

Summary

You've learned that working with memory is not as simple as you might have thought after reading Chapter 4. You got a feel for how much additional complication gets added to simple processors in order to improve memory usage. You now have a pretty complete idea of what's in a modern computer with the exception of I/O—which is the topic of Chapter 6.

6

COMMUNICATIONS BREAKDOWN

Computers don't compute just for the thrill of it. They take in input from various sources, do their computations, and produce output for use by a huge range of devices. Computers might be communicating with people, talking to each other, or running factories. Let's explore this a bit more.

I briefly mentioned input and output (I/O) in "Input and Output" on page 96, referring to getting things into and out of the processor core. Doing that isn't all that difficult; all we need are some *latches* (see "Latches" on page 71) for output and *tri-state buffers* (refer to Figure 2-38) for input. It used to be that each and every aspect of an I/O device would be hooked up to some bit on a latch or buffer, and the computer would be the puppeteer responsible for the articulation of every limb.

Processor cost reduction has changed that. Many formerly complex I/O devices now include their own microprocessors. For example, you can purchase a three-axis accelerometer or temperature sensor that provides a nice digital output for a few dollars. I won't bother talking about devices like those because they're not interesting from a programming standpoint—the interface is just reading and writing bytes as described in the device specification. But that doesn't get you off the hook. You might work on the code for a device with an integrated processor. If you're designing the next internet-connected hairbrush, you'll likely bristle at its hairy control algorithm.

This chapter examines techniques for interacting with some of the I/O devices that are still interesting from a programming standpoint. It also covers *sampling*, because that's how we convert real-world analog data into a digital form usable by computers and vice versa.

Low-Level I/O

The simplest forms of I/O involve connecting things to bits that can be read and written by the CPU. These forms began evolving into more complicated devices when they started getting used a lot. This section looks at a few examples.

I/O Ports

The easiest way to get a computer to talk to something is to hook it up to an I/O *port*. For example, Atmel makes the AVR family of small processors. They include a large number of built-in I/O devices. In Figure 6-1, we're hooking some things up to *port B*.

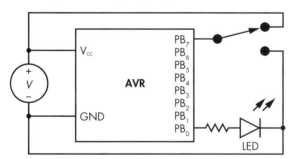

Figure 6-1: Light and switch on port B

You should recognize the switch in Figure 6-1 from Chapter 2. The *LED* is a light-emitting diode. A *diode* is a semiconductor device that works like an amusement park turnstile: it lets electricity through only in one direction, indicated by the direction of the hollow arrow. LEDs have the nice side effect that they glow.

Note the resistor in series with the LED. It's there to limit the amount of current that flows through the LED so that neither it nor PB_0 burns up. You can calculate the resistor value using Ohm's law, introduced in Chapter 2. Let's say that V is 5 volts. One of the characteristics of the silicon sandwiches discussed in "Transistors" on page 51 is that the voltage across one is 0.7 volts. The AVR processor's datasheet says that the output voltage for a logic 1 when V is 5 volts is 4.2 volts. We want to limit the current to 10 mA (0.01 A) because that's what the LED expects; the AVR is capable of 20 mA. Ohm's law says that resistance is voltage divided by current, so $(4.2 - 0.7) \div 0.01 = 350\Omega$. As you can see, PB_7 can be switched between the voltages for 0 and 1. No electricity flows through PB_0 when it's set to 0. Electricity flows through the LED when PB_0 is 1, making it glow. Make sure that you read the datasheet for any LED or other component that you use, because characteristics such as the voltage drop may be different.

Port B is controlled by three registers, as shown in Figure 6-2. *DDRB*, the data direction register, determines whether each pin is an input or an output. *PORTB* is a latch that holds the output data. *PINB* reads the values of the pins.

7	6	5	4	3	2	1	0	
DDB7	DDB6	DDB5	DDB4	DDB3	DDB2	DDB1	DDB0	DDRB

7	6	5	4	3	2	1	0	
PORTB7	PORTB6	PORTB5	PORTB4	PORTB3	PORTB2	PORTB1	PORTB0	PORTB

7	6	5	4	3	2	1	0	
PINB7	PINB6	PINB5	PINB4	PINB3	PINB2	PINB1	PINB0	PINB

Figure 6-2: AVR PORTB registers

This may appear really complicated, but as you can see in Figure 6-3, it's just another arrangement of our standard building blocks: demultiplexers, flip-flops, and tri-state buffers.

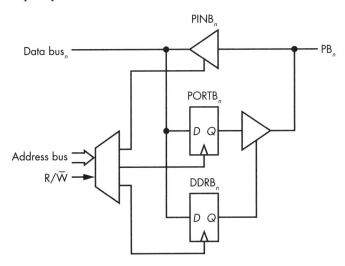

Figure 6-3: AVR port B construction

DDRB is the data direction register for port B. Putting a 1 in any bit turns the associated pin into an output; if set to 0, it's an input. PORTB is the output part of the port. Writing a 0 or a 1 into any bit makes the associated output a low voltage or a high voltage. Reading PINB supplies the state of the associated pins, so if pins 6 and 0 are pulled high and the rest are pulled low, it'll read 01000001, or 0x41.

As you can see, it's pretty easy to get data in and out of the chip. You can read the switch by looking at $PINB_7$ in the PINB register. You can turn the LED on and off by writing to $PORTB_0$ in the PORTB register. You could write a simple program to blink the LED for the perpetual entertainment of yourself and all your friends.

Push My Buttons

Lots of devices have buttons or switches of some sort. They're not as easy for a computer to read as you might think because of the way they're designed. A simple push button consists of a pair of electrical contacts and a piece of metal that connects them when the button is pressed. Take a look at the circuit in Figure 6-4.

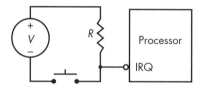

Figure 6-4: Simple push-button circuit

R is what's called a *pull-up* resistor, just like we saw earlier in Figure 2-37. When the button is not pushed, the resistor pulls the voltage on the processor *interrupt request (IRQ)* pin up to the voltage supplied by *V*, making it a logic 1. When the button is pressed, the resistor limits the current from *V* so that it doesn't burn up, allowing a logic 0 to be presented to IRQ.

Seems simple, but Figure 6-5 shows that it isn't. You would think that when you pushed and released the button, the signal at IRQ would look like the picture on the left, but it actually looks more like the one on the right.

Figure 6-5: Button bounce

What's going on here? When the piece of metal connected to the button hits the contacts, it *bounces* and comes off the contacts for a short time. It might bounce several times before settling down. Since we connected the button to an interrupt-generating pin on the processor, we might get several interrupts from a single button push, which is probably not what we want. We need to *debounce* the button. (You can get bounce-free buttons, but they often cost more.)

A simple way to debounce is to have the interrupt handler set a timer, and then you test the state of the button after the timer expires, as Figure 6-6 illustrates. We can approach this in two different ways: setting a timer on the first interrupt or replacing an existing timer with a new one on each interrupt.

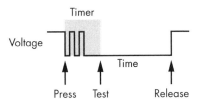

Figure 6-6: Button debounce timer

This approach works but isn't necessarily the best one. It's hard to choose a timer value because button bounce time can change over time due to mechanical wear. You've probably had a reviled alarm clock where the buttons were worn to the point that setting the time was difficult. Also, most devices have more than one button, and it's unlikely that a processor has enough interrupt pins to go around. We could build circuitry to share interrupts, but we'd rather do it cheaply in software. Most systems have some sort of timer that can generate periodic interrupts. We can piggy-back on that interrupt for button debouncing.

Let's assume that we have eight buttons hooked up to some I/O port, such as we saw in Figure 6-1, and that the state of the I/O port is available in a variable named INB that is an 8-bit unsigned char. We can construct a *finite impulse response (FIR)* filter out of an array, as shown in Figure 6-7. A FIR is a queue; on each timer tick, we discard the oldest element and shift in a new one. We OR the array elements together to form the current state as part of a two-element queue; current is moved to previous before we calculate the new current. All we have to do now is XOR the current and previous states to find out which buttons have changed state.

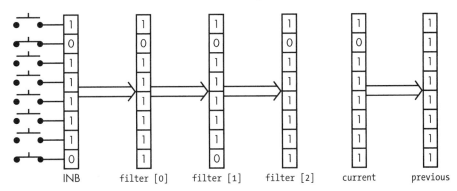

Figure 6-7: FIR filter button debouncer

It's a pretty simple piece of code, as shown in the C programming language in Listing 6-1.

```c
unsigned char   filter[FILTER_SIZE];
unsigned char   changed;
unsigned char   current;
unsigned char   previous;

previous = current;
current = 0;

for (int i = FILTER_SIZE - 1; i > 0; i--) {
        filter[i] = filter[i - 1];
        current |= filter[i];
}

filter[0] = INB;
current |= filter[0];
changed = current ^ previous;
```

Listing 6-1: FIR button debouncer

FILTER_SIZE is the number of elements in the filter, the choice of which depends on how noisy the buttons are and the timer interrupt rate.

Let There Be Lights

Many widgets have some sort of display. I'm not talking about things with computer screens here—more like alarm clocks and dishwashers. There are often several indicator lights and possibly some simple numeric displays.

A common type of simple indicator is the seven-segment display shown in Figure 6-8. These displays have seven LEDs arranged in a figure-8 pattern plus maybe an additional decimal point.

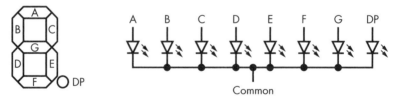

Figure 6-8: Seven-segment display

The eight LEDs in a display require 16 electrical connections (pins). But that's not how they're typically constructed; there's a pin for one end of each LED and a common connection for the other. Since we only need to control one end to turn an LED on or off, this common connection saves on pins, which reduces cost. Figure 6-8 shows a *common cathode* display in which the cathodes are all tied together and the anodes each have their own pins.

We could just hook up the anodes to output pins on a processor and the cathodes to the *ground* or negative end of the voltage source or *power supply*. A high (1) voltage on a pin would light up the corresponding LED. In practice, most processors don't supply enough current for that to work, so an additional driver circuit is used. Open-collector outputs (shown back in Figure 2-36) are often used.

The software to drive one of these displays is pretty simple. All we need is a table that maps numbers (and maybe letters) to the appropriate segments to light. But it should come as no surprise that there are complications. We rarely have a single display; for example, an alarm clock has four. Though we could hook each display up to its own I/O port, it's unlikely that there are that many ports. The solution is to *multiplex* the displays by connecting the anodes to port A and the cathodes to port B, as shown in Figure 6-9.

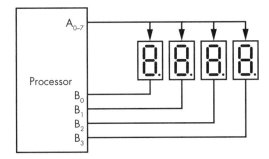

Figure 6-9: Multiplexed displays

The display anodes are wired in parallel; all of the A segments are connected together, all of the B segments are connected together, and so on. The cathode connection for each display is connected to its own output pin. A display segment can light up only if its anode is a 1 and its cathode a 0. You might wonder why, for example, segments A and B wouldn't light up if A were a 1 and B were a 0. Remember that the *D* in *LED* stands for *diode*, and diodes are one-way streets for electricity.

We take advantage of the human *persistence of vision* to make the displays work. A display doesn't have to be on all the time for us to perceive it as lit. Our eyes and brain will tell us that it's lit if it's on for as little as 1/24 of a second. This is the same effect that makes movies and video work. All we have to do is switch which display is on by setting the associated cathode pin to 0 and the segment anodes to whatever we want to display. We can switch displays in a timer interrupt handler similar to the one we used in the earlier push-button example.

Lights, Action, . . .

It's common for devices to include both buttons and displays. As it turns out, we can save some pins by multiplexing the buttons as well as the displays. Let's say we have a 12-button telephone-style keypad in addition to our four displays, as shown in Figure 6-10.

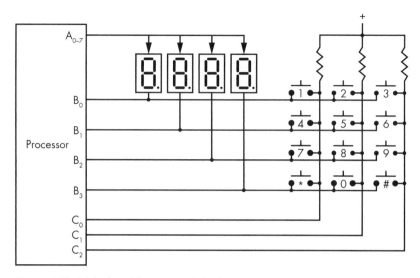

Figure 6-10: Multiplexed buttons and displays

What have we accomplished with all this complexity? We've only had to use three additional pins for the 12 push-buttons instead of 12. All the push-buttons are pulled up to logic 1s by the pull-up resistors. Pushing a button has no effect if no displays are selected, because the B outputs are also all 1s. When the leftmost display is selected, B_0 is low, and pushing any button in the top row will cause the associated C input to go low, and so on. Since the display and push buttons are scanned with the same set of signals, the code that does the scanning can be combined in the timer interrupt handler.

Note that Figure 6-10 is a simplified diagram. In practice, the B pins would need to be open-collector or *open-drain* (see "Output Variations" on page 58) devices; otherwise, if two buttons in different rows but the same columns were pushed, we'd be connecting a 1 to a 0, which might damage the parts. However, it's not normally implemented that way, since the aforementioned display driver circuitry handles that for us.

You can find out whether some device is constructed in a manner similar to Figure 6-10 by pushing multiple buttons at the same time and watching the displays. The displays will look strange. Think about why.

Bright Ideas

Your alarm clock might have a brightness adjustment for the display. How does that work? By varying the *duty cycle* of the display, illustrated in Figure 6-11.

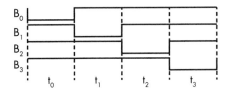 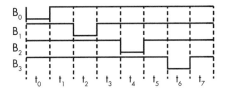

Figure 6-11: Duty cycle

Each display is lit one-quarter of the time in the left part of Figure 6-11. The right part shows each display lit only one-eighth of the time; no displays are lit half of the time. The result is that the displays on the right appear approximately half as bright as those on the left. The "brightness" is related to the average time that the display is on. Note that the relationship between duty cycle and perceived brightness is unlikely to be linear.

2^n Shades of Gray

A common sensor task is to determine the position of a rotating shaft— think motors, wheels, and knobs. We could determine the position by using switches on the shaft or by using black and white spots that could be read with a photosensor. Whatever approach we take, we'd encode each shaft position as a binary number. The encoder might look like Figure 6-12 if we cared about eight different positions. If the white sectors are 0s and the black sectors are 1s, then you can see how we can read the position value. The radial lines are not part of the encoder; they're just there to make the diagram easier to understand.

Figure 6-12: Binary rotary encoder

As usual, this seems simple, but it isn't. In this case, the problem is mechanical tolerances. Note that even with a perfectly aligned encoder, we'd still have issues resulting from propagation delay differences in the circuitry reading each bit. What happens if the encoder isn't perfectly aligned, as in Figure 6-13?

Figure 6-13: Binary rotary encoder alignment error

Rather than reading 01234567 as we'd expect, we get 201023645467. American physicist Frank Gray (1887–1969) at Bell Telephone Laboratories took a look at this problem and came up with a different encoding in which only the value of a single bit changes for each position. For the 3-bit encoder we've been looking at, the eponymous *Gray code* is 000, 001, 011, 010, 110, 111, 101, 100. The code can easily be translated to binary using a small table. Figure 6-14 shows a Gray code version of our encoder wheel.

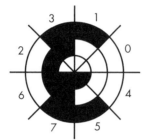

Figure 6-14: Gray code rotary encoder

Quadrature

There's a twist on 2-bit Gray codes we can use when we don't really need to know the absolute position of something, but need to know when the position changes and in which direction. Some of the knobs on your car dashboard, such as the volume control on the stereo, are likely to work this way. A good indicator is if turning a knob while the ignition is off has no effect once the car is started. The twist is called *quadrature encoding* because there are four states. The 2-bit Gray code pattern is repeated multiple times. For example, there are cheap quadrature encoders that are good to 1/4,096 of a revolution. Quadrature takes only two sensors, one for each bit. An absolute 4,096-position encoder would take 12 sensors.

The quadrature waveform is shown in Figure 6-15.

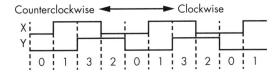

Figure 6-15: Quadrature waveform

As you can see, when the shaft is rotated clockwise, it produces the sequence 0132; counterclockwise yields 2310. We can form a 4-bit number out of the current position and the previous position. This number tells us the direction of rotation, as Table 6-1 shows.

Table 6-1: Quadrature Rotation Detection

Current	Previous	Combined	Meaning
00	00	0	Illegal
00	01	1	Clockwise
00	10	2	Counterclockwise
00	11	3	Illegal
01	00	4	Counterclockwise
01	01	5	Illegal
01	10	6	Illegal
01	11	7	Clockwise
10	00	8	Clockwise
10	01	9	Illegal
10	10	a	Illegal
10	11	b	Counterclockwise
11	00	c	Illegal
11	01	d	Counterclockwise
11	10	e	Clockwise
11	11	f	Illegal

Note that this is a state machine, where the combined value is the state.

What do you get when you take a pair of quadrature encoders, orient them at 90 degrees from each other, and stick a rubber ball in the middle? A computer mouse.

Parallel Communication

Parallel communication is an extension of what we saw earlier when lighting up LEDs. We could hook up eight LEDs to port B and flash ASCII character codes. *Parallel* means we have a wire for each component and can control them all at the same time.

You may have an IEEE 1284 *parallel port* on your computer if it's an old model. These were commonly used for printers and scanners before *Universal Serial Bus (USB)* came along. And yes, there were eight data lines on the parallel port so you could send ASCII character codes.

There's a problem with all of this, though: how do you know when the data is valid? Let's say you send the characters *ABC*. How do you know when it's the next character? You can't just look for some change, because it could be *AABC*. One way is to have another "look at me" signal. IEEE 1284 had a *strobe* signal for this purpose. In Figure 6-16, the data on bits 0 through 7 is valid whenever the strobe is low or 0.

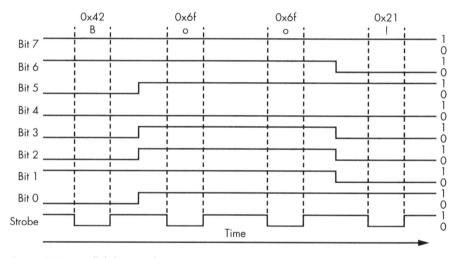

Figure 6-16: Parallel data strobe timing

Another parallel interface that has pretty much gone by the wayside is *IDE*. This is what's used to communicate with older disk drives.

Parallel interfaces are expensive because they require many I/O pins, connector pins, and wires. The parallel port had a 25-pin connector and a big fat cable. IDE had 40 wires. There's a limit to how fast a signal can be sent down a wire, and when that's exceeded, multiple wires are needed.

Serial Communication

It would be nice to be able to communicate using fewer wires because wires cost money, which adds up, especially when you're talking about long distances. Two wires is the minimum number required because we need a return signal path for the electricity, as you learned in Chapter 2. We're not going to show that return path in the diagrams for simplicity.

How could we send the eight signals over a single wire? We can get a hint by looking at the timing diagram in Figure 6-16. Even though each bit is on its own wire, the characters are spaced out in time. We can space out the bits in time too.

I talked about shift registers in "Shiftiness" on page 99. On the transmitting end, the strobe or *clock* signal shifts all the bits over one position and sends the bit that falls off the end out on the wire. On the receiving end, the clock shifts all the bits over by one position and puts the state of the data line into the newly vacated position, as shown in Figure 6-17.

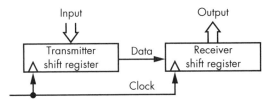

Figure 6-17: Serial communications using shift registers

We'd use a counter to tell us whenever we get to 8 bits, and then we could do something with the value. This approach takes two wires, not one, and it's pretty error-prone. It requires that the transmitter and receiver be synchronized, or *in sync*—which has nothing to do with the boy band. All we'd have to do is miss one clock, and everything would be garbled. We could add a third wire that said when we were starting a new character, but our goal is to minimize the number of wires.

A long time ago (in the early 1900s), the telegraph was married to the typewriter to make the *teletype*, a machine that allowed typing to a printer far away. Teletype machines were initially used to allow stock market information to be sent over telegraph wires.

The data was sent using a serial *protocol* (set of rules) that worked using just one wire in addition to the return path. The clever thing about this protocol is that it worked sort of like the timers at a swim meet. Everybody starts their individual timers when the starting gun goes off, and they're close enough that it works. Figure 6-18 illustrates the protocol.

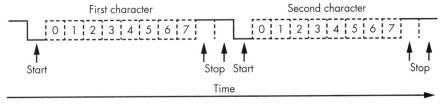

Figure 6-18: Mark-space signaling

The line here is in a 1, or *high*, state when nothing is happening. The high state is called *mark*, and the low state is called *space*, after the way early telegraph equipment either made a mark or left a space on a strip of paper. The line going low in Figure 6-18 is the starting gun, and it's called the *start bit*. Following the start bit, the 8 bits of data are sent. The character ends with a pair of high *stop bits*. Each bit is allotted the same amount of time. Synchronization errors can occur, but all the transmitter has to do is to be quiet for a *character time* and the receiver will sync up. We're dividing up time so that we have a slot for each bit and then multiplexing the data onto the single wire. This technique, called *time division multiplexing*, can be implemented using a selector (see "Building Selectors" on page 65) instead of a shift register. The speed in bits per second, by the way, is known as the *Baud rate*, named after French engineer Émile Baudot (1845–1903).

Teletypes were awesome machines. They didn't contain any electronics and worked by having a motor spin a shaft. An electromagnet released the shaft when a start bit came in so it could spin. At each place in the rotation for the bit position, all sorts of cams and levers and pushrods would move around, ultimately whacking a metal character onto an inked ribbon and then onto a piece of paper. You knew that a message was coming in when stuff started rattling off the shelves. The keyboard worked in a similar fashion. Pressing a key started a shaft spinning that would move an electrical contact, depending on which keys were pressed, to generate an ASCII code.

Another cool trick, called a *half-duplex* connection, is where a transmitter and a receiver on each end share the same wire. Only one can talk at a time, or gibberish results. That's why radio operators said things like "over." You know all about half-duplex communications if you've ever used a walkie-talkie. A *collision* results when more than one transmitter is active at the same time, garbling the data. A *full-duplex* connection is when there are two wires, one going in each direction.

All of the circuitry to implement this eventually became available in a single integrated circuit called a *UART*, which stands for *Universal Asynchronous Receiver-Transmitter*. Software can also implement a UART with an approach called *bit-banging*.

A standard called RS-232 defined the voltage levels used for mark and space on old serial ports, as well as many additional control signals. It's pretty much been replaced by USB now, although a variant called *RS-485*, which uses differential signaling (refer back to Figure 2-32) for greater noise immunity, is used in industrial environments. The parallel IDE interface to disks has been replaced by *SATA*, the serial equivalent. Electronics are now fast enough that we can do many things serially that we used to have to do in parallel. Also, wires remain expensive. The world is running low on copper extractable from the earth, which is what's used for the conductor in wires. Recycling existing copper products is now a major source of copper. Chips are mostly silicon, which is found in sand and very abundant.

There are a number of serial interfaces designed for connecting peripherals up to small microcomputers. These include *SPI*, *I2C*, *TWI*, and *OneWire*.

Catch a Wave

There's a big problem with mark-space signaling, which is that it's not good for very long distances. It doesn't work over telephone lines for reasons that are beyond the scope of this book. That was a big deal because once the telegraph was replaced by better technologies, the only remaining long-distance communication technologies were telephone and radio. This mark-space signaling problem is solved with the same trick that makes radio work.

The universe contains all kinds of different waves. There are waves in the ocean, sound waves, light waves, microwaves, and all sorts of stuff in between. The fundamental wave is a *sine wave*. All other wave shapes can be made from combinations of sine waves. You get a sine wave by plotting the height of a point on a circle versus the angle. It looks like Figure 6-19.

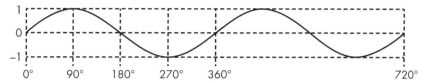

Figure 6-19: Sine wave

The height of the sine wave is the *amplitude*. The number of same-direction zero crossings per second is the *frequency*, measured in *Hertz*, after German physicist Heinrich Hertz (1857–1894). Hertz is abbreviated *Hz* and is synonymous with *cycles per second*. The distance between two same-direction zero crossings is the *wavelength*. They're related as follows:

$$\lambda = \frac{v}{f}$$

In this equation, λ is the wavelength in meters, f is the frequency in Hertz, and v is the speed of the wave in the medium in which it's traveling. That's the speed of light for radio waves. The higher the frequency, the shorter the wavelength. Just as a reference point, middle C is about 261 Hz these days.

If you stop to think about it, you'll realize that different waves have different properties. Sound waves don't travel very far and are stopped by a vacuum but go around corners. Light waves go a very long way but are stopped by a wall. Some frequencies of radio waves go through walls, but others don't. There's a lot of variation in between.

Time to surf. Let's find a wave that does what we want and hitch a ride. We'll call this wave the *carrier*, and what we want to do is *modulate* or change it based on the signal we care about, such as our mark-space *waveform*.

AT&T introduced the Bell 103A data set in the early 1960s. It provided full duplex communications at a whopping 300 Baud over a telephone line by using four audio frequencies; each end of the connection got its own pair of mark and space tones. This is called *frequency shift keying (FSK)* because the frequency shifts with the marks and spaces. You can see it in Figure 6-20.

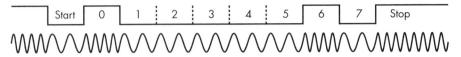

Figure 6-20: Frequency shift keying—ASCII letter A

The receiving end has to turn the audio back into marks and spaces, called *demodulation*, the opposite of modulation. Devices that do this are called *modems*. The weird noises you hear when someone uses a dial-up connection to the internet or sends a fax in a cheesy movie are the frequencies used by modems.

Universal Serial Bus

USB is not all that interesting, but it's worth a mention because it's so common. It features more incompatible and hard-to-use connectors than any other standard and is arguably more important for device charging than for data transfer.

USB replaced many of the bulky connectors that were proliferating on computers in the mid-1990s, such as the PS/2, RS-232, and parallel ports with a single four-wire connector. There were two power wires and a twisted pair for data using differential signaling. USB repeats the pattern we'll see more of soon of "can't stop there," so now USB Type-C is up to 24 wires, just shy of the old parallel port.

USB is not a free-for-all. There is a *controller* that is in charge of all of the *endpoints*, as opposed to everything having equal footing. The data transfer is structured; it's not just shoveling uninterpreted bits around. It uses a common technique: data is transferred in *packets*, which are equivalent to packages sent through the mail. Packets contain a *header* and optional *payload*. The header is essentially the information that you'd find on the outside of a package—where it came from, where it's going, the class of postage, and so on. The payload is the contents of the package.

USB handles audio and video via *isochronous transfers*. An endpoint can ask to reserve a certain amount of the *bandwidth* (data transfer rate), yielding a guarantee that data can be transferred. The controller refuses the request if there isn't enough bandwidth.

Networking

It's difficult to get a clear picture of the modern world of networking without knowing its origins. It drives me crazy when my daughter says, "The Wi-Fi is down" or, "The internet isn't working," because they're not the same thing. Attempts to explain this to her are met with the patented teenage eye roll and hair toss.

Two general classifications are used to describe networks. A *local area network (LAN)* is a network that covers a small geographic area such as a home or an office. A *wide area network (WAN)* covers a large geographic area. These terms are somewhat fuzzy since there is no exact definition of *small* and *large*.

The original network was the telegraph network, which evolved into the telephone network. It didn't start as a computer network because computers didn't exist at the time. The original telephone network was a *circuit-switched* network. When a call was made between parties, their wires were effectively connected together, forming a circuit. It was *switched* because that connection existed only for the duration of the conversation. Once a call was completed, new circuits could be created.

With a few exceptions, such as the remaining landlines, the phone system is now a *packet-switched* network. I mentioned packets in the last section. Communications are divided up into packets that include sender and recipient addresses. Packets can share wires using time division multiplexing (covered earlier in "Serial Communication" on page 152), which allows for more efficient use of circuits; this became possible when the amount of data that could be sent over a wire became more than was needed just for voice.

One of the earliest computer networks was part of *Semi-Automatic Ground Environment (SAGE)*, a Cold War–era defense system. It used modems on the telephone network for communications between sites.

Many organizations started experimenting with LANs in the late 1960s. For example, my lab at Bell was developing graphics terminals that were connected to our department's Honeywell DDP-516 computer using a LAN called the *ring*. At the time, peripherals such as tape drives and printers were very expensive, and most departments didn't have their own. But they were available in the main computer center. Our computer was connected to a modem, and when it needed something it didn't have, it would just call up the computer center. It was effectively a WAN. Not only could we send things off to be printed, we could also send programs that would be run, and the computer center would call our machine back with the results.

Similar activity was occurring at many research labs and companies. Many different LANs were invented. Each was its own private universe, though—they couldn't talk to each other. Modems and phone lines were the basis for wide-area communications.

A set of computer programs developed at Bell Labs called *UUCP* (for *UNIX-to-UNIX copy*) was released to the outside world in 1979. UUCP allowed computers to call each other to transfer data or run programs remotely. It formed the basis for early email and news systems such as USENET. These systems were an interesting hack. If you wanted to send data across the country, it would hop from machine to machine until it got to its destination. This usually allowed long-distance phone charges to be avoided.

Meanwhile, ARPA, the Advanced Research Projects Agency of the US Department of Defense, was funding the development of the ARPANET, a packet-switched WAN. The ARPANET evolved into the internet in the 1990s. Most people take the internet for granted today, and like my daughter, they probably think it's synonymous with networking. But its real nature is indicated right there in the name. It's a contraction of *inter* and *net*. The internet is a network of networks—it's the WAN that connects the LANs together.

Modern LANs

A lot of other stuff that we take for granted these days was invented at the Xerox Palo Alto Research Center (PARC) in the mid-1970s. For example, an American electrical engineer by the name of Bob Metcalfe invented *Ethernet*, which is a LAN because it's not designed to go very far.

NOTE *Check out Adele Goldberg's book* A History of Personal Workstations *(Addison-Wesley, 1988) for more about the history of PARC.*

The original Ethernet was a half-duplex system. Every computer was connected to the same wire. Each computer network interface had a unique 48-bit address called a *Media Access Control (MAC)* address, and that's still the case today. Data is organized into packets, called *frames*, of about 1,500 bytes. Frames have a *header* that includes the sender address, the recipient address, and some error checks (for example, cyclic redundancy checks, or CRCs, as discussed in "Error Detection and Correction" on page 88) along with the data payload.

Normally, one computer would talk, and the others would listen. Computers that didn't match the recipient's MAC address would ignore the data. Each machine listened to what was going on and didn't transmit if someone else was transmitting. When machines did start transmitting at the same time, the collision resulted in garbled packets, just like the half-duplex collisions described earlier. One of Metcalfe's big innovations was *random back-off-and-retry*. Each machine that was trying to talk would wait a random amount of time and then try to resend.

Ethernet is still in use today, though not the half-duplex version. Now machines are connected to *routers* that keep track of which machine is at which connection and routes packets to the right places. Collisions no longer happen. Wi-Fi is essentially a version of Ethernet that uses radio instead of wires. Bluetooth is another popular LAN system. Think of it as a version of USB that ditches the wires for radio.

The Internet

As you now know, the internet is not actually a physical network; it's a set of layered protocols. It's designed in such a way that the lower layers specifying the physical network can be replaced without affecting the upper layers. That design allows the internet to function over wires, radio, optical fibers, and whatever new technologies come along.

TCP/IP

Transmission Control Protocol/Internet Protocol (TCP/IP) is the pair of protocols on which the internet is built. IP gets packets from place to place. These packets, called *datagrams*, are like telegrams for computers. As with real telegrams, the sender doesn't know when or even whether the recipient got the message. TCP is built on top of IP and makes sure that packets get reliably delivered. This is a pretty complicated job, because large messages span many packets that may not arrive in order since they may have taken different routes—not much different from ordering some stuff and having it shipped in multiple boxes that may not all arrive on the same day or even be sent via the same carrier.

IP Addresses

Each computer on the internet has a unique address known as its *IP address*. Unlike MAC addresses, IP addresses aren't tied to the hardware and can change. The IP address system is a hierarchical system in which someone gives out blocks of addresses, who in turn give out blocks of addresses, and so on until it gets down to whoever gives your machine its address.

The internet pretty much runs on *IPv4*, version 4 of IP, which uses 32 bits of address. Addresses are written in *octet* notation of *xxx.xxx.xxx.xxx*, where each *xxx* is 8 of the 32 bits written in decimal. That's over 4 billion addresses, yet that's not enough. Now that everyone has an address for their desktop, their laptop, their tablet, their cell phone, and their other gadgets, there are no more addresses to give out. Hence, the world has been slowly migrating to *IPv6*, which has 128-bit addresses.

Domain Name System

How can you be found if your address can change? That's handled by the *Domain Name System (DNS)*, which is like a phone book, for those who remember what those are. DNS maps names to addresses. It knows that *whitehouse.gov* has the IP address 23.1.225.229 at the time that I'm writing this. It's sort of like the address book in your phone, except you have to keep that up-to-date; DNS takes care of everything whenever anybody moves.

The World Wide Web

Many other protocols are built on top of TCP/IP, such as the *Simple Mail Transfer Protocol (SMTP)* that makes email work. One of the most used protocols is *HTTP*, short for *HyperText Transfer Protocol*, which is used for web pages, along with *HTTPS* where the *S* stands for *secure*.

Hypertext is just text with links. American engineer Vannevar Bush (1890–1974) came up with the idea in 1945. It didn't really take off until Tim Berners-Lee, a scientist at CERN (the European Organization for Nuclear Research), invented the World Wide Web so that physicists could share information.

The HTTP standard defines how *web browsers* interact with *web servers*. Web browsers are what you use to view web pages. Web servers send you those pages upon request. Web pages are found and fetched by a *Uniform Resource Locator (URL)*, the website address in the address bar of your browser. It's how you locate the information you want and includes the domain name of a machine on the internet and a description of where to find the information on that machine.

Web pages typically start their lives as *HTML* (short for *HyperText Markup Language*), the most common language in which web pages are written. HTML has gotten a lot of stuff stuck onto it over time and is now a pretty complicated mess. More on this in Chapter 9.

Analog in the Digital World

Computers are in lots of entertainment devices, from audio players to televisions. You may have noticed that digital photos don't look very good when they're magnified beyond a certain point. Our real-world experience of sound and light is continuous, but computers have no way to store continuous things. The data must be *sampled*, which means we have to take readings at points in time and/or space. An analog (continuous) signal must then be reconstructed from those samples for playback.

NOTE *There's a good video called "Episode 1: A Digital Media Primer for Geeks" that you can find online that is a good introduction to sampling. There's a second episode, which is also good, but it's very misleading. While everything said is technically correct, it only applies to mono, not stereo. The presenter implies that it's good for stereo, but it isn't.*

Sampling isn't a new thing; even back in the days of silent movies, the scene was sampled at about 16 frames per second. There's an entire field called *discrete mathematics* that deals with sampling. Discreetly, of course.

We talked about the differences between analog and digital way back in Chapter 2. This book is about digital computers, and many real-world applications require computers to generate analog signals, interpret analog signals, or both. The following sections discuss how computers accomplish this.

Digital-to-Analog Conversion

How might we generate an analog voltage based on a digital number? The blithe and correct answer is: by using a digital-to-analog converter. How would we construct one of these?

Let's go back to Figure 6-1, where we have an LED connected to an I/O port. In Figure 6-21, we hook an LED to each of the eight pins of port B.

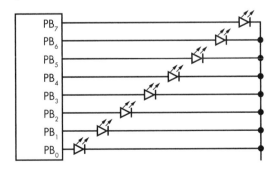

Figure 6-21: Digital-to-analog converter using LEDs

Now we can generate nine different light levels—from no LEDs on to eight LEDs on. But nine levels from 8 bits isn't a very good use of bits; with 8 bits, we should be able to get 256 different levels. How? Just like we do with numbers. Figure 6-22 hooks one LED to bit 0, two to bit 1, four to bit 2, and so on.

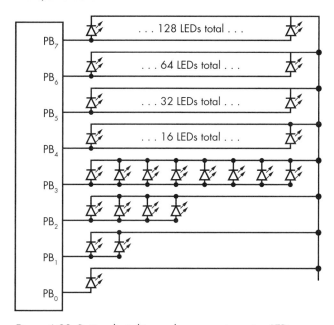

Figure 6-22: Better digital-to-analog converter using LEDs

That's a whole lotta LEDs. You could hang this circuit from a balloon to make a LED zeppelin. Moving on, you can see that this mirrors our binary representation of numbers. Bit 1 produces twice as much light as bit 0, bit 2 four times as much, and so on.

We used the LED example to illuminate the workings of a digital-to-analog converter. A real digital-to-analog converter (D/A or DAC) produces a voltage instead of light. The term *resolution* is loosely used to describe the number of "steps" a DAC can produce. I say "loosely" because it's common to say that a DAC has, for example, 10 bits of resolution, which really means that it has a resolution of 1 part in 2^{10}. To be completely correct, the resolution is the maximum voltage that the DAC can produce divided by the number of steps. For example, if a 10-bit DAC could produce 5V maximum, then it has a resolution of approximately 0.005V.

Figure 6-23 shows the symbol used for a DAC.

Figure 6-23: DAC
schematic symbol

We can generate analog waveforms using a DAC. This is how audio players and music synthesizers work. All we need to do is to change the DAC inputs at a regular rate. For example, if we had an 8-bit DAC connected to port B, we could generate the sawtooth wave shown in Figure 6-24.

```
int i = 0;

while (true)
    PORTB = i++;
```

Figure 6-24: Synthesized sawtooth wave

For more complex waveforms, devices usually incorporate memory that can be written with the data, which is then read out by additional circuitry. This ensures a constant data rate that is independent of whatever else the CPU is doing. A typical way of implementing this is by creating a *FIFO* ("first in, first out") configuration, as shown in Figure 6-25. Note that a FIFO is the same thing as a software queue.

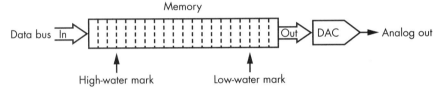

Figure 6-25: FIFO with high- and low-water marks

Two triggers are associated with the FIFO memory: a *high-water mark* and a *low-water mark*, which borrow their terminology from tides. The low-water mark triggers an interrupt when the FIFO is close to empty; the high-water mark triggers when it's close to full. This way, higher-level software can keep the memory filled so that the output is continuous. Though it's not exactly a FIFO because newly added water mixes with the old, this is how water towers work; when the water is below the low-water mark, the pump turns on to fill the tank; when the high-water mark is reached, the pump turns off. FIFOs are really handy for connecting things that operate at different speeds.

Analog-to-Digital Conversion

Analog-to-digital conversion, the opposite process, is done using an A/D, or ADC, which is more complicated than a DAC. The first problem that arises is getting the analog signal to hold still, because we can't measure it if it's wiggling around. (You know the problem if you've ever tried to take a little kid's temperature.) In Figure 6-26, we need to take a *sample* of the input waveform—more than one if we want our digitized version to resemble the analog original. We do this using a circuit called a *sample and hold*, which is the analog equivalent of a digital latch (see "Latches" on page 71).

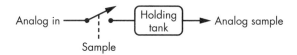

Figure 6-26: Sample and hold

When we take a sample by closing the switch, the current value of the analog signal is stored in the holding tank. Now that we have a stable signal in the holding tank, we need to measure it so we can generate a digital value. We need something that compares the signal to a threshold similar to what we saw in the right half of Figure 2-7, back in Chapter 2. Fortunately, an analog circuit called a *comparator* can tell us when one voltage is greater than another. It's just like a logic gate except that we can choose the threshold.

The schematic symbol for a comparator is shown in Figure 6-27.

Figure 6-27: Analog comparator

The output is 1 if the signal on the + input is greater than or equal to the signal on the – input.

We can use a stack of comparators with different *reference voltages* on the – inputs to build a *flash converter*, as shown in Figure 6-28.

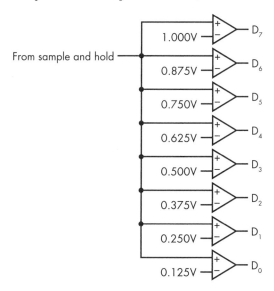

Figure 6-28: Flash converter

It's called a flash converter because it generates results quickly, in a flash. As you can see, the outputs are 00000000 for a voltage less than 0.125V, 000000001 for a voltage between 0.125V and 0.250V, 00000011 for a voltage between 0.250V and 0.375V, and so on. This works, but it has the same problem as our DAC in Figure 6-25: it doesn't use the bits very efficiently. Flash converters are also relatively expensive parts due to the number of comparators, but they're the way to go when extreme speed is required. How might we construct a cheaper ADC that better utilizes the bits?

Our flash converter used a set of fixed reference voltages, one for each comparator. We could use a single comparator if we had an adjustable reference voltage. Where might we get one of those? With a DAC!

In Figure 6-29, you can see that we're using a comparator to test the sampled value in the holding tank against the value of the DAC. Once cleared, the counter counts up until the DAC value hits the sampled value, at which time the counter is disabled and we're done. The counter contains the digitized value of the sample.

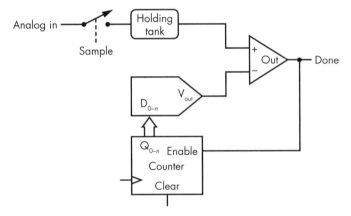

Figure 6-29: Analog-to-digital converter

Once cleared, the counter counts up until the DAC value hits the sampled value, at which time the counter is disabled and we're done. The counter contains the digitized value of the sample.

You can see how this works in Figure 6-30. The analog signal wiggles around, but the output of the holding tank is stable once a sample is taken. The counter is then cleared, and it counts up until the DAC output hits the sampled value, at which time the counter stops and we're done.

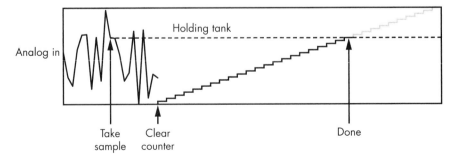

Figure 6-30: ADC in operation

This ADC is called a *ramp converter* because of the way in which the DAC output generates a ramp. One of the problems with a ramp converter is that it can take a long time since the conversion time is a linear function of the sampled signal value. If the sampled signal is at its maximum value and we have an n-bit ADC, conversion can take 2^n clocks.

One way around this is to use a *successive approximation* converter, which performs a *binary search* in hardware, as you can see in Figure 6-31.

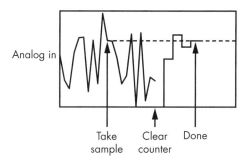

Figure 6-31: Successive approximation ADC in operation

The first clock sets the DAC to one-half of the full range. Since that's less than the sampled signal, it's adjusted upward by one-quarter of the full range. That's too much, so next it's adjusted downward by one-eighth of the full range. That's too low, so it's adjusted up by one-sixteenth of the full range, and we're there. Worst case, it takes $\log_2 n$ clocks. That's quite an improvement.

The term *resolution* is used for ADCs in a manner similar to how it's used for DACs. The schematic symbol is shown in Figure 6-32.

$$V_{in} \qquad D_{0-n}$$

Figure 6-32: ADC schematic symbol

Digital Audio

Audio involves *sampling* in one dimension—that is, measuring the *amplitude* or height of the signal at points in time. Look at the sine wave in Figure 6-33. We have a *square wave* with some *sampling frequency*, and we record the height of the signal on each *rising edge* using an A/D.

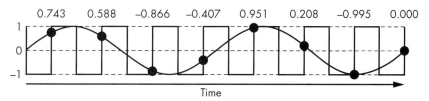

Figure 6-33: Sampling a sine wave

Now that we have a set of samples, we should be able to reconstruct the original signal by feeding them to a D/A. Let's give it a try, as shown in Figure 6-34.

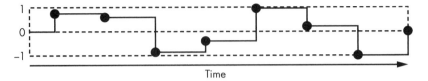

Figure 6-34: Reconstructed sine wave from samples

Wow, that looks terribly distorted. Looks like we'd need a lot more samples to improve the result so that it looked more like Figure 6-35.

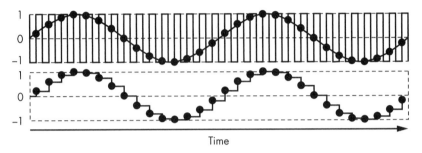

Figure 6-35: Higher-frequency sampling and reconstruction

But we don't need to. The sampling and reconstruction in Figures 6-33 and 6-34 is actually okay. I'm about to tell you why, but be warned: there's some heavy theory ahead.

A sine wave is relatively easy to describe, as mentioned in "Catch a Wave" on page 154. But we need a way to describe more complicated waveforms, such as the one in Figure 6-31.

The graphs so far plot amplitude against time, but we can look at it in other ways. Take a look at the musical score in Figure 6-36.

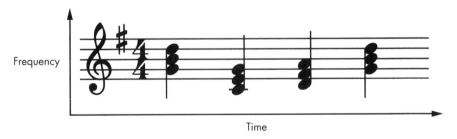

Figure 6-36: A musical score

You can see that the score plots musical notes against time, but there's more happening. We don't just have notes at each point in time; we have *chords*, which are constructed from multiple notes. Let's look at the first chord, which contains the notes G_4 (400 Hz), B_4 (494 Hz), and D_5 (587 Hz). Pretend we're playing the chord on a synthesizer that can generate sine waves for the notes. You can see in Figure 6-37 that although each note is a sine wave, the chord itself is a more complex waveform, being the sum of the three notes. It turns out that any waveform can be represented as the weighted (multiplied by some scale factor) sum of a set of sine waves. For example, if the square wave in Figure 6-33 has a frequency of f, it can be represented as the sum of sine waves:

$$\frac{\sin(f)}{1} + \frac{\sin(3f)}{3} + \frac{\sin(5f)}{5} + \frac{\sin(7f)}{7} + \dots$$

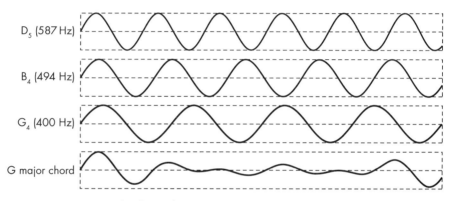

Figure 6-37: G major chord waveform

If you have a good ear, you can listen to a chord like this and pick out the component notes. Tone-deaf people have to rely on some mathematical acrobatics called the *Fourier transform*, invented by French mathematician and physicist Jean-Baptiste Joseph Fourier (1768–1830), who also discovered the greenhouse effect. All the graphs we've seen in this section so far plot amplitude against time. The Fourier transform allows us to plot amplitude against frequency. It's a different way of looking at things. The Fourier transform of our G major chord would look like Figure 6-38.

Figure 6-38: G major chord Fourier transform plot

You've probably seen this sort of thing before without knowing it. Many media players have spectrum analyzer eye candy that displays the volume in different frequency bands using the Fourier transform. Spectrum analyzers originated as complicated pieces of electronic equipment. Now they can be implemented on computers using the *Fast Fourier Transform (FFT)* algorithm. One of the coolest applications of Fourier analysis is the Hammond B-3 organ.

THE HAMMOND B-3 ORGAN

The Hammond B-3 is an amazing application of electromagnetics and Fourier analysis. The way it works is that a motor drives a shaft on which 91 "tone wheels" are mounted. Each tone wheel has an associated pickup, similar to what's used on electric guitars, that generates a specific frequency as determined by the bumps on the tone wheels. Since all of the tone wheels are mounted on the same shaft, they can't get out of tune with each other.

Pressing a key on a B-3 doesn't just generate the frequency produced by a tone wheel. There are nine eight-position "drawbars" that are used to mix the signal produced by the "fundamental" tone (the note being played) with signals from other tone wheels. The drawbars set the level of the sub-octave, fifth, fundamental, 8th, 12th, 15th, 17th, 19th, and 22nd harmonics.

The sound produced is the weighted sum of these nine signals as set by the drawbars in a manner similar to how we produced our G major chord in Figure 6-37.

Another feature of many media players is the *graphic equalizer*, which lets you adjust the sound to your taste. A graphic equalizer is a set of adjustable *filters*, devices that include or exclude certain frequencies. They're akin to the transfer functions that we saw in "Digital in an Analog World" on page 38, but for frequency instead of voltage or light. There are two main types of filters: *low pass*, which pass everything below a certain frequency, and *high pass*, which pass everything above a certain frequency. They can be combined to make *bandpass* filters that include everything between a low and high frequency, or *notch* filters that exclude a particular frequency. You can see in Figure 6-39 that the filter edges are not sharp; they *roll off*. Perfect filters don't exist. Note that the button debouncer in Figure 6-7 is a low-pass filter.

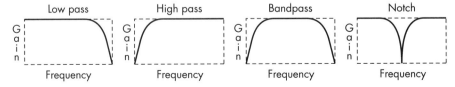

Figure 6-39: Filters

We could, for example, apply a low-pass filter to our G major chord, as seen in Figure 6-40. Applying a filter effectively multiplies the curves; the filter adjusts the sound level at different frequencies.

Figure 6-40: Low-pass filtered G major chord Fourier transform plot

As you can imagine, it no longer sounds the same. The B_4 is slightly quieter, and the D_5 is all but gone.

Why does all this matter? Figure 6-41 shows the Fourier transform of our reconstructed sine wave from Figure 6-34. I didn't completely specify everything in that figure, so let's assume that it's a 400 Hz sine wave sampled at 3 kHz.

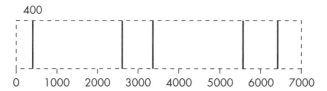

Figure 6-41: Reconstructed sine wave Fourier transform plot

Note that the x-axis goes on to infinity with frequencies at every multiple of the sampling frequency, plus or minus the frequency of the sampled signal.

What happens if we take that reconstructed sine wave and apply a low-pass filter, as shown in Figure 6-42?

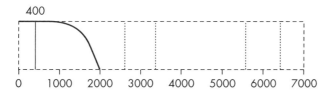

Figure 6-42: Low-pass filtered reconstructed sine wave Fourier transform plot

All the distortion disappears; what's left is our 400 Hz sine wave. It appears that sampling works, as long as we have appropriate filtering. How do we choose a sample rate and filter?

Harry Nyquist (1889–1976), a Swedish electronic engineer, came up with a theorem that says you have to sample at a rate at least twice the highest frequency if you want to be able to faithfully capture the signal. It's a nice theory, but because electronics doesn't follow ideal mathematics, it helps to sample faster than that in order to have the result sound good. The human hearing range is something like 20 to 20,000 Hz.

Based on all that, we should be able to capture anything that we can hear with a 40 kHz sampling rate. What if we accidentally get a 21 kHz sound, which is *undersampled* according to Nyquist's theorem? In that case, we get *folding* or *aliasing*. Imagine that the sampling frequency is a mirror and any information greater than that frequency is reflected. Looking back at Figure 6-41, you can see that there are *artifacts* at the sampling frequency plus or minus the sampled frequency. Because the sampling frequency is much greater than the sampled frequency, these artifacts are far away. A 21 kHz input sampled at 40 kHz would produce an artifact at 19 kHz (40–21). This false signal is called an *alias*. We don't get out what we put in. A low-pass filter must be applied before sampling to avoid aliasing.

Compact discs take 16-bit samples at 44,100 Hz—times 2, of course, because it's stereo. That produces a little more than 175KB/second. That's a lot of data. Some standard audio-sampling rates are 44.1 kHz, 48 kHz, 96 kHz, and 192 kHz. Why would we bother to sample at the higher rates, since doing so would generate a lot more data and Nyquist says it's not necessary?

Although the frequency and amplitude of a signal sampled near the Nyquist rate can be reconstructed, the *phase* cannot. Another new term! Think of the phase as a small shifting in time. You can see in Figure 6-43 that the fatter signal *lags* (as opposed to *leads*) the skinnier signal by 45 degrees, making it slightly later in time.

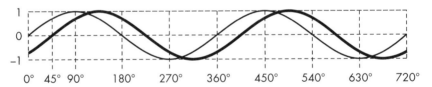

Figure 6-43: Phase difference in signals

Why does this matter? Well, it doesn't except for stereo. The *phase difference* causes a time delay between a signal hitting your left and right ears that tells you where it is in space, as illustrated in Figure 6-44.

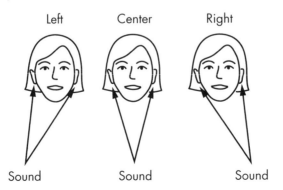

Figure 6-44: Phase difference in real life

You do a better job with high frequencies because they have shorter wavelengths relative to the thickness of your head. If your head were so narrow that your ears were in the same place, then there would be no time delay. Fat-headed people get better stereo! That's one of the reasons why you can get away with a single subwoofer: you can't really tell where the sound is coming from because the wavelength is so long compared to the thickness of your head that the phase difference is undetectable.

When you're listening to stereo sound, the phase difference between sounds coming out of the speakers creates the *image*, the ability to "see" where the musicians are in space. The image is "muddy" without accurate phase. Thus, the rationale for higher sampling rates is better reproduction of phase and stereo imaging. You may never notice this if your listening experience involves cheap earbuds on a cell phone.

SAMPLING AND FILTERING FOR FM STEREO

FM stereo is an interesting application of sampling and filtering. It's also a great example of how new functionality was wedged into a system that was never designed for it in a backward-compatible way, meaning that the old system still worked fine.

Back in Figure 6-20, you saw how bits could be used to modulate a frequency. FM stands for *frequency modulation*. FM radio works by modulating a carrier frequency by an analog signal instead of a digital one.

Carrier frequencies for FM radio stations are allocated every 100 kHz. You saw in Figure 6-41 that sampling generates additional frequencies up to infinity; the same thing happens with modulation. As a result, a low-pass filter has to be applied to the modulated signal or there will be interference with other stations. You saw filter rolloff in Figure 6-39. The steeper the rolloff, the more the filter perturbs the phase, which has a negative effect on the sound. This is shown in part of the radio spectrum in Figure 6-45.

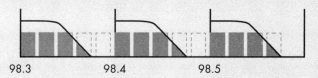

98.3   98.4   98.5

Figure 6-45: Radio spectrum

Before stereo, the audio information in a monaural FM signal occupied approximately 15 kHz above the carrier frequency. A receiver removed the carrier, resulting in the original audio. This characteristic had to be preserved in the move to stereo; otherwise, all existing receivers would have stopped working.

(continued)

Figure 6-46 gives an overview of how FM stereo works. A 38 kHz square wave is used to take alternate samples of the left and right channels. A 19 kHz pilot tone is generated that's synchronized with the sampling square wave. The pilot tone is mixed at a low level that's hard to hear over music and combined with the samples to make a composite signal that's broadcast.

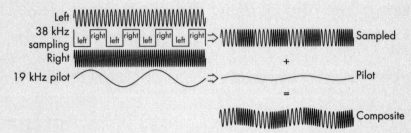

Figure 6-46: FM signal generation

The clever part is that if we look at the Fourier analysis result in Figure 6-47, the first set of frequencies on the left is the sum of the left and right channels—just what we want for mono. Not a problem for old receivers. The next set of frequencies is the difference between the left and right channels, which would not be picked up on an old mono receiver. However, a stereo receiver can use some simple arithmetic to separate out the left and right channels producing stereo.

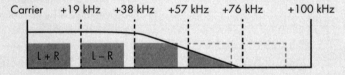

Figure 6-47: FM stereo spectrum

I mentioned earlier that audio involves a lot of data. It would be nice to be able to compress that data so that it takes up less space. There are two classes of compression: *lossless* and *lossy*. Lossless compression preserves all the original data. As a result, it can compress things only to about half of their original size. The most popular lossless compression today is *FLAC*, short for *Free Lossless Audio Codec*. A *codec* is a coder-decoder, which is sort of like a modem that knows how to translate things from one coding system to another.

MP3, AAC, Ogg, and their ilk are lossy compression codecs. Some fidelity is lost. They work on psychoacoustic principles. People who have studied the workings of the ear and brain have decided that there are certain things that you can't hear, like something quiet that happens right after a loud drum beat. These codecs work by removing these sounds, and that gives them a much better compression ratio than FLAC. But not everybody's ears are the same. I think MP3s sound horrible.

Digital Images

Visual images are more complicated than audio because we need to sample a two-dimensional space. Digital images are represented as rectangular arrays of picture elements, or *pixels*. Each pixel in a color image is a triad of red, green, and blue lights. Common displays available today have 8 bits each of red, green, and blue. We saw a commonly used representation back in Figure 1-20.

Computer displays use the *additive* color system, which can produce almost any color by combining (or adding, hence the name) different amounts of the red, green, and blue *primaries*. This differs from the *subtractive* color system used for printing, which makes colors by mixing different amounts of the cyan, magenta, and yellow primaries.

Sampling an image is akin to placing a window screen over the image and recording the color in each square. It's somewhat more complicated because of *point sampling*, which means we don't record the entire square, just a point in the center of each one. Figure 6-48 shows an image sampled using three screens of different resolutions.

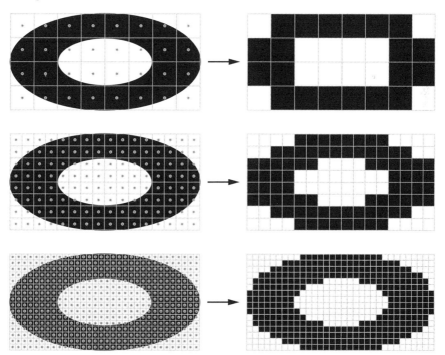

Figure 6-48: Sampling an image at different resolutions

You can see that the sampled image looks better with finer, higher-resolution screens, but of course that greatly increases the amount of data. Even with a high-resolution screen, however, we still get jaggy edges. This is due to undersampling and aliasing as per Nyquist, although the math for it is too advanced for this book. As with audio, maybe filtering helps. One way we can filter is by *supersampling*, or taking multiple samples per square and averaging them together, as shown in Figure 6-49.

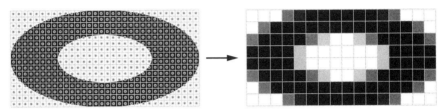

Figure 6-49: Supersampling

This doesn't look great all blown up, but if you hold it far away from your face, you'll see that it doesn't look too bad. If you think about it, supersampling is equivalent to upping the sampling rate, as we saw for audio in Figure 6-35.

Images are getting bigger and bigger and take up a lot of space. It's not clear if enough storage will ever exist for the world's cat photos and videos. As with audio, we'd like images to take less space so we can fit more of them in the same amount of memory and so they're faster to transmit over a network. This is addressed, once again, by compression.

The most common image compression right now is *JPEG*, a standard by the Joint Photographic Experts Group. It involves a lot of mathematical heavy lifting that I'm not going to cover here. A rough approximation of how JPEG works is that it looks for adjacent pixels that are pretty close to the same color and stores a description of that area instead of the individual pixels that it contains. You may have a camera that includes an image quality setting; this setting adjusts the definition of "pretty close." It's a color version of our example from "Stacks" on page 122.

JPEG uses knowledge about human perception in a manner similar to lossy audio codecs. For example, it takes advantage of the fact that our brains are more sensitive to changes in brightness than to changes in color.

Video

Yet another step up in multidimensional space, video is a sequence of two-dimensional images sampled at regular time intervals. The time interval is a function of the human visual system. Old movies got by with 24 frames per second (fps); the average person today is pretty happy with 48 fps.

Sampling video isn't much different than sampling images, except that different artifacts are visually annoying and therefore need to be minimized. The problem is that the sampling artifacts along edges, which we saw in Figure 6-48, don't stay still when objects are moving.

To understand this better, take a look at Figure 6-50, which shows a diagonal line that is moving from left to right over time. It's only moving a fraction of a pixel per frame, which means it doesn't get sampled the same every time. It still looks like an approximation of a line, but each one is a different approximation. This makes edges "swim," which is visually disturbing. Filtering using supersampling is one way to reduce such unpleasant visual artifacts.

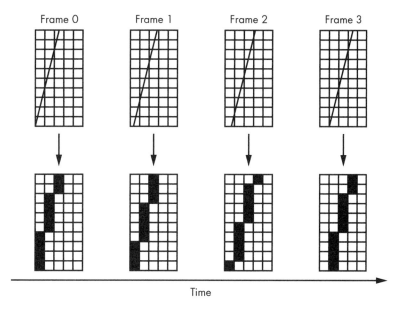

Figure 6-50: Swimming edges

Video produces a lot more data than images or audio. UHD video has a resolution of 3,840×2,160 pixels. Multiply that by 3 bytes per pixel and 60 frames per second, and you end up with a whopping 1,492,992,000 bytes per second! Obviously compression is very important.

The observation that only part of the image normally changes from frame to frame is the key to video compression. Look at Figure 6-51, in which Mr. Sigma is on his way to pick up a package.

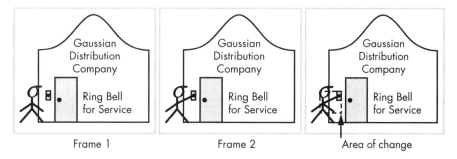

Figure 6-51: Interframe motion

As you can see, very little of the image changes between frames. Much less data needs to be stored or transmitted if we only need the data from the area of change. This technique is called *motion compression*.

One of the problems with representing video as a set of changes from an original image is that sometimes data can get garbled. You've probably seen some blocky artifacts on digital TV or when playing a damaged video disc.

We need some way to recover the data. This is done by regularly including *keyframes* in the data. A keyframe is a complete image, so even if damage accumulates due to corrupted change data, recovery takes place when the next keyframe is encountered.

The algorithms to detect differences between frames are complicated and very compute intensive. Newer compression standards such as MPEG4 include support for *layering*, which takes advantage of the fact that a lot of video is now computer generated. Layering works just like the old hand-drawn cel animation that we discussed in Chapter 1, where objects painted on transparencies were moved over a stationary background image.

Human Interface Devices

Computers are a lot like teenagers with cell phones. They spend most of their time messaging each other but occasionally have time to talk to people. This section covers some of how computers interact with people.

Terminals

Not that long ago, the keyboard, mouse, and display or touchscreen you're so used to were unimaginable luxuries.

There was a time when the way you interacted with a computer was to write a program or data down on paper using special coding forms. You'd hand those to someone who would use a keypunch to turn the forms into a stack of punched cards (refer back Figure 3-25). You'd take those cards, being careful not to drop them, and give them to a computer operator who would put them into a card reader, which would read them into the computer and run the program. This approach, known as *batch processing*, was used because computers were really slow and expensive, making computer time really valuable, so while your cards were being punched, somebody else's program was being run.

Computers got faster, smaller, and cheaper. By the late 1960s, it was possible to have a small computer for your company or department. Small as an RV. Computer time became a bit less scarce. The obvious thing happened, which is that people started hooking them up to *teletypes*. Teletypes were called *terminals* because they were at the end of the line. A particularly popular model, the Teletype ASR-33, had a keyboard, printer, paper tape (Figure 3-26) punch, and a paper tape reader. The paper tape was the equivalent of a USB memory stick. An ASR-33 was good for a jaw-dropping *10 characters per second*! The term TTY is still with us today as an abbreviation for teletype.

Time-sharing systems were invented to keep these smaller computers busy. Yes, they really were like time-share vacation rentals. You can pretend that it's your place, and it *is* your place while you're there, but other people use it when it's not your turn.

A time-sharing system has an *operating system* program that runs on the computer. The OS program is like the booking agent for a time-share rental. Its job is to allocate the various resources of the computer to each user. When it was your turn to use the machine, the other user's programs would get swapped out to disk, and yours would be loaded into memory and would run for a while. This all happened fast enough that you'd think that you had the machine to yourself, at least until things got busy. At some point, things would start to *thrash*, as the operating system spent more time swapping things in and out than it did running users' programs.

Thrashing made time-sharing systems pretty slow when there were a lot of users. Programmers started working late at night because they could have the machines to themselves after everybody else went home.

Time-sharing systems are *multitasking* in that the computer is presenting the illusion that it's doing more than one thing at a time. All of a sudden, lots of terminals were connected to the same machine. And the concept of a *user* appeared so that machines could tell what belonged to who.

Time marched on, and better versions of teletype-like things appeared, and each generation was faster and quieter. But they were still printing things on paper, or *hard copy*. And they were pretty much only good for text. The Teletype model 37 added Greek characters so that scientists could print math. IBM Selectric terminals had interchangeable *typeballs* that allowed the user to change fonts. This included a font with dots in different positions that enabled graph drawing.

Graphics Terminals

There were a lot of reasons to move away from hard-copy terminals, including speed, reliability, and noise. Screens existed for things like radar and television; it was time to make them work with computers. This happened slowly due to the evolution of electronics. Memory was just too expensive and slow.

Graphics terminals were originally built around a variation of the vacuum tube (see "Vacuum Tubes" on page 50) called a *cathode ray tube (CRT)*. The inside of the glass is coated with a chemical phosphor, which glows when it's hit by electrons. By having more than one grid or *deflection plate*, it's possible to draw pictures on the phosphor. It's like having a really talented batter who can hit any target with a ball.

There are actually two ways to make this display work. The deflection plate version, called *electrostatic deflection*, uses the same principle that gives you the dreaded static cling. The other option is the electromagnet version, called *electromagnetic deflection*. In either case, bits need to be translated into voltages, which is yet another application for our D/A building block.

Today the CRT is mostly a relic that has been replaced by the *liquid crystal display (LCD)*. Liquid crystals are substances that can change their light transmission properties when electricity is applied. A typical flat-screen display is much like a CRT in that there are three blobs of liquid crystal at every raster point with red, green, and blue filters and a light that shines through from the back. We still talk to LCD devices as if they're CRTs, but that's just a historical artifact. LCDs are now ubiquitous and have replaced CRTs in most applications; LCDs have made cell phones, laptops, and flat-screen TVs possible.

Early screen-based terminals were called *glass ttys* because they could display only text. These terminals displayed 24 rows of 80 characters each, for a total of 1,920 characters. Since a character fit into a byte, that was less than 2 KiB of memory, which was affordable at the time. Over time, more features got added, such as on-screen editing and cursor motion, which were eventually standardized as part of ANSI X3.64.

Vector Graphics

A CRT works pretty much like a piece of graph paper. An electron beam moves to some point based on the x- and y-axis voltages. There's also a z-axis that determines the brightness. Originally there was no color, so these were black-and-white, or *grayscale*, displays. The number of coordinate locations per inch is called the *resolution*.

Vector graphics is all about drawing lines, or *vectors*. You make a picture by drawing a set of lines from here to there. The skinny arrows in Figure 6-52 are drawn with the brightness all the way down or off.

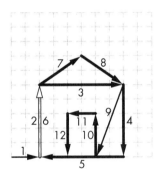

Figure 6-52: House of vector graphics

The white arrow with the black outline is drawn twice, once with the brightness on and then again with the brightness off. Drawing the same line twice with the brightness on makes it twice as bright, which we don't want to do just because we're changing position.

The house in Figure 6-52 is drawn from a *display list*, which is a list of drawing instructions. It looks like Figure 6-53.

1. Move to (2, 0)
2. Draw to (2, 5)
3. Draw to (7, 5)
4. Draw to (7, 0)
5. Draw to (2, 0)
6. Move to (2, 5)
7. Draw to (8, 7)
8. Draw to (7, 5)
9. Move to (6, 0)
10. Draw to (5, 3)
11. Draw to (4, 3)
12. Draw to (4, 0)
13. Restart at step 1

Figure 6-53: Display list

Note the last instruction. We start over again because the image on the screen fades pretty quickly. This works only because of the *persistence* of the CRT phosphor, which is how long it stays lit once the beam moves away, and the slow response of the human eye. We have to keep doing this over and over to keep the image displayed on the screen.

There's more to this instruction, however. There's a lot of 60 Hz radiation around us because that's the frequency of American alternating current electric power (it's 50 Hz in some other countries). Despite our best attempts at shielding, this radiation affects our display and makes it wiggle. Thus, graphics terminals like the *GLANCE G* developed at Bell Telephone Laboratories had a "restart at step 1 after the next time the power line crosses 0 from the positive to the negative" instruction. This synchronized the drawing to the interference so that it always wiggled exactly the same and therefore wasn't noticeable.

Drawing the image took time, a nasty side effect of which was that everything looked fine until the display list got long enough that it couldn't be drawn in one-sixtieth of a second. It suddenly got very flickery when it drew only once every one-thirtieth of a second.

A company called Tektronix had an interesting solution to the flicker problem, called the *storage tube*. This was the electronic equivalent of an *Etch-a-Sketch*. You could draw very complicated images, but you had to electronically shake it up to erase it. It was very hard to draw solid images on a GLANCE G because it took huge numbers of vectors and ended up with display flicker. Storage tubes could handle solid images since there was no limit to the number of vectors, but the centers of the solid areas tended to fade. You could erase a single line on a GLANCE G by removing it from the display list. That wasn't possible on a storage tube. It gave off a bright green flash when the screen was erased, which has been burned into many an aging programmer's eyeballs.

Raster Graphics

Raster graphics is a completely different approach than vector graphics. It's how television originally worked. The raster is a continually drawn pattern, as shown in Figure 6-54.

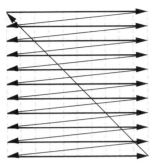

Figure 6-54: A raster

The raster starts at the upper left and goes across the screen. Then a *horizontal retrace* takes it down to the start of the next line. Finally, a *vertical retrace* takes it back to the beginning once the last line is drawn.

This works very much like the starting-gun analogy I used earlier when discussing serial communications. Once the raster is off and running, all you have to do is to change the brightness at exactly the right time to get the image you want, as you can see in Figure 6-55.

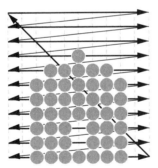

Figure 6-55: House of raster graphics

I also used the analogy of a window screen back in "Digital Images" on page 173. A raster display is an *actual* screen, which means we can't draw between the dots. This can result in unpleasant visual artifacts, such as the roof not looking quite right. That's because the resolution of a typical raster display is fairly low—on the order of 100 dots per inch. The low resolution results in undersampling and aliasing similar to what we saw for digital images. Sufficient compute power now exists to make *anti-aliasing* commonplace using techniques such as supersampling.

Raster scanning is also used for things like fax machines, laser printers, and scanners. Pull up the lid of a scanner and watch it go. Wear sunglasses. Back when printers had more moving parts and were louder, people figured out how to play *raster music* on them by carefully choosing what to print.

Raster displays don't use display lists, although display lists are still used behind raster displays. As we'll see later, web pages are display lists. The OpenGL graphics language includes display lists, and support for the language is often included in graphics hardware. Monochrome displays use a piece of memory with 1 bit for each position on the raster. This was a huge amount of memory back in the day; now, it's not such a big deal. Of course, that memory could get big fast. If you wanted a raster display that could do 256 different levels of gray, you'd need 8 bits of memory for each raster position.

Color was discovered in the Land of Oz and quickly made it onto the screen. Monochrome or grayscale displays were easy: all you had to do was to coat the inside of the screen with a layer of phosphor. Color displays needed three different color dots at each location on the raster—red, green, and blue—and three electron beams that could hit these spots with great precision. This meant you needed three times the display memory for a typical display.

Keyboard and Mouse

Terminals have a way for you to input data in addition to the display that outputs data to you. You know them as the keyboard and mouse, the touchpad on your laptop, and the touchscreen on your phone and tablet.

Keyboards are pretty easy. They're just a bunch of switches and some logic. A common way to build a keyboard is to put the key switches on a grid, multiplexing them kind of like in Figure 6-10. Power is sequentially applied to the rows of the grid, and the values of the columns are read out.

The mouse as we know it was invented by American engineer Douglas Engelbart (1925–2013) at the Stanford Research Institute. I mentioned in "Quadrature" on page 150 that you can make a mouse using a pair of quadrature encoders, one each for the x and y directions.

There are a lot of touchpad and touchscreen technologies. The main difference is that touchscreens have to be transparent so that the display can be seen. Touch devices are row- and column-scanning devices, like keyboards but on a much finer scale.

Summary

In this chapter, you learned about the interrupt system that allows processors to handle I/O efficiently. We talked about how various types of I/O devices work and how they interact with computers. We also discussed the complex area of sampling analog data so that it can be processed using digital computers. At this point, you know enough about how computers work, so starting with the next chapter, we'll look at the relationship between hardware and software with the goal of learning how to write software that runs well on the hardware.

7

ORGANIZING DATA

If you've been paying attention, you may have noticed a bit of an obsession when it comes to dealing with memory. Back in Chapter 3, you learned that the order in which memory devices such as DRAM, flash memory, and disk drives are accessed affects their speed. And in Chapter 5, you learned that performance also depends on whether or not the data that you need is present in cache memory. Keeping these characteristics of the memory system in mind when organizing your data leads to better performance. To help you do this, in this chapter we'll examine a number of *data structures*, or standard ways of organizing data. Many of these exist to support the efficient use of different types of memory. This often involves a space/time trade-off wherein more memory is used to make certain operations faster. (Note that higher-level data structures are provided by programming languages, not the computer hardware itself.)

The phrase *locality of reference* sums up much of what this chapter covers in a fully buzzword-compliant manner. Or "keep the data you need close, the data you'll need soon even closer."

Primitive Data Types

Programming languages offer a variety of primitive data *types*. There are two aspects to these types: their size (number of bits) and their interpretation (signed, unsigned, floating point, char, pointer, Boolean). Figure 7-1 shows the data types available to programmers on a typical modern machine via the C programming language. Different implementations of C on the same machine, as well as different languages such as Pascal or Java, may present these data types differently. Some language environments include facilities that allow the programmer to query the endianness (see Figure 4-4 on page 96), number of bits per byte, and more.

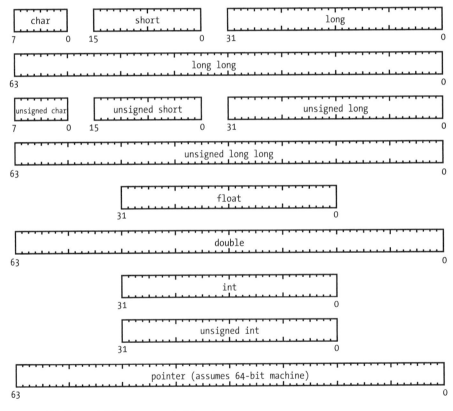

Figure 7-1: Typical C language primitive data types

We saw all of these in Chapter 1 except the pointer; the only difference here is that we're using the C language names for them.

American engineer Harold Lawson invented the pointer for the PL/I (Programming Language One) in 1964. A *pointer* is just an unsigned integer of some architecture-dependent size, but it's interpreted as a memory address. It's like the address of your house—it's not the house itself, but it can be used to find your house. We've seen how this works before; it's indirect addressing from "Addressing Modes" on page 104. A zero-valued, or *NULL*, pointer is not generally considered a valid memory address.

C popularized pointers. Some languages have implemented more abstract *references* in order to try to avoid problems resulting from sloppy pointer use, a subject I'll touch on this later in the chapter. Pointers tend to be the size of the natural word on a machine so that they can be accessed in a single cycle.

Advances in chip technology spurred the development of a large number of new machines in the 1980s, which included the transition from 16-bit to 32-bit computers. A lot of code written in the 1970s and early 1980s was very cavalier about pointer use; for example, it assumed that pointers and integers were the same size and used them interchangeably. This code broke in often difficult-to-debug ways when ported to these new machines, spawning two independent remediation approaches. First, people started paying a lot more attention to portability issues. This solution was quite successful; portability and pointer issues are much less of a problem today. Second, languages that eliminated pointers were developed, such as Java. This approach has helped in some places but is not always worth the price.

Arrays

The data types you saw in the previous section are simple; you can think of them as houses. Languages also support *arrays*, which can instead be likened to apartment buildings. Apartment buildings have an address, and the individual apartments have unit numbers. Programmers call the unit number the *index* (starting at 0, unlike most apartments), and the individual apartments are called array *elements*. Typical computer building codes mandate that all apartments in a building be identical. Figure 7-2 shows a building that contains ten 16-bit apartments in C.

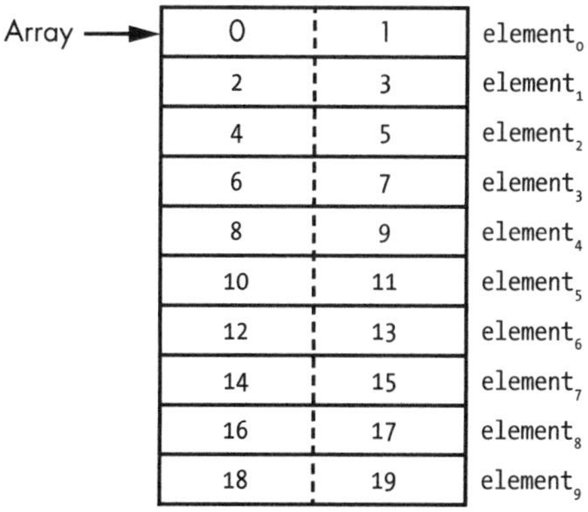

Figure 7-2: Ten-element array of 16-bit numbers

Each box in Figure 7-2 is a byte. In this array of 16-bit items, therefore, each element occupies two 8-bit bytes. The element subscript indicates the array's index.

An alternative way to view an array is the through the lens of relative addressing (see "Relative Addressing" on page 128). Each element is an offset from the address of the 0th element, or *base address*. Thus, $element_1$ is 2 bytes away from $element_0$.

The array in Figure 7-2 is a *one-dimensional* array—an ugly one-story building with all the apartments on one hall. Programming languages also support *multidimensional* arrays—for example, a building with four floors of three byte-sized apartments. This would be a two-dimensional array with two indices, one for the floor number and another for the apartment number on that floor. We can even make three-dimensional buildings with indices for wing, floor, and apartment; four-dimensional buildings with four indices; and so on.

It's important to know how multidimensional arrays are laid out in memory. Let's say we're putting a flyer under every door in a 4×3 apartment building. We could do that in one of two ways. We could start on floor 0 and put a flier in apartment 0, then go to floor 1 and put a flier into apartment 0, and so on. Or we could start on floor 0 and put a flier under every door on that floor, then do the same on floor 1, and so on. This is a *locality of reference* issue. The second approach (doing all the doors on one floor) has better locality of reference and is much easier on the legs. You can see this in Figure 7-3, where the numbers in parentheses are the addresses relative to the start of the array.

Array

$element_0$	$element_{0,0}$ (0)	$element_{0,1}$ (1)	$element_{0,2}$ (2)
$element_1$	$element_{1,0}$ (3)	$element_{1,1}$ (4)	$element_{1,2}$ (5)
$element_2$	$element_{2,0}$ (6)	$element_{2,1}$ (7)	$element_{2,2}$ (8)
$element_3$	$element_{3,0}$ (9)	$element_{3,1}$ (10)	$element_{3,2}$ (11)

Figure 7-3: Two-dimensional array layout

The column index moves between adjacent columns, whereas the row index moves between rows, which are farther apart in the address space.

This approach extends to higher dimensions. If we had a five-building complex with four floors of three apartments per floor, Figure 7-3 would be replicated five times, once for each building. In address space, adjacent buildings are farther apart than adjacent rows, which are farther apart than adjacent columns.

Going back to Figure 7-2, think about what would happen if you tried to access $element_{10}$. Some programming languages, such as Pascal, check to make sure that array indices are within the bounds of the array, but many others (including C) don't. Without being checked, $element_{10}$ would land us at bytes 20 and 21 relative to the start of the array. That could crash a program if there's no memory at that address, or it could be a security hole allowing unintended access to data stored past the end of the array. It's your job as a programmer to stay within bounds if the language doesn't do it for you.

Bitmaps

You've seen how you can construct arrays out of the primitive data types, but sometimes there isn't a primitive data type that's small enough for your purposes. For example, say Santa needs to track naughty versus nice for a large number of innocent children. Two values means that we need only 1 bit per child. We could easily use a byte for each value, but that's less efficient—which translates into more warming at the North Pole and bad news for Frosty the Snowman because meltness is considered a preexisting condition and not covered. What we really need is an array of bits, or a *bitmap*.

Bitmaps are easy to create. For example, say we want to keep track of 35 bits. We know that an array of five 8-bit bytes would be enough memory, as shown in Figure 7-4.

$bits_0$	7	6	5	4	3	2	1	0
$bits_1$	15	14	13	12	11	10	9	8
$bits_2$	23	22	21	20	19	18	17	16
$bits_3$	31	30	29	28	27	26	25	24
$bits_4$						34	33	32

Figure 7-4: Array as bitmap

There are four basic operations that we can do on bitmaps: set a bit, clear a bit (set it to 0), test a bit to see if it is set, and test a bit to see if it is clear.

We can use integer division to find the byte containing a particular bit; all we have to do is divide by 8. We can do that quickly on machines with barrel shifters (see "Shiftiness" on page 99) by right-shifting the desired bit number by 3. For example, bit number 17 would be in the third byte because $17 \div 8$ is 2 in integer division, and byte 2 is the third byte counting from 0.

The next step is to make a mask for the bit position. Similar to its physical counterpart, a *mask* is a bit pattern with holes that we can "see through." We start by ANDing our desired bit number with a mask of 0x07 to get the lower three bits; for 17, that's 00010001 AND 00000111, which yields 00000001, or bit position 1. We then left-shift a 1 by that amount, giving us a mask of 00000010, which is the position of bit 17 in byte 2.

Using the array index and bit mask, we can easily perform the following operations:

Set a bit	$bits_{index} = bits_{index}$ OR mask
Clear a bit	$bits_{index} = bits_{index}$ AND (NOT mask)
Test for set bit	$(bits_{index}$ AND mask$) \neq 0$
Test for clear bit	$(bits_{index}$ AND mask$) = 0$

There's another useful application of bitmaps: to indicate whether resources are available or busy. If a set bit represents a busy resource, we can scan the array looking for a byte that's not all 1s. This lets us test eight at a time. Of course, we would need to find the clear bit once we find a byte that contains one, but that's much more efficient than testing each bit individually. Note that in cases like this, it's more efficient to use an array of the largest primitive data type, such as C's unsigned long long, instead of an array of bytes.

Strings

You learned about encoding characters in "Representing Text" on page 22. A sequence of characters, such as those in this sentence, is called a *string*.

As with arrays, we often need to know a string's length in order to be able to operate on it. Usually, it's not enough to just make an array for each string, because many programs operate on variable-length string data; large arrays are often used when the length of a string isn't known in advance. Since the array size is unrelated to the string length, we need some other method to track the string length. The most convenient way to do that is to somehow bundle the string length in with the string data.

One approach is to store the length in the string itself—for example, in the first byte. This works well but limits the length of the string to a maximum of 255 characters, which is insufficient for many applications. More bytes can be used to support longer strings, but at some point, the amount of overhead (bookkeeping bytes) exceeds the length of many strings. Also, because strings are bytes, they can have any alignment, but if multibyte counts are needed, strings would have to be aligned on those boundaries.

C uses a different approach, borrowed from the PDP-11 assembly language's .ASCIZ pseudo-instruction, which doesn't have a special data type for strings like some languages do. It just uses one-dimensional arrays of bytes; the fact that strings are arrays of characters is why the byte-sized data type in C is a char. But there's a twist: C doesn't store a string length. Instead, it adds an extra byte at the end of the array of characters for a NUL terminator. C uses the ASCII NUL character (refer back to Table 1-11), which has a value of 0, as a *string terminator*. In other words, the NUL terminator is used to mark the end of a string. This works both for ASCII and UTF-8, and it looks like Figure 7-5.

0	1	2	3	4	5	6
C	h	e	e	s	e	NUL

Figure 7-5: C string storage and termination

As you can see, C uses 7 bytes of memory for the string, even though it's only six characters long, because an extra byte is needed for the terminator.

NUL turns out to be a good choice for the terminator because most machines include an instruction that tests whether or not a value is 0. Any other choice would involve extra instructions to load the value against which we'd be testing.

The use of a string terminator instead of an explicit length has its benefits and drawbacks. On one hand, storage is compact, which is important, and there's essentially no overhead to do something like "print each character in the string until the end is reached." But when you need the string's length, you have to scan the string for the end, counting the characters. Also, with this approach you can't have a NUL character in a string.

Compound Data Types

Although simple rooms are good for some things, the market often demands fancier accommodations, such as suites. Most modern languages include facilities that allow you to roll your own data types—the "suites," often called *structures*. The various rooms in each suite are its *members*.

Let's say we're writing a calendar program that includes a list (array) of events with their starting and ending dates and times. If we were doing this in C, the day, month, hours, minutes, and seconds would each be held in an `unsigned char`, but the year would need to be in an `unsigned short`. Figure 7-6 creates a structure for the date and time.

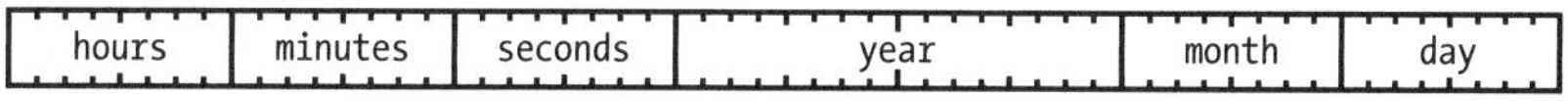

hours	minutes	seconds	year	month	day

Figure 7-6: Structure for date and time

Note that this isn't strictly necessary; we could just have arrays of hours, minutes, and so on. But it's certainly more convenient to have an array of date-time structures, and it makes programs easier to read and understand. British computer scientist Peter Landin coined the term *syntactic sugar* in 1964 for constructs such as this that make programs "sweeter." Of course, one person's sweetener is often another person's essential functionality, leading to intense philosophical debates. Many would argue that syntactic sugar is limited to things like replacing a = a + 1 with a += 1 or a++, while fewer would claim that arrays of structures are syntactic sugar for sets of arrays. Time further complicates this fuzzy definition: a += 1 and a++ were not syntactic sugar when they were introduced, as compilers weren't as good and these constructs generated better machine language. On the other hand, structures were more sugary when they were introduced, because prior code used arrays; they're more essential now that programs are designed with structures in mind.

We can use compound data types, such as our date-time structure, as if they're primitive data types. Figure 7-7 combines a pair of date-time structures with a small array to hold an event name string to make a complete calendar event structure.

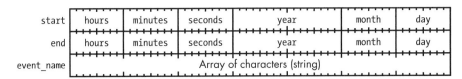

Figure 7-7: Structure for calendar entry

Structures often take up more memory space than you might expect. I discussed aligned and nonaligned memory in "Memory" on page 94. Say we built our date-time structure in an area zoned for 32-bit computers, as in Figure 4-2 on page 95. The language keeps the structure members in the order specified by the programmer because it might matter. But the language also has to respect the alignment (Figure 4-3 on page 95), which means that it can't put the year in the fourth and fifth bytes, as shown in Figure 7-7, because that crosses a boundary. The language tools solve this problem by automatically adding *padding* as needed. The actual memory layout of our structure would look like Figure 7-8.

hours	minutes	seconds	padding	year	month	day

Figure 7-8: Structure for date and time with padding

You could rearrange the structure members to make sure that you ended up with a 7-byte structure with no padding. Of course, when you combine a pair of these into the calendar structure, the language tools will likely pad them out to 8 bytes anyway.

It's worth mentioning that this is a contrived example and you shouldn't necessary handle dates and times this way. The standard in many systems, which came from UNIX, is to use a 32-bit number to represent the number of seconds since the "UNIX epoch" began on January 1, 1970. This scheme will run out of bits in 2038, but many systems have expanded this to 64 bits in preparation.

Figure 1-21 showed a way to use four 8-bit values to represent color with transparency. That's a great use for a structure, but it's not always the best way to view that data. For example, if we needed to copy a color, it would be much more efficient to copy all 32 bits at once rather than doing four 8-bit copies. Another compound data type to the rescue.

Not only can we have suites, as we saw in the previous section, but we can also have offices with movable partitions, which are called *unions* in C. A union allows multiple views of the same space or content. The difference between a structure and a union is that everything in a structure takes memory, whereas everything in a union shares memory. Figure 7-9 combines the RGBα structure with an unsigned long to form a union.

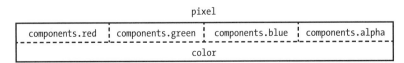

Figure 7-9: Pixel union

Using the union and C language syntax, we could set the pixel.color to 0x12345678 and then pixel.components.red would be 0x12, pixel.components.green would be 0x34, and so on.

Singly Linked Lists

Arrays are the most efficient way to keep lists of things. They only hold actual data, without requiring any additional bookkeeping information. But they don't work as well for arbitrary amounts of data, because if we didn't make the array large enough, then we have to create a new, larger array and copy all the data into it. And they waste space if we make them larger than necessary. Similarly, copying is required if you need to insert an element into the middle of a list or delete an element.

Linked lists can perform better than arrays when you don't know in advance how many things you'll be tracking. Singly linked lists, implemented using structures, look like Figure 7-10.

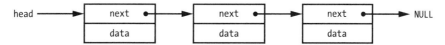

Figure 7-10: Singly linked list

Note that next is a pointer that holds the address of the next element in the list. The first thing in the list is known as the *head*; the last thing is the *tail*. We can recognize the tail because next is a value that can't be another list element, usually a NULL pointer.

A big difference between the list shown in Figure 7-10 and an array is that all array elements are contiguous in memory. List elements can be anywhere in memory and look more like Figure 7-11.

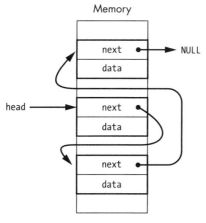

Figure 7-11: Singly linked list in memory

Adding an element to a list is easy; just pop it on the head, as shown in Figure 7-12.

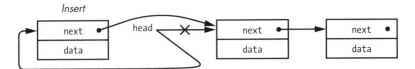

Figure 7-12: Singly linked list insertion

Deleting an element is a bit more complicated because we need to make the next of the previous element point to the following element, as shown in Figure 7-13.

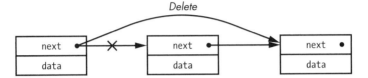

Figure 7-13: Singly linked list deletion

One way to do that is by using a pair of pointers, as shown in Figure 7-14.

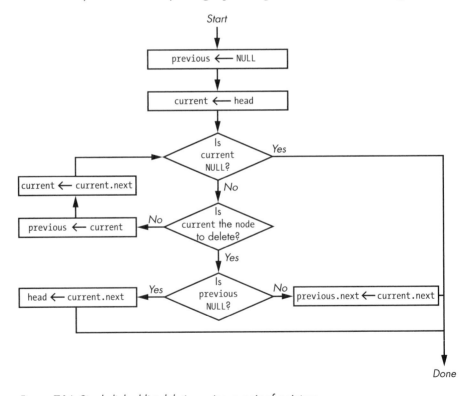

Figure 7-14: Singly linked list deletion using a pair of pointers

The current pointer walks the list looking for the node to delete. The previous pointer allows us to adjust the next of the node before the one to delete. We use a dot (.) to indicate a member of a structure, so current.next means the next member of the current node.

Figure 7-14 isn't a great example; although to be fair, I looked online while writing this section and found algorithms that were much worse. The problem with the code shown here is that it's complicated because a special test is needed for the list head.

The algorithm in Figure 7-15 shows how the power of *double indirect addressing* eliminates the special case, resulting in simpler code.

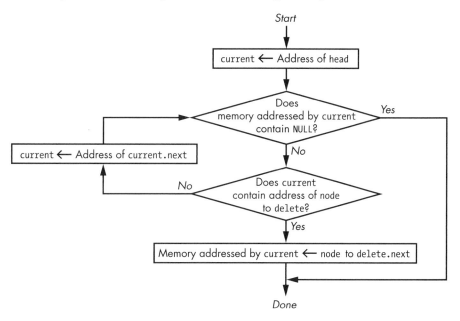

Figure 7-15: Singly linked list deletion using indirect addressing

Let's examine how this algorithm works in more detail. Have a look at Figure 7-16. The subscripts show how current changes as the algorithm proceeds.

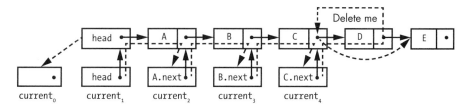

Figure 7-16: Singly linked list deletion in action

The steps shown in Figure 7-16 are complicated, so let's walk through them.

1. We start by setting $current_0$ to the address of head, which results in $current_1$, which in turn points to head. This means that current points to head, which points to list element A.

2. We're not looking for element A, so we move along.

3. As shown by the dashed arrow, we set current to the address of the next pointer in the element pointed to by whatever current points to. Since current$_1$ points to head, which points to element A, current$_2$ ends up pointing to A.next.

4. It's still not the element that we want to delete, so we do it all again, causing current$_3$ to reference B.next.

5. It's still not the element that we want to delete, so we do it all again, causing current$_4$ to reference C.next.

6. C.next points to element D, which is the one we want to delete. Following the light dashed arrow, we follow current to C.next to D, and replace C.next with the contents of D.next. Since D.next points to element E, C.next now points to E as shown by the heavy dashed arrow, removing D from the list.

We could modify the preceding algorithm to insert links into the middle of the list. That might be useful if we, for example, wanted the list to be ordered by date, name, or some other criteria.

Earlier I mentioned that this second algorithm produced better code. Let's compare the two as written in the C programming language. You don't have to understand this code to see the difference between Listing 7-1 and Listing 7-2.

```
struct node {
    struct node *next;
    // data
};

struct node *head;
struct node *node_to_delete;
struct node *current;
struct node *previous;

previous = (struct node *)0;
current = head;

while (current != (struct node *)0) {
    if (current == node_to_delete) {
        if (previous == (struct node *)0)
            head = current->next;
        else
            previous->next = current->next;
        break;
    }
    else {
            previous = current;
            current = current->next;
    }
}
```

Listing 7-1: C language code for singly linked list deletion using a pair of pointers

```
struct node {
    struct node *next;
    // data
};

struct node *head;
struct node *node_to_delete;
struct node **current;

for (current = &head; *current != (struct node *)0; current = &((*current)->next))
    if (*current == node_to_delete) {
            *current = node_to_delete->next;
            break;
    }
}
```

Listing 7-2: C language code for singly linked list deletion using double indirect addressing

As you can see, the indirect addressing version of this code in Listing 7-2 is much simpler than the code using a pair of pointers in Listing 7-1.

Dynamic Memory Allocation

Our discussion of linked list insertion conveniently omitted something important. I showed how to insert a new node but didn't say where the memory for that node came from.

We saw back in Figure 5-16 that program data space starts with a section for statically allocated data followed by the heap that the runtime library sets up for the program. This is all of the data memory available to a program (except for the stack and interrupt vectors) on machines that don't have memory management units (MMUs). On systems with MMUs, the runtime library requests the amount of memory it thinks it needs, because tying up all of the main memory doesn't make sense. The *break* is the end of the memory available to a program, and there are some system calls that grow or shrink the amount of available memory.

Memory for variables such as arrays is static; that is, it's assigned an address that doesn't change. Things like list nodes are dynamic; they come and go as needed. We get memory for them from the heap.

A program needs some way to manage the heap. It needs to know what memory is in use and what's available. There are library functions for this so that you don't have to write your own. In C, they're the malloc and free functions. Let's look at how they can be implemented.

One implementation of malloc works by using a singly linked list data structure. The heap is divided up into blocks, each of which has a size and a pointer to the next block, as shown in Figure 7-17.

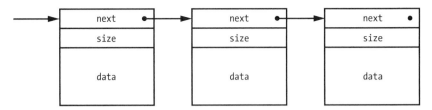

Figure 7-17: malloc structure for heap management

Initially there's just one block for the entire heap. When a program asks for memory, malloc looks for a block that has enough space, returns the caller a pointer to the requested space, and adjusts the size of the block to reflect the memory that it gave away. When a program frees memory using the free function, it just puts the block back in the list.

At various times, malloc scans the list for adjacent free blocks and coalesces them into a single larger block. One way of doing this is when allocating memory (calling malloc) because allocation requires going through the list looking for a large enough block. Over time, the memory space can become *fragmented*, which means there's no available block of memory large enough to satisfy a request, even if not all memory has been used up. On systems with MMUs, the break is adjusted to get more memory if needed.

You can see that there's a certain amount of overhead to this approach: next and size add 16 bytes to each block on a 64-bit machine.

Freeing unallocated memory is a common error that inexperienced programmers make. Another is continuing to use memory that has already been freed. As you can see in Figure 7-17, if you write data outside the bounds of allocated memory, you can corrupt the size and next fields. That's particularly insidious because the problems this causes may not show up until a later operation needs to use the information in those fields.

One side effect of technological advances is that small machines often come with way more RAM than your program needs. In these cases, it's better to just statically allocate everything because that reduces overhead and eliminates memory allocation bugs.

More Efficient Memory Allocation

Linked lists that include text strings are common. Suppose we have a linked list where the node includes a pointer to a string, as shown in Figure 7-18.

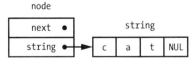

Figure 7-18: List node with string

We have to allocate memory not only for each node but also for the string attached to the node. The `malloc` overhead can be significant, especially on a 64-bit machine where we would have 16 bytes of overhead for the 16-byte node, and then another 16 bytes of overhead for a string such as the 4-byte cat in Figure 7-18.

We can reduce the overhead by allocating the node and string at the same time. Instead of allocating the node and then the string, we can allocate space for the sum of the node and string sizes plus whatever padding might be necessary for alignment. This means that nodes are of variable size, which is okay. This trick cuts the overhead in half. The result looks like Figure 7-19, with a string of cat.

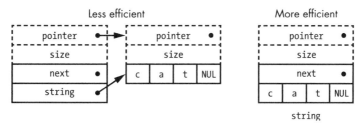

Figure 7-19: More efficient memory allocation

This approach is also more efficient when you are deleting nodes. In the less efficient case, two calls to `free` would be required, one for the string and another for the node. In the more efficient case, both get freed with a single call.

Garbage Collection

Two problems can arise from explicit dynamic memory management that are really problems of sloppy pointer use. Remember, a pointer is just a number that represents a memory address. But not all numbers are valid memory addresses. Using a pointer to try to access nonexistent memory or memory that doesn't meet the processor alignment rules can cause an exception and crash a program.

You might be learning a programming language such as Java or JavaScript that doesn't have pointers but supports dynamic memory allocation without equivalents to `malloc` and `free`. These languages instead implement *garbage collection*, a technique invented in 1959 by American computer and cognitive scientist John McCarthy (1927–2011) for the LISP programming language. Garbage collection has experienced a renaissance, partly as a proscriptive remedy for bad pointer use.

Languages like Java use references instead of pointers. *References* are an abstraction for pointers that provide much of the same functionality without actually exposing memory addresses.

Garbage-collected languages often have a new operator that creates items and allocates memory for them (this operator also appears in non-garbage-collected languages such as C++). There is no corresponding operator for item deletion. Instead, the language runtime environment tracks the use of variables and automatically deletes those it deems no longer in use. There are many ways in which this is done, one of which is to keep a count of references to variables so the variables can be deleted when there are no references left.

Garbage collection is a trade-off; it's not without its issues. One issue is similar to the LSI-11 refresh problem (see "Random-Access Memory" on page 82) in that the programmer doesn't have much control over the garbage collection system, which may decide to run even though the program needs to do something more important. Also, programs tend to take a lot of memory because it's easy to leave unnecessary references around, which prevents memory from being reclaimed. This makes programs run slowly as opposed to just crashing due to bad pointers. It turns out that despite good intentions of solving the pointer problem, tracking down unnecessary references is actually harder to debug.

Doubly Linked Lists

Our singly linked list delete function can be pretty slow because we have to find the element before the one we want to delete so that we can adjust its pointer. This could involve traversing a very long list. Fortunately, there's a different type of list that solves this problem at the expense of some extra memory.

A doubly linked list includes a link not only to the next element but also to the previous element, as you can see in Figure 7-20. This doubles the per-node overhead, but it eliminates the need for list walking in the delete case, so it's a space/time trade-off.

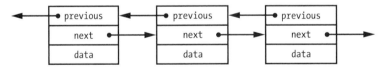

Figure 7-20: Doubly linked list

The advantage of a doubly linked list is that you can insert and delete anywhere without having to spend time traversing the list. Figure 7-21 shows how you'd add a new node into a list after element A.

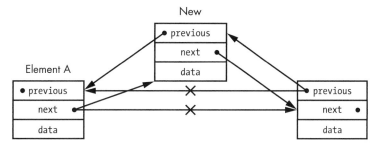

Figure 7-21: Doubly linked list insertion

Figure 7-22 shows that deleting an element is just as simple.

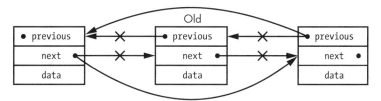

Figure 7-22: Doubly linked list deletion

As you can see, these operations on doubly linked list elements don't require traversal.

Hierarchical Data Structures

So far, we've looked only at *linear* data structures. They're great for many applications, but at some point their linearity can be a problem. That's because storing data is only half of the work; we also need to be able to retrieve it efficiently. Let's say we have a list of things stored in a linked list. We might need to walk the entire list to find a particular one; for a list of length n, it could take n lookups. This is fine for small numbers of things but impractical for large values of n.

Earlier we saw how pointers could be used to connect nodes into linked lists. We're not restricted to any number of pointers, so the ways in which we can organize data are limited only by our imagination and memory space. For example, we could come up with a hierarchical arrangement of nodes, as in the example back in Figure 5-4.

The simplest hierarchical data structure is the *binary tree*—"binary" not because of binary numbers but because a node can connect to two other nodes. Let's make a node that contains a number arranged as shown in Figure 7-23.

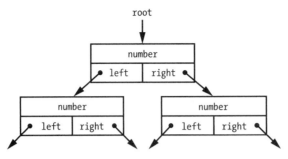

Figure 7-23: Binary tree nodes containing numbers

The *root* is the tree equivalent of a linked list's head.

We're going to hang out in a bingo parlor and record the numbers in a binary tree as they're called out. We'll then be able to look up numbers to see if they've been called. Figure 7-24 shows an algorithm that inserts a number into a tree. It works in a manner similar to our singly linked list deletion in that it relies on indirect addressing.

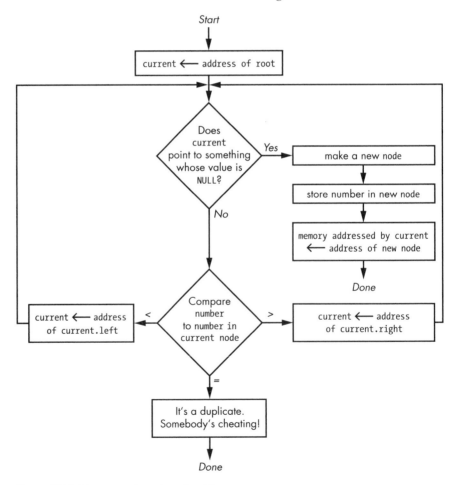

Figure 7-24: Binary tree insertion algorithm

Let's look at this in action by inserting the numbers 8, 6, 9, 4, and 5. Nothing is attached to the root when we insert the 8, so we attach it there. When we insert the 6, the root spot is taken, so we compare that node; then because 6 is less than 8, we hit the left side. It's vacant, so we plop a new node there. The 9 goes on the right-hand side of the 8, the 4 on the left-hand side of the 6, and so on, as shown in Figure 7-25.

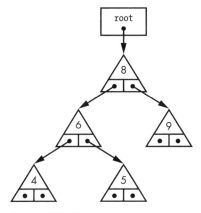

Figure 7-25: Binary tree

You can see that even though there are five things in this data structure, worst case we can find one by checking three nodes. This beats a linked list, where we may have to check all five. It's easy to look something up in a binary tree, as shown in Figure 7-26. Note that we don't need a pointer to a pointer to a node here because we don't have to modify the tree.

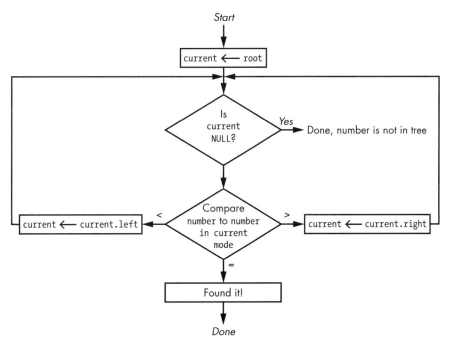

Figure 7-26: Binary tree look-up algorithm

You may have noticed that the arrangement of the tree depends on insertion order. Figure 7-27 shows what happens if we insert the numbers in order: 4, 5, 6, 8, and 9.

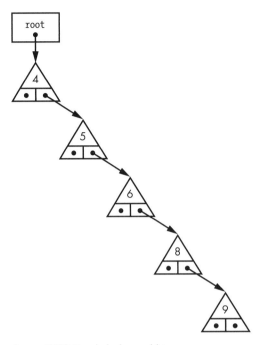

Figure 7-27: Poorly balanced binary tree

This degenerate case looks a lot like a singly linked list. Not only do we lose the benefits of a binary tree, but now we have the additional overhead of the unused left pointers as well. We'd really prefer that our tree ended up looking like the one on the right in Figure 7-28.

Figure 7-28: Unbalanced versus balanced binary trees

Searching for something in a binary tree is a function of the depth in the tree; if it's n levels down, then it takes n tests to find it. It takes only $\log_2 n$ in a balanced binary tree as opposed to n in a linked list. Putting that in perspective, in the worst case you'd have to visit 1,024 nodes in a linked list containing 1,024 nodes, but you'd need to visit only 10 nodes in a balanced binary tree.

There are numerous tree-balancing algorithms, which I'm not going to cover here in detail. It takes time to rebalance a tree, so there's a trade-off between algorithm speed, insert/lookup time, and rebalancing time. Tree-balancing algorithms have more computational overhead, and some have additional storage overhead. That overhead is quickly overcome, however, as the size of the tree increases, because $\log_2 n$ becomes much smaller than n.

Storage for the Masses

We talked about disk drives back in "Block Devices" on page 85. Let's look at them in more detail so we can understand their data organization peculiarities. Warning: we're going to go pointer-crazy here!

I mentioned that the basic unit on a disk is a *block* and consecutive blocks are called *clusters*. It would be nice if we could just store data in clusters, which are contiguous sectors on a track. Although that's done in certain circumstances where very high performance is required, it's not a good general-purpose solution, and there might be more data than would fit on a track anyway. Instead, data is stored in whatever sectors are available; the operating system's device driver provides the illusion of contiguous storage. Now we're sort of in familiar territory, with a twist: instead of finding a block of storage to hold an object, we now have to find enough fixed-size blocks to hold an object and divide the object up among them.

Linked lists are not a great solution for keeping track of which disk blocks are free and which are in use, because traversing a list would be too slow. An 8 TiB disk has almost 2 billion blocks, and with worst-case behavior, 250 blocks can be accessed per second. That adds up to more than 15 years, which makes it impractical. That sounds really bad, but keep in mind that's 1 MiB of data per second.

When we're managing data in memory, it suffices to reference it using a pointer. But those are transient, and because disks are used for long-term data storage, we need something more persistent. You've already seen the answer: *filenames*. We need some way to both store those filenames on the disk and associate them with the blocks used to store the file data.

One way to manage all of this comes from—yup, you guessed it—UNIX. A number of blocks are set aside as *inodes*, a contraction of the disk block *index* and *node*; thus, inodes are index nodes. An inode contains various pieces of information about a file, such as its owner, size, and permissions. It also contains the indices of the blocks containing the file data, as you can see in Figure 7-29.

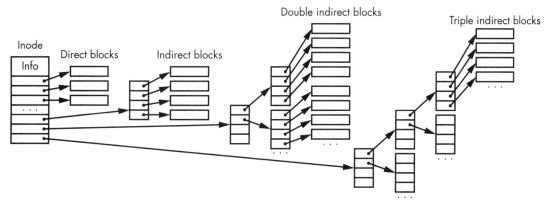

Figure 7-29: Filesystem data structure

This looks really complicated, but it isn't. An inode typically has 12 *direct block* pointers (they're really not pointers, just block indices), which support files up to 4,096 × 12 = 49,152 bytes in length. That's good enough for most files. If a file is larger, it uses *indirect blocks*. Assuming 32-bit indices (though these will need to be 64-bit soon), 1,024 indirect blocks which at 4 bytes each fit in one block, add another 4 MiB to the maximum file size. If that's not enough, 4 GiB are available via the *double indirect* blocks, and finally another 4 PiB via the *triple indirect* blocks.

One piece of information an inode indicates is whether the blocks contain *directory* information instead of other data. A directory maps filenames to the inodes that reference the file data. One of the nice things about the way UNIX does things is that a directory is really just another type of file. That means a directory can reference other directories, which is what gives us our familiar tree-structured *hierarchical filesystems.*

At this point, you may be thinking that all this looks a lot like an arbitrary tree, which was true for a while. One of the features of this arrangement is that multiple inodes can reference the same blocks. Each reference is called a *link*. Links allow the same file to appear in multiple directories. It turns out that it's very convenient to also be able to link to directories, so *symbolic links* were invented to make that possible. But symbolic links allow loops in the filesystem graph, so we need special code to detect that to prevent infinite looping. In any case, we have this complex structure that tracks the blocks used, but we're still missing an efficient way to track the *free space*.

One way to accomplish this is by using a bitmap (see "Bitmaps" on page 187) with 1 bit for each disk block. A bitmap can be pretty large: an 8 TB disk drive would need almost 2 billion bits, which would consume about 256 MiB. It's still a reasonable way to go—it's way less than 0.01 percent of the total disk space, and it doesn't all have to be in memory at the same time.

Working with bitmaps is pretty simple and efficient, especially if they're stored in 64-bit words. Assuming that a 1 indicates a block in use and a 0 indicates a free block, we can easily look for words that are not all 1s to find free blocks.

But there is a problem with this approach: it's possible for the filesystem graph and the free space bitmap to get out of sync. For example, the power could fail while data is being written to the disk. In the dark ages when computers had front panels with switches and blinking lights, you'd have to repair a damaged filesystem by inputting inode numbers through the front panel switches. This ordeal was remedied by programs such as fsck, which traverse the filesystem graph and compare it to the free block data. That's a better approach, but it's increasingly time-consuming as disks get larger. New journaling filesystem designs make damage control more efficient.

Databases

Binary trees are a great way to store data in memory, but they don't work as well when it comes to storing huge amounts of data that doesn't fit in memory. That's partly because tree nodes tend to be small and therefore don't map well to disk sectors.

A *database* is just a collection of data organized in some way. A *database management system (DBMS)* is a program that allows information to be stored in and retrieved from a database. A DBMS usually includes a number of interfaces layered on top of the underlying storage mechanism.

Databases are a common application of the *B-tree* data structure invented by German computer scientist Rudolf Bayer and American computer scientist Ed McCreight at Boeing in 1971. The B-tree is a balanced tree, but not a binary tree. It's a bit less space efficient than a balanced binary tree but performs better, especially when data is stored on disk. This is yet another case where an understanding of memory architecture leads to more efficient code.

Say we have a balanced binary tree of names sorted alphabetically. It would look something like Figure 7-30.

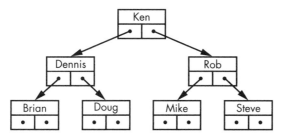

Figure 7-30: Balanced binary tree

A B-tree node has many more legs (children) than a binary tree node. The number of legs is chosen such that a node fits exactly into a disk block, as shown in Figure 7-31.

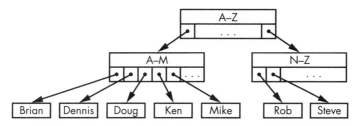

Figure 7-31: B-tree

As you can see, the interior nodes are balanced, which yields a predictable search time. There are unused child links in Figure 7-31 that consume space. You can easily rebalance the tree when child links run out by changing the range covered by the node. For example, if the A-M node ran out of children, it could be subdivided into A-G and H-M nodes. This isn't a great example, because power-of-2 subdivision is most often used but we don't have an even number of things to subdivide here.

More keys per node means less fetching of nodes. The larger nodes aren't a problem because they're the size of a disk block, which is fetched as a unit. There is some wasted space because of unused child links, but it's a reasonable trade-off.

Indices

Accessing sorted data is efficient, but we often need to access data sorted in more than one way. We might have both first and last names, or names and favorite bands.

Figure 7-31 shows nodes organized by name. These nodes are often referred to as the *primary index*. But we can have more than one index, as shown in Figure 7-32, which allows us to efficiently search for things in different ways.

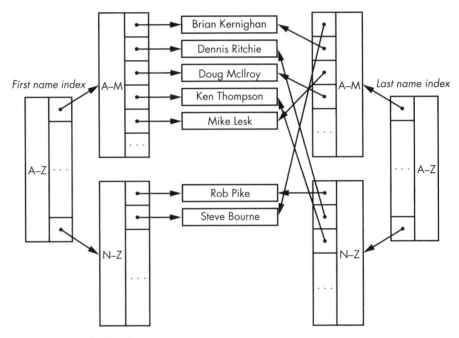

Figure 7-32: Multiple indices

The trade-off with indices is that they need maintenance. Every index must be updated when the data changes. That's a worthwhile cost when searching is a more common activity than modification.

Moving Data Around

I mentioned earlier that using arrays instead of linked lists requires copying data if the array needs to grow in size. You need copying in order to move page tables in and out of MMUs, free disk bitmaps on and off disk, and so on. Programs spend a lot of time moving data from one place to another, so it's important to do it efficiently.

Let's start with a half-measure: setting a block of length memory bytes to all 0s, as shown in Figure 7-33.

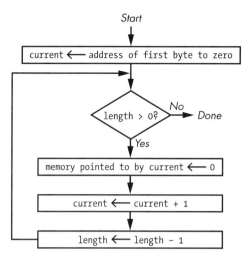

Figure 7-33: Zeroing a block of memory

That algorithm works fine, but it's not very efficient. Assuming that each box in Figure 7-33 takes the same amount of time to execute, we spend more time bookkeeping than zeroing memory locations. The *loop unrolling* technique can make this more efficient, as shown in Figure 7-34. For example, assuming that length is an even number, we can unroll the loop so that now more of the time is spent zeroing and less is spent on other things.

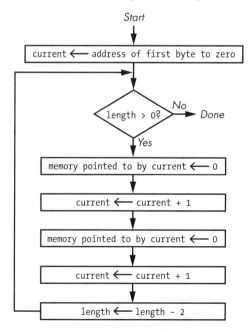

Figure 7-34: Zeroing a block of memory with loop unrolling

It would be nice to have a more general implementation, and fortunately there is one. When he worked at Lucasfilm, Canadian programmer

Tom Duff invented *Duff's Device* to speed up the copying of data; Figure 7-35 shows a variant for zeroing memory. This approach works only if the length is greater than zero.

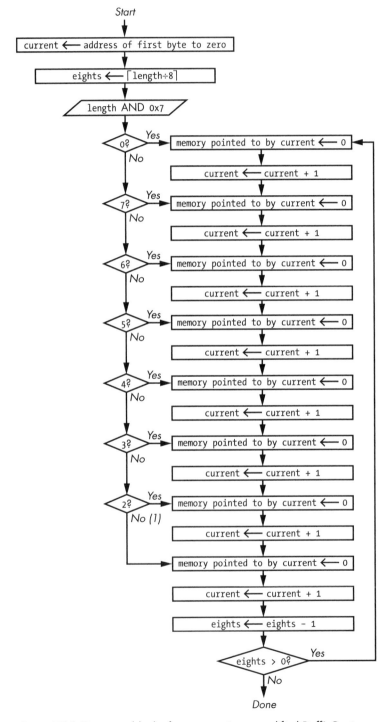

Figure 7-35: Zeroing a block of memory using a modified Duff's Device

Duff's Device unrolls the loop eight times and jumps into the middle to handle any leftover bytes. Though you might be tempted to unroll the loop further, this approach must be balanced with the code size because having it fit into the instruction cache is worth a lot of speed.

You can see on the loop side of the figure that the ratio of memory-zeroing time to bookkeeping time is much improved. Though the initial setup and branching to the proper place in the loop looks complicated, it really isn't. It doesn't take a pile of conditional branches, just some address manipulation as follows:

1. Mask off all but the lower 3 bits of the length by ANDing with 0x7.
2. Subtract the result from 8.
3. Mask off all but the lower 3 bits by ANDing with 0x7.
4. Multiply by the number of bytes between zeroing instructions.
5. Add the address of the first zeroing instruction.
6. Branch to that address.

Another way to increase the efficiency is to recognize that, for example, on a 64-bit machine, 8 bytes can be zeroed at a time. Of course, a bit of extra code is needed to handle leftover bytes at the beginning and the end. We need to use the algorithm from Figure 7-36 without the loop on the eights for the beginning and end. In the middle, we zero as many 8-byte chunks as possible.

This all becomes more complicated when we're copying a block of data instead of just setting it to a value, because chances are, the source and destination won't have the same byte alignment. It's often worth testing for the case where both the source and destination are word aligned because it's a pretty common case.

Copying has yet another complication, which is that it's common to use copying to move data around in a region of memory. For example, we may have a buffer full of space-separated words in which we want to read the first word out of the buffer and then cram everything else down so that there's room for more at the end. You have to take care when copying data in overlapping regions; sometimes you have to copy backward in order to avoid overwriting the data.

An interesting historical case was an early raster graphics terminal (see "Raster Graphics" on page 180) called the *blit*, designed by Canadian programmer Rob Pike at Bell Telephone Laboratories in the early 1980s, an era before it became practical to make custom integrated circuits to do this sort of thing. Source and destination data could overlap, such as in the case of dragging a window, and the data could be of any bit alignment. Performance was very important because processors weren't very fast compared to today; the blit used a Motorola 68000. There was no MMU, so Pike wrote code that looked at the source and destination and generated optimal code on the fly to do the fastest copy. I did a similar implementation on a system that used the Motorola 68020. This achieved even better performance because the 68020 had an instruction cache into which the generated code fit, so it didn't have to keep accessing instruction memory. Note that this was a precursor to the JIT (just-in-time) techniques used in many virtual machines, including Java.

Vectored I/O

Copying data efficiently is important for system performance, but avoiding copying altogether helps even more. A lot of data is moved through the operating system to and from user space programs, and this data is often not in contiguous memory.

For example, say we're generating some audio data in the mp3 format that we want to write to an audio device. Like many file formats, mp3 files consist of a number of *frames*, each of which includes a *header* followed by some data. A typical audio file contains multiple frames that, in many cases, have identical headers, as shown in Figure 7-36.

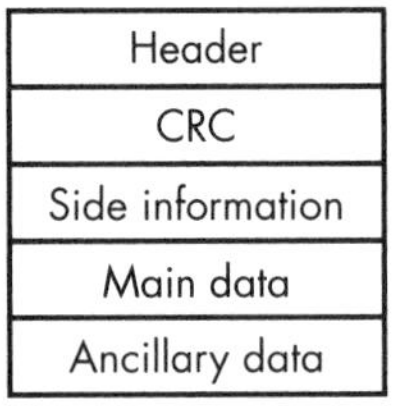

Header
CRC
Side information
Main data
Ancillary data

Figure 7-36: mp3 frame layout

We could build each frame by copying all the data into a buffer, but then when we write that data to an audio device, we'll have to copy it yet again. Alternatively, we could write each portion of each frame separately, but that would increase the context-switching overhead and might cause problems for an audio device if only a partial frame gets written.

It would be more efficient if we could just hand the system a set of pointers to each piece of the frame and let the system gather the pieces together as they're written, as shown in Figure 7-37. This is sufficiently worthwhile to justify system call (`readv`, `writev`) support.

Vector
size
size
size
size
size
Header
CRC
Side information
Main data
Ancillary data

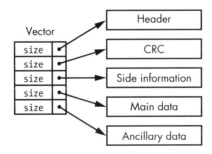

Figure 7-37: Data gather

The idea is to hand a vector of sizes and data pointers to the operating system, which then assembles them in order. There are versions for both reading and writing: writing is known as *gathering* because data is collected from many places, while reading is known as *scattering* because data is dispersed to many places. The whole concept is called *scatter/gather*.

Scatter/gather became mainstream with the Berkeley networking code that became a foundation of the internet. I mentioned back in "TCP/IP" on page 158 that IP data is sent in packets and TCP is responsible for making sure that the packets arrive and are in the correct order. Packets arriving from a communications endpoint (well, it might be a communications endpoint to you, but it's a socket to me) are gathered into a contiguous stream for presentation to user programs.

Object-Oriented Pitfalls

Since you're learning to code, you may be learning an *object-oriented* language such as Java, C++, Python, or JavaScript. Object-oriented programming is a great methodology, but it can lead to performance issues if not used judiciously.

Object-oriented programming first gained serious traction with C++. C++ is an interesting case because it was initially built on top of C, which gives us an opportunity to see how it works.

Objects have *methods*, which are equivalent to functions, and *properties*, which are equivalent to data. Everything needed for an object can be collected into a single data structure. C's support for type casting and pointers, especially pointers to functions, wins big here. A C structure for an object might look something like Figure 7-38.

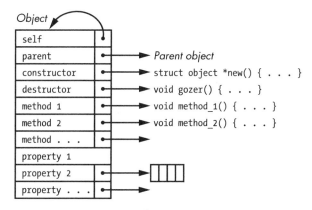

Figure 7-38: A C structure for an object

Some properties, such as those with integer values (`property 1`), reside in the object structure itself, whereas others require additional memory allocation (`property 2`) that's referenced by the object structure.

Clearly this structure could get quite large, especially if there are a lot of methods. We can address that by breaking the methods out into a separate structure—another space/time trade-off—as shown in Figure 7-39.

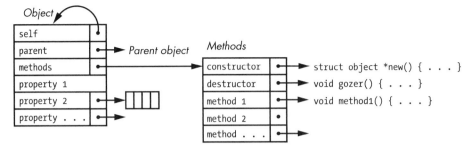

Figure 7-39: Separate method structure

Programmers used this sort of approach to object-oriented programming long before Danish programmer Bjarne Stroustrup invented C++. The original C++ was a wrapper around C that did things like this.

Why does this matter? Object-oriented ideologues believe that objects are the answer for everything. But as you can see in the previous figures, there's a certain amount of overhead associated with objects. They have to carry around their own methods instead of using globally available functions. The upshot is that objects don't pack as densely as pure data types, so stick to classic arrays when performance is paramount.

Sorting

There are many reasons to sort data. Sometimes we just want sorted results, like when we alphabetize names to make them easier for people to find. Many times we want to store data in sorted form because it speeds up searching by reducing the number of memory accesses.

I'm not going to go into sorting algorithms in depth here, because it's a pretty mature subject covered in many books. And plenty of good sort functions are available, so it's not likely that you'll need to write your own except as a homework problem. But there are a few important points to keep in mind.

One is that if the size of the things you're sorting is larger than the size of a pointer, you should sort by rearranging the pointers to the data instead of by moving the data itself around.

Also, a convention for sorting has evolved. Our bingo parlor tree example enabled decisions based on an arithmetic comparison; we made decisions based on whether one number was less than, equal to, or greater than another. This method of decision making is rooted in the FORTRAN programming language from 1956, which included a statement that looked like Listing 7-3.

```
IF (expression) branch1, branch2, branch3
```

Listing 7-3: A FORTRAN arithmetic IF statement

This IF statement evaluated the expression and went to branch1 if the result was less than zero, branch2 if it was zero, and branch3 if it was greater than zero; the branches are similar to what we saw in "Branching" on page 105.

Sorting numbers is straightforward. It would be nice to apply this same methodology to sorting other things. We saw back in Figure 7-10 that a list node can include arbitrary data; the same is true with tree nodes and other data structures.

UNIX version III introduced a library function called qsort that implemented a variation of the classic *quicksort* algorithm. The interesting thing about the qsort implementation is that although it knew how to sort things, it didn't know how to compare them. Therefore, it took advantage of C's pointers to functions; when calling qsort with a list of things to sort, you also provided a comparison function that returned <0, 0, or >0 for less than, equal to, or greater than, just like the FORTRAN arithmetic IF. This approach allowed the caller to use qsort to sort things however they wanted. For example, if a node contained both a name and an age, the supplied function could compare first by age and then name so that qsort would produce results organized by age first and name second. This approach worked well and has been copied by many other systems.

The standard C library string comparison function strcmp was designed with this in mind; it returns a value of less than, equal to, or greater than zero. This has also become the de facto way of doing things.

The original ASCII version of strcmp just walked the strings, subtracting the character of one from the other. It kept going if the value was zero and returned 0 if the end of the strings was reached. Otherwise, it returned the subtraction result.

This is all well and good if you're just sorting to distribute data in a tree, but it falls apart if you're sorting to put things into alphabetical order. It worked in the ASCII days—you can see in Table 1-10 that the numerical order and alphabetical order are the same. Where it falls apart is with support for other *locales*. A side effect of support for other languages coming later is that only the ASCII characters are numerically in the correct *collating order*, or language-specific sorting rules.

For example, what value should be assigned to the German letter *ß*, the sharp S (*Eszett* or *scharfes S*)? Its Unicode value is 0x00DF. Because of that, the word *Straße* would get sorted after the word *Strasse* using a vanilla string comparison. But these are actually different representations of the same word. The *ß* is equivalent to *ss*. A string comparison that heeded the locale would say that the two words are equal.

Making a Hash of Things

All the searching methods we've seen so far involve repeated testing while traversing a data structure. There's another approach that performs better in some circumstances, called *hashing*. Hashing has many applications. We're talking about in-memory storage and retrieval here, not mass storage. The general concept is to apply some *hash function* to the search keys that evenly splatter them onto the wall. If the hash function is easy to compute and transforms a key into a splat in a unique location on the wall, then single-step lookup should be fast. Of course, there are some practical realities to consider.

Each splat represents the storage for the object associated with the key. The hash function must produce values that fit in memory. And it shouldn't splatter things across too much memory or performance will suffer, both from using too much memory and from lack of locality of reference. Coming up with a perfect hash function isn't really possible because we don't have any prior knowledge of our keys.

One way to bound the storage is to have a hash function that maps keys into array indices. The array is called a *hash table*, shown in Figure 7-40. The array elements are called *buckets*.

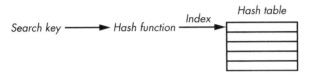

Figure 7-40: Hashing

What makes a good hash function? It needs to be easy to compute, and it needs to distribute keys evenly into the buckets. A simple hash function that works pretty well for text is just to sum up the character values. That's not quite enough, because the sum might produce an index that's beyond the end of the hash table, but we can easily solve this by making the index the sum modulo the hash table size. Let's look at how this works in practice. We'll use a table size of 11; prime numbers make good table sizes because multiples of the sum end up in different buckets, improving the splatter pattern.

Say we have an application that keeps track of songs played at our favorite jam band concerts. Maybe it stores the last played date. We'll just use the first word of each song name.

As you can see in Figure 7-41, we start with *Hell* in a bucket—in this case, bucket 4. Next is *Touch* in bucket 9, followed by *Scarlet* in 3. But when we get to *Alligator*, we have a problem because the value of the hash function is the same as it was for *Scarlet*. This is called a *collision*.

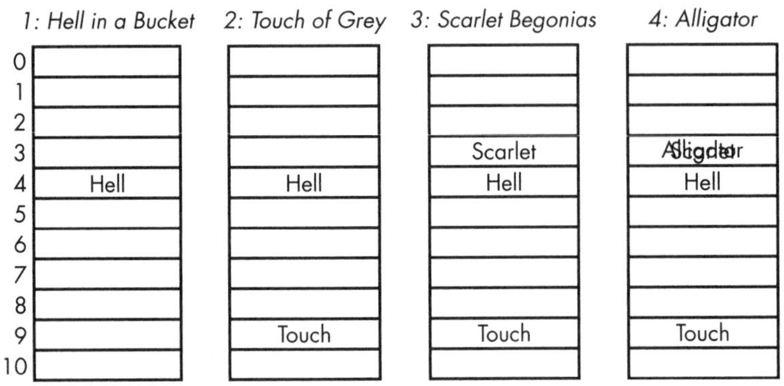

	1: Hell in a Bucket	2: Touch of Grey	3: Scarlet Begonias	4: Alligator
0				
1				
2				
3			Scarlet	Alligator
4	Hell	Hell	Hell	Hell
5				
6				
7				
8				
9		Touch	Touch	Touch
10				

Figure 7-41: Hash collision

We solve this by replacing the buckets with *hash chains*, which in their simplest form are singly linked lists, as shown in Figure 7-42.

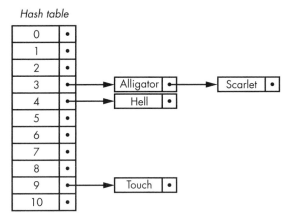

Figure 7-42: Hash chains

There are a number of trade-offs in hash chain management. We can just insert collisions at the head of the chain, as in Figure 7-42, because it's fast. But lookup can slow down as the chains get longer, so we could also do an insertion sort, which takes longer but means we don't have to traverse a chain to the end to determine whether or not an item exists. There are also many different collision-handling methods—for example, eliminating hash chains and using some algorithm to find an empty slot in the table.

It's difficult to pick a good hash table size without knowing the expected number of symbols in advance. You can keep track of chain length and grow the hash table if the chains are getting too long. This can be an expensive operation, but it can pay off because it doesn't need to be done very often.

There are many variations on hash functions. The holy grail of hash functions is the *perfect hash*, which maps each key to a unique bucket. It's pretty much impossible to create a perfect hash function unless all of the keys are known in advance, but mathematicians have come up with much better functions than the one used in this example.

Efficiency vs. Performance

A lot of effort has gone into making efficient search algorithms. Much of this work was done in an era when computers were expensive. Performance and efficiency were linked.

The cost of electronics has plunged so dramatically that it's almost impossible to purchase anything that doesn't include a gratuitous blue LED. Performance and efficiency are decoupled; there are cases where better performance can be achieved by using less efficient algorithms on more processors than more efficient algorithms on fewer processors.

One application of this decoupling is database *sharding*, also called *horizontal partitioning*. Sharding involves breaking up a database into multiple shards, each of which lives on its own machine, as shown in Figure 7-43.

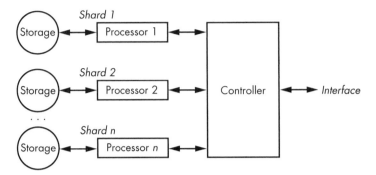

Figure 7-43: Database sharding

Database operations requested over the interface are sent to all of the shards, and the results are assembled by a controller. This technique improves performance because operations are split across multiple workers.

A variation on sharding is called *MapReduce*, which essentially allows you to provide code to the controller for assembly of the intermediate results. This makes it possible to do operations such as "count the number of students in all math classes" without having to first request a list of students and then count them.

Databases aren't the only application of this multiple processor approach. A historically interesting use is the Electronic Frontier Foundation's DES (Data Encryption Standard) cracker built in 1998; see the book *Cracking DES* (O'Reilly, 1998) for the full story. A machine was constructed that used 1,856 custom processor chips, each of which tried a range of keys on the encrypted data. Any "interesting" results were forwarded to a controller for further analysis. This machine could test 90 billion keys per second.

Summary

This chapter introduced you to a number of ways in which data can be organized to take advantage of what you've learned so far about computer hardware. In the next chapter, you'll see how your programs get converted into forms that computer hardware can understand.

8

LANGUAGE PROCESSING

It's pretty clear that only crazy people would try to write computer programs. That's always been true, but *programming languages* at least make the job a lot easier.

This chapter examines how programming languages are implemented. Its aim is to help you develop an understanding of what happens with your code. You'll also learn how the code you write is transformed into an executable form called *machine language*.

Assembly Language

We saw a machine language implementation of a program to compute Fibonacci numbers back in Table 4-4 on page 108. As you might imagine, figuring out all the bit combinations for instructions is pretty painful. Primitive computer programmers got tired of this and came up with a better way to write computer programs, called *assembly language*.

Assembly language did a few amazing things. It let programmers use *mnemonics* for instructions so they didn't have to memorize all the bit combinations. It allowed them to give names or *labels* to addresses. And it allowed them to include *comments* that can help other people read and understand the program.

A program called an *assembler* reads assembly language programs and produces *machine code* from them, filling in the values of the labels or *symbols* as it goes. This is especially helpful because it prevents dumb errors caused by moving things around.

Listing 8-1 shows what the Fibonacci program from Table 4-4 looks like in the hypothetical assembly language from Chapter 4.

```
          load    #0        ; zero the first number in the sequence
          store   first
          load    #1        ; set the second number in the sequence to 1
          store   second
again:    load    first     ; add the first and second numbers to get the
          add     second    ; next number in the sequence
          store   next
                            ; do something interesting with the number
          load    second    ; move the second number to be the first number
          store   first
          load    next      ; make the next number the second number
          store   second
          cmp     #200      ; are we done yet?
          ble     again     ; nope, go around again
first:    bss     1         ; where the first number is stored
second:   bss     1         ; where the second number is stored
next:     bss     1         ; where the next number is stored
```

Listing 8-1: Assembly language program to compute the Fibonacci sequence

The bss (which stands for *block started by symbol*) *pseudo-instruction* reserves a chunk of memory—in this case, one address—without putting anything in that location. Pseudo-instructions don't have a direct correspondence with machine language instructions; they're instructions to the assembler. As you can see, assembly language is much easier to deal with than machine language, but it's still pretty tedious stuff.

Early programmers had to pull themselves up by their own bootstraps. There *was* no assembler to use when the first computer was made, so programmers had to write the first one the hard way, by figuring out all the bits by hand. This first assembler was quite primitive, but once it worked, it could be used to make a better one, and so on.

The term *bootstrap* has stuck around, although it's often shortened to *boot*. Booting a computer often involves loading a small program, which loads a bigger one, which in turn loads an even bigger one. On early computers, people had to enter the initial bootstrap program by hand, using switches and lights on the front panel.

High-Level Languages

Assembly language helped a lot, but as you can see, doing simple things with it still takes a lot of work. We'd really like to be able to use fewer words to describe more complicated tasks. Fred Brooks's 1975 book *The Mythical Man-Month: Essays on Software Engineering* (Addison-Wesley) claims that on average, a programmer can write 3 to 10 lines of documented, debugged code per day. So a lot more work could get done if a line of code did more.

Enter *high-level languages*, which operate at a higher level of abstraction than assembly language. Source code in high-level languages is run through a program called a *compiler*, which translates or *compiles* it into machine language, also known as *object* code.

Thousands of high-level languages have been invented. Some are very general, and some are designed for specific tasks. One of the first high-level languages was called FORTRAN, which stood for "formula translator." You could use it to easily write programs that solved formulas like $y = m \times x + b$. Listing 8-2 shows what our Fibonacci sequence program would look like in FORTRAN.

```
C   SET THE INITIAL TWO SEQUENCE NUMBERS IN I and J
    I=0
    J=1
C   GET NEXT SEQUENCE NUMBER
5   K=I+J
C   DO SOMETHING INTERESTING WITH THE NUMBER
C   SHIFT THE SEQUENCE NUMBERS TO I AND J
    I=J
    J=K
C   DO IT AGAIN IF THE LAST NUMBER WAS LESS THAN 200
    IF (J .LT. 200) GOTO 5
C   ALL DONE
```

Listing 8-2: Fibonacci sequence program in FORTRAN

Quite a bit simpler than assembly language, isn't it? Note that lines that begin with the letter C are comments. And although we have labels, they must be numbers. Also note that we don't have to explicitly declare memory that we want to use—it just magically appears when we use *variables* such as *I* and *J*. FORTRAN did something interesting (or ugly, depending on your point of view) that still reverberates today. Any variable name that began with the letter *I, J, K, L, M,* or *N* was an integer, which was borrowed from the way mathematicians write proofs. Variables beginning with any other letter were floating-point, or REAL in FORTRAN-speak. Generations of former FORTRAN programmers still use *i, j, k, l, m,* and *n* or their upper-case equivalents as names for integer variables.

FORTRAN was a pretty cumbersome language that ran on the really big machines of the time. As smaller, cheaper machines became available (that is, ones that only took up a small room), people came up with other languages. Most of these new languages, such as BASIC (which stood for

"Beginner's All-purpose Symbolic Instruction Code"), were variations on the FORTRAN theme. All of these languages suffered from the same problem. As programs increased in complexity, the network of line numbers and GOTOs became an unmanageable tangle. People would write programs with the label numbers all in order and then have to make a change that would mess it up. Many programmers started off by using labels 10 or 100 apart so that they'd have room to backfill later, but even that didn't always work.

Structured Programming

Languages like FORTRAN and BASIC are called *unstructured* because there is no structure to the way that labels and GOTOs are arranged. You can't build a house by throwing a pile of lumber on the ground in real life, but you can in FORTRAN. I'm talking about original FORTRAN; over time, the language has evolved and incorporated structured programming. It's still the most popular scientific language.

Structured programming languages were developed to address this *spaghetti code* problem by eliminating the need for the nasty GOTO. Some went too far. For example, Pascal got rid of it completely, resulting in a programming language that was useful only for teaching elementary structured programming. To be fair, that's actually what it was designed to do. C, the successor to the Ken Thompson's B, was originally developed by Dennis Ritchie at Bell Telephone Laboratories. It was very pragmatic and became one of the most widely used programming languages. A large number of later languages—including C++, Java, PHP, Python, and JavaScript—copied elements from C.

Listing 8-3 shows how our Fibonacci program might appear in JavaScript. Note the absence of explicit branching.

```
var first;    // first number
var second;   // second number
var next;     // next number in sequence

first = 0;
second = 1;

while ((next = first + second) < 200) {
    // do something interesting with the number
    first = second;
    second = next;
}
```

Listing 8-3: JavaScript program to compute Fibonacci sequence

The statements inside the curly brackets {} are executed as long as the while condition in the parentheses is true. Execution continues after the } when that condition becomes false. The flow of control is cleaner, making the program easier to understand.

Lexical Analysis

Now let's look at what it takes to process a language. We'll start with *lexical analysis*, the process of converting *symbols* (characters) into *tokens* (words).

A simple way of looking at lexical analysis is to say that a language has two types of tokens: words and separators. For example, using the above rules, *lex luthor* (the author of all evil programming languages) has two word tokens (*lex* and *luthor*) and one separator token (the space). Figure 8-1 shows a simple algorithm that divides its input into tokens.

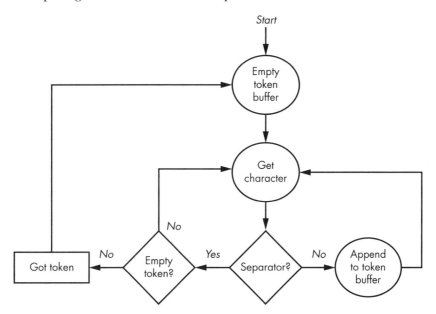

Figure 8-1: Simple lexical analysis

It's not enough to just extract tokens; we need to classify them because practical languages have many different types of tokens, such as names, numbers, and operators. Languages typically have operators and operands, just like math, and operands can be variables or constants (numbers). The free-form nature of many languages also complicates things—for example, when separators are implied, as in A+B as opposed to A + B (note the spaces). Both forms have the same interpretation, but the first form doesn't have any explicit separators.

Numeric constants are astonishingly hard to classify, even if we ignore the distinctions among octal, hexadecimal, integer, and floating-point numbers. Let's diagram what constitutes a legitimate floating-point number. There are many ways to specify a floating-point number, including 1., .1, 1.2, +1.2, -.1, 1e5, 1e+5, 1e-5, and 1.2E5, as shown in Figure 8-2.

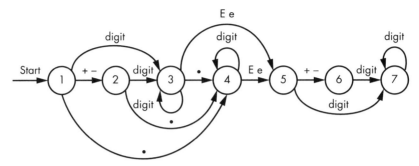

Figure 8-2: Diagram for floating-point numbers

We start at the bubble labeled 1. A + or - character brings us to bubble 2, while a . sends us to bubble 4. We leave bubble 2 for bubble 4 when we get a . character, but we go to bubble 3 when we receive a digit. Bubbles 3 and 4 accumulate digits. We're done if we get a character for which no transition is shown. For example, if we received a space while at any of the bubbles, we'd be done. Of course, leaving bubble 2 without a digit or decimal point, bubble 6 without a digit, or bubble 5 without a sign or digit is an error because it doesn't produce a complete floating-point number. These paths are absent from the diagram for simplicity's sake.

This is a lot like trying to find treasure using a pirate map. As long as you're following directions, you can get from one place to another. If you don't follow directions—for example, with a Z at bubble 1—you fall off the map and get lost.

You could view Figure 8-2 as the specification for floating-point numbers and write software to implement it. There are other, more formal ways to write specifications, however, such as Backus-Naur form.

BACKUS-NAUR FORM

Backus-Naur form (BNF) has its roots in the work of Indian Sanskrit scholar Pāṇini (approximately fifth century BCE). BNF is named after American computer scientist John Backus (1924–2007), who was also the inventor of FORTRAN, and Danish computer scientist Peter Naur (1928–2016). It's a formal way to specify languages. We're not going to go into great detail about it here, but it's something you should be familiar with because it's used in the *RFC* (request for comments) documents that define internet protocols, among other things. Here's the BNF for a floating-point number:

```
<digit>        ::= "0" | "1" | "2" | "3" | "4" | "5" | "6" | "7" | "8" | "9"
<digits>       ::= <digit> | <digits> <digit>

<e>            ::= "e" | "E"
<sign>         ::= "+" | "-"
```

```
<optional-sign>      ::= <sign> | ""
<exponent>           ::= <e> <optional-sign> <digits>
<optional-exponent>  ::= <exponent> | ""

<mantissa>           ::= <digits> | <digits> "." | "." <digits> | <digits> "." <digits>
<floating-point>     ::= <optional-sign> <mantissa> <optional-exponent>
```

Things on the left of the ::= can be substituted for things on the right. The |
indicates a choice, and things inside of quotes are literals, meaning that they
must appear exactly as written.

State Machines

Based just on the complexity of numbers, you can imagine that it would
take a substantial amount of special case code to extract language tokens
from input. Figure 8-2 gave us a hint that there's another approach. We
can construct a *state machine*, which consists of a set of states and a list of
what causes a transition from one state to another—exactly what we saw in
Figure 8-2. We can arrange this information as shown in Table 8-1.

Table 8-1: State Table for Floating-Point Numbers

Input	State						
	1	**2**	**3**	**4**	**5**	**6**	**7**
0	3	3	3	4	7	7	7
1	3	3	3	4	7	7	7
2	3	3	3	4	7	7	7
3	3	3	3	4	7	7	7
4	3	3	3	4	7	7	7
5	3	3	3	4	7	7	7
6	3	3	3	4	7	7	7
7	3	3	3	4	7	7	7
8	3	3	3	4	7	7	7
9	3	3	3	4	7	7	7
e	error	error	5	5	error	error	done
E	error	error	5	5	error	error	done
+	2	error	done	done	6	error	done
–	2	error	done	done	6	error	done
.	4	4	4	done	error	error	done
other	error	error	done	done	error	error	done

Looking at the table, you can see that when we're in state 1, digits move us to state 3, e or E moves us to state 5, + or - to state 2, and . to state 4—anything else is an error.

Using a state machine allows us to classify the input using a simple piece of code, as shown in Listing 8-4. Let's use Table 8-1, replacing done with 0 and error with -1. For simplicity, we'll have an other row in the table for each of the other characters.

```
state = 1;
while (state > 0)
    state = state_table[state][next_character];
```

Listing 8-4: Using a state machine

This approach could easily be expanded to other types of tokens. Rather than have a single value for done, we could have a different value for each type of token.

Regular Expressions

Building tables like Table 8-1 from diagrams like Figure 8-2 is very cumbersome and error-prone for complicated languages. The solution is to create languages for specifying languages. American mathematician Stephen Cole Kleene (1909–1994) supplied the mathematical foundation for this approach way back in 1956. Ken Thompson first converted it into software in 1968 as part of a text editor and then created the UNIX grep (which stands for "globally search a regular expression and print") utility in 1974. This popularized the term *regular expression*, which is now ubiquitous. Regular expressions are languages themselves, and of course there are now several incompatible regular expression languages. Regular expressions are a mainstay of *pattern matching*. Figure 8-3 shows a regular expression that matches the pattern for a floating-point number.

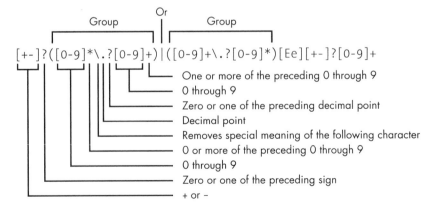

Figure 8-3: Regular expression for floating-point number

This looks like gibberish but really only relies on a few simple rules. It's processed from left to right, meaning that the expression abc would match the string of characters "abc". If something in the pattern is followed by ?, it means zero or one of those things, * means zero or more, and + means one or more. A set of characters enclosed in square brackets matches any single character in that set, so [abc] matches a, b, or c. The . matches any single character and so needs to be *escaped* with a backslash (\) so that it matches the . character only. The | means either the thing on the left or the thing on the right. Parentheses () are for grouping, just like in math.

Reading from left to right, we start with an optional plus or minus sign. This is followed by either zero or more digits, an optional decimal point, and one or more digits (which handles cases like 1.2 and .2), or by one or more digits, an optional decimal point, and zero or more digits (which handles the 1 and 1. cases). This is followed by the exponent, which begins with an E or e, followed by an optional sign and one or more digits. Not as horrible as it first looked, is it?

Having a regular expression language that processed input into tokens would be more useful if it automatically generated state tables. And we have one, thanks again to research at Bell Telephone Laboratories. In 1975, American physicist Mike Lesk—along with intern Eric Schmidt, who today is executive chairman of Google's parent company, Alphabet—wrote a program called lex, short for "lexical analyzer." As The Beatles said in "Penny Lane:" "It's a *Kleene* machine." An open source version called flex was later produced by the GNU project. These tools do exactly what we want. They produce a state table driven program that executes user-supplied program fragments when input matches regular expressions. For example, the simple lex program fragment in Listing 8-5 prints ah whenever it encounters either ar or er in the input and prints er whenever it encounters an a at the end of a word.

```
[ae]r      printf("ah");
a/[ .,;!?]  printf("er");
```

Listing 8-5: Bostonian lex program fragment

The / in the second pattern means "only match the thing on its left if it is followed by the thing on its right." Things not matched are just printed. You can use this program to convert regular American English to Bostonian: for example, inputting the text Park the car in Harvard yard and sit on the sofa would produce Pahk the cah in Hahvahd yahd and sit on the sofer as output.

Classifying tokens is a piece of cake in lex. For example, Listing 8-6 shows some lex that matches all of our number forms plus variable names and some operators. Instead of printing out what we find, we return some values defined elsewhere for each type of token. Note that several of the characters have special meaning to lex and therefore require the backslash escape character so that they're treated as literals.

```
0[0-7]*                                                   return (INTEGER);
[+-]?[0-9]+                                               return (INTEGER);
[+-]?(([0-9]*\.?[0-9]+)|([0-9]+\.?[0-9]*))([Ee][+-]?[0-9]+)?  return (FLOAT);
0x[0-9a-fA-F]+                                            return (INTEGER);
[A-Za-z][A-Za-z0-9]*                                      return (VARIABLE);
\+                                                        return (PLUS);
-                                                         return (MINUS);
\*                                                        return (TIMES);
\/                                                        return (DIVIDE);
=                                                         return (EQUALS);
```

Listing 8-6: Classifying tokens using lex

Not shown in the listing is the mechanism by which lex supplies the actual values of the tokens. When we find a number, we need to know its value; likewise, when we find a variable name, we need to know that name.

Note that lex doesn't work for all languages. As computer scientist Stephen C. Johnson (introduced shortly) explained, "Lex can be easily used to produce quite complicated lexical analyzers, but there remain some languages (such as FORTRAN) which do not fit any theoretical framework, and whose lexical analyzers must be crafted by hand."

From Words to Sentences

So far, we've seen how we can turn sequences of characters into words. But that's not enough for a language. We now need to turn those words into sentences according to some *grammar.*

Let's use the tokens from Listing 8-6 to create a simple four-function calculator. Expressions such as 1 + 2 and a = 5 are legal, whereas 1 + + + 2 isn't. We once again find ourselves in need of pattern matching, but this time for token types. Maybe somebody has already thought about this.

That somebody would be Stephen C. Johnson, who also—unsurprisingly—worked at Bell Labs. He created yacc (for "yet another compiler compiler") in the early 1970s. The name should give you an idea of how many people were playing with these sorts of things back then. It's still in use today; an open source version, called bison, is available from the GNU project. Just like lex, yacc and bison generate state tables and the code to operate on them.

The program yacc generates is a *shift-reduce* parser using a stack (see "Stacks" on page 122). In this context, *shift* means pushing a token onto the stack, and *reduce* means replacing a matched set of tokens on the stack with a token for that set. Look at the BNF for the calculator in Listing 8-7— it uses the token values produced by lex in Listing 8-6.

```
<operator>      ::= PLUS | MINUS | TIMES | DIVIDE
<operand>       ::= INTEGER | FLOAT | VARIABLE
<expression>    ::= <operand> | <expression> PLUS <operand>
                             | <expression> MINUS <operand>
                             | <expression> TIMES <operand>
                             | <expression> DIVIDE <operand>
```

```
<assignment>   ::= <variable> EQUALS <expression>
<statement>    ::= <expression> | <assignment>
<statements>   ::= "" | <statements> <statement>
<calculator>   ::= <statements>
```

Listing 8-7: Simple calculator BNF

Shift-reduce is easy to understand once you see it in action. Look at what happens when our simple calculator is presented with the input 4 + 5 - 3 in Figure 8-4. Referring back to "Different Equation Notations" on page 125, you can see that processing infix notation equations requires a deeper stack than postfix (RPN) requires because more tokens, such as parentheses, must be shifted before anything can be reduced.

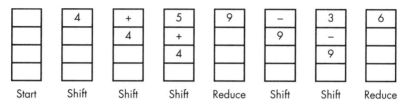

Figure 8-4: Shift-reduce in action

Listing 8-8 shows what our calculator would look like when coded in yacc. Note the similarity to the BNF. This is for illustration only; it's not a fully working example, as that would introduce far too many nitpicky distractions.

```
calculator  : statements
            ;

statements  : /* empty */
            | statement statements
            ;

operand     : INTEGER
            | FLOAT
            | VARIABLE
            ;

expression  : expression PLUS operand
            | expression MINUS operand
            | expression TIMES operand
            | expression DIVIDE operand
            | operand
            ;

assignment  : VARIABLE EQUALS expression
            ;

statement   : expression
            | assignment
            ;
```

Listing 8-8: Partial yacc for a simple calculator

The Language-of-the-Day Club

Languages used to be difficult. In 1977, Canadian computer scientist Alfred Aho and American computer scientist Jeffrey Ullman at Bell Labs published *Principles of Compiler Design*, one of the first computer-typeset books published using the troff typesetting language. One can summarize the book as follows: "languages are hard, and you had better dive into the heavy math, set theory, and so on." The second edition, published in 1986 along with Indian computer scientist Ravi Sethi, had a completely different feel. Its attitude was more like "languages are a done thing, and here's how to do them." And people did.

That edition popularized lex and yacc. All of a sudden, there were languages for everything—and not just programming languages. One of my favorite small languages was chem, by Canadian computer scientist Brian Kernighan at Bell Labs, which drew pretty chemical structure diagrams from input like C double bond O. The diagrams in the book you're reading, in fact, were created using Brian Kernighan's picture-drawing language pic.

Creating new languages is fun. Of course, people started making new languages without understanding their history and reintroduced old mistakes. For example, many consider the handling of *whitespace* (the spaces between words) in the Ruby language to be a replay of a mistake in the original C language that was fixed long ago. (Note that one of the classic ways to deal with a mistake is to call it a feature.)

The result of all this history is that a huge number of languages are now available. Most don't really add much value and are just demonstrations of the designer's taste. It's worth paying attention to *domain-specific* languages, particularly *little languages* such as pic and chem, to see how specific applications are addressed. American computer scientist Jon Bentley published a wonderful column about little languages called "Programming Pearls" in *Communications of the ACM* back in 1986. These columns were collected and published in updated book form in 1999 as *Programming Pearls* (Addison-Wesley).

Parse Trees

Earlier I talked about compiling high-level languages, but that's not the only option. High-level languages can be compiled or *interpreted*. The choice is not a function of the design of the language but rather of its implementation.

Compiled languages produce machine code like you saw back in Table 4-4 page 108. The compiler takes the source code and converts it into machine language for a particular machine. Many compilers allow you to compile the same program for different target machines. Once a program is compiled, it's ready to run.

Interpreted languages don't result in machine language for a real machine ("real" as in hardware). Instead, interpreted languages run on *virtual machines*, which are machines written in software. They may have their own machine language, but it's not a computer instruction set implemented in hardware. Note that the term *virtual machine* has become overloaded recently; I'm using it to mean an abstract computing machine. Some interpreted languages are executed directly by the *interpreter*. Others are compiled into an *intermediate language* for later interpretation.

In general, compiled code is faster because once it's compiled, it's in machine language. It's like translating a book. Once it's done, anyone who speaks that language can read it. Interpreted code is ephemeral, like someone reading a book aloud while translating it into the listener's language. If another person later wants the book read to them in their own language, it must be translated again. However, interpreted code allows languages to have features that are really difficult to build in hardware. Computers are fast enough that we can often afford the speed penalty that comes with interpreters.

Figure 8-4 depicted the calculator directly executing the input. Although this is fine for something like a calculator, it skips a major step used for compilers and interpreters. For those cases, we construct a *parse tree*, which is a DAG (directed acyclic graph) data structure from the calculator grammar. We'll build this tree out of node structures, as depicted in Figure 8-5.

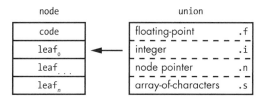

Figure 8-5: Parse tree node layout

Each node includes a code that indicates the type of node. There is also an array of leaves; the interpretation of each leaf is determined by the code. Each leaf is a union since it can hold more than one type of data. We're using C language syntax for the member naming, so, for example, .i is used if we're interpreting a leaf as an integer.

We'll assume the existence of a makenode function that makes new nodes. It takes a leaf count as its first argument, a code as its second, and the values for each leaf afterward.

Let's flesh out the code from Listing 8-8 a bit more while still omitting some of the picky details. To keep things simple, we'll only handle integer numbers. What was missing earlier was code to execute when matching grammar rules. In yacc, the value of each of the right-hand-side elements is available as $1, $2, and so on, and $$ is what gets returned by the rule. Listing 8-9 shows a more complete version of our yacc calculator.

calculator	: statements	{ do_something_with($1); }
	;	
statements	: /* empty */	
	| statement statements	{ $$.n = makenode(2, LIST, $1, $2); }
	;	
operand	: INTEGER	{ $$ = makenode(1, INTEGER, $1); }
	| VARIABLE	{ $$ = makenode(1, VARIABLE, $1); }
	;	
expression	: expression PLUS operand	{ $$.n = makenode(2, PLUS, $1, $3); }
	| expression MINUS operand	{ $$.n = makenode(2, MINUS, $1, $3); }
	| expression TIMES operand	{ $$.n = makenode(2, TIMES, $1, $3); }
	| expression DIVIDE operand	{ $$.n = makenode(2, DIVIDE, $1, $3); }
	| operand	{ $$ = $1; }
	;	
assignment	: VARIABLE EQUALS expression	{ $$.n = makenode(2, EQUALS, $1, $3); }
	;	
statement	: expression	{ $$ = $1; }
	| assignment	{ $$ = $1; }
	;	

Listing 8-9: Simple calculator parse tree construction using yacc

Here, all the simple rules just return their values. The more complicated rules for statements, expression, and assignment create a node, attach the children, and return that node. Figure 8-6 shows what gets produced for some sample input.

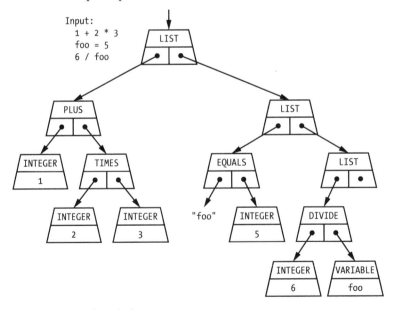

Figure 8-6: Simple calculator parse tree

As you can see, the code generates a tree. At the top level, we use the calculator rule to create a linked list of statements out of tree nodes. The remainder of the tree consists of statement nodes that contain the operator and operands.

Interpreters

Listing 8-9 includes a mysterious do_something_with function invocation that is passed the root of the parse tree. That function causes an interpreter to "execute" the parse tree. The first part of this execution is the linked-list traversal, as shown in Figure 8-7.

The second part is the evaluation, which we do recursively using depth-first traversal. This function is diagrammed in Figure 8-8.

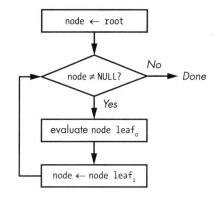

Figure 8-7: Parse tree linked-list traversal

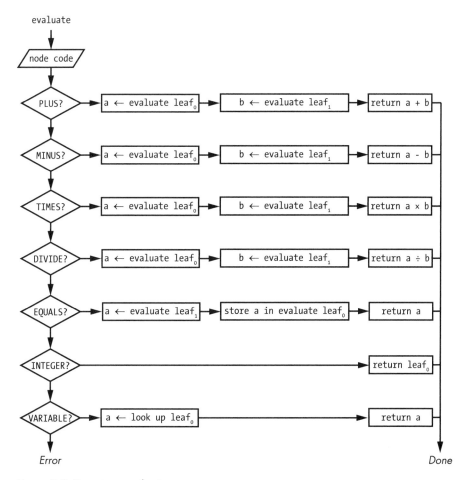

Figure 8-8: Parse tree evaluation

As you can see, it's easy to decide what to do since we have a code in our node. Observe that we need an additional function to store a variable (symbol) name and value in a *symbol table* and another to look up the value associated with a variable name. These are commonly implemented using hash tables (see "Making a Hash of Things" on page 213).

Gluing the list traversal and evaluation code into yacc allows us to immediately execute the parse tree. Another option is to save the parse tree in a file where it can be read and executed later. This is how languages such as Java and Python work. For all intents and purposes, this is a set of machine language instructions, but for a machine implemented in software instead of hardware. A program that executes the saved parse tree must exist for every target machine. Often the same interpreter source code can be compiled and used for multiple targets.

Figure 8-9 summarizes interpreters.

The front end generates the parse tree, which is represented by some *intermediate language*, and the back ends are for various machines to execute that language in their target environments.

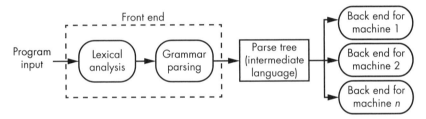

Figure 8-9: Interpreter structure

Compilers

Compilers look a lot like interpreters, but they have code generators instead of backend execution code, as shown in Figure 8-10.

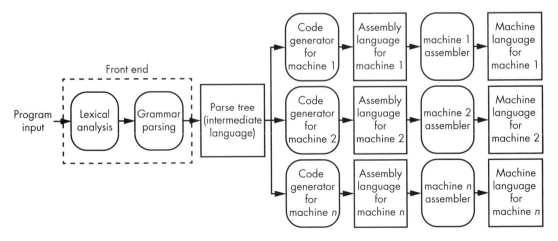

Figure 8-10: Compiler structure

A *code generator* generates machine language for a particular target machine. The tools for some languages, such as C, can generate the actual assembly language (see "Assembly Language" on page 217) for the target machine, and the assembly language is then run through that machine's assembler to produce machine language.

A code generator looks exactly like the parse tree traversal and evaluation we saw in Figures 8-7 and 8-8. The difference is that the rectangles in Figure 8-8 are replaced by ones that generate assembly language instead of executing the parse tree. A simplified version of a code generator is shown in Figure 8-11; things shown in bold monospace font (like **add tmp**) are emitted machine language instructions for our toy machine from Chapter 4. Note that the machine there didn't have multiply and divide instructions but, for this example, we pretend that it does.

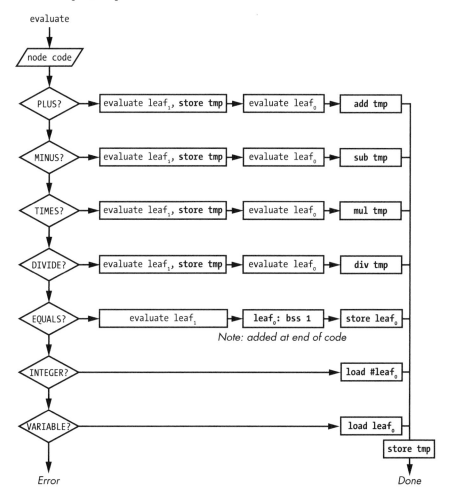

Figure 8-11: Assembler generation from parse tree

Applying Figure 8-11 to the parse tree in Figure 8-6, we get the assembly language program shown in Listing 8-10.

```
                                       ; first list element
              load     #3            ; grab the integer 3
              store    tmp           ; save it away
              load     #2            ; grab the integer 2
              mul      tmp           ; multiply the values subtree nodes
              store    tmp           ; save it away
              load     #1            ; grab the integer 1
              add      tmp           ; add it to the result of 2 times 3
              store    tmp           ; save it away
                                       ; second list element
              load     #5            ; grab the integer 5
              store    foo           ; save it in the space for the "foo" variable
              store    tmp           ; save it away
                                       ; third list element
              load     foo           ; get contents of "foo" variable
              store    tmp           ; save it away
              load     #6            ; grab the integer 6
              div      tmp           ; divide them
              store    tmp           ; save it away
tmp:          bss      1             ; storage space for temporary variable
foo:          bss      1             ; storage space for "foo" variable
```

Listing 8-10: Machine language output from code generator

As you can see, this generates fairly bad-looking code; there are a lot of unnecessary loads and stores. But what can you expect from a contrived simple example? This code would be much improved via optimization, which is discussed in the next section.

This code can be executed once it's assembled into machine language. It will run much faster than the interpreted version because it's a much smaller and more efficient piece of code.

Optimization

Many language tools include an additional step called an *optimizer* between the parse tree and the code generator. The optimizer analyzes the parse tree and performs transformations that result in more efficient code. For example, an optimizer might notice that all the operands in the parse tree on the left in Figure 8-12 are constants. It can then evaluate the expression in advance at compile time so that evaluation doesn't have to be done at runtime.

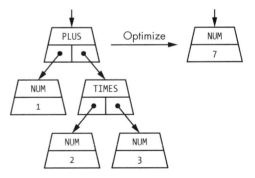

Figure 8-12: Optimizing a parse tree

The preceding example is trivial because our example calculator doesn't include any way to do conditional branching. Optimizers have a whole bag of tricks. For example, consider the code shown in Listing 8-11 (which happens to be in C).

```
for (i = 0; i < 10; i++) {
    x = a + b;
    result[i] = 4 * i + x * x;
}
```

Listing 8-11: C loop code with assignment in loop

Listing 8-12 shows how an optimizer might restructure it.

```
x = a + b;
optimizer_created_temporary_variable = x * x;
for (i = 0; i < 10; i++) {
    result[i] = 4 * i + optimizer_created_temporary_variable;
}
```

Listing 8-12: Loop code with loop invariant optimization

This example gives the same results as Listing 8-11 but is more efficient. The optimizer determined that a + b was *loop invariant*, meaning that its value didn't change inside the loop. The optimizer moved it outside the loop so it would need to be computed only once instead of 10 times. It also determined that x * x was constant inside the loop and moved that outside.

Listing 8-13 shows another optimizer trick called *strength reduction*, which is the process of replacing expensive operations with cheaper ones—in this case, multiplication with addition.

```
x = a + b;
optimizer_created_temporary_variable = x * x;
optimizer_created_4_times_i = 0;
for (i = 0; i < 10; i++) {
    result[i] = optimizer_created_4_times_i + optimizer_created_temporary_variable;
    optimizer_created_4_times_i = optimizer_created_4_times_i + 4;
}
```

Listing 8-13: C loop code with loop-invariant optimization and strength reduction

Strength reduction could also take advantage of relative addressing to make the calculation of result[i] more efficient. Going back to Figure 7-2, result[i] is the address of result plus i times the size of the array element. Just like with the optimizer_created_4_times_i, we could start with the address of result and add the size of the array element on each loop iteration instead of using a slower multiplication.

Be Careful with Hardware

Optimizers are wonderful, but they can cause unexpected problems with code that manipulates hardware. Listing 8-14 shows a variable that's actually a hardware register that turns on a light when bit 0 is set, like we saw back in Figure 6-1.

```
void
lights_on()
{
    PORTB = 0x01;
    return;
}
```

Listing 8-14: Example of code that shouldn't be optimized

This looks great, but what's the optimizer going to do? It will say, "Hey, this is being written but never read, so I can just get rid of it." Likewise, say we have the code in Listing 8-15, which turns on the light and then tests to see whether or not it's on. The optimizer would likely just rewrite the function to return 0x01 without ever storing it in PORTB.

```
unsigned int
lights_on()
{
    PORTB = 0x01;
    return (PORTB);
}
```

Listing 8-15: Another example of code that shouldn't be optimized

These examples demonstrate that you need to be able to turn off optimization in certain cases. Traditionally, you'd do so by splitting up the software into general and hardware-specific files and running the optimizer only on the general ones. However, some languages now include mechanisms that allow you to tell the optimizer to leave certain things alone. For example, in C the volatile keyword says not to optimize access to a variable.

Summary

So far in this book, you've learned how computers work and how they run programs. In this chapter, you saw how programs get transformed so that they can be run on machines and learned that programs can be compiled or interpreted.

In the next chapter, you'll meet a monster of an interpreter called a *web browser* and the languages that it interprets.

9

THE WEB BROWSER

You probably don't think of it this way, but the web browser you use every day is a *virtual machine*—an abstract computer with an incredibly complicated instruction set implemented entirely in software. In other words, it's one of those interpreters you learned about in the last chapter.

In this chapter, you'll learn about some of the functionality of this virtual machine. You'll learn about the input language and how it's interpreted by the browser. Browsers are extremely complicated beasties, however, so I can't cover every feature.

One thing that makes browsers interesting to learn about is that, on one hand, they're big, complex applications, and on the other, they're software-implemented computers that you can program. Browsers have a *developer console*, which you can use while playing with the examples from this chapter. This allows you to get a real-time view of how the browser operates.

Understanding the web browser also teaches us something about system design, which is arguably more important than programming (Chapter 15 covers system design in more detail). The popularity of the web has turned the browser into a magnet for new features. Many of these features have extended browser functionality in a compatible manner by adding to the original instruction set. Other features have duplicated existing functionality in incompatible ways, the result being that browsers now support multiple instruction sets, and the complete set of features is not available in any of them. It should become clear in this chapter that I'm not thrilled by the latter category of features—those that are merely different instead of adding value.

For starters, having multiple ways to do things means you as a programmer have a lot more to learn, which isn't a great use of your time for features that don't add value. And you need to expend energy choosing which way to do your code. Adding multiple approaches also increases the complexity of programs. Industry statistics show a direct relationship between the amount of code in a program and the number of bugs. Browsers crash often. And, as Chapter 13 covers in more detail, more complex code is more likely to contain security problems.

Incompatible ways of doing things makes programmers more prone to errors. It's like an American driving a car in New Zealand: some of the controls are in different places because New Zealanders drive on the left-hand side of the road. People from countries where you drive on the right are easy to spot, as they turn on their windshield wipers when making a turn. You don't want to program in an environment that facilitates these sorts of avoidable errors.

In my opinion, the fact that many of the web standards have become *living documents* is a clear sign of trouble. If you're not familiar with that term, I'm referring to online documents that are constantly being updated. Standards exist to provide stability and interoperability. Living documents don't; at best, they capture a moment in time. It's difficult to program to constantly changing specifications. In this context, living documents make life easier for a few document creators (because those documents and the software that they reference never have to be "done") and more difficult for a much larger number of consumers.

Markup Languages

Had this book been written 15 years earlier, this chapter would have started with an introduction to HTML, the HyperText Markup Language. But, as I've already implied, the browser has a lot in common with the Great Pacific Garbage Patch: it keeps getting bigger by attracting features that stick to it. Among these are multiple markup languages, so we'll begin with an overview of them.

Markup is a system for annotating or adding marks to text in a way that can be distinguished from that text—like homework that a teacher has written snarky comments in red pencil on.

Markup languages are not new; they existed long before computers. They were developed as a side effect of the printing press so that authors and editors could describe what they wanted to the "pressmen" who set the type. This useful notion was carried forward when computers automated typesetting. Today's markup languages are just the latest incarnations of an old idea.

There are a large number of markup languages. For example, I originally wrote this book in a markup language for typesetting called troff. The source for this paragraph is shown in Listing 9-1.

```
.PP
There are a large number of markup languages.
For example, I originally wrote this book in a markup language for
typesetting, called \fCtroff\fP.
The source for this paragraph is shown in Listing 9-1.
```

Listing 9-1: troff for the preceding paragraph

As you can see, most of it is just the text, but there are three elements of markup. The `.PP` tells troff to start a paragraph. The `\fC` tells troff to push the current font onto a stack and replace it with font C, for Courier. The `\fP` tells troff to pop the font stack (see "Stacks" on page 122), which restores the previous font.

Web pages are regular text files, just like the troff example. You don't need a fancy program to create them; you can do it in any text editor. As a matter of fact, fancy web page creation programs produce bloated results that you can easily beat by handcrafting them yourself.

How do you mark up a regular text file when the only tool available is more text? By giving superpowers to some characters, the way Superman has superpowers even though he's also a mild-mannered reporter. For example, troff gives superpowers to any line that begins with a `.` or `'` and to anything that begins with a `\`.

IBM rolled its own markup language, called *GML* (short for *Generalized Markup Language*, though it's really named for its developers, Goldfarb, Mosher, and Lorie), which the company used for its ISIL publishing tool. This work was expanded into the *Standard Generalized Markup Language (SGML)*, which was adopted by the International Standards Organization in the 1980s. SGML was so "generalized" that it's not clear that anybody was ever able to produce a complete working implementation of the standard.

eXtensible Markup Language (XML) is a more practical subset of SGML. Support for it was a later addition to browsers.

HTML and XML both have their roots in SGML. They borrow some of the same syntax but don't conform to the standard.

XHTML is a modified form of HTML that conforms to the XML rules.

Uniform Resource Locators

The first web browser (called WorldWideWeb), invented by English engineer and computer scientist Sir Tim Berners-Lee in 1990, was pretty straightforward in how it worked, as shown in Figure 9-1. The browser used a *Uniform Resource Locator (URL)* to request a document from a server using the HTTP protocol discussed in "The World Wide Web" on page 159. The server sent the document to the browser, which would display it. The document used to be written in HTML, but now it can be written in a variety of languages.

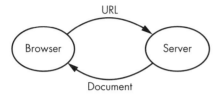

Figure 9-1: Web browser interaction with web server

URLs are text strings that have some structure. Right now we just care about the three parts of that structure shown in Figure 9-2.

Figure 9-2: Anatomy of a URL

The *scheme* indicates the communication mechanism—for example, https selects HyperText Transfer Protocol (Secure). The server that we want to communicate with is the *host*. It can be a numeric internet address (see "IP Addresses" on page 159) but is most commonly specified as a domain name (see "Domain Name System" on page 159). The location of the document to be retrieved is the *path*, which looks just like a filesystem path.

One of the schemes is file. When it's used, the host/path portion of the URL is a local filename—the name of a file on the same system on which the browser is running. In other words, the file scheme points to a file on your computer.

There are an ever-growing number of schemes, such as bitcoin for cryptocurrencies and tv for television broadcasts. These are similar, and in many cases identical, to the protocols that we saw back in "The World Wide Web."

HTML Documents

As mentioned, the first web pages were documents written in HTML. HTML utilized *hypertext*—text that links to something else, such as other web pages. Sci-fi buffs can think of it like combining hyperspace with text: you hit a link and, *zap*, you're someplace else. Hypertext has been around for quite some time, but the web was its compelling application.

Take a look at the simple HTML document in Listing 9-2.

```
<html>
    <head>
        <title>
            My First Web Page
        </title>
    </head>
    <body>
        This is my first web page.
        <b>
            <big>
                Cool!
            </big>
        </b>
    </body>
</html>
```

Listing 9-2: My First Web Page

Enter the HTML shown in Listing 9-2 into a file and open it in your browser. You should see something like Figure 9-3.

Figure 9-3: Browser display of My First Web Page

You can see that the display in Figure 9-3 doesn't look much like the text in Listing 9-2. That's because the less-than sign (<) is a character with superpowers. In this case, it begins an *element* of markup. You might notice that elements come in pairs; for each start <tag> there is a matching end </tag>.

The tag determines how the browser interprets the markup element. Tags are essentially virtual machine instructions. For example, <title> puts its contents—what's between the start and end tags—into the browser title bar. The <b> and <big> elements make the word "Cool!" bold and big, and it's part of the <body> of the web page.

Because the < has superpowers, you may wonder how to use that character without the superpowers—for example, if you wanted to display This is my first web page with a <. HTML includes its own form of kryptonite called an *entity reference*, which is an alternate form of a character. In this case, the sequence < represents the < character without triggering its superpowers. (Of course, now there's a new superpowered character &, which can itself be represented using the & sequence.) Using an entity reference, you could type This is my first web page with a < and it would look correct.

HTML elements aren't quite as simple. There are a number of random exceptions where end tags are not required, and there's a <tag/> form for elements with no content. XHTML eliminates these exceptions. The only complication that we care about here is *attributes*, which are optional sets of name/value pairs, as shown in Listing 9-3.

```
<tag name1="value1" name2="value2" ...>
    element content
</tag>
```

Listing 9-3: HTML elements with attributes

Some attribute names have predefined behaviors; you can include arbitrary attributes for any that aren't predefined. Attribute values are treated identically, with the exception of class, whose value is treated as a space-separated list of values.

The Document Object Model

Web browsers process documents according to the *Document Object Model (DOM)*. You can think of a web page as a series of elements that enclose other elements as illustrated by the indentation in the Listing 9-2 HTML. Figure 9-4, which looks sort of like an aerial cutaway view of a twisted *matryoshka* (Russian nesting) doll, shows what this structure looks like for the code in Listing 9-2.

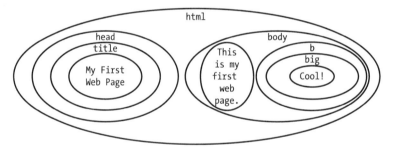

Figure 9-4: Nested elements in an HTML document

Let's grab that picture by the edge of the HTML and tilt it so that all of the innards hang out the bottom, as shown in Figure 9-5.

Look familiar? It's our old friend, the directed acyclic graph, or DAG (from "Stacks" on page 122), and a tree structure too (see "Hierarchical Data Structures" on page 199). Not only that, but the HTML can be processed using techniques from Chapter 8 and the result is a parse tree (see "Parse Trees" on page 228).

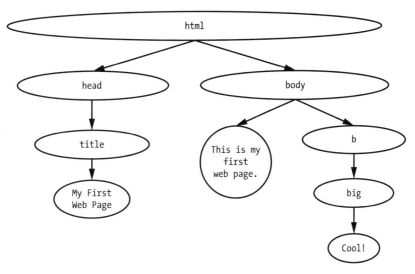

Figure 9-5: HTML document as a tree structure

Tree Lexicon

Tree structures like the DOM are so common that an entire lexicon has developed around them. The examples in Table 9-1 are taken from Figure 9-5.

Table 9-1: Tree Lexicon

Term	Definition	Example
Node	An element in the tree	html, head, body
Interior node	An element in the tree that has arrows entering and leaving	title
Terminal node	An element in the tree that has no arrows leaving it	Cool!
Root	The top of the tree	html
Parent	A node whose arrow points directly to another node	html is the parent of head and body
Child	A node directly pointed to by another node	head and body are children of html
Descendant	A node directly or indirectly pointed to by another node	title is a descendent of html
Ancestor	A node that directly or indirectly points to a node	body is an ancestor of big
Sibling	A node with a common parent	head is a sibling of body

Nodes in a tree are ordered. For example, head is the first child of html, and body is the second and also last child of html.

Interpreting the DOM

What does a browser do with a document tree? Although it's possible that someone could build a piece of computing hardware with instructions corresponding to the HTML elements, nobody has done so yet. That rules out compiling the DOM parse tree into machine language. The other choice is to interpret it using *depth-first traversal*, as shown in Figure 9-6.

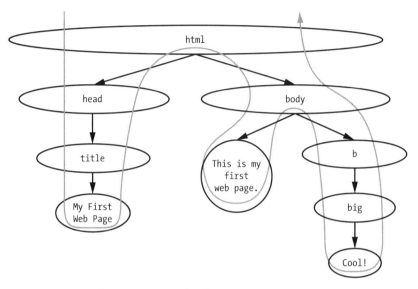

Figure 9-6: HTML document traversal order

As you can see, the browser starts at the root, descends to the first child, then to its first child, and so on until it hits a terminal node. It then goes up to the closest ancestor that has another child and does the same thing from there, and so on until every node in the tree is visited. Note that the ordering follows the way in which the HTML is written. Depth-first traversal is yet another application of stacks.

Cascading Style Sheets

An original idea behind HTML was that authors wrote web pages and browsers figured out how to display them. This made sense because there was no way for the author to know things like the size of a browser's window, the screen resolution, or the number of available colors and fonts.

Once the web became popular, the marketing types got their hands on it. Glitz became important. All sorts of stuff got added (mostly via the creation of a new CSS specification) to allow authors to finely control how their pages are displayed. Of course, this is exactly the opposite of the original intent. The result is messy.

HTML web pages originally included styling information. For example, the font element that selected a text font had a size attribute that controlled the size. This approach didn't work as well when pages were displayed on a diverse set of devices from desktops to cell phones. *Cascading Style Sheets (CSS)* separates the styling from the HTML so that the HTML can be written once and have different styles applied depending on the target device.

Figure 9-7 shows a data structure that could be used to represent an HTML element in memory.

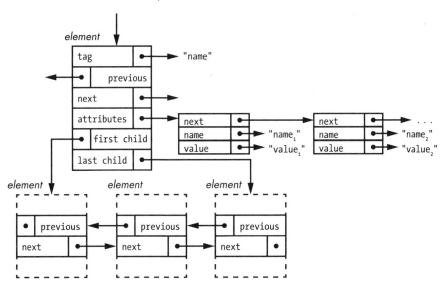

Figure 9-7: HTML element data structure

This diagram looks really complicated, but it simply glues together a few things you've already learned about. There's a compound data type (see "Compound Data Types" on page 189) for elements and another for attributes. The attributes are organized as a singly linked list (see "Singly Linked Lists" on page 191). Elements are arranged in a tree (see "Hierarchical Data Structures" on page 199). Because there are an arbitrary number of children whose ordering matters, they're organized using a doubly linked list (see "Doubly Linked Lists" on page 198).

This organization matters because CSS uses a variation of regular expressions (see "Regular Expressions" on page 224) called *selectors* to locate elements in the DOM, similar to how yacc matches tokens on a stack. CSS then allows attributes to be associated with the selected elements. This enables a web page designer, for example, to change the text size depending on the target device or to collapse a side menu into a drop-down menu for devices with smaller screens.

CSS muddies up the terminology. It defines a large number of *properties*—things like color, font size, and so on. Once these properties are associated with a DOM element, they're called *attributes*.

Table 9-2 shows some of the CSS selectors. Originally there were only a few, but new ones are being added at an alarming rate.

Table 9-2: CSS Selectors

Pattern	Meaning
*	Matches any element
E	Matches any element of type E (that is, `<E>...</E>`)
F	Matches any element of type F (that is, `<F>...</F>`)
E F	Matches any element F that is a descendent of an E element
E > F	Matches any element F that is a child of an E element
E + F	Matches any element F with an immediate sibling element E
E - F	Matches any element F preceded by any sibling element E
E[name]	Matches any element E that has attribute name
E[name=value]	Matches any element E that has attribute name with value
E[name~="value"]	Matches any E element whose name attribute is a space-separated list of words, one of which matches value
E#id	Matches any E element that has an ID attribute with a value of `id`
E.class	Matches any E element that has a class attribute with a value of `class`
E:first-child	Matches element E if it is the first child of its parent
E:last-child	Matches element E if it is the last child of its parent
E:*n*th-child(*n*)	Matches element E if it is the *n*th child of its parent
E:empty	Matches element E if it has no children
E:link	Matches element E if it is a hyperlink anchor such as `<a>`
E:visited	Matches element E if it is a hyperlink anchor such as `<a>` that has been visited
E:hover	Matches element E when the mouse hovers over it
E:active	Matches element E on which the mouse is down
E:focus	Matches element E if it has the input focus, meaning that it's listening to the keyboard

HTML includes a `<link>` element that can be used to associate a separate file containing CSS with a web page. That's the preferred usage because it conforms to the principle of keeping the content separate from the styling. But that's overkill for what we're doing here. HTML also includes a `<style>` element that allows CSS to be embedded directly in HTML documents. That's what we'll use for our examples.

Let's modify our web page from Listing 9-1 to include some simple styling, which is shown in **bold** in Listing 9-4.

```
<html>
    <head>
        <title>
            My First Web Page
        </title>
        <style>
```

```
        body {
            color:      blue;
        }
        big {
            color:      yellow;
            font-size: 200%;
        }
    </style>
</head>
<body>
    This is my first web page.
    <b>
        <big>
            Cool!
        </big>
    </b>
</body>
</html>
```

Listing 9-4: Web page with embedded CSS

You can see that there are two selectors in Listing 9-4: body and big. Each selector is followed by a list of property names and values; a colon separates each name from its value, there is a semicolon after the value, and the list of names and values for each selector is enclosed in curly brackets. First, we set the color of all text in the document body to blue. Next, we set the color of the text inside the <big> element to yellow, and we set the font-size to 200% of normal. Give it a try!

CSS was an afterthought; nobody had it in mind when developing HTML. There are some quirks as a result. HTML has all sorts of elements with defined meanings. For example, there is a <b> element that makes text **bold** and a <i> element for *italics*. But the CSS snippet in Listing 9-5 changes their meanings to be the opposite.

```
b {
    font-style:  italic;
    font-weight: normal;
}
i {
    font-style:  normal;
    font-weight: bold;
}
```

Listing 9-5: Swapping bold and italic using CSS

For all intents and purposes, CSS eliminates the distinction between many HTML elements. You can think of HTML elements as having a default set of styles, but once those styles are changed via CSS, the element name may no longer have any relation to to its original purpose.

CSS originally just provided a more flexible mechanism for attaching attributes to elements, but then it started adding new attributes. These new attributes were not retrofitted into HTML. As a result, some attributes can be specified in both HTML and CSS, and others only in CSS. There's a bit of an attitude among the programming community that the old way should no longer be used, but that ignores the issues of maintaining existing code.

XML and Friends

XML looks a lot like HTML. However, like SGML it requires *well-formed* elements. This means that each <tag> must have a matching </tag>. Implicit end tags are not permitted. The big distinction between HTML and XML is that HTML was created for a specific application: web pages. XML is a general-purpose markup language that can be used for many different applications.

Most XML tags don't have preassigned meanings. You can assign any meaning to them that you want. XML provides structure you can use to create your own application-specific markup languages. For example, suppose you want to keep track of vegetables in your garden. You could create a Vegetable Markup Language (VML) that looks like Listing 9-6.

```
<xml>
    <garden>
        <vegetable>
            <name>tomato</name>
            <variety>Cherokee Purple</variety>
            <days-until-maturity>80</days-until-maturity>
        </vegetable>
        <vegetable>
            <name>rutabaga</name>
            <variety>American Purple Top</variety>
            <days-until-maturity>90</days-until-maturity>
        </vegetable>
        <vegetable>
            <name>rutabaga</name>
            <variety>Helenor</variety>
            <days-until-maturity>100</days-until-maturity>
        </vegetable>
        <vegetable>
            <name>rutabaga</name>
            <variety>White Ball</variety>
            <days-until-maturity>75</days-until-maturity>
        </vegetable>
        <vegetable>
            <name>rutabaga</name>
            <variety>Purple Top White Globe</variety>
            <days-until-maturity>45</days-until-maturity>
            </vegetable>
    </garden>
</xml>
```

Listing 9-6: XML-based markup language example

Conflicts can arise from allowing people to create their own markup languages, however. For example, suppose that in addition to VML, someone else creates a Recipe Markup Language (RML) that also includes a <name> element, as in Listing 9-7.

```
<xml>
    <garden>
        <vegetable>
            <name>tomato</name>
            <variety>Cherokee Purple</variety>
            <days-until-maturity>80</days-until-maturity>
            <name>Purple Tomato Salad</name>
        </vegetable>
    </garden>
</xml>
```

Listing 9-7: XML-based markup language example with name conflict

There is no way to tell whether the <name> elements are vegetable names or recipe names. We need a mechanism to allow us to combine VML and RML without confusing the <name> elements. This mechanism is an element tag prefix known as a *namespace*.

As you'd expect from something browser related, there are multiple ways to specify namespaces, but I cover only one of them here. Each namespace is associated with a URL, although there's no requirement that it be a valid URL; it just has to be distinct from the others. The xmlns attribute on the <xml> element associates a namespace prefix with a URL. Listing 9-8 shows our combined garden and recipe markups with distinguishing namespaces.

```
<xml xmlns:vml="http://www.garden.org" xmlns:rml="http://www.recipe.org">
    <vml:garden>
        <vml:vegetable>
            <vml:name>tomato</vml:name>
            <vml:variety>Cherokee Purple</vml:variety>
            <vml:days-until-maturity>80</vml:days-until-maturity>
            <rml:name>Purple Tomato Salad</rml:name>
        </vml:vegetable>
    </vml:garden>
</xml>
```

Listing 9-8: XML-based markup language example with namespaces

You can see that the elements from both fictitious markup languages are combined and that they are distinguished by prefix. The namespace prefix is arbitrary and left up to whatever is combining the different markup languages together. There's no requirement that rml be the prefix for the Recipe Markup Language; we could choose recipe if we needed to combine this code with another RML, such as Ridiculous Markup Language.

Plenty of tools are available to help you write applications that understand custom markup languages such as the ones just described. There are also libraries for many programming languages that create and operate on parse trees from XML documents.

One tool is a *Document Type Definition (DTD)*. You can think of this as meta-markup. A DTD is an XML-looking document (there are no ending tags for some reason) that defines the legal elements in a markup language. XML includes a mechanism that allows an XML document to reference a DTD. You could, for example, make a DTD that says that one or more <vegetable> elements are allowed in a <garden> element and that a <vegetable> can contain only <name>, <variety>, and <days-until-maturity> elements. XML parsers can validate the XML against the DTD. Although this is useful, it doesn't do the most important part. For example, although a DTD can ensure that a required <variety> exists, it can't test for a valid variety.

The *XML Path Language (XPath)* provides selectors for XML documents by, as you might guess, creating yet another incompatible syntax; it has essentially the same functionality of CSS selectors but in a completely different syntax that you may need to learn. XPath isn't very useful by itself but is an important component of *Xtensible Stylesheet Language Transformations (XSLT)*.

XSLT is yet another XML-based language. When combined with XPath, it allows you to write a piece of XML that transforms an XML document into other forms by searching and modifying the parse tree. Listing 9-9 shows a simple example where an XPath expression is used to match any vegetable in the garden and then output the name and variety of each, separated by a space.

```
<xsl:stylesheet xmlns:xsl="http://www.w3.org/1999/XSL/Transform" version="1.0">
    <xsl:template match="/garden/vegetable">
        <xsl:value-of select="variety"/>
        <xsl:text> </xsl:text>
        <xsl:value-of select="name"/>
    </xsl:template>
</xsl:stylesheet>
```

Listing 9-9: Call any vegetable using XSLT and XPath

Applying the XSLT in Listing 9-9 to the XML in Listing 9-6 produces the results in Listing 9-10.

```
Cherokee Purple tomato
American Purple Top rutabaga
Helenor rutabaga
White Ball rutabaga
Purple Top White Globe rutabaga
```

Listing 9-10: Call any vegetable results

Another example is shown in Listing 9-11, which selects only vegetables when the value of the name is rutabaga.

```
<xsl:stylesheet xmlns:xsl="http://www.w3.org/1999/XSL/Transform" version="1.0">
    <xsl:template match="/garden/vegetable[name/text()='rutabaga']">
        <xsl:value-of select="name"/>
        <xsl:text> </xsl:text>
    </xsl:template>
```

```
    <xsl:template match="text()"/>
</xsl:stylesheet>
```

Listing 9-11: Call it by name

Applying the XSLT from Listing 9-11 to the XML in Listing 9-6 produces what you see in Listing 9-12.

```
rutabaga rutabaga rutabaga rutabaga
```

Listing 9-12: Call it by name results

XSLT is especially useful for transforming markup containing arbitrary data into HTML for display in a browser.

JavaScript

Our example web page is static—that is, all it does is display some formatted text. Going back to Figure 9-1, the only way to change what's displayed is to send another URL to a web server to get a new document. Not only is this a slow process, but it also wastes resources. If you entered a phone number into a form, the data would have to be sent to a server to determine whether it contained all numbers, and the server would have to send back a page with an error message if it didn't.

In 1993, Mark Andreesen created the graphical Mosaic web browser, which fueled the consumer internet boom. He went on to found Netscape, which released the Netscape Navigator browser in 1994. Realizing the need for more interactive web pages, Netscape introduced the JavaScript programming language in 1995. JavaScript has since been standardized by the Ecma International standards organization, formerly the European Computer Manufacturers Association, as ECMA-262. It's also known as ECMAScript, which sounds like a skin condition and has since been known to make browsers flaky. JavaScript borrowed from both the C programming language and from Java, which itself borrowed from C.

JavaScript allows web pages to contain actual programs that run on your computer instead of on the server. These programs can modify the DOM and can communicate directly with a web server, as shown in Figure 9-8.

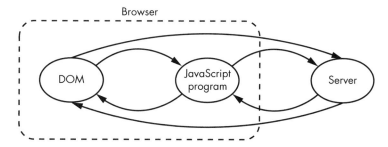

Figure 9-8: Web browser interaction with JavaScript and web server

The interaction between the JavaScript program and the server is not the same as the browser/server communication we saw in Figure 9-1. Instead, it takes place via *Asynchronous JavaScript and XML (AJAX)*. Let's break that down. *Asynchronous* is related to what we saw with ripple counters in "Counters" on page 77; in this instance, it means the browser has no control over when (and if) a server responds. The *JavaScript* part just means it's under the control of a JavaScript program. I'm not going to explain the *and*. Finally, the data from the server to the JavaScript program was initially encoded using *XML*, not HTML.

You can include JavaScript in an HTML document by enclosing it in <script> elements. Let's add some to what we had in Listing 9-4, again showing the changes in bold, in Listing 9-13.

```
<html>
    <head>
        <title>
            My First Web Page
        </title>
        <style>
            body {
                color: blue;
            }
            big {
                color:     yellow;
                font-size: 200%;
            }
        </style>
        <script>
            window.onload = function() {
                var big = document.getElementsByTagName('big');
                big[0].style.background = "green";
            }
        </script>
    </head>
    <body>
        This is my first web page.
        <b>
            <big>
                Cool!
            </big>
        </b>
    </body>
</html>
```

Listing 9-13: Web page with embedded JavaScript

Let's see what this does without going into all the nitpicky details. Part of the browser definition is that there is a `window.onload` variable that can be set to a function to execute when the initial page has finished loading. Another part of the definition says that there is a `document.getElementsByTagName` function that returns an array of all matching elements in the DOM. Here it returns the one <big> element. Finally, it allows us to change various element properties. In this case, we set the background color to green.

There are a large number of defined functions for DOM manipulation. They allow us to do more than just change CSS styles from a program. There are also functions that allow you to rearrange the DOM tree, including the ability to add and delete elements.

jQuery

Using the browser DOM functions from the previous section has two problems. First, the DOM functions don't have exactly the same behavior on different browsers. Second, they're pretty cumbersome to use—not exactly a user-friendly interface.

Enter *jQuery*, a library introduced by American software engineer John Resig in 2006. It solved both of the problems just mentioned. It smoothed over the incompatibilities between browsers so that the programmers using it didn't have to. And it supplied a DOM manipulation interface that was much easier to use.

The jQuery library combines selectors with *actions*. The code in Listing 9-14 does exactly the same thing as the code in Listing 9-13 but in a more programmer-friendly way.

```
<html>
  <head>
    <title>
      My First Web Page
    </title>
    <style>
      body {
        color:      blue;
      }
      big {
        color:      yellow;
        font-size:  200%;
      }
    </style>
    <script type="text/javascript" src="https://code.jquery.com/jquery-3.2.1.min.js"> </script>
    <script>
      $(function() {
        $('big').css('background', 'green');
      });
    </script>
  </head>
  <body>
    This is my first web page.
      <b>
        <big>
        Cool!
      </big>
      </b>
  </body>
</html>
```

Listing 9-14: Web page with embedded JavaScript and jQuery

The first `<script>` element imports the jQuery library; the second contains our code. The "document ready" function that the browser calls when the page is loaded contains a single jQuery statement. The first part of it, `$('big')`, is a selector. It's similar to the CSS selectors we saw in Table 9-2. The remainder of the statement, `.css('background', 'green')`, is an action to perform on the selected elements. In this case, the `css` function modifies the background property, setting it to green.

Let's add the piece of jQuery in Listing 9-15 to the document ready function to add some interactivity.

```
$('big').click(function() {
    $('big').before('<i>Very</i>');
    $('big').css('font-size', '500%');
});
```

Listing 9-15: jQuery event handler

This simple piece of code attaches an *event handler* to the `<big>` element that is executed when the mouse clicks it. This handler does two things: it inserts a new `<i>` element before the `<big>` element, and it increases the `<big>` font size.

As you can see in this example, jQuery makes it easy to manipulate the DOM using JavaScript. You can open up your browser's debugging console and watch these changes occur when you click.

jQuery blazed a path, and a very popular one at that; the library is very widely used. However, as seems endemic in the web community, some programmers decided to create parallel, incompatible paths. There are now a number of JavaScript libraries that do the same things, only differently.

SVG

Scalable Vector Graphics (SVG) is kind of an odd duck in the collection of browser additions. It's yet another completely different language that allows you to produce nice-looking graphics and text in a manner that is completely incompatible with everything else.

John Warnock and Chuck Geschke founded Adobe Systems in 1982 and developed the PostScript language. Warnock had been working on more complicated versions of the ideas in PostScript for years, and the development of PostScript was similar to the way that the overly complex SGML was simplified to HTML. The duo caught a lucky break when Steve Jobs requested that they use PostScript to drive laser printers. The PostScript-based Apple LaserWriter was a major factor in the formation of the desktop publishing industry and was responsible for Adobe's success.

PostScript had some issues with *portability*—getting the same results everywhere. The *Portable Document Format (PDF)*, based on PostScript, was created to address these issues. SVG is more or less PDF wedged into browsers. Of course, SVG and PDF aren't completely compatible because that would make too much sense.

In general, SVG is more automatic than the recently added canvas (covered in the next section). You can tell it to do things, and it will, whereas with a canvas you have to write a program to manipulate it. Add the contents of Listing 9-16 to the body of your web page and give it a spin, because every web page needs a red pulsing circle.

```
<br>
<svg xmlns="http://www.w3.org/2000/svg" width="400" height="400">
  <circle id="c" r="10" cx="200" cy="200" fill="red"/>
  <animate xlink:href="#c" attributeName="r" from="10" to="200" dur="5s" repeatCount="indefinite"/>
</svg>
```

Listing 9-16: SVG animated circle

HTML5

As I mentioned at the beginning of this chapter, it seems that in the browser world, there's no idea that should be implemented only once. HTML5 is the latest incarnation of HTML. Among other things, it adds a big pile of *semantic* elements, including `<header>`, `<footer>`, and `<section>`, which—if used as intended—would add consistent structure to documents.

HTML5 introduces the *canvas*, which provides pretty much the same functionality as SVG but in a completely different way. The major difference is that canvases can be manipulated only with a new set of JavaScript functions, unlike SVG, which can use the existing DOM functions. In other words, you would have to write a JavaScript program in order to duplicate Listing 9-16 using a canvas.

HTML5 also adds `<audio>` and `<video>`, which provide somewhat standard mechanisms for audio and video.

JSON

I touched on AJAX back in "JavaScript" on page 251 and mentioned that asynchronous XML-formatted data is sent from the server to the browser JavaScript program. Well, that's *so* four sections ago. The *X* in AJAX is now a *J* for JSON. Although the acronym AJAJ floats around, the technique is still called AJAX.

JSON stands for JavaScript Object Notation. It's essentially a human-readable text format for a JavaScript *object*, which is one of JavaScript's compound data types. The theory is that data in this format can be exchanged in an interoperable manner, although problems with the specification mean that this exchange is possible only if you adhere to certain unspecified rules such as avoiding certain characters. Programmers also need to work around the fact that JSON doesn't support all the JavaScript data types.

Listing 9-17 builds a JavaScript object and converts it to JSON format. It then shows the result that was stored in the variable **the_quest**, shown in bold below.

```
var argonauts = {};
argonauts.goal = "Golden Fleece";
argonauts.sailors = [];
argonauts.sailors[0] = { name: "Acastus", father: "Pelias" };
argonauts.sailors[1] = { name: "Actor", father: "Hippasus" };
argonauts.sailors[2] = { name: "Admentus", father: "Pheres" };
argonauts.sailors[3] = { name: "Amphiarus", father: "Oicles" };
argonauts.sailors[4] = { name: "Ancaeus", father: "Poseidon" };

var the_quest = JSON.stringify(argonauts);

"{
    "goal": "Golden Fleece",
    "sailors": [
        { "name": "Acastus", "father": "Pelias" },
        { "name": "Actor", "father": "Hippasus" },
        { "name": "Admentus", "father": "Pheres" },
        { "name": "Amphiarus", "father": "Oicles" },
        { "name": "Ancaeus", "father": "Poseidon" }
    ]
}"
```

Listing 9-17: JSON and the Argonauts

JSON has an advantage over XML when using JavaScript, and not just because converting JavaScript objects into JSON is trivial, as shown in Listing 9-17. The companion JavaScript eval function can execute JSON directly, because it's data, as if it's a JavaScript program. JSON is popular because it eliminates the need for extra code to handle data export and import.

Just because it's easy to use JSON doesn't mean you can be cavalier about it, however. Blithely importing JSON data using eval can allow an attacker to execute arbitrary code in a browser. More recently, a companion JSON.parse function has been added that safely converts JSON back into a JavaScript object.

Summary

In this chapter, you've learned the basics of how many of the components comprising a web browser work. Figure 9-9 illustrates the pieces we've discussed. Of course, browsers include a lot more functionality that isn't particularly interesting, such as bookmarks and history.

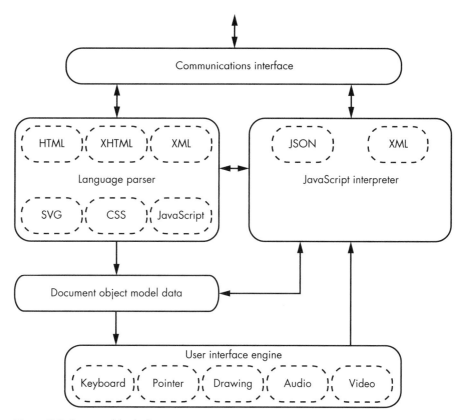

Figure 9-9: Browser block diagram

The diagram may look pretty complicated, but it's just an assemblage of parts that you've already seen. These include language parsers, parse trees, regular expressions, interpreters, networking, input, and output.

It also illustrates a distinction between hardware and software design. Designing hardware is more expensive than designing software. It's unlikely that a hardware designer would construct a system that used six different incompatible methods to do the same thing before breakfast. But because there isn't the same up-front cost in software, software designers are often less careful. The result is often a larger, more complex result that might cost less up front but often costs more later because of the number of complicated interoperating parts that must be maintained.

Now that you've learned something about the workings of this complex interpreter, in the next chapter we'll write some programs for it. You'll see a program written for a browser in JavaScript and the same program written in C. This will illustrate some of the important system-level considerations that are hidden from web programmers but are important for system-level programming.

10

APPLICATION AND SYSTEM PROGRAMMING

Chapter 9 covered how web browsers work. You learned that browsers are complex application programs that provide software-implemented "computers" that support very high-level "instructions." In this chapter, we'll write a program that runs in a browser, followed by a similar program that doesn't use the browser. The structure of the two programs is shown in Figure 10-1.

The operating system hides much of the I/O device complexity from user programs. In a similar manner, a complex user program such as a browser hides much of the complexity of dealing with operating systems from application programs that are built on top of them. This is fine if you're going to limit yourself to being a high-level application writer. But you need to know more if you're going to be a system programmer.

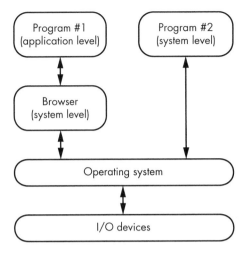

Figure 10-1: Two program scenarios

This chapter includes lengthier JavaScript and C code examples than you've seen before. Don't worry if you're not fluent in these languages—you don't need to know all the details to follow along.

Let's look at a game in which the computer asks the user a series of questions to try to guess an animal. New animals and questions that distinguish them are added to the program as needed. The program "learns" by constructing a binary tree of knowledge.

The interaction between the *computer* (the literal text) and the *user* (the **literal bold** text) looks something like this:

```
Think of an animal.
Does it bark?
Yes
Is it a dog?
Yes
I knew it!
Let's play again.
Think of an animal.
Does it bark?
Yes
Is it a dog?
No
I give up. What is it?
giant purple snorklewhacker
What's a question that I could use to tell a giant purple snorklewhacker from a dog?
Does it live in an anxiety closet?
Thanks. I'll remember that.
Let's play again.
Think of an animal.
Does it bark?
```

Yes
Is it a dog?
No
Does it live in an anxiety closet?
Yes
Is it a giant purple snorklewhacker?
Yes
I knew it!
Let's play again.

Figure 10-2 shows the implementation plan.

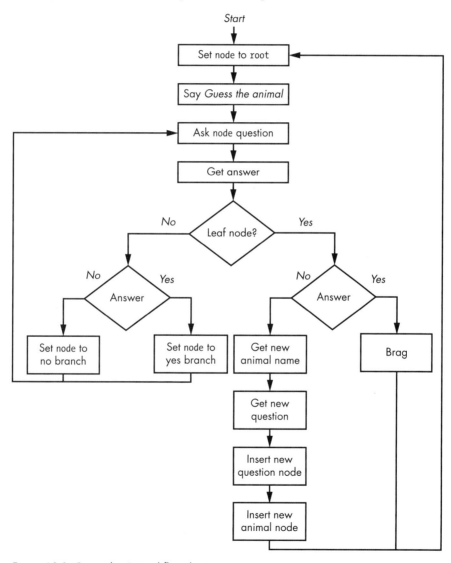

Figure 10-2: Guess the Animal flowchart

As you can see, we ask questions that guide our descent through the tree of knowledge. We congratulate ourselves when we guess correctly. Otherwise, we ask the user to supply the answer and a question, add them to the tree, and start over.

The program follows a path down the tree of knowledge on the left side. When it reaches the end of the path on the right, it either brags or adds to the knowledge base.

Guess the Animal Version 1: HTML and JavaScript

On to the program. We'll go about this in a way that, although convenient, will upset some of my colleagues. This is a *clever hack*—something that works but is a bit twisted and ugly. As you saw in the previous chapter, the DOM is a tree that is a subset of a DAG—same with a binary tree. We're going to build the binary tree of knowledge in the DOM as a set of nested, invisible <div>s. We could create a data structure in JavaScript, but the browser already has something easy that works. As Figure 10-3 shows, our program starts off with an initial question and two answers in the knowledge tree.

```
<div string="Does it bark?">
    <div string="dog"></div>
    <div string="cat"></div>
</div>
```

Figure 10-3: Initial knowledge tree

Let's play the game. We answer yes in response to Does it bark? and when the program guesses Is it a dog? we answer no. The program then asks What is it? and we respond with giant purple snorklewhacker. The program then asks us what question would distinguish a giant purple snorkle-whacker from a dog and uses our response of Does it live in an anxiety closet? to modify the knowledge tree, as shown in Figure 10-4.

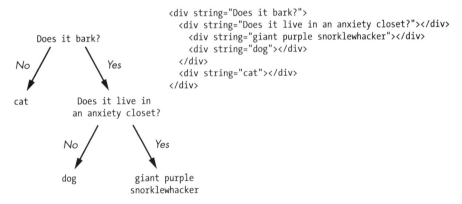

```
<div string="Does it bark?">
    <div string="Does it live in an anxiety closet?"></div>
        <div string="giant purple snorklewhacker"></div>
        <div string="dog"></div>
    </div>
    <div string="cat"></div>
</div>
```

Figure 10-4: Modified knowledge tree

Application-Level Skeleton

Listing 10-1 shows the web page skeleton into which we'll add the code. Purists would be very upset at this because it combines HTML, CSS, and JavaScript into a single file. But we're building a simple program, not a website, so it's convenient to have everything in one place.

```
1  <html>
2    <head>
3      <!-- include jQuery -->
4      <script type="text/javascript" src="https://code.jquery.com/jquery-3.1.1.min.js"> </script>
5
6      <title>Web Page Skeleton</title>
7
8      <style>
9        <!-- CSS goes here -->
10     </style>
11
12     <script type="text/javascript">
13
14       <!-- JavaScript goes here -->
15
16       $(function() {
17         <!-- JavaScript to run when document ready -->
18       });
19
20     </script>
21   </head>
22
23   <body>
24     <!-- HTML goes here -->
25   </body>
26 </html>
```

Listing 10-1: Web page skeleton

You can change the title to something like `Guess the Animal` yourself.

You learned about web browser components in the last chapter (see Figure 9-9). Now we'll put some of them to use.

Web Page Body

Let's start by looking at the `<body>` of the program in Listing 10-2. This replaces the `<!-- HTML goes here -->` from line 24 of Listing 10-1.

```
1  <!-- This is the knowledge tree that is never visible -->
2
3  <div id="root" class="invisible">
4    <div string="Does it bark">
5      <div string="dog"></div>
6      <div string="cat"></div>
7    </div>
8  </div>
9
```

```
10 <div id="dialog">
11   <!-- The conversation will go here -->
12 </div>
13
14 <!-- Get new animal name dialog -->
15
16 <div id="what-is-it" class="start-hidden">
17   <input id="what" type="text"/>
18   <button id="done-what">Done</button>
19 </div>
20
21 <!-- Get new animal question dialog -->
22
23 <div id="new-question" class="start-hidden">
24   What's a good question that I could use to tell a
25   <span id="new"></span> from a <span id="old"></span>?
26   <input id="question" type="text"/>
27   <button id="done-question">Done</button>
28 </div>
29
30 <!-- Yes and no buttons -->
31
32 <div id="yesno" class="start-hidden">
33   <button id="yes">Yes</button>
34   <button id="no">No</button>
35 </div>
```

Listing 10-2: Guess the Animal HTML

You can see in lines 3 through 8 that the knowledge tree is preloaded with an initial question and answers. The string attribute is the question, except for leaf nodes where it is the animal name. The question contains two <div>s, the first being for the yes answer and the second for the no. The tree is wrapped in a <div> styled so that it's never visible.

The dialog in lines 10 through 12 holds the conversation between the computer and the player. Then what-is-it (lines 16–19) contains a text field for the name of a new animal and a button the player presses when done. After that, new-question (lines 23–28) contains a text field for the new question and a button the player presses when done. The yes and no buttons are in yesno (lines 32–35). The three user input <div>s (lines 16, 23, and 32) have a start-hidden class that is used to make these values invisible at the beginning of a game.

The JavaScript

Let's move on to the actual JavaScript. The first part is shown in Listing 10-3.

The first thing we do is declare the variable node where the skeleton says <!-- JavaScript goes here --> on line 14 of Listing 10-1. Although it could go inside the document ready function, putting it outside makes it easier to access using the browser developer console. We also declare two functions outside of the document ready function since they don't rely on the page being loaded.

```
1 var node; // current position in tree of knowledge
2
3 // Append the supplied html to the dialog. Bail if the new node has
4 // no children because there is no question to ask. Otherwise, make
5 // the new node the current node and ask a question using the string
6 // attribute of the node. Turn the animal name into a question if a
7 // leaf node. Returns true if the new node is a leaf node.
8
9 function
10 question(new_node, html)
11 {
12    $('#dialog').append(html);      // add the html to the dialog
13
14    if ($(new_node).length == 0) { // no question if no children
15      return (true);
16    }
17    else {
18      node = new_node;              // descend to new node
19
20      if ($(node).children().length == 0)
21        $('#dialog').append('Is it a ' + $(node).attr('string') + '?');
22      else
23        $('#dialog').append($(node).attr('string') + '?');
24
25      return (false);
26    }
27 }
28
29 // Restarts the game. Hides all buttons and text fields, clears
30 // the text fields, sets the initial node and greeting, asks the
31 // first question, displays the yes/no buttons.
32
33 function
34 restart()
35 {
36    $('.start-hidden').hide();
37    $('#question,#what').val('');
38    question($('#root>div'), '<div><b>Think of an animal.</b></div>');
39    $('#yesno').show();
40 }
```

Listing 10-3: Guess the Animal JavaScript variable and functions

Next, the <!-- JavaScript to run when document ready --> from line 17 of Listing 10-1 gets the five things shown in Listing 10-4.

```
1 restart(); // Sets everything up the first time through.
2
3 // The user has entered a new question. Make a node with that
4 // question and put the old no-node into it. Then, make a node
5 // with the new animal and put it into the new question node ahead
6 // of the old no-node so that it becomes the yes choice. Start over.
7
```

```
 8 $('#done-question').click(function() {
 9   $(node).wrap('<div string="' + $('#question').val() + '"></div>');
10   $(node).parent().prepend('<div string="' + $(what).val() + '"></div>');
11   $('#dialog').append("<div>Thanks! I'll remember that.</div><p>");
12   restart();
13 });
14
15 // The user has entered a new animal name and clicked done. Hide
16 // those items and make the new-question text field and done button
17 // visible. Plug the old and new animal names into the query.
18
19 $('#done-what').click(function() {
20   $('#what-is-it').hide();
21   $('#new').text($('#what').val());
22   $('#old').text($(node).attr('string'));
23   $('#new-question').show();
24   $('#dialog div:last').append(' <i>' + $('#what').val() + '</i>');
25 });
26
27 // The user clicked yes in answer to a question. Descend the tree
28 // unless we hit bottom in which case we boast and start over.
29
30 $('#yes').click(function() {
31   if (question($(node).children(':first-child'), ' <i>yes</i><br>')) {
32     $('#dialog').append("<div>I knew it! I'm so smart!</div><p>");
33     restart();
34   }
35 });
36
37 // The user clicked no in answer to a question. Descend the tree
38 // unless we hit bottom, in which case we hide the yes/no buttons
39 // and make the what-is-it text field and done button visible.
40
41 $('#no').click(function() {
42   if (question($(node).children(':last-child'), ' <i>no</i><br>')) {
43     $('#yesno').hide();
44     $('#dialog').append('<div>I give up. What is it?</div>');
45     $('#what-is-it').show();
46   }
47 });
```

Listing 10-4: Guess the Animal document ready function JavaScript

We invoke the restart function (line 1) to start the game. The other four things are *event handlers*, the JavaScript equivalent of the interrupt handlers introduced in Chapter 5. There is one event handler for each of the four button elements. Each handler calls an anonymous function (an inline function that doesn't have a name) when the associated button is pressed.

Practice your text-editing skills by typing in the program. Save the results in a file named something like *gta.html* and then open the file in your browser. Play the game. Open up the developer tools in your browser and find the HTML inspector; this allows you to look at the HTML that makes up the web page. Watch the tree of knowledge get built as you play.

The CSS

As we touched on in Chapter 9, classes give us a way to label elements so that they can be easily selected. CSS is primarily used for static declarations of properties; it becomes dynamic mostly via programmatic manipulation. The HTML in Listing 10-2 has two CSS classes: start-hidden is dynamic, and invisible is static.

The class attribute is used to make several of the HTML elements in Listing 10-5 members of the start-hidden class. This isn't just to make our program classy; it's to give us a way to locate all of these elements with a simple selector. These elements are made invisible whenever the program is started or restarted. They're made visible as the program runs, and start-hidden allows us to reset everything simply.

The element with the invisible class is always invisible, as it's the tree of knowledge. Thus, the CSS shown in Listing 10-5 replaces the `<!-- CSS goes here -->` in line 9 of Listing 10-1.

```
1 invisible {
2   display: none; /* elements with this class are not displayed */
3 }
```

Listing 10-5: Guess the Animal CSS

Note that you can use *inline style* for simple CSS instead, because of course there has to be more than one way to do things in a browser. Writing line 3 of Listing 10-2 as `<div id="root" style="display: none">` would have the same effect.

Guess the Animal Version 2: C

As I've mentioned, browsers are high-level virtual machines—all their functionality is implemented in software. This enables us to quickly and easily construct our program in part by hiding some of the important underpinnings. Let's rewrite the program in C so that more of the primitive actions that browsers hide are exposed. This discussion assumes a UNIX-derived operating system.

Terminals and the Command Line

Our C program is going to be extremely retro in that it's not going to have any fancy buttons or graphics. It will use the command line in a manner similar to the ancient game of *Adventure*. This is a great opportunity to learn more about how input and output work rather than relying on the fancy widgets built into browsers.

What do I mean by "retro" and "command line"? As Chapter 1 mentions, human language likely started as sounds and gestures, with writing being invented *much* later. Computer language is the opposite. While interaction did start with pushing buttons and flipping switches when computers still had front panels, it quickly evolved to written language, with gesture and sound recognition coming later. Humans would type and computers would "type back" on terminals (see "Terminals" on page 176).

You probably use a *graphical user interface (GUI)* to communicate with your computer. It's actually pretty Stone Age if you think about it. *"Ugh! Look! Button! Press! Friend! Cat video! Like! Tweet Tweet Tweet!"* GUIs mostly use gestural language, which works well for casual computer users because it doesn't rely too much on users' memories—or at least it didn't in the days before all the icons were changed to be universally unrecognizable.

Most computer systems still support a written command line interface behind all the fancy graphics. Terminals are now implemented in software instead of being a piece of hardware external to the computer. You'll get a *command prompt* if you open up the terminal application on your computer; you can type in it, and it will respond.

Instead of using buttons for yes and no, the C version of our program expects the player to type y or n into the terminal program, followed by the ENTER, RETURN, or ⏎ key (depending on keyboard). The player similarly types in new animal names and questions. The program also accepts q to quit.

Building the Program

Because C is a compiled language, we can't just "run" the source code like we could with the interpreted JavaScript version. We have to convert it into machine language first. We can do this pretty easily using the command line. If the source is in a file named, for example, *gta.c*, you can generate a machine language file called *gta* by typing the command shown in Figure 10-5 into your terminal.

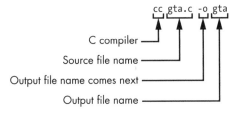

Figure 10-5: Building the program

Once you have the output file, you can typically just type its name to run it.

Terminals and Device Drivers

A terminal is an I/O device, and—as mentioned in "System and User Space" on page 133—user programs don't talk to I/O devices directly; the operating system mediates, as shown in Figure 10-6.

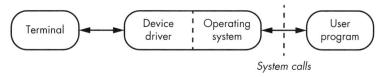

Figure 10-6: I/O device mediation

Back when terminals were separate devices, the computer and the terminal were connected through an RS-232 serial connection (see "Serial Communication" on page 152). There were physical wires connecting terminals and computers. Operating systems still pretend that this type of connection exists today, mimicking it in software so that legacy programs continue to work unmodified.

Context Switching

The device driver is more complicated than it seems because a primary reason we have operating systems is so that more than one user program can run at the same time. Because the computer has only one set of registers, the OS must save and restore their contents when switching between user programs. There's actually a lot of stuff that needs to be saved and restored other than the CPU registers, including the MMU registers and state of any I/O. The whole pile is called the *process context*, or just *context*. We don't want to do *context switching* frivolously because the size of the context makes it comparatively expensive. The system call process is shown in Figure 10-7.

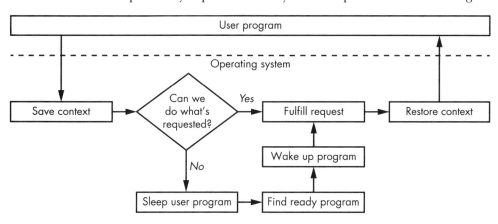

Figure 10-7: Context switching

As you can see, a lot of work happens behind the scenes when a system call is made. And, as mentioned back in "Relative Addressing" on page 128, sometimes the OS will *sleep* a user program, even when it can fulfill a request, in order to give another user program a chance to run.

We don't want to do a context switch every time a user presses a key. One way to minimize context switching in this case is to realize we usually don't care what the user is typing until they hit ENTER. The user program uses a system call to indicate that it wants to *read* from the terminal. This puts the user program to sleep, because it can't do anything while it's waiting, which allows the OS to perform some other operation, such as switching to run another program. The *device driver* that handles the idiosyncrasies of the physical device can save characters from the terminal in a *buffer* and *wake up* the user program only when the user hits ENTER instead of on every keypress.

What's a buffer? We saw one back in Figure 6-25; it's a *first-in, first-out (FIFO)* data structure, at least in software land. (In hardware land, a buffer is often a circuit used to protect delicate components from buffoons.) Figure 10-8 depicts a FIFO, also known as a *queue*, which is similar to being in line at the grocery store. As with stacks, a FIFO can overflow by running out of space and underflow by fetching from an empty queue.

Figure 10-8: Dog in queue

Terminals usually operate in full-duplex mode (see "Serial Communication" on page 152), which means there is no direct connection between the keyboard and the display; the keyboard sends data to the computer, and the display receives data from the computer. Originally, as mentioned earlier, there were separate physical wires for each direction. It's not enough, then, for the terminal device driver to buffer up the input because the user will get confused unless what they type is *echoed* so they can see it. And terminals are often slower than programs that write to them, so an *output buffer* is used in addition to the *input buffer*. A program is put to sleep if it tries to write to a full output buffer. The driver might provide the user some feedback, such as beeping if the input buffer becomes full. The part of the driver that we've been discussing looks like Figure 10-9.

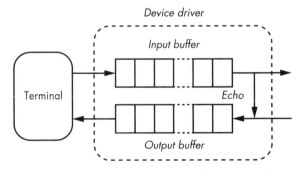

Figure 10-9: Terminal device driver buffering and echoing

Real device drivers are more complicated. Additional system calls are used to modify the driver settings. Echoing can be turned on and off. Buffering can be turned off, which is known as *raw* mode, whereas turning it on is known, of course, as *cooked* mode. The key(s) that wake up the user program can be set, along with much more, such as which key erases characters (usually BACKSPACE or DELETE).

Standard I/O

Buffering in the device driver solves only part of the problem. User programs have similar issues. It doesn't do any good to have the device driver buffer up input just to have a user program make a system call for each character. The output buffer doesn't help too much if the user program makes a system call to write each character. This is a common enough situation that it prompted the creation of the *standard input/output* library (stdio), which contains buffered I/O functions for user programs.

The stdio library supports buffered input, in which as much input as possible is read from the device driver in a single system call and placed into a buffer. The user program gets characters from the buffer until it's empty, then tries to get more. On the output side, characters are buffered until either the buffer is full or an important character such as a newline occurs. Together it looks like Figure 10-10.

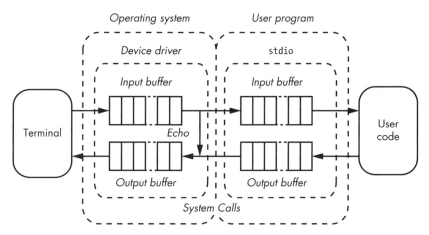

Figure 10-10: User program with stdio buffering

Seems like a lot of work just to make things run efficiently! And we're not done yet. How does the user program get connected to the terminal device driver?

It's way easier to reference someone by their name than it is to provide their complete description, and operating systems take a similar approach to access files. The open system call converts a filename into a *handle* or *file descriptor* that can be used to reference the file until it is closed via the close system call. This is akin to getting a claim ticket when you check your backpack in a museum. The stdio library includes analogous fopen and fclose functions that use the system calls but also set up and tear down the buffering system. Because the UNIX abstractions treat devices just like files, you can open a special file such as */dev/tty* to access a terminal device.

Circular Buffers

Earlier I said queues are like being in line at a grocery store. Although they do have that outward appearance, that's not how buffers such as the stdio output buffer in Figure 10-10 are actually implemented.

Think about what happens in a grocery line. When the person in front is done, everybody else in line must move forward one position. Let's queue up a frog, as shown in Figure 10-11. As you can see, we need to keep track of the end of the line so we know where to insert things.

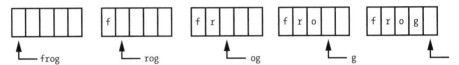

Figure 10-11: Inserting into a queue

Now let's look at what happens when the frog is removed from the queue (Figure 10-12).

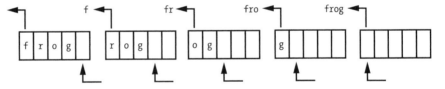

Figure 10-12: Removing from a queue

As you can see, a lot of work is involved. When the f is removed, the r must be copied to where the f was, then the o to where the r was, and so on. Let's try a different approach. Rather than everyone in the line moving, let's have the checker get some exercise in Figure 10-13.

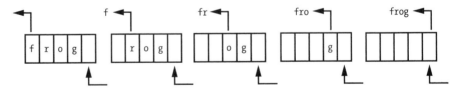

Figure 10-13: Removing from a queue by moving the checker

This is a lot less work, except for the checker. But it causes a new problem. At some point, the line backs up to the door even though there's space at the front. Nobody else can get in line.

What we need is some way to funnel new people into the space at the front of the line. We can do this by bending the line so that it's circular, as shown in Figure 10-14.

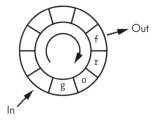

Figure 10-14: Circular buffer

As you can see, data can be added to the queue as long as the *in* arrow is clockwise from the *out* arrow. Likewise, data in the queue can be removed as long as the out arrow is counterclockwise from the in arrow. A bit of arithmetic is needed to wrap around from the end of the buffer to the beginning. The next location is the current one plus 1, modulo the buffer size.

These structures have many names, including *circular buffers*, *circular queues*, and *ring buffers*. They're a pretty standard approach, and not just in stdio or device drivers.

Better Code Through Good Abstractions

Every time we play the Guess the Animal game, we start over from scratch with a program that knows only about cats and dogs. It would be nice if we could remember our game and continue where we left off. That's easy to do in our C program; it's a side benefit that results from the file abstraction.

Adding such a feature to the JavaScript version is much more difficult. Figure 10-15 illustrates why.

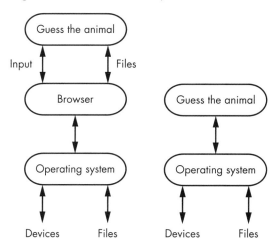

Figure 10-15: Browser and operating system interfaces

You can see that the OS has a single interface that works for both devices and files. This interface is used both by the browser on the left and by the C version of the program on the right. That means the C program, like the browser, can use the same code to read input from a file as it does to read user input from a device. But the browser doesn't pass this abstraction on to the JavaScript programmer. Instead, a completely separate piece of code using a completely different interface would be needed to add the new feature there. The choice of interface can have a big impact on both the ease of programming and the clarity of the result.

Some Mechanics

Back to our C program. Getting a C program ready to run requires compiling it and then *linking* it to other code that it uses, such as the stdio library. The section "Running Programs" on page 137 mentions that a runtime library is also included; the C version is often named crt0. It's responsible for tasks like setting up the stack and the heap so they're ready to use. It also opens up a pair of files that are connected to the terminal device driver by default, one for input and one for output.

The stdio library maps the system file descriptors into *file pointers*, addresses that reference the data structures that it uses for buffering and bookkeeping. It starts with three: stdin (standard input), stdout (standard output), and stderr (standard error). The intent is for things that are important to go to stderr instead of stdout; they both go to the same place, but stderr is unbuffered and stdout is buffered. If you use stdout for error messages, they get buffered, and you may never see them if your program crashes. The file pointers stdout and stderr share the same file descriptor, as shown in Figure 10-16, unless changed.

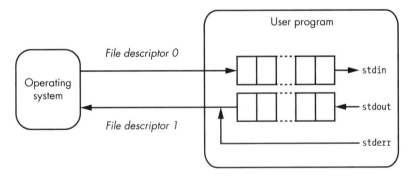

Figure 10-16: The file pointers stdin, stdout, and stderr

Invention is often sparked by strange events. According to Steve Johnson, stderr was not part of the original stdio library; it was added as a side effect of the development of the first computer typesetting software (troff, written by Joseph Ossanna, 1928–1977) for the C/A/T photoypesetter. You take laser and inkjet printing for granted, but this beast projected images onto silver photographic paper, which then had to be developed. That became very expensive when the Hunt brothers cornered the silver market, and folks were asked to cut down on phototypesetter use. It was not uncommon to send a job to the typesetter only to get back a beautifully formatted page containing a `cannot open file` error message. The `stderr` file pointer was born so that error messages could go to the terminal instead of to the typesetter in order to save money.

Buffer Overflow

As long as we're on the subject of `stdio`, let's talk about a class of very serious system programming errors called *buffer overflow*. When `stdio` was originally written, it included a function called `gets` that read a string up to the next newline character from `stdin` into a user-supplied buffer. We could use it as shown in Listing 10-6 to read the y, n, or q response; there's room in `buffer` for the character and a NUL terminator.

```
1 char buffer[2];
2
3 gets(buffer);
```

Listing 10-6: Using gets to read input

Why might this be a problem? Because gets doesn't check to make sure that the input doesn't run off the end of the buffer. Say we have a more serious program that also has a variable named `launch_missiles`, which just happens to be the next thing in memory (Figure 10-17).

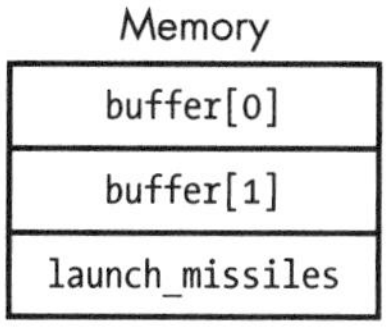

Memory

| buffer[0] |
| buffer[1] |
| launch_missiles |

Figure 10-17: Buffer overflow in memory

A malicious user might discover that answering yyy would store a y in `launch_missiles`, which for all intents and purposes is the same as the non-existent `buffer[2]`. That could get really ugly. As a matter of fact, it has. A very large number of discovered security issues result from exactly this sort of buffer overflow bug. This was fixed in `stdio` by the addition of an `fgets` function that checks bounds. But be careful—there are many, many ways in which buffer overflow bugs can occur. *Never, ever assume that buffer sizes are big enough!* There's more detail about buffer overflows in Chapter 13.

The C Program

There are many C libraries in addition to `stdio`. The `string` library, for example, includes functions for comparing and copying strings, and the catchall standard library `stdlib` includes functions for memory management.

Listing 10-7 shows the C program for our game's prologue. The first part brings in the library information we need (lines 1–3). Next, a node structure is declared (lines 5–9) that contains pointers to two leaves and a placeholder for the question or animal string. Note that we didn't have to do something like this in our JavaScript version because we took advantage of the existing HTML <div>; had we not done that, there would have been a JavaScript equivalent. Notice that the node structure is defined such that we can allocate the node and string together, as in "More Efficient Memory Allocation" on page 196.

```
1 #include <stdio.h>  // standard I/O library
2 #include <stdlib.h> // standard library for exit and malloc
3 #include <string.h> // string library
4
5 struct node {
6    struct node *no;  // references no answer node
7    struct node *yes; // references yes answer node
8    char string[1];   // question or animal
9 };
```

Listing 10-7: Guess the Animal in C: prologue

Next, we define a function to help with memory allocation (Listing 10-8). Although memory allocation is no big deal, we need to do it in several places, and it gets tedious to check for errors each time. More recent languages include exception-handling constructs that make this sort of thing simpler.

Since the only time that we need to allocate memory is when making a new node, we use a function that takes the string to install in the node. In addition to allocating memory, the string is copied into the node, and the yes and no pointers are initialized.

```
10 struct  node    *
11 make_node(char *string)
12 {
13     struct  node    *memory;        // newly allocated memory
14
15     if ((memory = (struct node *)malloc(sizeof (struct node) + strlen(string))) == (struct node *)0) {
16         (void)fprintf(stderr, "gta: out of memory.\n");
17         exit(-1);
18     }
19
20     (void)strcpy(memory->string, string);
21     memory->yes = memory->no = (struct node *)0;
22
23     return (memory);
24 }
```

Listing 10-8: Guess the Animal in C: memory allocator

We use the fprintf function in stdio for our error message because, as discussed earlier, things sent to stderr are unbuffered, which gives us a better chance of seeing the message if the program fails unexpectedly.

Note that the cast operator is used to cast the fprintf as void on line 16. When fprintf returns a value that we're ignoring, the cast tells the compiler that we're doing it deliberately, instead of forgetting to check something, so that it doesn't generate warning messages. It also informs someone reading the code that the return value is being deliberately ignored, so it's not a mistake. Recent changes to some compilers eliminate these warnings unless explicitly requested.

The call to exit on line 17 terminates the program. That's the only reasonable option when there isn't enough memory available to continue running the program.

The printf (*print formatted*) function is part of stdio and has made its way into many other languages. The first argument is a *format string* that determines the interpretation of the remainder of the arguments. A % followed by a code means "replace me with the next argument according to the code." In this case, %s means "treat the next argument as a string."

The rest of the program is shown in Listing 10-9.

```
25 int
26 main(int argc, char *argv[])
27 {
28     char          animal[50];     // new animal name buffer
29     char          buffer[3];      // user input buffer
30     int           c;              // current character from buffer
31     struct  node  **current;      // current tree traversal node
32     FILE          *in;            // input file for training data or typing
33     struct  node  *new;           // newly created node
34     FILE          *out;           // output file for saving training data
35     char          *p;             // newline removal pointer
36     char          question[100];  // new question buffer
37     struct  node  *root;          // root of the tree of knowledge
38
39     //  Process the command line arguments.
40
41     in = out = (FILE *)0;
42
43     for (argc--, argv++; argc > 1 && argc % 2 == 0; argc -= 2, argv += 2) {
44         if (strcmp(argv[0], "-i") == 0 && in == (FILE *)0) {
45             if ((in = fopen(argv[1], "r")) == (FILE *)0) {
46                 (void)fprintf(stderr, "gta: can't open input file `%s'.\n", argv[1]);
47                 exit(-1);
48             }
49         }
50
51         else if (strcmp(argv[0], "-o") == 0 && out == (FILE *)0) {
```

```
52          if ((out = fopen(argv[1], "w")) == (FILE *)0) {
53              (void)fprintf(stderr, "gta: can't open output file `%s'.\n", argv[1]);
54              exit(-1);
55          }
56       }
57
58       else
59           break;
60   }
61
62   if (argc > 0) {
63       (void)fprintf(stderr, "usage: gta [-i input-file-name] [-o output-file-name]\n");
64       exit(-1);
65   }
66
67   //  Read from standard input if no input file was specified on the command line.
68
69   if (in == (FILE *)0)
70       in = stdin;
71
72   //  Create the initial tree of knowledge.
73
74   root = make_node("Does it bark");
75   root->yes = make_node("dog");
76   root->no = make_node("cat");
77
78   for (;;) {        // play games until the user quits.
79
80       if (in == stdin)
81           (void)printf("Think of an animal.\n");
82
83       current = &root;     //  start at the top
84
85       for (;;) {            // play a game
86
87           for (;;) {        // get valid user input
88               if (in == stdin) {
89                   if ((*current)->yes == (struct node *)0)
90                       (void)printf("Is it a ");
91
92                   (void)printf("%s?[ynq] ", (*current)->string);
93               }
94
95               if (fgets(buffer, sizeof (buffer), in) == (char *)0 || strcmp(buffer, "q\n") == 0) {
96                   if (in != stdin) {
97                       (void)fclose(in);
98                       in = stdin;
99                   }
100                  else {
101                      if (in == stdin)
102                          (void)printf("\nThanks for playing.  Bye.\n");
103                      exit(0);
104                  }
105              }
```

```
106                    else if (strcmp(buffer, "y\n") == 0) {
107                        if (out != (FILE *)0)
108                            fputs("y\n", out);
109
110                        current = &((*current)->yes);
111
112                        if (*current == (struct node *)0) {
113                            (void)printf("I knew it!\n");
114                            break;
115                        }
116                    }
117                    else if (strcmp(buffer, "n\n") == 0) {
118                        if (out != (FILE *)0)
119                            fputs("n\n", out);
120
121                        if ((*current)->no == (struct node *)0) {
122                            if (in == stdin)
123                                (void)printf("I give up.  What is it? ");
124
125                            fgets(animal, sizeof (animal), in);
126
127                            if (out != (FILE *)0)
128                                fputs(animal, out);
129
130                            if ((p = strchr(animal, '\n')) != (char *)0)
131                                *p = '\0';
132
133                            if (in == stdin)
134                                (void)printf(
135                                "What's a good question that I could use to tell a %s from a %s? ",
136                                    animal, (*current)->string);
137                            fgets(question, sizeof (question), in);
138
139                            if (out != (FILE *)0)
140                                fputs(question, out);
141
142                            if ((p = strchr(question, '\n')) != (char *)0)
143                                *p = '\0';
144
145                            new = make_node(question);
146                            new->yes = make_node(animal);
147                            new->no = *current;
148                            *current = new;
149
150                            if (in == stdin)
151                                (void)printf("Thanks!  I'll remember that.\n");
152
153                            break;
154                        }
155
156                        else
157                            current = &((*current)->no);
158                    }
159                    else {
```

```
160                     if (in == stdin)
161                         (void)printf("Huh?  Please answer y for yes, n for no, or q for quit.\n");
162
163                     while ((c = getc(in)) != '\n' && c != EOF)
164                         ;
165                 }
166             }
167
168         break;
169     }
170
171     if (in == stdin)
172         (void)printf("Let's play again.\n\n");
173 }
174 }
```

Listing 10-9: Guess the Animal in C: mainline

There's nothing particularly interesting about this code except the memory management, as the program does pretty much the same thing as the JavaScript version. Lines 28 through 37 declare variables. Lines 74 through 76 create the initial nodes depicted in Figure 10-18. Note that all the strings are NUL-terminated ('\0').

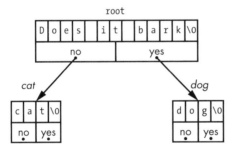

Figure 10-18: Guess the Animal in C: initial nodes

Let's play the game as we did earlier in "Guess the Animal Version 1: HTML and JavaScript" on page 262. After the player supplies a new question, a new node is allocated for it. There are a couple of points of interest here. Be careful getting the length of a string using the strlen (*string length*) function. It returns the actual length of the string, not the amount of memory used, which is 1 byte more to account for the NUL terminator. But notice that we don't add 1 when allocating memory for strings because of the way we're allocating memory for the node, which already includes the extra byte.

Whenever we descend the tree in response to a yes or no answer, we keep a current pointer to make it easy to insert the new question node. We need to detach either the yes or no, which we do by having current point to whatever node pointer is being replaced. Because current points to a node pointer, it's a pointer to a pointer. When we say *current = new; we're dereferencing the pointer and saying "replace whatever the pointer is pointing to." In Figure 10-19, the no pointer in the new node is set to current, which is the old answer, and current points to the yes pointer in the root node, which gets replaced with the pointer to the new node.

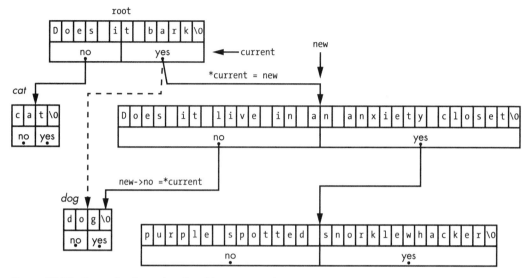

Figure 10-19: Guess the Animal in C: adding new nodes

Training

Recall that our C program can be run with command line options for reading and writing training data. We can run the program as follows:

```
prompt> gta -o training
Think of an animal.
Does it bark?
n
Is it a dog?
n
I give up. What is it?
giant purple snorklewhacker
What's a question that I could use to tell a giant purple snorklewhacker from a dog?
Does it live in an anxiety closet?
Thanks. I'll remember that.
Let's play again.
Think of an animal.
Does it bark?
q
Thanks for playing. Bye.
```

Now, if you look in the training file, you'll see that it contains exactly what you typed:

```
n
n
giant purple snorklewhacker
Does it live in an anxiety closet?
```

If we rerun the program as:

```
prompt> gta -i training
```

the contents of the training file will get read in so that the program starts where we left off.

Way back in "What Is Computer Programming?" on page xxix, I mentioned that you need to know a lot about everything in order to be a good programmer. Our program isn't very good grammatically. It works fine if the animal is a dog, because it will ask Is it a dog?. But what if it's an elephant? It's not grammatically correct to ask Is it a elephant?. What are the rules for making sure the grammar is correct? Can you modify the code to make it grammatically more better?

Summary

In this chapter, you've seen a program written in two ways: once as a high-level application and once as a lower-level system program. On one hand, writing high-level application programs can be easier because many small details are handled automatically. On the other hand, some features, such as recording and playback, are much more difficult to implement in environments that don't include uniform interfaces.

Furthermore, using very complex application environments for simple applications increases the likelihood of bugs. The probability of bugs is the sum of your application code and the code for the environment in which it runs. How many times has your browser begun running very slowly and needed to be restarted, usually due to internal memory management errors? How often has your browser just crashed?

You've seen that system programming involves much more attention to detail, such as the management of strings, memory, and buffers. But these details are important when the goal is to craft code that is concise and secure. In the next chapter, we'll look at a different type of detail: structuring problems so that they're easier to solve.

11

SHORTCUTS AND APPROXIMATIONS

So far, we've spent a lot of time looking at how to compute efficiently, especially with regard to memory usage. But there's one thing that's better than computing efficiently, and that's not computing at all. This chapter looks at two ways to avoid computing: taking shortcuts and approximating.

We think of computers as very exact and precise. But, as we saw in "Representing Real Numbers" on page 14, they really aren't. We can write code to be as exact as we want. For example, the UNIX bc utility is an arbitrary precision calculator that's perfect if you need lots of accuracy, but it's not a very efficient approach because computer hardware doesn't support arbitrary precision. This leads to the question, how close is good enough for a particular application? Effective use of computing resources means not doing more work than necessary. Calculating all the digits of π before using it is just not rational!

Table Lookup

Many times it's simpler and faster to look something up in a table than to do a calculation. We'll look at a few examples of this approach in the following subsections. Table lookup is similar to the loop-invariant optimization that was discussed in Chapter 8 in that if you're going to use something a lot, it often makes sense to calculate it once in advance.

Conversion

Suppose we need to read a temperature sensor and display the result in tenths of a degree Celsius (°C). A clever hardware designer has given us a circuit that produces a voltage based on the measured temperature that we can read using an A/D converter (see "Analog-to-Digital Conversion" on page 162). The curve looks like Figure 11-1.

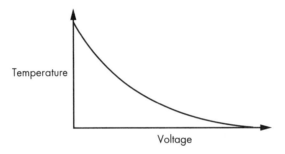

Figure 11-1: Temperature sensor curve

You can see that the curve is not a convenient straight line. We can calculate the temperature (t) from the voltage (v) using the following formula, where A, B, and C are constants determined by the particular model of sensor:

$$t = \frac{1}{A + B \times \log_e v + \left(C \times \log_e v\right)^2}$$

As you can see, a lot of floating-point arithmetic is involved, including natural logarithms, which is costly. So let's skip it all. Instead, let's build a table that maps voltage values into temperatures. Suppose we have a 10-bit A/D and that 8 bits is enough to hold our temperature value. That means we only need a 1,024-byte table to eliminate all the calculation, as shown in Figure 11-2.

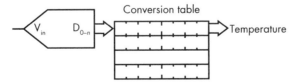

Figure 11-2: Table lookup conversion

Texture Mapping

Table lookup is a mainstay of *texture mapping*, a technique that helps provide realistic-looking images in video games and movies. The idea behind it is that pasting an image onto an object such as a wall takes a lot less computation than algorithmically generating all the detail. This is all well and good, but it has its own issues. Let's say we have a brick wall texture such as the one in Figure 11-3.

Figure 11-3: Brick wall texture

Looks pretty good. But video games aren't static. You might be running away from a brick wall at high speed because you're being chased by zombies. The appearance of the brick wall needs to change based on your distance from it. Figure 11-4 shows how the wall looks from a long distance away (on the left) and from very close (on the right).

Figure 11-4: Brick wall texture at different distances

As you might expect, adjusting the texture for distance is a lot of work. As the viewpoint moves farther away from the texture, adjacent pixels must be averaged together. It's important to be able to do this calculation quickly so that the image doesn't jump around.

Lance Williams (1949–2017) at the New York Institute of Technology Graphics Language Laboratory devised a clever approach called *MIP mapping* (named from the Latin *multum in parvo*, meaning "many things in a small place"). His paper on this topic, entitled "Pyramidal Parametrics," was published in the July 1983 SIGGRAPH proceedings. His method is still in use today, not only in software but also in hardware.

As we saw in "Representing Colors" on page 27, a pixel has three 8-bit components, one each for red, green, and blue. Williams noticed that on 32-bit systems, a quarter of the space was left over when these components were arranged in a rectangular fashion, as shown in Figure 11-5.

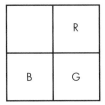

Figure 11-5: Color component
arrangement with leftover space

He couldn't just let that space go to waste, so he put it to good use in a different way than Tom Duff and Thomas Porter did (see "Adding Transparency" on page 29). Williams noticed that because it was one-fourth of the space, he could put a one-fourth-size copy of the image into that space, and then another one-fourth-size copy into *that* space, and so on, as shown in Figure 11-6. He called this arrangment a MIP map.

Figure 11-6: Multiple
image layout

Making a MIP map out of our brick wall texture results in the image shown in Figure 11-7 (you'll have to imagine the color components in this grayscale image).

Figure 11-7: MIP mapped texture

As you can see, there's a lot more detail in the closer-up images, where it's important. This is interesting, but other than being a clever storage mechanism, what use is it? Take a look at Figure 11-8, which unfolds one of the colors of the MIP map into a pyramid.

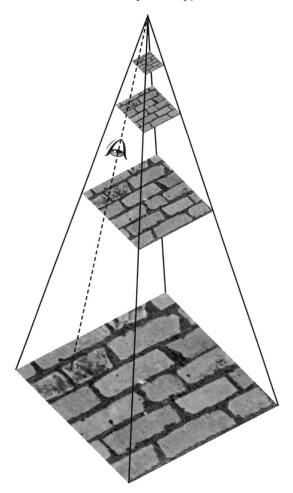

Figure 11-8: MIP map pyramid

The image at the tip of the pyramid is what things look like from far away, and there's more detail as we head toward the base. When we need to compute the actual texture to display for the position of the eye in Figure 11-8, we don't need to average together all the pixels in the base image; we just need to use the pixels in the nearest layer. This saves a lot of time, especially when the vantage point is far away.

Precomputing information that's going to be used a lot—in this case, the lower-resolution versions of the texture—is equivalent to loop-invariant optimization.

Character Classification

Table lookup methods had a big influence on the addition of libraries to the programming language C. Back in Chapter 8, we saw that *character classification*—deciding which characters were letters, numbers, and so on—is an important part of lexical analysis. Going back to the ASCII code chart in Table 1-10, you could easily write code to implement classification, such as that shown in Listing 11-1.

```
int
isdigit(int c)
{
  return (c >= '0' && c <= '9');
}

int
ishexdigit(int c)
{
  return (c >= '0' && c <= '9' || c >= 'A' && c <= 'F' || c >= 'a' && c <= 'f');
}

int
isalpha(int c)
{
  return (c >= 'A' && c <= 'Z' || c >= 'a' && c <= 'z');
}

int
isupper(int c)
{
  return (c >= 'A' && c <= 'Z');
}
```

Listing 11-1: Character classification code

Some at Bell Labs suggested putting commonly useful functions, such as the ones in Listing 11-1, into *libraries*. Dennis Ritchie (1941–2011) argued that people could easily write their own. But Nils-Peter Nelson in the computer center had written an implementation of these routines that used a table instead of a collection of if statements. The table was indexed by character value, and each entry in the table had bits for aspects like uppercase, lowercase, digit, and so forth, as shown in Figure 11-9.

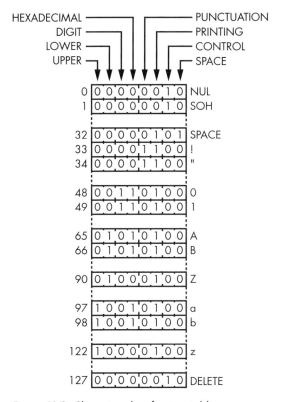

Figure 11-9: Character classification table

Classification, in this case, involved looking up the value in the table and checking the bits, as shown in Listing 11-2.

```
unsigned char table[128] = [ ... ];

#define isdigit(c)    (table[(c) & 0x7f] & DIGIT)
#define ishexdigit(c) (table[(c) & 0x7f] & HEXADECIMAL)
#define isalpha(c)    (table[(c) & 0x7f] & (UPPER | LOWER))
#define isupper(c)    (table[(c) & 0x7f] & UPPER)
```

Listing 11-2: Table-driven character classification code

As you can see, the functions in Listing 11-2 are simpler than those in Listing 11-1. And they have another nice property, which is that they're all essentially the same code; the only difference is the value of the constants that are ANDed with the table contents. This approach was 20 times faster than what anybody else had done, so Ritchie gave in and these functions were added as a library, setting the stage for additional libraries.

You'll notice that I use macros *in Listing 11-2 but* functions *in Listing 11-1. In case you haven't seen macros before, they're a language construct that substitutes the code on the right for the code on the left. So, if your source code included* isupper('a'), *the language* preprocessor *would replace it with* table[('a') & 0x7f] & UPPER. *This is great for small chunks of code because there's no function call overhead. But the code in Listing 11-1 couldn't reasonably be implemented using macros because we have to handle the case where someone does* isupper(*p++). *If the code in Listing 11-1 were implemented as macros, then in* ishexdigit, *for example,* p *would be incremented six times, which would be a surprise to the caller. The version in Listing 11-2 references the argument only once, so that doesn't happen.*

Integer Methods

It should be obvious from the earlier discussion of hardware that some operations are cheaper to perform in terms of speed and power consumption than others. Integer addition and subtraction are inexpensive. Multiplication and division cost more, although we can multiply and divide by 2 cheaply using shift operations. Floating-point operations are considerably more expensive. Complex floating-point operations, such as the calculation of trigonometric and logarithmic functions, are much more expensive. In keeping with the theme for this chapter, it would be best if we could find ways to avoid using the more expensive operations.

Let's look at some visual examples. Listing 11-3 modifies the web page skeleton from Listing 10-1 to have style, a script fragment, and a body.

```
 1 <style>
 2    canvas {
 3      border: 5px solid black;
 4    }
 5 </style>
 6 ...
 7 <script>
 8    $(function() {
 9      var canvas = $('canvas')[0].getContext('2d');
10
11      // Get the canvas width and height.  Force them to be numbers
12      // because attr yields strings and JavaScript often produces
13      // unexpected results when using strings as numbers.
14
15      var height = Number($('canvas').attr('height'));
16      var width = Number($('canvas').attr('width'));
17
18      canvas.translate(0, height);
19      canvas.scale(1, -1);
20    });
21 </script>
22 ...
23 <body>
24    <canvas width="500" height="500"></canvas>
25 </body>
```

Listing 11-3: Basic canvas

I briefly mentioned canvases back in "HTML5" on page 255. A *canvas* is an element on which you can do free-form drawing. You can think of it as a piece of graph paper.

The canvas "graph paper" isn't exactly what you're used to because it doesn't use the standard Cartesian coordinate system by default. This is an artifact of the direction in which the raster was drawn on televisions (see "Raster Graphics" on page 180); the raster starts at the upper left. The x-coordinate behaves normally, but the y-coordinate starts at the top and increases downward. This coordinate system was kept when television monitors were repurposed for computer graphics.

Modern computer graphics systems support arbitrary coordinate systems for which graphics hardware often includes support. A *transformation* is applied to every (x, y) coordinate you specify and maps your coordinates to the screen coordinates (x', y') using the following formulas:

$$x' = Ax + By + C$$
$$y' = Dx + Ey + F$$

The C and F terms provide *translation*, which means they move things around. The A and E terms provide *scaling*, which means they make things bigger and smaller. The B and D terms provide *rotation*, which means they change the orientation. These are often represented in matrix form.

For now, we just care about translation and scaling to convert the canvas coordinate system into a familiar one. We translate downward by the height of the canvas on line 13 and then flip the direction of the y-axis on line 14. The order matters; if we did these translations in the reverse order, the origin would be above the canvas.

Graphics are effectively created from blobs of primary colors plopped on a piece of graph paper (see "Representing Colors" on page 27). But how fine a piece of graph paper do we need? And how much control do we need over the color blob composition?

The width and height attributes on line 19 set the size of the canvas in pixels (see "Digital Images" on page 173). The *resolution* of the display is the number of pixels per inch (or per centimeter). The size of the canvas on your screen depends on the resolution of your screen. Unless it's a real antique, you probably can't see the individual pixels. (Note that the resolution of the human eye isn't a constant across the field of vision; see "A Photon Accurate Model of the Human Eye," Michael Deering, SIGGRAPH 2005.) Even though current UHD monitors are awesome, techniques such as supersampling are still needed to make things look really good.

We'll start by drawing things at a very low resolution so we can see the details. Let's make some graph paper by adding a JavaScript function that clears the canvas and draws a grid, as shown in Listing 11-4. We'll also use a scaling transformation to get integer value grid intersections. The scale applies to everything drawn on the canvas, so we have to make the line width smaller.

```
1  var grid = 25;                                 // 25 pixel grid spacing
2
3  canvas.scale(grid, grid);
4  width = width / grid;
5  height = height / grid;
6  canvas.lineWidth = canvas.lineWidth / grid;
7  canvas.strokeStyle = "rgb(0, 0, 0)";           // black
8
9  function
10 clear_and_draw_grid()
11 {
12   canvas.clearRect(0, 0, width, height);        // erase canvas
13   canvas.save(); // save canvas settings
14   canvas.setLineDash([0.1, 0.1]);               // dashed line
15   canvas.strokeStyle = "rgb(128, 128, 128)";    // gray
16   canvas.beginPath();
17
18   for (var i = 1; i < height; i++) {            // horizontal lines
19     canvas.moveTo(0, i);
20     canvas.lineTo(height, i);
21   }
22
23   for (var i = 1; i < width; i++) {             // vertical lines
24     canvas.moveTo(i, 0);
25     canvas.lineTo(i, width);
26   }
27
28   canvas.stroke();
29   canvas.restore();                             // restore canvas settings
30 }
31
32 clear_and_draw_grid();                          // call on start-up
```

Listing 11-4: Drawing a grid

Straight Lines

Now let's draw a couple of lines by placing colored circles on the grid in
Listing 11-5. One line is horizontal, and the other has a slope of 45 degrees.
The diagonal line blobs are slightly bigger so we can see both lines at the
point where they intersect.

```
1  for (var i = 0; i <= width; i++) {
2    canvas.beginPath();
3    canvas.fillStyle = "rgb(255, 255, 0)";       // yellow
4    canvas.arc(i, i, 0.25, 0, 2 * Math.PI, 0);
5    canvas.fill();
6
7    canvas.beginPath();
8    canvas.fillStyle = "rgb(255, 0, 0)";         // red
9    canvas.arc(i, 10, 0.2, 0, 2 * Math.PI, 0);
10   canvas.fill();
11 }
```

Listing 11-5: Horizontal and diagonal lines

As you can see in Figure 11-10 and by running the program, the pixels are farther apart on the diagonal line than they are on the horizontal line ($\sqrt{2} - 1$ farther apart, according to Pythagoras). Why does this matter? Because both lines have the same number of pixels emitting light, but when the pixels are farther apart on the diagonal line, the light density is less, making it appear dimmer than the horizontal line. There's not much you can do about it; designers of displays adjust the shape of the pixels to minimize this effect. It's more of an issue on cheaper displays than on desktop monitors and phones.

Figure 11-10: Pixel spacing

The horizontal, vertical, and diagonal lines are the easy cases. How do we decide what pixels to illuminate for other lines? Let's make a line-drawing program. We'll start by adding some controls after the canvas element in the body, as shown in Listing 11-6.

```
1  <div>
2    <label for="y">Y Coordinate: </label>
3    <input type="text" size="3" id="y"/>
4    <button id="draw">Draw</button>
5    <button id="erase">Erase</button>
6  </div>
```

Listing 11-6: Basic line-drawing program body

Then, in Listing 11-7, we'll replace the code from Listing 11-5 with event handlers for the draw and erase buttons. The draw function uses the dreaded $y = mx + b$, with b always being 0 in our case. Surprise! Some stuff from math is actually used.

```
1  $('#draw').click(function() {
2    if ($('#y').val() < 0 || $('#y').val() > height) {
3      alert('y value must be between 0 and ' + height);
4    }
5    else if (parseInt($('#y').val()) != $('#y').val()) {
6      alert('y value must be an integer');
7    }
8    else {
9      canvas.beginPath();                    // draw ideal line
10     canvas.moveTo(0, 0);
11     canvas.setLineDash([0.2, 0.2]);        // dashed line
12     canvas.lineTo(width, $('#y').val());
13     canvas.stroke();
14
15     var m = $('#y').val() / width;         // slope
```

```
16
17      canvas.fillStyle = "rgb(0, 0, 0)";
18
19      for (var x = 0; x <= width; x++) {    // draw dots on grid
20        canvas.beginPath();
21        canvas.arc(x, Math.round(x * m), 0.15, 0, 2 * Math.PI, 0);
22        canvas.fill();
23      }
24
25      $('#y').val('');                       // clear y value field
26    }
27  });
28
29  $('#erase').click(function() {
30    clear_and_draw_grid();
31  });
```

Listing 11-7: Floating-point line-drawing and erase functions

Let's try this with a y-coordinate of 15. The result should look like Figure 11-11.

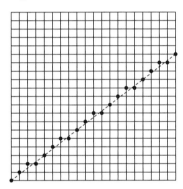

Figure 11-11: Line drawn using floating-point arithmetic

This looks pretty bad, but if you stand way back, it looks like a line. It's as close as we can get. This is not just a computer graphics problem, as anyone who does cross-stitching can tell you.

Although the program we just wrote works fine, it's not very efficient. It's performing floating-point multiplication and rounding at every point. That's at least an order of magnitude slower than integer arithmetic, even on modern machines. We do get some performance from computing the slope once in advance (line 15). It's a loop invariant, so there's a good chance that an optimizer (see "Optimization" on page 234) would do this for you automatically.

Way back in 1962, when floating-point was cost-prohibitive, Jack Bresenham at IBM came up with a clever way to draw lines without using floating-point arithmetic. Bresenham brought his innovation to the IBM patent office, which didn't see the value in it and declined to pursue a patent. Good thing, since it turned out to be a fundamental computer graphics algorithm, and the lack of a patent meant that everybody could use it.

Bresenham recognized that the line-drawing problem could be approached incrementally. Because we're calculating y at each successive x, we can just add the slope (line 9 in Listing 11-8) each time through, which eliminates the multiplication. That's not something an optimizer is likely to catch; it's essentially a complex strength-reduction.

```
1  var y = 0;
2
3  canvas.fillStyle = "rgb(0, 0, 0)";
4
5  for (var x = 0; x <= width; x++) {          // draw dots on grid
6    canvas.beginPath();
7    canvas.arc(x, Math.round(y), 0.15, 0, 2 * Math.PI, 0);
8    canvas.fill();
9    y = y + m;
10 }
```

Listing 11-8: Incrementally calculating y

We need floating-point arithmetic because the slope $\frac{\Delta y}{\Delta x}$ is a fraction. But the division can be replaced with addition and subtraction. We can have a *decision variable* d and add Δy on each iteration. The y value is incremented whenever $d \geq \Delta x$, and then we subtract Δx from d.

There is one last issue: rounding. We want to choose points in the middle of pixels, not at the bottom of them. That's easy to handle by setting the initial value of d to ½m instead of 0. But we don't want to introduce a fraction. No problem: we'll just get rid of the ½ by multiplying it and everything else by 2 using $2\Delta y$ and $2\Delta x$ instead.

Replace the code that draws the dots on the grid with Listing 11-9's "integer-only" version (we have no control over whether JavaScript uses integers internally, unlike in a language like C). Note that this code works only for lines with slopes in the range of 0 to 1. I'll leave making it work for all slopes as an exercise for you.

```
1  var dx = width;
2  var dy = $('#y').val();
3  var d = 2 * dy - dx;
4  var y = 0;
5
6  dx *= 2;
7  dy *= 2;
8
9  canvas.fillStyle = "rgb(255, 255, 0)";
10 canvas.setLineDash([0,0]);
11
12 for (var x = 0; x <= width; x++) {
13   canvas.beginPath();
14   canvas.arc(x, y, 0.4, 0, 2 * Math.PI, 0);
15   canvas.stroke();
16
17   if (d >= 0) {
18     y++;
19     d -= dx;
```

```
20   }
21   d += dy;
22 }
```

Listing 11-9: Integer line drawing

One interesting question that arises from Listing 11-9 is, why isn't the decision arithmetic written as shown in Listing 11-10?

```
1  var dy_minus_dx = dy - dx;
2
3  if (d >= 0) {
4    y++;
5    d -= dy_minus_dx;
6  }
7  else {
8    d += dy;
9  }
```

Listing 11-10: Alternate decision code

At first glance, this approach seems better because there's only one addition to the decision variable per iteration. Listing 11-11 shows how this might appear in some hypothetical assembly language such as the one from Chapter 4.

```
        load    d                       load    d
        cmp     #0                      cmp     #0
        blt     a                       blt     a
        load    y                       load    y
        add     #1                      add     #1
        store   y                       store   y
        load    d                       load    d
        sub     dx_plus_dy              sub     dx
        bra     b
a:      add     dy              a:      add     dy
        store   d                       store   d
b:      ...                             ...
```

Listing 11-11: Alternate decision code assembly language

Notice that the alternate version is one instruction longer than the original. And in most machines, integer addition takes the same amount of time as a branch. Thus, the code we thought would be better is actually one instruction time slower whenever we need to increment y.

The technique used in Bresenham's line algorithm can be applied to a large variety of other problems. For example, you can produce a smoothly changing color *gradient*, such as that shown in Figure 11-12, by replacing y with a color value.

Figure 11-12: Color gradient

The gradient in Figure 11-12 was generated using the code shown in Listing 11-12 in the document ready function.

```
1  var canvas = $('canvas')[0].getContext('2d');
2  var width = $('canvas').attr('width');
3  var height = $('canvas').attr('height');
4
5  canvas.translate(0, height);
6  canvas.scale(1, -1);
7
8  var m = $('#y').val() / width;
9
10 var dx = width;
11 var dc = 255;
12 var d = 2 * dc - dx;
13 var color = 0;
14
15 for (var x = 0; x <= width; x++) {
16   canvas.beginPath();
17   canvas.strokeStyle = "rgb(" + color + "," + color + "," + color + ")";
18   canvas.moveTo(x, 0)
19   canvas.lineTo(x, height);
20   canvas.stroke();
21
22   if (d >= 0) {
23     color++;
24     d -= 2 * dx;
25   }
26   d += 2 * dc;
27 }
```

Listing 11-12: Color gradient code

Curves Ahead

Integer methods aren't limited to straight lines. Let's draw an ellipse. We'll stick to the simple case of ellipses whose axes are aligned with the coordinate axes and whose center is at the origin. They're defined by the following equation, where a is one-half the width and b is one-half the height:

$$\frac{x^2}{a^2} + \frac{y^2}{b^2} = 1$$

Assuming that we're at the solid black point in Figure 11-13, we need to decide which of the three possible next points is closest to the ideal ellipse.

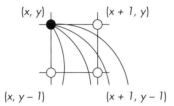

Figure 11-13: Ellipse decision points

Defining $A = b^2$ and $B = a^2$, we can rearrange the ellipse equation as $Ax^2 + By^2 - AB = 0$. We won't be able to satisfy this equation most of the time because the points we need to draw on the integer grid aren't likely to be the same as those on the ideal ellipse. When we're at (x, y), we want to choose our next point to be the one in which $Ax^2 + By^2 - AB$ is closest to 0. And we'd like to be able to do it without the seven multiplications in that equation.

Our approach is to calculate the value of the equation at each of the three possible points and then choose the point where the equation value is closest to 0. In other words, we'll calculate a distance variable d at each of the three points using $d = Ax^2 + By^2 - AB$.

Let's start by figuring out how to calculate d at the point $(x + 1, y)$ without the multiplications. We can plug $(x + 1)$ into the equation for x, as follows:

$$d_{x+1} = A(x + 1)^2 + By^2 - AB$$

Of course, squaring something is just multiplying it by itself:

$$d_{x+1} = A(x + 1)(x + 1) + By^2 - AB$$

Multiplying it all out, we get:

$$d_{x+1} = x^2 + 2Ax + A + By^2 - AB$$

Now, if we subtract that from the original equation, we see that the difference between the equation at x and $x + 1$ is:

$$dx = 2Ax + A$$

We can add dx to d to get d_{x+1}. That doesn't quite get us where we want to be, though, because there's still a multiplication. So let's evaluate dx at $x + 1$:

$$dx_{x+1} = 2A(x+1) + A$$

$$dx_{x+1} = 2Ax + 2A + A$$

Just like before, subtraction gives us:

$$d2x = 2A$$

This yields a constant, which makes it easy to calculate d at $(x + 1, y)$ without multiplication by using the intermediates dx and $d2x$:

$$2A_{x+1} = 2Ax + d2x$$

That gets us the horizontal direction—the vertical is almost identical, except there's a sign difference since we're going in the $-y$ direction:

$$dy = -2By + B$$

$$d2y = 2B$$

Now that we have all these terms, deciding which of the three points is closest to the ideal curve is simple. We calculate the horizontal difference dh to point $(x + 1, y)$, the vertical difference dv to the point $(x, y - 1)$, and the diagonal difference dd to the point $(x + 1, y - 1)$ and choose the smallest. Note that although dx is always positive, dv and dd can be negative, so we need to take their absolute value before comparing, as shown in Figure 11-14.

Our ellipse-drawing algorithm draws the ellipse only in the first quadrant. That's okay because there's another trick that we can use: symmetry. We know that each quadrant of the ellipse looks the same as the first; it's just flipped horizontally, vertically, or both. We could draw the whole ellipse by drawing $(-x, y)$, $(-x, -y)$, and $(x, -y)$ in addition to drawing (x, y). Note that we could use eight-way symmetry if we were drawing circles.

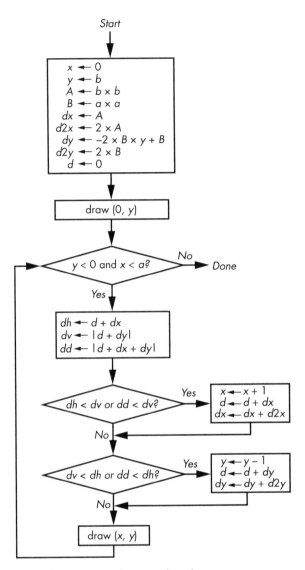

Figure 11-14: Ellipse-drawing algorithm

This algorithm includes some comparisons that could be simplified, which result from drawing one-quarter of the ellipse. The one-quarter ellipse could be partitioned into two sections at the point where the slope of the curve is 1. By doing so, we'd have one piece of code that only had to decide between horizontal and diagonal movements and another that had to decide between vertical and diagonal movements. Which one got executed first would depend on the values of a and b. But a lot more time is spent inside the loop making decisions than in the setup, so it's a good trade-off.

The preceding algorithm has one serious deficiency: because it starts from the half-width (a) and half-height (b), it can draw only ellipses that are odd numbers of pixels in width and height, since the result is $2a$ wide and $2b$ high plus 1 for the axes.

Polynomials

The method we used to draw ellipses by incrementally calculating differences doesn't scale well beyond conic sections (squared things). That's because higher-order equations can do strange things, such as change direction several times within the space of a single pixel—which is pretty hard to test for efficiently.

But incrementally calculating differences can be generalized to any polynomials of the form $y = Ax^0 + Bx^1 + Cx^2 + \ldots Dx^n$. All we have to do is generate n sets of differences so that we start our accumulated additions with a constant. This works because, unlike with the ellipse-drawing code, the polynomials have only a single independent variable. You may remember Charles Babbage's difference engine from "The Case for Digital Computers" on page 34. It was designed to do just this: evaluate equations using incremental differences.

Recursive Subdivision

We touched briefly on *recursive subdivision* back in "Stacks" on page 122. It's a technique with many uses. In this section, we'll examine how to use it to get by with the minimum amount of work.

Spirals

Our line-drawing code can be leveraged for more complicated curves. We can calculate some points and connect them together using lines.

Your math class has probably covered the measurement of angles in degrees, so you know that there are 360 degrees in a circle. You may not be aware that there are other systems of measurement. A commonly used one is *radians*. There are 2π radians in a circle. So 360 degrees is 2π radians, 180 degrees is π radians, 90 degrees is $\pi/2$ radians, 45 degrees is $\pi/4$ radians, and so on. You need to know this because many trigonometric functions available in math libraries, such as the ones in JavaScript, expect angles in radians instead of degrees.

We'll use curves drawn in polar coordinates for our examples because they're pretty. Just in case you haven't learned this yet, *polar coordinates* use radius r and angle θ instead of x and y. Conversion to Cartesian coordinates is easy: $x = r\cos\theta$ and $y = r\sin\theta$. Our first example draws a spiral using $r = \theta \times 10$; the point that we draw gets farther away from the center as we sweep through the angles. We'll make the input in degrees because it's not as intuitive for many people to think in radians. Listing 11-13 shows the body for the controls.

```
<canvas width="500" height="500"></canvas>
<div>
  <label for="degrees">Degrees: </label>
  <input type="text" size="3" id="degrees"/>
  <button id="draw">Draw</button>
  <button id="erase">Erase</button>
</div>
```

Listing 11-13: Spiral body

We'll skip the grid here because we need to draw more detail. Because we're doing polar coordinates, Listing 11-14 puts (0, 0) at the center.

```
canvas.scale(1, -1);
canvas.translate(width / 2, -height / 2);

$('#erase').click(function() {
  canvas.clearRect(-width, -height, width * 2, height * 2);
});

$('#draw').click(function() {
  if (parseFloat($('#degrees').val()) == 0)
    alert('Degrees must be greater than 0');
  else {
    for (var angle = 0; angle < 4 * 360; angle += parseFloat($('#degrees').val())) {
      var theta = 2 * Math.PI * angle / 360;
      var r = theta * 10;
      canvas.beginPath();
      canvas.arc(r * Math.cos(theta), r * Math.sin(theta), 3, 0, 2 * Math.PI, 0);
      canvas.fill();
    }
  }
});
```

Listing 11-14: Dotted spiral JavaScript

Enter a value of 10 for degrees and click Draw. You should see something like Figure 11-15.

Notice that the dots get farther apart as we get farther from the origin, even though they overlap near the center. We could make the value of degrees small enough that we'd get a good-looking curve, but that means we'd have a lot of points that overlap, which is a lot slower, and it's difficult to guess the value needed for an arbitrary function.

Let's try drawing lines between the points. Swap in Listing 11-15 for the drawing code.

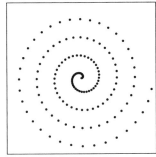

Figure 11-15: Dotted spiral

```
canvas.beginPath();
canvas.moveTo(0, 0);

for (var angle = 0; angle < 4 * 360; angle += parseFloat($('#degrees').val())) {
  var theta = 2 * Math.PI * angle / 360;
  var r = theta * 10;
  canvas.lineTo(r * Math.cos(theta), r * Math.sin(theta));
}

canvas.stroke();
```

Listing 11-15: Spiral line JavaScript

Enter a value of 20 for degrees and click Draw. Figure 11-16 shows what you should see.

Not very pretty. Again, it looks good near the center but gets worse as we progress outward. We need some way to compute more points as needed—which is where our old friend recursive subdivision comes into play. We're drawing lines using the spiral function between two angles, θ_1 and θ_2. What we'll do is have some *close enough* criterion, and if a pair of points is not close enough, we'll halve the difference in the angles and try again until we do get close enough. We'll use the *distance formula* $d = \sqrt{\left(x_2 - x_1\right)^2 + \left(y_2 - y_1\right)^2}$ to find the distance between points, as shown in Listing 11-16.

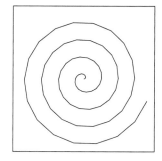

Figure 11-16: Spiral line

```
var close_enough = 10;

function
plot(theta_1, theta_2)
{
  var r;

  r = theta_1 * 10;
  var x1 = r * Math.cos(theta_1);
  var y1 = r * Math.sin(theta_1);

  r = theta_2 * 10;
  var x2 = r * Math.cos(theta_2);
  var y2 = r * Math.sin(theta_2);

  if (Math.sqrt(((x2 - x1) * (x2 - x1) + (y2 - y1) * (y2 - y1))) < close_enough) {
    canvas.moveTo(x1, y1);
    canvas.lineTo(x2, y2);
  }
  else {
    plot(theta_1, theta_1 + (theta_2 - theta_1) / 2);
    plot(theta_1 + (theta_2 - theta_1) / 2, theta_2);
  }
}

$('#draw').click(function() {
  if (parseFloat($('#degrees').val()) == 0)
    alert('Degrees must be greater than 0');
  else {
    canvas.beginPath();

    for (var angle = 0; angle < 4 * 360; angle += parseFloat($('#degrees').val())) {
      var old_theta;
      var theta = 2 * Math.PI * angle / 360;
```

```
    if (angle > 0)
      plot(old_theta, theta);
    old_theta = theta;
  }
 }

 canvas.stroke();
});
```

Listing 11-16: Recursive spiral line JavaScript

You'll notice that as long as `close_enough` is small enough, the size of the increment in degrees doesn't matter because the code automatically generates as many intermediate angles as needed. Play around with different values for `close_enough`; maybe add an input field so that it's easy to do.

The determination of close enough is very important for certain applications. Though it's beyond the scope of this book, think about curved objects that you've seen in movies. Shining light on them makes them look more realistic. Now imagine a mirrored sphere approximated by some number of flat faces just like the spiral was approximated by line segments. If the flat faces aren't small enough, it turns into a disco ball (a set of flat surfaces approximating a sphere), which reflects light in a completely different manner.

Constructive Geometry

Chapter 5 briefly mentioned quadtrees and showed how they could represent shapes. They're an obvious use of recursion because they're a hierarchical mechanism for dividing up space.

We can perform Boolean operations on quadtrees. Let's say we want to design something like the engine gasket in Figure 11-17.

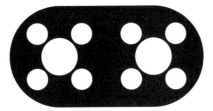

Figure 11-17: Engine gasket

We'll need a data structure for a quadtree node, plus two special leaf values—one for 0, which we're coloring white, and one for 1, which we're coloring black. Figure 11-18 shows a structure and the data it represents. Each node can reference four other nodes, which is a good use for pointers in languages such as C.

Figure 11-18: Quadtree node

We don't need to keep track of the size of a node. All operations start from the root, the size of which is known, and each child node is one-quarter the size of its parent. Figure 11-19 shows us how to get the value at a location in the tree.

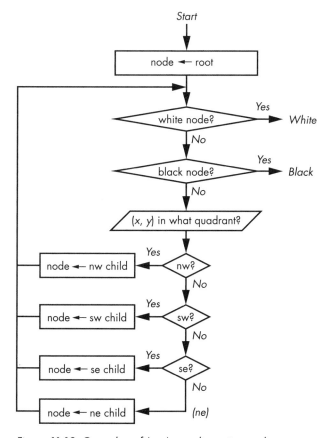

Figure 11-19: Get value of (x, y) coordinate in quadtree

Figure 11-20 shows how we would set the value of (that is, make black) an (x, y) coordinate in a quadtree. Note that "done" means "return from the function" since it's recursive.

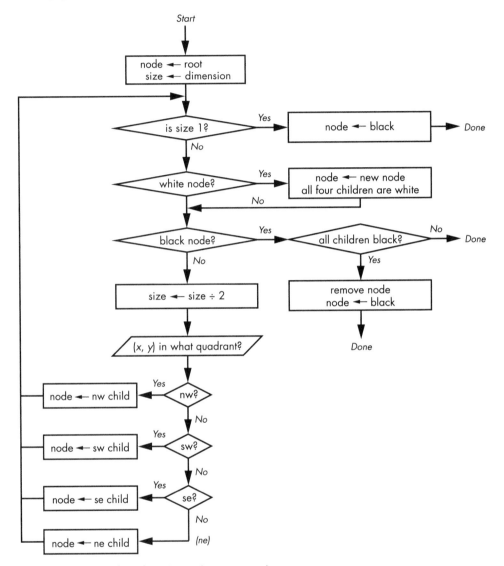

Figure 11-20: Set value of (x, y) coordinate in quadtree

This is similar to the value-getting code in Figure 11-19. At a high level, it descends the tree, subdividing as it goes, until it reaches the 1×1 square for the (x, y) coordinate and sets it to black. Any time it hits a white node, it replaces it with a new node having four white children so there's a tree to keep descending. On the way back up, any nodes having all black children are replaced by a black node. This happens any time a node with three black children has the fourth set to black, as shown in Figure 11-21.

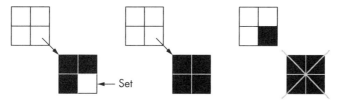

Figure 11-21: Coalescing a node

Coalescing nodes not only makes the tree take less memory, but it also makes many operations on the tree faster because it's not as deep.

We need a way to clear (that is, make white) the value of an (x, y) coordinate in a quadtree. The answer is fairly similar to the setting algorithm. The differences are that we partition black nodes instead of white ones and we coalesce white nodes instead of black ones.

We can build some more complicated drawing functions on top of our value-setting function. It's easy to draw rectangles by invoking the set function for each coordinate. We can do the same for ellipses using the algorithm from "Curves Ahead" on page 298 and symmetry.

Now for the fun stuff. Let's create quadtree versions for some of our Boolean logic functions from Chapter 1. The NOT function is simple: just descend the tree and replace any black nodes with white ones and vice versa. The AND and OR functions in Figure 11-22 are more interesting. These algorithms aren't designed to perform the equivalents of $C = a$ AND b and $C = a$ OR b. Instead, they implement dst &= src and dst |= src, as in the assignment operators found in many languages. The dst operand is the one modified.

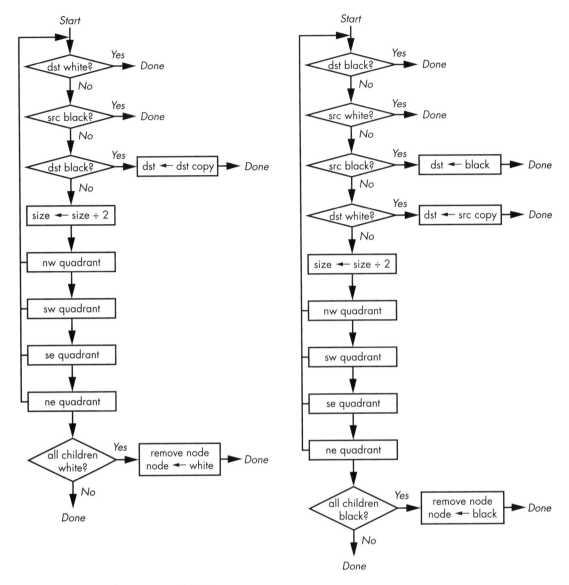

Figure 11-22: Quadtree AND and OR functions

Now that we have all these tools, let's build our gasket. We'll do it at low resolution so the details are visible. We'll start with an empty gasket quadtree on the left and a scratch quadtree in the center in which we draw a big circle. The scratch quadtree is OR'd with the gasket, producing the result on the right as shown in Figure 11-23. Note how the coalescing keeps the number of subdivisions to a minimum.

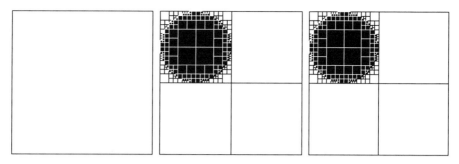

Figure 11-23: Gasket, circle, circle OR gasket

Next we'll make another circle in a different position and combine it with the partially completed gasket, as shown in Figure 11-24.

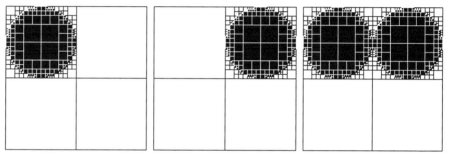

Figure 11-24: Adding to the gasket

Continuing on, we'll make a black rectangle and combine it with the gasket, as shown in Figure 11-25.

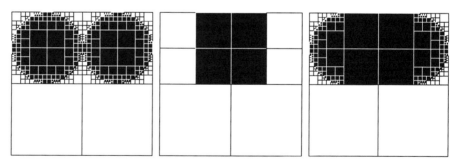

Figure 11-25: Adding the rectangle

The next step is to make a hole. This is accomplished by making a black circle and then inverting it using the NOT operation to make it white. The result is then ANDed with the partially completed gasket, resulting in the hole as seen in Figure 11-26.

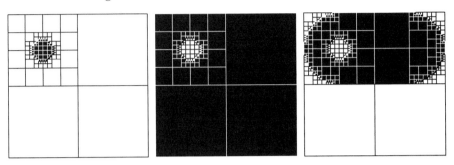

Figure 11-26: ANDing a NOT-hole

It's getting boring at this point. We need to combine another hole, in the same way as shown in Figure 11-26, and then eight smaller holes in a similar fashion. You can see the result in Figure 11-27.

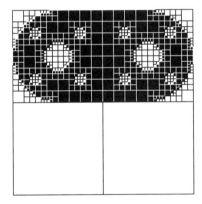

Figure 11-27: Completed gasket

As you can see, we can use Boolean functions on quadtrees to construct objects with complicated shapes out of simple geometric pieces. Although we used a two-dimensional gasket as our example, this is more commonly done in three dimensions. Twice as many nodes are needed for three dimensions, so the quadtree is extended into an *octree*, an example of which is shown in Figure 11-28.

Building complex objects in three dimensions using the preceding techniques is called *constructive solid geometry*. The three-dimensional counterpart to a two-dimensional pixel is called a *voxel*, which sort of means "volume pixel."

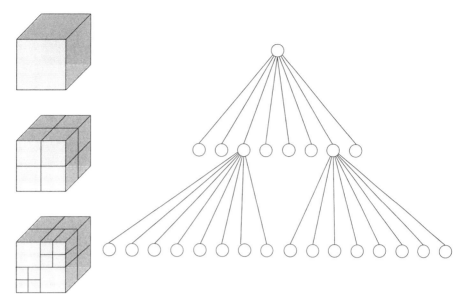

Figure 11-28: Octree

Octrees are a common storage method for CAT scan and MRI data. These machines generate a stack of 2D slices. It's a simple matter to peel away layers to obtain cutaway views.

Shifting and Masking

One of the downsides of quadtrees is that the data is scattered around memory; they have terrible locality of reference. Just because two squares are next to each other in the tree doesn't mean they're anywhere near each other in memory. This becomes a problem when we have to convert data from one memory organization to another. We could always move data 1 bit at a time, but that would involve a large number of memory accesses—which we want to minimize, because they're slow.

One task where this situation arises is displaying data. That's because the display memory organization is determined by the hardware. As mentioned back in "Raster Graphics" on page 180, each row of the raster is painted one at a time in a particular order. A raster row is called a *scan line*. The whole collection of scan lines is called a *frame buffer*.

Let's say we want to paint our completed gasket from Figure 11-27 on a display. For simplicity, we'll use a monochrome display that has 1 bit for each pixel and uses 16-bit-wide memory. That means the upper-leftmost 16 pixels are in the first word, the next 16 are in the second, and so on.

The upper-left square in Figure 11-27 is 4×4 pixels in size and is white, which means we need to be clearing bits in the frame buffer. We'll use the coordinates and size of the quadtree square to construct a mask, as shown in Figure 11-29.

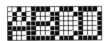

Figure 11-29: AND mask

We can then AND this mask with all the affected rows, costing only two memory accesses per row: one for read and one for write. We would do something similar to set bits in the frame buffer; the mask would have 1s in the area to set, and we would OR instead of AND.

Another place where this comes into play is when drawing text characters. Most text characters are stored as *bitmaps*, two-dimensional arrays of bits, as shown in Figure 11-30. Character bitmaps are packed together to minimize memory use. That's how text characters used to be provided; now they come as geometric descriptions. But for performance reasons, they're often converted into bitmaps before use, and those bitmaps are usually cached on the assumption that characters get reused.

*Figure 11-30: Bitmap
text characters*

Let's replace the character *B* on the display shown in Figure 11-31 with a *C*.

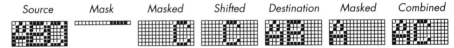

*Figure 11-31: Bitmap
text characters*

The *C* is located in bits 10 through 14 and needs to go into bits 6 through 10. For each row, we need to grab the *C* and then mask off everything else in the word. Then we need to shift it into the destination position. The destination must be read and the locations that we want to overwrite masked off before combining with the shifted *C* and being written, as shown in Figure 11-32.

| Source | Mask | Masked | Shifted | Destination | Masked | Combined |

Figure 11-32: Painting a character

This example uses three memory accesses per row: one to fetch the source, one to fetch the destination, and one to write the result. Doing this bit by bit would take five times that amount.

Keep in mind that there are often additional complications when the source or destination spans word boundaries.

More Math Avoidance

We discussed some simple ways to avoid expensive math in "Integer Methods" on page 290. Now that we have the background, let's talk about a couple of more complicated math-avoidance techniques.

Power Series Approximations

Here's another take on getting close enough. Let's say we need to generate the sine function because we don't have hardware that does it for us. One way to do this is with a *Taylor series*:

$$\sin(x) = x - \frac{x^3}{3!} + \frac{x^5}{5!} - \frac{x^7}{7!} + \frac{x^9}{9!}$$

Figure 11-33 shows a sine wave and the Taylor series approximations for different numbers of terms. As you can see, the more terms, the closer the result is to an ideal sine.

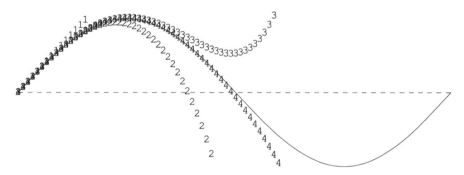

Figure 11-33: Taylor series for sine

It's a simple matter to add terms until you get the desired degree of accuracy. It's also worth noting that fewer terms are needed for angles more acute than 90 degrees, so you can be more efficient by using symmetry for other angles.

Note that we can reduce the number of multiplications required by initializing a *product* to x, precomputing $-x^2$, and multiplying the *product* by $-x^2$ to get each term. All the denominators are constants that could reside in a small table indexed by the exponent. Also, we don't have to compute all of the terms. If we need only two digits of accuracy, we can stop when computing more terms doesn't change those digits.

The CORDIC Algorithm

Jack Volder at Convair invented the *Coordinate Rotation Digital Computer (CORDIC)* algorithm in 1956. CORDIC was invented to replace an analog part of the B-58 bomber navigation system with something more accurate. CORDIC can be used to generate trigonometric and logarithmic functions using integer arithmetic. It was used in the HP-35, the first portable scientific calculator, released in 1972. It was also used in the Intel 80x87 family of floating-point coprocessors.

The basic idea of CORDIC is illustrated in Figure 11-34. Because it's a unit circle (radius of 1) the x- and y-coordinates of the arrow ends are the cosine and sine of the angle. We want to rotate the arrow from its original position along the x-axis in smaller and smaller steps until we get to the desired angle and then grab the coordinates.

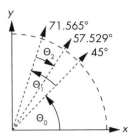

Figure 11-34: CORDIC algorithm overview

Let's say we want $\sin(57.529°)$. As you can see, we first try 45 degrees, which isn't enough, so we take another step of 25.565 degrees, getting us to 71.565 degrees, which is too much. We then go backward by 14.036 degrees, which gets us to our desired 57.529 degrees. We're clearly performing some sort of subdivision but with weird values for the angles.

We saw the equations for transformation earlier in "Integer Methods," where we cared only about translation and scaling. The CORDIC algorithm is based on rotation. The following equations, the general form of which you've seen, show us how (x, y) is rotated by angle θ to get a new set of coordinates (x', y'):

$$x' = x \times \cos(\theta) - y \times \sin(\theta)$$

$$y' = x \times \sin(\theta) + y \times \cos(\theta)$$

Although this is mathematically correct, it seems useless because we wouldn't be discussing an algorithm that generates sines and cosines if they were already available.

Let's make it worse before making it better by rewriting the equations in terms of tangents using the trigonometric identity:

$$\tan(\theta) = \frac{\sin(\theta)}{\cos(\theta)}$$

Because we're dividing by $\cos(\theta)$, we need to multiply the result by the same:

$$x' = \cos(\theta) \times \left[x \frac{\cos(\theta)}{\cos(\theta)} - y \frac{\sin(\theta)}{\cos(\theta)} \right] = \cos(\theta) \times \left[x - y \times \tan(\theta) \right]$$

$$y' = \cos(\theta) \times \left[x \frac{\sin(\theta)}{\cos(\theta)} + y \frac{\cos(\theta)}{\cos(\theta)} \right] = \cos(\theta) \times \left[x \times \tan(\theta) + y \right]$$

That looks pretty ugly. We're making a bad situation worse, but that's because we haven't talked about the trick, which goes back to the weird angles. It turns out that $\tan(45°) = 1$, $\tan(26.565°) = \frac{1}{2}$, and $\tan(14.036°) = \frac{1}{4}$. That sure looks like some simple integer division by 2, or as Maxwell Smart might have said, "the old right shift trick." It's a binary search of the tangents of the angles.

Let's see how this plays out for the example in Figure 11-34. There are three rotations that get us from the original coordinates to the final ones. Keep in mind that, per Figure 11-34, $x_0 = 1$ and $y_0 = 0$:

$$x_1 = \cos(45°) \times \left[x_0 - y_0 \times \tan(45°)\right] = \cos(45°) \times \left[x_0 - \frac{y_0}{1}\right]$$

$$y_1 = \cos(45°) \times \left[x_0 \times \tan(45°) + y_0\right] = \cos(45°) \times \left[\frac{x_0}{1} + y_0\right]$$

$$x_2 = \cos(26.565°) \times \left[x_1 - y_1 \times \tan(26.565°)\right] = \cos(26.565°) \times \left[x_1 - \frac{y_1}{2}\right]$$

$$y_2 = \cos(26.565°) \times \left[x_1 \times \tan(26.565°) + y_1\right] = \cos(26.565°) \times \left[\frac{x_1}{2} + y_1\right]$$

$$x_3 = \cos(-14.036°) \times \left[x_2 - y_2 \times \tan(-14.036°)\right] = \cos(-14.036°) \times \left[x_2 + \frac{y_2}{4}\right]$$

$$y_3 = \cos(-14.036°) \times \left[x_2 \times \tan(-14.036°) + y_2\right] = \cos(-14.036°) \times \left[-\frac{x_2}{4} + y_2\right]$$

Note the sign change in the last set of equations that result from going the other (clockwise) direction; when we're going clockwise, the sign of the tangent is negative. Plugging the equations for (x_1, y_1) into the equations for (x_2, y_2) and plugging that into the equations for (x_3, y_3) and then factoring out the cosines (and cleaning out the multiplications by 1) gives us the following:

$$x_3 = \cos(45°) \times \cos(26.565°) \times \cos(-14.036°) \times \left\{(x_0 - y_0) - \frac{x_0 - y_0}{2} + \frac{\frac{x_0 - y_0}{2} + (x_0 + y_0)}{4}\right\}$$

$$y_3 = \cos(45°) \times \cos(26.565°) \times \cos(-14.036°) \times \left\{\frac{-(x_0 - y_0) - \frac{(x_0 + y_0)}{2}}{4} + \frac{(x_0 - y_0)}{2} + (x_0 + y_0)\right\}$$

So what about those cosines? Skipping the mathematical proof, it turns out that as long as we have enough terms:

$$\cos(45°) \times \cos(26.565°) \times \cos(-14.036°) \times \ldots = 0.607252935008881$$

That's a constant, and we like constants. Let's call it C. We could multiply it at the end like this:

$$x_3 = C \times \left\{ [x_0 - y_0] - \frac{x_0 - y_0}{2} + \frac{\dfrac{x_0 - y_0}{2} + [x_0 + y_0]}{4} \right\}$$

$$y_3 = C \times \left\{ -\frac{[x_0 - y_0] - \dfrac{(x_0 + y_0)}{2}}{4} + \frac{(x_0 - y_0)}{2} + [x_0 + y_0] \right\}$$

But we could save that multiplication by just using the constant for x_0, as shown next. We'll also eliminate y_0, since it's 0. It ends up looking like this:

$$x_3 = C - \frac{C}{2} + \frac{\dfrac{C}{2} + C}{4} = 0.531$$

$$y_3 = -\frac{C - \dfrac{C}{2}}{4} + \frac{C}{2} + C = 0.834$$

If you check, you'll discover that the values for x_3 and y_3 are pretty close to the values of the cosine and sine of 57.529 degrees. And that's with only three terms; more terms gets us closer. Notice that this is all accomplished with addition, subtraction, and division by 2.

Let's turn this into a program that gives us a chance to introduce several additional tricks. First, we'll use a slightly different version of CORDIC called *vectoring mode*; so far, we've been discussing *rotation mode* because it's a little easier to understand. We've seen that in rotation mode we start with a vector (arrow) along the x-axis and rotate it until it's at the desired angle. Vectoring mode is sort of the opposite; we start at our desired angle and rotate it until we end up with a vector along the x-axis (angle of 0). Doing it this way means we can just test the sign of the angle to determine the direction of rotation for a step; it saves a comparison between two numbers.

Second, we're going to use table lookup. We'll precompute a table of angles with tangents of 1, ½, ¼, and so on. We only need to do this once. The final algorithm is shown in Figure 11-35.

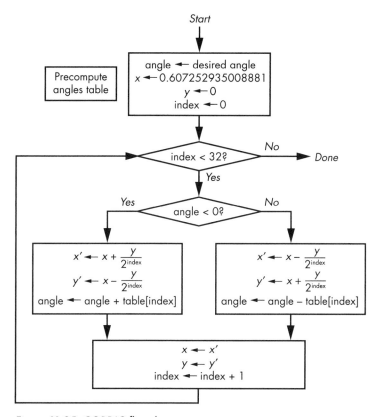

Figure 11-35: CORDIC flowchart

Now let's write a C program that implements this algorithm using even more tricks. First, we're going to express our angles in radians instead of in degrees.

The second trick is related to the first. You may have noticed that we haven't encountered any numbers greater than 1. We can design our program to work in the first quadrant (between 0 and 90 degrees) and get the others using symmetry. An angle of 90 degrees is $\pi/2$, which is ≈ 1.57. Because we don't have a wide range of numbers, we can use a fixed-point integer system instead of floating-point.

We're going to base our sample implementation on 32-bit integers. Because we need a range of $\approx \pm 1.6$, we can make bit 30 be the ones, bit 29 the halves, bit 28 the quarters, bit 27 the eighths, and so on. We'll use the MSB (bit 31) as the sign bit. We can convert floating-point numbers (as long as they're in range) to our fixed-point notation by multiplying by our version of 1, which is 0x40000000, and casting (converting) that into integers. Likewise, we can convert our results into floating-point by casting them as such and dividing by 0x40000000.

Listing 11-17 shows the code, which is quite simple.

```
1  const int angles[] = {
2    0x3243f6a8, 0x1dac6705, 0x0fadbafc, 0x07f56ea6, 0x03feab76, 0x01ffd55b, 0x00fffaaa, 0x007fff55,
3    0x003fffea, 0x001ffffd, 0x000fffff, 0x0007ffff, 0x0003ffff, 0x0001ffff, 0x0000ffff, 0x00007fff,
4    0x00003fff, 0x00001fff, 0x00000fff, 0x000007ff, 0x000003ff, 0x000001ff, 0x000000ff, 0x0000007f,
5    0x0000003f, 0x0000001f, 0x0000000f, 0x00000008, 0x00000004, 0x00000002, 0x00000001, 0x00000000
6  };
7
8  int angle = (desired_angle_in_degrees / 360 * 2 * 3.14159265358979323846) * 0x40000000;
9
10 int x = (int)(0.6072529350088812561694 * 0x40000000);
11 int y = 0;
12
13 for (int index = 0; index < 32; index++) {
14   int x_prime;
15   int y_prime;
16
17   if (angle < 0) {
18     x_prime = x + (y >> index);
19     y_prime = y - (x >> index);
20     angle += angles[index];
21   }
22   else {
23     x_prime = x - (y >> index);
24     y_prime = y + (x >> index);
25     angle -= angles[index];
26   }
27
28   x = x_prime;
29   y = y_prime;
30 }
```

Listing 11-17: CORDIC implementation in C

Implementing CORDIC uses many of the goodies in our growing bag of tricks: recursive subdivision, precomputation, table lookup, shifting for power-of-two division, integer fixed-point arithmetic, and symmetry.

Somewhat Random Things

It's very difficult to do completely random things on computers because they have to generate random numbers based on some formula, and that makes it repeatable. That kind of "random" is good enough for most computing tasks though, except for cryptography, which we'll discuss in

Chapter 13. In this section, we'll explore some approximations based on *pseudorandomness*. We're choosing visual examples because they're interesting and printable.

Space-Filling Curves

Italian mathematician Giuseppe Peano (1858–1932) came up with the first example of a *space-filling curve* in 1890. Three iterations of it are shown in Figure 11-36.

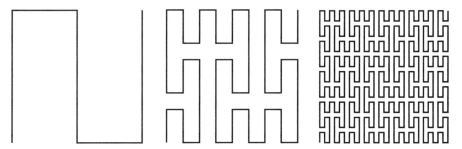

Figure 11-36: Peano curve

As you can see, the curve is a simple shape that is shrunk and repeated at different orientations. Each time that's done, it fills more of the space.

Space-filling curves exhibit *self-similarity*, which means they look about the same both up close and far away. They're a subset of something called *fractals*, which were popularized when Benoit Mandelbrot (1924–2010) published *The Fractal Geometry of Nature* (W. H. Freeman and Company, 1977). Many natural phenomena are self-similar; for example, a coastline has the same jaggedness when observed from a satellite and from a microscope.

The term *fractal* comes from *fraction*. Geometry includes numerous integer relationships. For example, doubling the length of the sides of a square quadruples its area. But an integer change in lengths in a fractal can change the area by a fractional amount, hence the name.

The Koch snowflake is an easy-to-generate curve first described in 1904 by Swedish mathematician Helge von Koch (1870–1924). It starts with an equilateral triangle. Each side is divided into thirds, and the center third is replaced by a triangle one-third of the size, with the edge in line with the original side omitted, as shown in Figure 11-37.

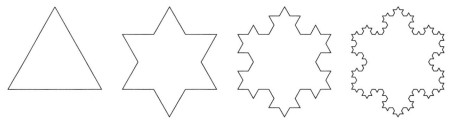

Figure 11-37: Four iterations of the Koch snowflake

You can see that complex and interesting shapes can be generated with a tiny amount of code and recursion. Let's look at slightly more complex example: the Hilbert curve, first described in 1891 by German mathematician David Hilbert (1862–1943), as shown in Figure 11-38.

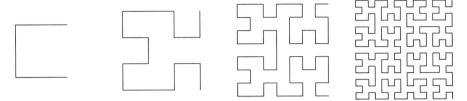

Figure 11-38: Four iterations of the Hilbert curve

The rules for the next iteration of the Hilbert curve are more complicated than for the Koch snowflake, because we don't do the same thing everywhere. There are four different orientations of the "cup" shape that are replaced by smaller versions, as shown in Figure 11-39. There's both a graphical representation and one using letters for right, up, left, and down. For each iteration, each corner of the shape on the left is replaced with the four shapes on the right (in order) at one-quarter the size of the shape on the left and then connected by straight lines.

Figure 11-39: Hilbert curve rules

L-Systems

The rules in Figure 11-39 are similar to the regular expressions we saw back in "Regular Expressions" on page 224, but backward. Instead of defining what patterns are matched, these rules define what patterns can be produced. They're called *L-systems* or *Lindenmayer systems*, after Hungarian botanist Aristid Lindenmayer (1925–1989), who developed them in 1968. Because they define what can be produced, they're also called *production grammars*.

You can see from Figure 11-39 that replacing an *R* with the sequence *U R R U* transforms the leftmost curve in Figure 11-38 into the one next to it.

The nice thing about production grammars is that they're compact and easy to both specify and implement. They can be used to model a lot of phenomena. This became quite the rage when Alvy Ray Smith at Lucasfilm published "Plants, Fractals, and Formal Languages" (SIGGRAPH, 1984); you couldn't go outside without bumping into L-System-generated shrubbery. Lindenmayer's work became the basis for much of the computer graphics now seen in movies.

Let's make some trees so this book will be carbon-neutral. We have four symbols in our grammar, as shown in Listing 11-18.

```
E draw a line ending at a leaf
B draw a branch line
L save position and angle, turn left 45°
R restore position and angle, turn right 45°
```

Listing 11-18: Symbols for tree grammar

In Listing 11-19, we create a grammar that contains two rules.

```
B → B B
E → B L E R E
```

Listing 11-19: Tree grammar rules

You can think of the symbols and rules as a genetic code. Figure 11-40 shows several iterations of the grammar starting from *E*. Note that we're not bothering to draw leaves on the ends of the branches. Also, beyond the first three, the set of symbols that define the tree are too long to show.

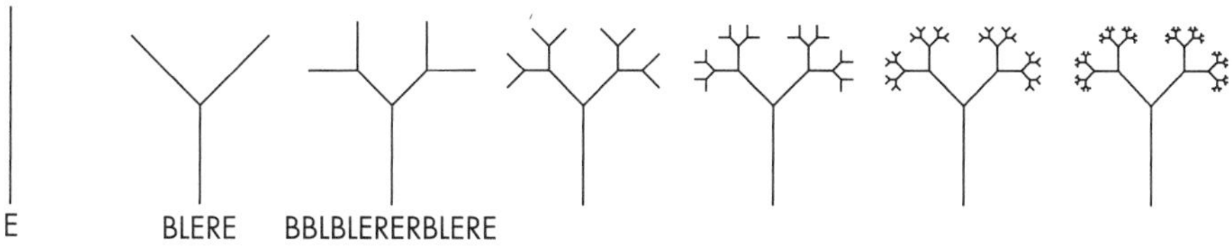

```
E        BLERE    BBLBLERERBLERE
```

Figure 11-40: Simple L-system tree

As you can see, we get pretty good-looking trees without much work. L-systems are a great way to generate natural-looking objects.

Production grammars have been used to generate objects since long before computers. Knitting instructions are production grammars, for example, as shown in Listing 11-20.

```
k = knit
p = purl
s = slip first stitch purl wise
row₁ → s   p  k k p p k k p p  k  p p k k p p k k   p   k k p p k k p p  k  p p k k p p k k   p   k
row₂ → s   k  p p k k p p k k  p  k k p p k k p p   k   p p k k p p k k  p  k k p p k k p p   k   k
row₅ → s   p p k k p p k k   p p p k k p p k k   p p p k k p p k k   p p p k k p p k k   p p k
row₆ → s   k k p p k k p p   k k k p p k k p p   k k k p p k k p p   k k k p p k k p p   k k k
section → row₁ row₂ row₁ row₂ row₅ row₆ row₅ row₆ row₂ row₂ row₂ row₂ row₆ row₅ row₆ row₅
scarf → section ...
```

Listing 11-20: Production grammar for scarf in Figure 11-41

Executing the grammar in Listing 11-20 using the knitting needle I/O device for some number of sections yields a scarf, as shown in Figure 11-41.

Figure 11-41: Scarf produced by production grammar

Going Stochastic

Stochastic is a good word to use when you want to sound sophisticated and *random* just won't do. Alan Fournier and Don Fussell at the University of Texas at Dallas introduced the notion of adding randomness to computer graphics in 1980. A certain amount of randomness adds variety. For example, Figure 11-42 shows a stochastic modification of the L-system trees from the last section.

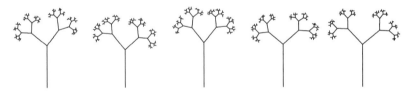

Figure 11-42: Stochastic L-system trees

As you can see, it generates a nice set of similar-looking trees. A forest looks more realistic when the trees aren't all identical.

Loren Carpenter at Boeing published a paper that pioneered a simple way to generate fractals ("Computer Rendering of Fractal Curves and Surfaces," SIGGRAPH, 1980). At SIGGRAPH 1983, Carpenter and Mandelbrot engaged in a very heated discussion about whether Carpenter's results were actually fractals.

Carpenter left Boeing and continued his work at Lucasfilm. His fractal mountains produced the planet in *Star Trek II: The Wrath of Khan.* An interesting factoid is that the planet took about six months of computer time to generate. Because it was generated using random numbers, Spock's coffin ended up flying through the side of the mountain for several frames. Artists had to manually cut a notch in the mountain to fix this.

Carpenter's technique was simple. He randomly selected a point on a line and then moved that point a random amount. He recursively repeated this for the two line segments until things were close enough. It's a bit like adding randomness to the Koch curve generator. Figure 11-43 shows a few random peaks.

Figure 11-43: Fractal mountains

Once again, pretty good for not much work.

Quantization

Sometimes we don't have a choice about approximating and must do the best we can. For example, we may have a color photograph that needs to be printed in a black-and-white newspaper. Let's look at how we might make this transformation. We'll use the grayscale image in Figure 11-44, since this book isn't printed in color. Because it's grayscale, each of the three color components is identical and in the range of 0 to 255.

Figure 11-44: Tony Cat

We need to perform a process called *quantization*, which means taking the colors that we have available in the original image and assigning them to colors in the transformed image. It's yet another sampling problem, as we have to take an analog (or *more* analog, in our case) signal and divide it among a fixed set of buckets. How do we map 256 values into 2?

Let's start with a simple approach called *thresholding*. As you might guess from the name, we pick a threshold and assign anything brighter than that to white, and anything darker to black. Listing 11-21 makes anything greater than 127 white, and anything not white is black.

```
for (y = 0; y < height; y++)
  for (x = 0; x < width; x++)
    if (value_of_pixel_at(x, y) > 127)
      draw_white_pixel_at(x, y);
    else
      draw_black_pixel_at(x, y);
```

Listing 11-21: Threshold pseudocode

Running this pseudocode on the image in Figure 11-44 produces the image in Figure 11-45.

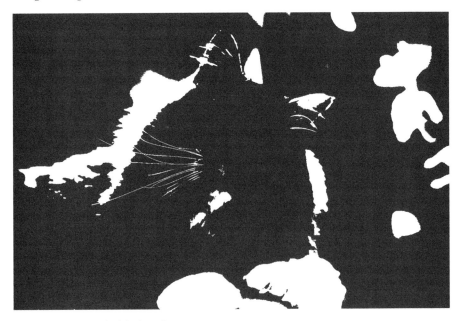

Figure 11-45: Threshold algorithm

That doesn't look very good. But there's not a lot we can do; we could monkey around with the threshold, but that would just give us different bad results. We'll try to get better results using optical illusions.

British scientist Henry Talbot (1800–1877) invented *halftone printing* in the 1850s for just this reason; photography at the time was grayscale, and printing was black and white. Halftone printing broke the image up into dots of varying sizes, as shown in the magnified image on the left in Figure 11-46. As you can see on the right, your eye interprets this as shades of gray.

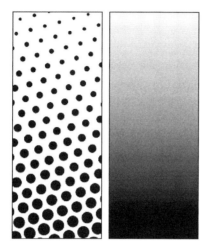

Figure 11-46: Halftone pattern

We can't vary the dot size on a computer screen, but we want the same type of effect. Let's explore some different ways to accomplish this. We can't change the characteristics of a single dot that can be either black or white, so we need to adjust the surrounding dots somehow to come up with something that your eye will see as shades of gray. We're effectively trading off image resolution for the perception of more shades or colors.

The name for this process is *dithering*, and it has an amusing origin going back once again to World War II analog computers. Someone noticed that the computers worked better aboard flying airplanes than on the ground. It turns out that the random vibration from the plane engines kept the gears, wheels, cogs, and such from sticking. Vibrating motors were subsequently added to the computers on the ground to make them work better by trembling them. This random vibration was called *dither*, based on the Middle English verb *didderen*, meaning "to tremble." There are many dithering algorithms; we'll examine only a few here.

The basic idea is to use a pattern of different thresholds for different pixels. In the mid-1970s, American scientist Bryce Bayer (1929–2012) at Eastman Kodak invented a key technology for digital cameras, the eponymous *Bayer filter*. The *Bayer matrix* is a variation that we can use for our purposes. Some examples are shown in Figure 11-47.

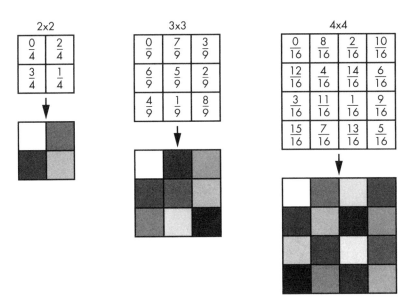

Figure 11-47: Bayer matrices

These matrices are *tiled* over the image, meaning they repeat in both the x and y directions, as shown in Figure 11-48. Dithering using tiled patterns is called *ordered dithering*, as there's a predictable pattern based on position in the image.

Figure 11-48: 2×2
Bayer matrix tiling pattern

Listing 11-22 shows the pseudocode for the Bayer matrices from Figure 11-47.

```
for (y = 0; y < height; y++)
 for (x = 0; x < width; x++)
  if (value_of_pixel_at(x, y) > bayer_matrix[y % matrix_size][x % matrix_size])
    draw_white_pixel_at(x, y);
  else
    draw_black_pixel_at(x, y);
```

Listing 11-22: Bayer ordered dithering pseudocode

On to the important question: what does Tony Cat think of this? Figures 11-49 through 11-51 show him dithered using the three matrices just shown.

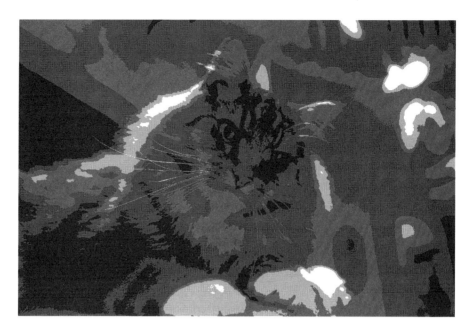

Figure 11-49: Tony dithered using the 2×2 Bayer matrix

Figure 11-50: Tony dithered using the 3×3 Bayer matrix

Figure 11-51: Tony dithered using the 4×4 Bayer matrix

As you can see, these are somewhat acceptable if you squint, and they improve with larger matrices. Not exactly the cat's meow, but a lot better than thresholding. Doing more work by using larger matrices yields better results. But the tiling pattern shows through. Plus it can produce really trippy artifacts called *moiré* patterns for certain images. You might have seen these if you've ever grabbed a stack of window screens.

How can we eliminate some of these screening artifacts? Instead of using a pattern, let's just compare each pixel to a random number using the pseudocode in Listing 11-23. The result is shown in Figure 11-52.

```
for (y = 0; y < height; y++)
  for (x = 0; x < width; x++)
    if (value_of_pixel_at(x, y) > random_number_between_0_and_255())
      draw_white_pixel_at(x, y);
    else
      draw_black_pixel_at(x, y);
```

Listing 11-23: Random-number dithering pseudocode

Figure 11-52: Tony dithered using random numbers

This eliminates the patterning artifacts but is pretty fuzzy, which is not unusual for cats. It's not as good as the ordered dither.

The fundamental problem behind all these approaches is that we can only do so much making decisions on a pixel-by-pixel basis. Think about the difference between the original pixel values and the processed ones. There's a certain amount of *error* for any pixel that wasn't black or white in the original. Instead of discarding this error as we've done so far, let's try spreading it around to other pixels in the neighborhood.

Let's start with something really simple. We'll take the error for the current pixel and apply it to the next horizontal pixel. The pseudocode is in Listing 11-24, and the result is shown in Figure 11-53.

```
for (y = 0; y < height; y++)
  for (error = x = 0; x < width; x++)
    if (value_of_pixel_at(x, y) + error > 127)
      draw_white_pixel_at(x, y);
      error = -(value_of_pixel_at(x, y) + error);
    else
      draw_black_pixel_at(x, y);
      error = value_of_pixel_at(x, y) + error;
```

Listing 11-24: One-dimensional error propagation pseudocode

Figure 11-53: Tony dithered using one-dimensional error propagation

Not great, but not horrible—easily beats thresholding and random numbers and is somewhat comparable to the 2×2 matrix; they each have different types of artifacts. If you think about it, you'll realize that error propagation is the same decision variable trick that we used earlier for drawing lines and curves.

American computer scientists Robert Floyd (1936–2001) and Louis Steinberg came up with an approach in the mid-1970s that you can think of as a cross between this error propagation and a Bayer matrix. The idea is to spread the error from a pixel to some surrounding pixels using a set of weights, as shown in Figure 11-54.

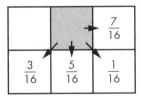

*Figure 11-54: Floyd-Steinberg
error distribution weights*

Listing 11-25 shows the Floyd-Steinberg pseudocode. Note that we have to keep two rows' worth of error values. We make each of those rows 2 longer than needed and offset the index by 1 so that we don't have to worry about running off the end when handling the first or last columns.

```
for (y = 0; y < height; y++)
  errors_a = errors_b;
  errors_b = 0;
  this_error = 0;

  for (x = 0; x < width; x++)
    if (value_of_pixel_at(x, y) > bayer_matrix[y % matrix_size][x % matrix_size])
      draw_white_pixel_at(x, y);
      this_error = -(value_of_pixel_at(x, y) + this_error + errors_a[x + 1]);
    else
      draw_black_pixel_at(x, y);
      this_error = value_of_pixel_at(x, y) + this_error + errors_a[x + 1];

    this_error = this_error * 7 / 16;

    errors_b[x] += this_error * 3 / 16;
    errors_b[x + 1] += this_error * 5 / 16;
    errors_b[x + 2] += this_error * 1 / 16;
```

Listing 11-25: Floyd-Steinberg error propagation code

This is a lot more work, but the results, as shown in Figure 11-55, look pretty good. (Note that this is unrelated to the Pink Floyd–Steinberg algorithm that was used to make album covers in the 1970s.)

Figure 11-55: Tony dithered using the Floyd-Steinberg algorithm

Post–Floyd-Steinberg, numerous other distribution schemes have been proposed, most of which do more work and distribute the error among more neighboring pixels.

Let's try one more approach, this one published by Dutch software engineer Thiadmer Riemersma in 1998. His algorithm does several interesting things. First, it goes back to the approach of affecting only one adjacent pixel. But it keeps track of 16 pixels' worth of error. It calculates a weighted average so that the most recently visited pixel has more effect than the least recently visited one. Figure 11-56 shows the weighting curve.

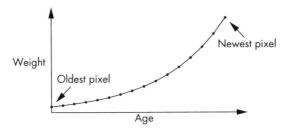

Figure 11-56: Riemersma pixel weights

The Riemersma algorithm doesn't use the typical adjacent pixels grid that we've seen before (see Listing 11-26). Instead, it follows the path of a Hilbert curve, which we saw in Figure 11-38.

```
for (each pixel along the Hilbert curve)
  error = weighted average of last 16 pixels

  if (value_of_pixel_at(x, y) + error > 127)
    draw_white_pixel_at(x, y);
  else
    draw_black_pixel_at(x, y);

  remove the oldest weighted error value
  add the error value from the current pixel
```

Listing 11-26: Riemersma error propagation pseudocode

The result is shown in Figure 11-57. Still not purr-fect, but at this point we've seen enough cats. Try the example code on a gradient such as the one in Figure 11-12. You've learned that there are many different ways to deal with approximation required by real-life circumstances.

Figure 11-57: Tony dithered using the Riemersma algorithm

Summary

In this chapter, we've examined a number of tricks you can use to increase performance and efficiency by avoiding or minimizing computation. As Jim Blinn, one of the giants in the field of computer graphics, said, "A technique is just a trick that you use more than once." And just as you saw with hardware building blocks, these tricks can be combined to solve complex problems.

12

DEADLOCKS AND RACE CONDITIONS

We've talked about *multitasking*, or computers doing more than one thing at a time. Originally we were just pretending that computers could do this, because really there was only one computer switching between tasks. But now that multicore processors are the norm, computers *are* actually doing more than one thing at a time. Multiprocessing isn't a particularly new concept; single-core processors have long been connected together to achieve higher performance. It's just easier and more common now. A multiprocessor system isn't an expensive special-purpose machine anymore—it's your phone.

Sometimes the order in which things are done is important. For example, let's say you have a joint bank account (one that you share with someone else) that has a balance of $100. The other account owner goes to an ATM to withdraw $75 at the same time that you go into the bank to withdraw $50. This is what's known as a *race condition*. The bank software needs to be able to *lock* one of you out so that only one withdrawal can be processed at a time to prevent the account from becoming overdrawn. This essentially means turning off multitasking for certain operations. It's tricky to do that without losing the benefits of multitasking, however, as this chapter will show.

What Is a Race Condition?

A race condition occurs when two (or more) programs access the same resource and the outcome is dependent on timing. Take a look at Figure 12-1, where two programs are trying to deposit money into a bank account.

Program 1	Program 2	Balance
		$100
read $100		$100
add $10		$100
write $110		$110
	read $110	$110
	add $50	$110
	write $160	$160

Correct result

Program 1	Program 2	Balance
		$100
read $100		$100
add $10		$100
	read $100	$100
	add $50	$100
write $110		$110
	write $150	$150

Incorrect result

Figure 12-1: Race condition example

The *shared resource* in this example is the account balance. As you can see, the result depends on the timing of the two programs accessing this resource.

Another way of looking at it is best expressed by the T-shirt shown in Figure 12-2.

Figure 12-2: Racing attire

Shared Resources

What resources can be shared? Pretty much anything. In the previous section, we saw memory being shared. Memory is always involved in sharing, even if the end result of the sharing isn't memory. That's because there must be some indication that a shared resource is in use. This memory may not be what we typically think of as memory; it may just be a bit in some piece of input/output (I/O) device hardware.

Sharing I/O devices is also very common—for example, sharing a printer. It obviously wouldn't work very well to mix pieces of different documents together. I mentioned back in "System and User Space" on page 133 that operating systems handle I/O for user programs. That really only applies to I/O devices that are part of the machine, like the USB controller. While the operating system ensures that USB-connected devices communicate correctly, it often leaves the control of these devices up to user programs.

Field-programmable gate arrays, or *FPGAs* (see "Hardware vs. Software" on page 90), are an exciting frontier in resource sharing. You might want to program an FPGA to provide a special hardware function to speed up a particular piece of software. You'd want to make sure that nothing replaces the hardware programming that's expected by the software.

It's less obvious that programs running on different computers communicating with each other can also share resources.

Processes and Threads

How can multiple programs get access to the same data? We briefly touched on operating systems back in "Relative Addressing" on page 128. One of the functions of an operating system is to manage multiple tasks.

Operating systems manage *processes*, which are programs running in *user space* (see "System and User Space" on page 133). Multiple programs can be running simultaneously with multicore processors, but that's not enough for a race condition by itself—programs must have shared resources.

There's no magic way, at least since Thor took the Tesseract back to Asgard, for processes to share resources; they must have some kind of arrangement to do so. This implies that processes sharing resources must somehow communicate, and this communication can take many forms. It must be prearranged either by being built into a program or via some sort of configuration information.

Sometimes a process needs to pay attention to multiple things. A good example is a *print server*—a program that other programs can communicate with to get things printed. Before networking, it was difficult to use a printer that wasn't connected to an I/O port on the machine you wanted to print from. The networking code developed in the 1980s at the University of California, Berkeley, made it easier to for computers to communicate with each other by adding several system calls. In essence, a program could wait for incoming activity from multiple sources and run the appropriate handler code. This approach worked pretty well, mainly because the handler code was fairly simple and was run before waiting for the next activity. Print server code could print an entire document before worrying about the next one.

Interactive programs with graphical user interfaces changed all that. Activity handlers were no longer simple tasks that ran from start to finish; they may have to pause and wait for user input in multiple places. Although programs could be implemented as a swarm of cooperating processes, that's pretty cumbersome because they need to share a lot of data.

What's needed is a way for handlers to be interruptible—that is, for them to be able to stop where they are, saving their state so that they can resume execution where they left off at a later time. Well, this is nothing new. Where is that state? On the stack. Problem is, there's only one stack per process, and it sounds like we need one for every handler in a process. Enter threads of execution. We saw how operating systems arrange process memory in "Arranging Data in Memory" on page 136. A *thread* is a piece of a program that shares the static data and heap but has its own stack, as shown in Figure 12-3. Each thread believes it has sole access to the CPU registers, so the *thread scheduler* must save and restore them when switching from one thread to another, in a manner similar to what the OS does when switching from one process to another. Threads are also called *lightweight processes* because they have much less context than a regular process, so switching between threads is faster than switching between processes.

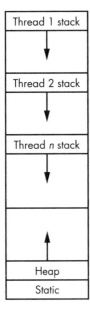

Figure 12-3: Memory layout for threads

Early implementations of threads involved some custom assembly language code that was by definition machine specific. Threads turned out to be sufficiently useful that a machine-independent API was standardized.

Threads are interesting to us here because they make race conditions within a single process possible. Not only is this an issue in low-level C programs, but JavaScript event handlers are also threads.

But just because threads exist doesn't mean they're the right solution for everything. Thread abuse is responsible for a lot of bad user experience. When Microsoft first introduced Windows, it was a program that ran on top of MS-DOS, which was not a state-of-the-art operating system that supported multitasking. As a result, Microsoft built parts of an operating system into each of its applications so that users could, for example, have several documents open at once. Unfortunately, some people brought this approach to programs running on complete operating systems. This method shows up in tabbed applications (for example, LibreOffice and Firefox) and user interfaces (for example, GNOME).

Why is that a bad idea? First of all, threads share data, so it's a security issue. Second, as you've probably experienced, a bug or problem with one tab often kills the entire process, resulting in lost work in what should be unrelated tasks. Third, as you've also likely experienced, a thread that takes a long time to complete prevents all other threads from running, so, for example, a slow-loading web page often hangs multiple browser instances.

The moral of the story here is to code smartly. Use the operating system; that's why it's there. If it doesn't perform as needed or is missing a critical feature, fix that. Don't make a mess of everything else.

Locks

The problem at hand isn't really sharing resources. It's how to make operations *atomic* (that is, indivisible, uninterruptible) when they're made up of a series of smaller operations.

We wouldn't be having this discussion if computers had instructions like adjust the bank balance. But of course they don't, because we'd need an infinite number of such instructions. Instead, we have to make critical sections of code appear atomic using some sort of *mutual exclusion* mechanism. We do that by creating *advisory locks* that programs follow to avoid conflicts (see Figure 12-4).

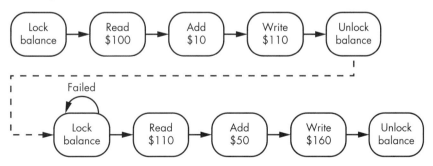

Figure 12-4: Advisory lock

As you can see in Figure 12-4, the upper program grabbed the lock first, so the lower program had to wait until the lock was released. The lock is *advisory* because it's up to the programs to follow it; there is no enforcement mechanism. This might seem pretty useless because it wouldn't stop anyone from robbing a bank. But it's a matter of where the lock resides. As you can see in Figure 12-5, the lock is at the bank, which does the enforcement, so that makes it work.

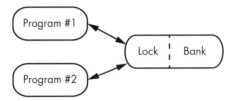

Figure 12-5: Lock location

This solves one problem but creates others. What happens if the communication between program #1 and the bank is slow? Clearly, program #2 is going to have to wait a while, which means we're losing some of the benefits of multitasking. And what happens if program #1 dies or just behaves badly and never releases the lock? What does program #2 do while it's waiting?

We'll look at these issues in the next few sections.

Transactions and Granularity

Every operation performed by program #1 in Figure 12-5 requires some sort of communication with the bank. This needs to be two-way communication because we need to know whether or not each operation succeeds before doing the next. The easy way to improve the performance is to bundle the set of operations into a *transaction*, which is a group of operations that either all succeed or all fail (see Figure 12-6). The term *transaction* stems from the database world. Rather than sending each operation separately, we'll bundle them.

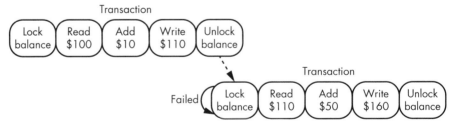

Figure 12-6: Transactions

An obvious guideline is to minimize the amount of time in which something is locked, because that reduces concurrency. One guideline that's not quite so obvious, however, is to minimize the *granularity* of locks—that is, the amount of stuff covered by the lock. We're locking the balance in our example; it's implied that we're just locking the balance of one account. Locking the entire bank every time one customer needs to update a balance would not be a great solution. The X Window System is an example of poorly designed locking. Although it has many types of locks, there are many instances where locking everything is the only option, but that eliminates concurrency.

Locks that cover a small part of a system are called *fine-grained*; locks covering larger parts are called *coarse-grained*.

Processor interrupt handling includes a locking mechanism. When an interrupt is received, a mask *is set that prevents the processor from receiving any more interrupts of the same type, unless explicitly allowed, until the interrupt handler is done.*

Waiting for a Lock

It doesn't do a lot of good to use transactions and fine-grained locks if a program waiting for a lock can't do anything useful while waiting. After all, the "multi" is the whole point of multitasking.

Sometimes there's nothing useful to do while waiting for a lock, which is why you have to stand in the rain waiting for an ATM to respond. There are two ways of doing nothing, though. We can *spin*, which means we can try the lock over and over until we successfully grab it. Spinning often involves using a timer to space out the tries. Going full speed on a machine chews up a lot of power unnecessarily. Going full speed on a network can be like having a mob of people trying to get into a store on Black Friday. In some circumstances—and this is the second way of doing nothing—an entity requesting a lock can *register* that request with the lock authority and *get notified* when the request is granted. This allows the requestor to go do something more useful while waiting. This approach doesn't scale particularly well and is explicitly not supported by the architecture of the internet, although it can be layered on top.

We learned in Chapter 6 that Ethernet takes an interesting approach to waiting. It doesn't have locks, but if multiple devices collide while trying to access the shared resource (the wire), they each wait a random amount of time and then try again.

Some operating systems provide locking functionality, usually associated with a handle similar to a file descriptor. Locking can be attempted in blocking or nonblocking modes. *Blocking* means that the system suspends the calling program (that is, stops it from executing) until the lock is available. *Nonblocking* means that the program keeps running and receives some indication that it did not get the lock.

Deadlocks

You've seen that programs must do some sort of waiting around when they need locks that aren't available. Complicated systems often have multiple locks, though, so what happens in the case shown in Figure 12-7?

Program #1 successfully grabs Lock A, and program #2 successfully grabs Lock B. Next, program #1 tries to grab Lock B but can't because program #2 has it. Likewise, program #2 tries to grab Lock A but can't because program #1 has it. Neither program can proceed to the point where it releases the locks it holds. This is situation is called a *deadlock*, which is not a multi-threaded hairstyle.

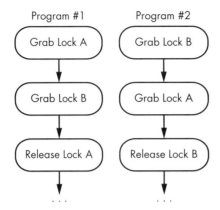

Figure 12-7: Deadlock

There are few great solutions to deadlocks other than to write code well. In some situations, it's possible to manually clear a lock without causing a lot of damage. You've probably come across some situation where a program refuses to run because it can't get a lock and prompts you as to whether or not you'd like to clear it. This situation arises when a program that holds a lock croaks unexpectedly without releasing it.

Short-Term Lock Implementation

There is really only one way to implement locks, but there are many ways to present them to programs. Lock implementation requires hardware support in the form of special instructions to support locking. Software solutions designed decades ago no longer work due to advances in processor technology, such as out-of-order execution and multiple cores.

Many processors have a *test and set* instruction that exists explicitly for locking. This is an atomic instruction that tests to see whether a memory location is 0 and sets it to 1 if it isn't. It returns a 1 if it was successful in changing the value and 0 otherwise. Thus, it directly implements a lock.

An alternate version that works better in situations where lots of programs are contending for a lock is *compare and swap*. This instruction is similar to test and set, but instead of just using a single value, the invoker provides both an old and a new value. If the old value matches what's in the memory location, it's replaced by the new value and the lock is grabbed.

Use of these instructions is usually restricted to system mode, so they're not available to user programs. Some of the more recent language standards, such as C11, have added user-level support for atomic operations. Various locking operations have also been standardized and made available in libraries.

Additional code can be attached to locks to make them more efficient. For example, queues can be associated with locks to register programs waiting for locks.

Long-Term Lock Implementation

We've mostly been talking about locks that are held for as short a time as possible, but sometimes we want to hold a lock for a long time. This is usually in situations where access by multiple programs is never permitted—for example, a word processor that's designed to prevent multiple parties from editing the same document at the same time.

Long-term locks need to be kept in more persistent storage than memory. They're often implemented through files. System calls exist that allow exclusive file creation, and whatever program gets there first succeeds. This is equivalent to acquiring a lock. Note that system calls are a high-level abstraction that uses atomic instructions underneath the hood.

Browser JavaScript

Writing JavaScript programs that run in a browser is the first place where, as a new programmer, you're likely to have to pay attention to concurrency. This may sound surprising if you've read any JavaScript documentation, because JavaScript is defined as single-threaded. So how can concurrency be an issue?

The reason is that JavaScript wasn't originally designed for the uses it's being put to today. One of its original purposes was to provide faster user feedback and to reduce internet traffic, back when the internet was much slower. For example, imagine a web page containing a field for a credit card number. Before JavaScript, the number would have to be sent to a web server that would verify that it contained only digits and either send an error response or further process the number if it was okay. JavaScript allowed the credit card number to be checked for digits in the web browser. This meant that the user didn't have to wait in the event of a typo and that no internet traffic was required in order to detect and report the typo. Of course, there's still lots of bad JavaScript out there that can't handle spaces in card numbers, as you've probably discovered.

Since JavaScript was created to run short programs in response to user events, it's implemented using an *event loop* model, the workings of which are shown in Figure 12-8.

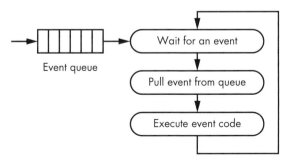

Figure 12-8: JavaScript event loop

What happens is that tasks to be performed are added to the *event queue*. JavaScript pulls these tasks from the queue one at a time and executes them. These tasks are not interruptible because JavaScript is single-threaded. But you as the programmer don't have control over the order in which events are added to the queue. For example, say you have an event handler for each mouse button. You don't control the order in which mouse buttons are clicked, so you can't control the ordering of events. Your program must reliably deal with events in any order.

Asynchronous communications weren't designed into JavaScript when it debuted in 1995. Up until that point, browsers submitted forms and servers returned web pages. Two things changed that. First came the publication of the Document Object Model (DOM) in 1997, although it didn't become stable (more or less) until around 2004. The DOM allowed existing web pages to be modified instead of just being replaced. Second, the XMLHttpRequest (XHR) arrived on the scene in 2000, which became the basis of AJAX. It provided background browser-server communications outside of the existing "load a page" model.

These changes triggered a dramatic increase in the complexity of web pages. Much more JavaScript was written, making it a mainstream programming language. Web pages became increasingly reliant on background asynchronous communication with servers. There were a lot of growing pains, because this wasn't something JavaScript was designed to do, especially because the single-threaded model was at odds with asynchronous communications.

Let's contrive a simple web application to display the art for an album by an artist. We'll use some hypothetical website that first requires us to convert the album and artist name into an album identifier and then uses that identifier to fetch the album art. You may try writing the program as shown in Listing 12-1, where the code in italics is supplied by the user.

```
var album_id;
var album_art_url;

// Send the artist name and album name to the server and get back the album identifier.

$.post("some_web_server", { artist: artist_name, album: album_name }, function(data) {
  var decoded = JSON.parse(data);
  album_id = decoded.album_id;
});

// Send the album identifier to the server and get back the URL of the album art image.
// Add an image element to the document to display the album art.

$.post("some_web_server", { id: album_id }, function(data) {
  var decoded = JSON.parse(data);
  album_art_url = decoded.url;
});

$(body).append('<img src="' + album_art_url + '"/>');
```

Listing 12-1: First-try album art program

The jQuery post function sends the data from the second argument to the URL in the first argument, and calls the function that's the third argument when it gets a response. Note that it doesn't really call the function—it adds the function to the event queue, so that the function gets called when it reaches the front.

This seems like a nice, simple, orderly program. But it won't work reliably. Why not? Let's look at what's happening in detail. Check out Figure 12-9.

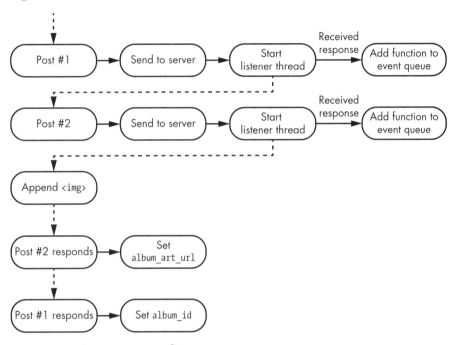

Figure 12-9: Album art program flow

As you can see, the program doesn't execute in order. The post operations start threads internally that wait for the server to respond. When the response is received, the callback functions are added to the event queue. The program shows the second post responding first, but it could just as easily be the first post responding first; that's out of our control.

There's a good chance, then, that our program will request the album art before it obtains the album_id from the first post. And it's almost guaranteed that it will append the image to the web page before it obtains the album_art_url. That's because, although JavaScript itself is single-threaded, we have concurrent interactions with web servers. Put another way: although the JavaScript interpreter presents a single-threaded model to the programmer, it's actually multithreaded internally.

Listing 12-2 shows a working version.

```
$.post("some_web_server", { artist: artist_name, album: album_name }, function(data) {
  var decoded = JSON.parse(data);

  $.post("some_web_server", { id: decoded.id }, function(data) {
    var decoded = JSON.parse(data);
    $(body).append('<img src="' + decoded.url + '"/>');
  });
});
```

Listing 12-2: Second-try album art program

Now we've moved the image append to be inside of the second post callback, and we've moved the second post callback to be inside of the first post callback. This means we won't make the second post until the first one has completed.

As you can see, nesting is required to ensure that the dependencies are met. And it gets uglier with error handling, which I didn't show. The next section covers a different way to approach this issue.

Asynchronous Functions and Promises

There's absolutely nothing wrong with the program in Listing 12-2. It works correctly because jQuery implemented the post function correctly. But just because jQuery did it correctly doesn't mean other libraries do, especially in the Node.js world, where bad libraries are being created at an astonishing rate. Programs that use libraries that don't properly implement callbacks are very difficult to debug. That's become a problem because, as I mentioned in the book's introduction, so much of programming is now taught as if it's just the process of gluing together functions in libraries.

JavaScript has recently addressed this by adding a new construct called a *promise*. The computing concept of a promise stems from the mid-1970s and is having a renaissance since its addition to JavaScript. Promises move the mechanics of asynchronous callbacks into the language proper so that libraries can't screw them up. Of course, it's a moving target because you can't add to the language every time a programmer makes a mistake. This particular case, however, seemed common enough to be worthwhile.

Explanations of JavaScript promises can be hard to understand because two independent things are jumbled together. Promises are easier to understand if these components are separated out. The important part is that there's a better chance that libraries for asynchronous operations will function correctly if they use promises. The less important part, which gets talked about more, is a change in the programming paradigm. There's a lot of "religion" around programming paradigms, which I talk about more in the final chapter. At some level, the promise construct is *syntactic sugar*, a sweetener that makes certain types of programming easier at the expense of fattening the programming language.

Taken to extremes, code for JavaScript asynchronous requests starts to look like what some call the *pyramid of doom*, as shown in Listing 12-3. I personally don't see anything wrong with writing code this way. If indenting offends you, then stay away from the Python programming language; it'll bite your legs off.

```
$.post("server", { parameters }, function() {
  $.post("server", { parameters }, function() {
    $.post("server", { parameters }, function() {
      $.post("server", { parameters }, function() {
        ...
      });
    });
  });
});
```

Listing 12-3: Pyramid of doom

Of course, some of this results from the way the program was written. The anonymous functions require all the code to be written inline. These can be eliminated, as shown in Listing 12-4, which eliminates the pyramid of doom but is harder to follow.

```
$.post("some_web_server", { artist: artist_name, album: album_name }, got_id);

function
got_id(data)
{
  var decoded = JSON.parse(data);
  $.post("some_web_server", { id: decoded.id }, got_album_art);
}

function
got_album_art(data)
{
  var decoded = JSON.parse(data);
  $(body).append('<img src="' + decoded.url + '"/>');
}
```

Listing 12-4: Rewrite eliminating anonymous functions

What programmers really want is a more straightforward way of writing code. This is easy in many other programming languages but difficult in JavaScript because of its single-threaded model. In a hypothetical multithreaded version of JavaScript, we would just create a new thread to run the code in Listing 12-5. This code assumes that the post blocks until completed; it's synchronous instead of asynchronous. The code is clear and easy to follow.

```
var data = $.post("some_web_server", { artist: artist_name, album: album_name } );
var decoded = JSON.parse(data);

var data = $.post("some_web_server", { id: decoded.id }, got_album_art);
var decoded = JSON.parse(data);

$(body).append('<img src="' + decoded.url + '"/>');
```

Listing 12-5: Hypothetical blocking JavaScript example

If you could write code like this in JavaScript, it wouldn't work well. The single-threaded nature of JavaScript would prevent other code from running while the posts were waiting, which means that event handlers for mouse clicks and other user interactions wouldn't get run in a timely manner.

JavaScript promises have some similarity to Listing 12-4 in that the definition of a promise is akin to the function definitions; the definition of a promise is separated out from its execution.

A promise is created as shown in Listing 12-6. Although this doesn't look much different from other JavaScript code, such as a jQuery post that takes a function as an argument, the function is not executed. This is the setup phase of a promise.

```
var promise = new Promise(function(resolve, reject) {
  if (whatever it does is successful)
    resolve(return_value);
  else
    reject(return_value);
});
```

Listing 12-6: Promise creation

Let's look at this in more detail. You supply the promise with a function that performs some asynchronous operation. That function has two arguments that are also functions: one (resolve in Listing 12-6) that's appended to the JavaScript event queue when the asynchronous operation completes successfully, and one (reject in Listing 12-6) that's added to the JavaScript event queue if the asynchronous operation fails.

The program executes a promise using its then method, as shown in Listing 12-7. This method takes a pair of functions as arguments that are matched to the resolve and reject functions supplied during promise creation.

```
promise.then(
  function(value) {
    do something with the return_value from resolve
  },
  function(value) {
    do something with the return_value from reject
  }
);
```

Listing 12-7: Promise execution

This isn't very exciting. We could write code to do this without using promises, as we did before. So why bother? Promises come with a bit of syntactic sugar called *chaining*. It allows code to be written in a something().then().then().then() ... style. This works because the then method returns another promise. Note that, in a manner similar to exceptions, the second argument to then can be omitted and errors can be fielded with a catch. Listing 12-8 shows the album art program rewritten using promise chaining.

```
function
post(host, args)
{
  return (new Promise(function(resolve, reject) {
    $.post(host, args, function(data) {
      if (success)
        resolve(JSON.parse(data));
      else
        reject('failed');
    });
  }));
}

post("some-web-server, { artist: artist_name, album: album_name } ).then(function(data) {
  if (data.id)
    return (post("some-web-server, { id: data.id });
  else
    throw ("nothing found for " + artist_name + " and " + album_name);
}).then(function(data) {
  if (data.url)
    $(body).append('<img src="' + data.url + '"/>');
  else
    throw (`nothing found for ${data.id}`);
}).catch(alert);
```

Listing 12-8: Album art program using promise chaining

Now, I don't find this code easier to follow than the pyramid-of-doom version, but you may feel differently. The versions of code in Listings 12-2 and 12-8 raise another point about the art of programming: trading off the ease of code development versus maintenance. In the grand scheme of a product's lifecycle, maintainability is more important than writing code in some personally preferred style. I talk about this a little more in Chapter 15. Promise chaining allows you to write code in a *function().function().function()* . . . style instead of the pyramid-of-doom style. While the first style makes keeping track of parentheses slightly easier, JavaScript—unlike Ruby, for example— was designed with the second style, and having two styles in the same language likely increases confusion, resulting in decreased programmer productivity. Although promises might reduce the instances of one class of programming errors, don't mistake them as a cure-all for poorly written code.

Promises are syntactic sugar that reduce the amount of nesting. But if we really want code that's easier to follow, we want something more like Listing 12-5. JavaScript includes yet another way to write "asynchronous" programs that builds on promises but mirrors the synchronous coding style: async and await.

Listing 12-9 shows an implementation of the album art program using async and await.

```
function
post(host, args)
{
  return (new Promise(function(resolve, reject) {
    $.post(host, args, function(data) {
      if (success)
        resolve(JSON.parse(data));
      else
        reject('failed');
    });
  }));
}

async function
get_album_art()
{
  var data = await post("some-web-server, { artist: artist_name, album: album_name } );

  if (data.id) {
    var data = await post("some-web-server, { id: data.id });

    if (data.url)
      $(body).append('<img src="' + data.url + '"/>');
  }
}
```

Listing 12-9: Album art program using async and await

To me, this looks more straightforward than Listing 12-8.

Of course, what's going on here is that the single-threaded JavaScript model has been severely bent, if not broken. Asynchronous functions are essentially threads that are not interruptible.

Summary

In this chapter, you learned about some of the issues that result from using shared resources. You learned about race conditions and deadlocks, and about processes and threads. You also learned a little bit about concurrency in JavaScript and new ways in which it's being approached. At this point, we've covered the basics. We'll move on to one of our two advanced topics—security—in the next chapter, which uses many of the technologies that you've learned about so far.

13

SECURITY

Security is an advanced topic. The cryptography component in particular involves lots of esoteric mathematics. But it's a really important topic. Rather than go into all the gory details, this chapter gives you the lay of the land. While this isn't enough for you to qualify as a security expert, it should enable you to ask questions about the viability of security implementations. And there are lots of things that you can do without having to be a security expert to make both you and your code more secure.

For the most part, computer security is not very different from regular old security, such as home security. In many respects, the advent of networked computers transformed security issues from those needed for a small apartment to those required to secure a large castle. As you can imagine, a large castle has many more entrances that need guarding and more inhabitants who can compromise the defenses. And it's bigger, so a lot more trash accumulates, making it harder to keep clean and giving bugs more places to hide.

At its core, security is about keeping you and your stuff safe by *your* definition of *safe*. It's not just a technological issue—it's a social issue. You and your stuff, along with your definition of safe, must be balanced against everybody else, their stuff, and their definitions.

Security and privacy are intertwined, in part because security comes from keeping your information private. For example, your bank account wouldn't be secure if everybody had the password. Privacy is difficult to maintain given the number of inane practices at organizations with which we are forced to interact. Every time I see a new doctor, their office asks me for all my personally identifying information. I always ask them, "Why do you need this information?" They always reply, "To protect your privacy." To which I always ask, "How does giving you and everybody else who asks for it all my personal information protect my privacy?" They just give an exasperated sigh and say, "We just need it." And whether they do or not, they're not required to give you a truthful answer. Nowadays, privacy is also impacted by the ease of connecting disparate pieces of information (a topic covered in more detail in the next chapter) resulting from pervasive data collection, which includes surveillance cameras, automatic license plate readers (ALPRs), cell phone surveillance including IMSI catchers (StingRays), internet surveillance (room 641A), facial recognition, and so on. Protecting your privacy is increasingly difficult, which negatively impacts your security.

Good security is hard. The old adage that "a chain is only as strong as its weakest link" describes the situation perfectly. Think about online banking. There are many components ranging from computer hardware, software, and communications networks to people. The best technology won't protect you if you leave your password written down next to your computer!

Overview of Security and Privacy

This section provides a nontechnical introduction to the issues involved in security and privacy. It defines many of the terms that later sections cover in more depth.

Threat Model

We wouldn't be talking about security in the absence of threats. There wouldn't be security worries if everybody behaved nicely. But they don't.

Security doesn't exist in a vacuum; it's relative to a *threat model*, which lists the things to be secured and enumerates the possible attacks on whatever needs securing so that appropriate defenses can be designed. Contrary to what you might infer from the behavior of "smart devices" such as internet-connected televisions, security cameras, light bulbs, and such, "What could possibly go wrong?" is not a valid threat model.

For example, at the time of writing, Fender had recently introduced a Bluetooth-enabled guitar amplifier. But the company didn't bother to implement the Bluetooth pairing protocol, which would secure the wireless connection between a performer's guitar and amp. That means a crafty audience member could connect to the stage amp as well from a cell phone if they were close enough, broadcasting whatever they wanted. (This could become a new art form, but that was likely not Fender's intent.)

Understanding the threat model is important because there's no such thing as 100 percent security. You have to design defenses that are appropriate for the threat model. For example, it might be nice to have your own personal armed guard to keep your backpack safe when you're in class, but it's not cost-effective and probably wouldn't go over well with the school administration. A locker is a more appropriate defense for this particular threat.

Here's another example: I live on a farm in the middle of nowhere. I can put all the expensive locks I want on the doors, but if someone wanted to cut through a wall with a chainsaw or dynamite their way in, nobody would notice because those are normal country sounds. Of course, I do have locks, but in this case, carrying good insurance is a large component of my security because I'm protecting the value of my property, which would be too expensive to secure by physical means.

Many of my neighbors don't really understand this and engage in practices that decrease their security. It's unfortunately common for people to move to the country and immediately install streetlights on their property. I've asked many of them why they installed the lights, because part of living in the country is being able to see the stars at night and light pollution interferes. The answer is always "for security." I've tried to explain that those lights are just a big advertisement that something is worth stealing and that nobody is home.

Self-defeating security measures are common in the computer world too. For example, many organizations choose to have rules dictating the composition of passwords and how often they must be changed. The result is that people either choose easily guessable passwords or write them down because they can't remember them.

The upshot is that you can't do effective security without defining the threat model. There has to be a balance between threats and defending against them. The goal is have inexpensive defenses that are expensive to attack. A side effect of the internet is that it has dramatically reduced attack costs but not defense costs.

Trust

One of the hardest things to do when determining a threat model is deciding what you can *trust*. Trust in a bygone era came from face-to-face interactions, although people still got taken by charismatic grifters. Deciding who and what to trust is much harder in the modern world. Can you recognize an honest Wi-Fi access point by looking it in the eyes? Not very likely, even if you know where to find its eyes.

You know how important trust is if you've ever asked friends to keep a secret. There's a 50/50 chance that a friend will violate your trust. Probability math tells us that there's a 75 percent chance that your secret will get out if you tell it to two friends. The odds of your secret getting out increase with each friend; it's 87 percent with three friends, 94 with four, 97 with five, and so on. You can see that putting trust in anything that you don't control reduces security; it starts off bad and gets worse from there.

With friends, you get to decide who is worthy of your trust. Your ability to make that choice is very limited in the networked computer world. For example, if you're one of those rare people who reads terms and conditions before accepting, you might have noticed that almost all of them say something like "Your privacy is very important to us. As a result, you're going to hold us harmless for breaches of your privacy." Doesn't sound very trustworthy. But you have no choice if you want to use the service.

In the computer security world, *trust* refers to those components that you have no choice but to rely on. Your security depends on the security of those components. As you saw earlier, you want to keep these to the absolute minimum necessary for the greatest security.

When you're using computers, you're relying on a huge collection of third-party hardware and software. You don't have access to the hardware or the software and have no choice but to rely on them, even though they've done nothing to earn your trust. Even if you had access, would you really have the time and knowledge to review it all?

The notion of trust comes up again and again in security. For now, consider three classes of trust violations:

Deliberate   Examples include the 2005 *rootkit* (a collection of software that bypasses protections) that Sony BMG installed on customers' computers and the pop-up ad delivering *malware* (malicious software) in Lenovo laptops a few years ago. These weren't programs accidentally installed by users; they were installed by the computer suppliers.

Incompetent   Examples of incompetence include unencrypted wireless tire pressure sensors that make it possible for your car to be targeted, the unencrypted RFID tags in newer U.S. passports that make it simple to detect someone carrying one or the proposed vehicle-to-vehicle communications standards being discussed for "safety" that would allow vehicles to be targeted by bad information. Attackers have found a way to get access to and change the settings in a large number of Wi-Fi routers without having to know the administrator password. In the extremely dangerous category, Siemens included a hardcoded password in some of its industrial control systems, meaning that anyone with that password could access equipment that was thought to be supposedly secured. A hardcoded password was just found in some of Cisco's products as well. The largest DDoS (discussed shortly) attack to date leveraged default passwords in IoT devices made by Hangzhou XiongMai. These sadly all harken back to the "What could possibly go wrong?" threat model combined with the "security by obscurity" mindset (more on this in a moment).

Disingenuous   This is when people flat out lie. I talk about this more in "The Social Context" on page 359. A good example is when the American National Institute of Standards and Technology (NIST) was working on encryption standards with the assistance of "experts" from the American National Security Agency (NSA). It turns out that the NSA experts deliberately weakened the standard instead of strengthening it. This made it easier for them to spy while also making it easier for someone to break into your bank account. Trust violations are so common that the term *kleptography* has been coined to describe the class of violations in which an adversary secretly and securely steals information.

The phrase *security by obscurity* is used to categorize claims that things are secure because the secret sauce is, well, secret. That's been repeatedly demonstrated not to be the case. In fact, better security comes from *transparency* and *openness*. When as many people as possible are educated about the security methods being used, it fosters discussion and discovery of flaws. History tells us that no one person is perfect or will think of everything. In computer programming, we sometimes call this the *thousands of eyeballs principle*. This is evident in the industry statistic that Windows has a hundred times more critical vulnerabilities than Linux.

This stuff isn't easy; it sometimes takes years or even decades to discover security issues, even when smart people are looking for them. For example, the recent "Spectre" and "Meltdown" exploits have their genesis in CPU architectural design decisions made in the 1960s.

Physical Security

Think about a school locker. You put your belongings in it to keep them safe from other people. It's made of fairly heavy steel and designed to be hard to pry open. Security folks would call the door an *attack surface* because it's something that someone trying to break into your locker can attack. It's a pretty good response to the threat of theft, because you can't break it open without making a lot of noise. Lots of people are around during the day when your stuff is in your locker, and they would probably notice. Although someone could break in after hours, it's less likely that things of value would be in the locker at those times.

The combination lock on the door opens only with the correct combination, which you know. When the school gave you the combination, they gave you *authorization* to open that particular locker. The lock is another attack surface. The lock is designed so that breaking the dial off doesn't cause it to open and so that it's hard to get to the innards of the lock with the locker closed. Of course, now some new issues arise. You need to keep the combination secret. You can write it down on a piece of paper somewhere, but someone else might find it. You have to make sure that someone else doesn't learn your combination by watching you open your locker. And, as you know from watching movies, safecrackers can open combination locks, and it's not practical for the school to spend the money for really good locks. Devices called *autodialers* can be attached to a combination lock to try all the possible combinations. They used to be specialty devices, but people have built their own using small, inexpensive microcomputers such as Arduinos combined with cheap stepper motors. But just like with the door, enough people are roaming the halls that a break-in attempt would likely be noticed. It would take either a talented safecracker or a bad lock design (as many "tough-looking" locks are all show). Note that there is a popular brand of combination lock that can easily be opened in less than a minute by anyone with easily obtainable knowledge.

There's a third attack surface that may have escaped your notice. There's a keyhole in the middle of the lock. It's what security people would call a *backdoor*, even though in this case it's on the front door. It's another way of getting into your locker that's not under your control. Why is it there? Obviously the school knows the combination to your locker, or they wouldn't have been able to give it to you. This backdoor is there for their convenience so that they can quickly open everybody's lockers. But it reduces everybody's security. Locks with keyholes are pretty easy to pick in seconds. And because one key opens everybody's locker, they're all vulnerable if someone gets a copy of the key, which isn't as hard as you might think.

When the school gave you the combination to your locker, they conferred a *privilege* on you—namely, the ability to get into your locker. Someone with the key has a higher *privilege level*, as they're authorized to open all lockers, not just one. Acquiring a copy of the key would raise your privilege level. Many budding engineers, including this author, discovered locksmithing and found ways to become "privileged" in our youths.

Communications Security

Now that we've learned a little about keeping stuff secure, let's tackle a harder problem. How do you transfer something of yours to someone else? Let's start with an easy case. You have a homework assignment about Orion that's due, but you have to miss class for a doctor's appointment. You see your friend Edgar in the hall and ask him to turn in your homework for you. Seems simple enough.

The first step in this process is *authentication*. This is you recognizing that the person you're handing your homework to is indeed Edgar. But in your rush, you may have forgotten that Edgar has an evil twin brother. Or "Edgar" could be something wearing Edgar, like an Edgar suit. You really don't want to accidentally authenticate something buggy (see the 1997 movie *Men in Black*)!

Edgar impersonators aren't the only attack surface. All bets are off once your homework is out of your hands; you're trusting Edgar to act in your best interest. But Edgar could space out and forget to hand it in. Evil Edgar could change your homework so that some of the answers are wrong, or worse, he could make it look like you copied someone else's work. There's no way to prove *authenticity*—that Edgar turned in what you handed him. If you had planned ahead, you could have put your homework into an envelope secured by a wax seal. Of course, these can often be opened and resealed without leaving a trace.

This becomes a much more difficult problem when you don't have an authenticated, *trusted* courier delivering your homework. Maybe you had an unplanned absence and your teacher said that you could mail in your homework. Any number of unknown people may handle your letter, making it vulnerable to a *man-in-the-middle attack*, which is when an attacker gets between parties and intercepts and/or modifies their communications. You don't know who's handling your mail, and, unlike with Edgar, you don't even have an opportunity for authentication.

The solution to these issues is *cryptography*. You can *encrypt* your communication using a secret code known only to you and the intended recipient, who can use that code to *decrypt* it. Of course, like your locker combination, the secret code must be kept secret. Codes can be broken, and you have no way to know if someone knows or broke your code. A properly designed *cryptosystem* reduces the need to trust components between parties; leaked communications that can't be read aren't as big a risk.

Codes get changed when their users figure out that they've been broken. An interesting aspect of World War II code breaking was the various ruses concocted to camouflage actions resulting from broken codes. For example, sending out an airplane to "accidentally" spot fleet movements so that the fleet could be attacked hid the fact that code breaking was how the location of the fleet was actually determined. Neal Stephenson's novel *Cryptonomicon* is a highly entertaining read about this type of information security.

Modern Times

The "connected computer" age combines the problems of physical security with those of communications security. Psychedelic cowboy, poet, lyricist, and futurist John Perry Barlow (1947–2018) remarked that "cyberspace is where your money is" during a 1990 SIGGRAPH panel. And it's not just your money. People used to purchase music on records or CDs and movies on videotape or DVDs. Now, this entertainment is mostly just bits on a computer. And of course, banking has moved online.

It would be one thing if those bits were just sitting on your various computers. But your computers, including your phone, are connected to the global internet. This is such a huge attack surface that you have to assume that trust will be violated in at least one place. And the attackers are essentially invisible.

In ancient times, someone who wanted to annoy you could ring your doorbell and run away. You had a good chance of catching them if you were in the right place at the right time and could see them. And there was a limit to how many times someone could do that in a day. On the internet, even if you could see the annoying attacker, there's not much you could do about it. The attackers are rarely even people anymore; they're programs. Because they're programs, they can try to break into your machines thousands of times per second. That's a whole different game.

Attackers don't need to break into a machine in order to cause problems. If our doorbell ringer were persistent enough, they'd block others from reaching your door. This is called a *denial of service (DoS)* attack, because it keeps legitimate folks away. This could put you out of business if you're running a store. Most attacks of this nature today are *distributed denial of service (DDoS)*, where large numbers of bell ringers coordinate their actions.

One of the things that makes tracking attackers mostly useless is that they're often using *proxies*. Launching millions of attacks from their own computer would leave a trail that would be easy to follow. Instead, attackers break into a few machines, install their software (often called *malware*), and let these other machines do their dirty work for them. This often takes the form of a multilevel tree containing millions of compromised machines. It's much harder to catch the relatively few *command and control* messages that tell the other compromised machines what to do. And attack results don't have to be sent back to the attacker; they can just be posted on some public website in encrypted form, where the attacker can fetch them at their convenience.

How is all this possible? Primarily because a large number of machines in the world run software from Microsoft, which set a standard for buggy and insecure software. This wasn't accidental. In an October 1995 *Focus* magazine interview, Bill Gates said, "I'm saying we don't do a new version to fix bugs. We don't. Not enough people would buy it." Microsoft has made some recent improvements, and it's also losing market dominance in the insecure software sector to Internet-of-Things devices, many of which have more processing power than was available on a desktop computer not that long ago.

There are two major classes of attacks. The first, breaking a cryptography system, is relatively rare and difficult in a well-designed system. Much more common are "social" attacks in which a user is tricked into installing software on their system. The best cryptography can't protect you if some malicious piece of code that you installed is watching you type your password. Some common social attack mechanisms represent some of the dumbest things ever done by supposedly smart people—running arbitrary programs sent via email or contained on whatever USB drive you find on the ground, for example, or plugging your phone into a random USB port. What could possibly go wrong? These avoidable mechanisms are being replaced by attacks via web browsers. Remember from Chapter 9 how complex these are.

One example of an extremely clever and dangerous attack was a 2009 online banking exploit. When someone logged into their bank account, the attack would transfer some of their money out of their account. It would then rewrite the web page coming back from the bank so that the transfer wouldn't be detected by the account owner. This made the theft something you'd never notice unless you still received paper statements and carefully checked them.

Another modern-era problem is that messing with bits can have physical repercussions. In the name of progress or convenience, all sorts of critical infrastructure is connected to the internet now. This means an attacker can make a power plant fail or simply turn off the heat in your house in winter so the pipes freeze. And, with the rise of robotics and the Internet of Things, an attacker could potentially program your vacuum cleaner to terrorize your cats or set off burglar alarms when you're away.

Finally, modern technology has greatly complicated the ability to determine whether something is authentic. It's pretty trivial to create *deep fakes*—realistic fake photographs, audio, and video. There's a theory that a lot of the current batch of robocalls is just harvesting voice samples so that they can be used elsewhere. How long will it be before voice-search data is converted into robocalls that sound like one of your friends is calling?

Metadata and Surveillance

There's another big change brought about by modern technology. Even if cryptography can keep the contents of communications secret, you can learn a lot by observing patterns of communication. As the late Yogi Berra said, "You can observe a lot by just watching." For example, even if nobody ever opens your letters, someone can glean a lot by examining who you're writing to and who's writing to you, not to mention the size and weight of the envelopes and how often they're sent. This is unavoidable in America where the post office photographs every piece of mail.

The information on the outside of the envelope is called *metadata*. It's data about the data, not the data itself. Someone could use this information to deduce your network of friends. That may not sound so bad to you if you live in a modern Western society. But imagine for a minute if you and your friends lived in a more oppressive society, where having this information about you known could endanger your friends. An example of this is China's "social credit" score.

Of course, hardly anybody needs to do such things by tracking mail anymore. They can just look at your social media friends. Makes the job much easier. Also, tracking you and yours no longer depends on having a lot of manpower. Nobody has to follow you when you leave your house because your online activities can be tracked remotely, and your movements in the real world can be tracked using an increasing variety of spy cameras. Of course, if you carry a cell phone, you're tracked all the time because the information that's used to make the cell phone system function is metadata too.

The Social Context

It's hard to talk about security without getting political. That's because there are really two prongs to security. One is the techniques for building robust security. The other is trading off one's personal security against the security of society as a whole. That's where it gets complicated, because it's hard to discuss technical measures absent societal goals.

Not only is security a social issue, but it's different from country to country because of different laws and norms. That gets especially complicated in an age where communications easily cross national borders and are subject to different regulations. There's no intent to start a political argument here; it's just that you can't discuss security from a solely technological perspective. The political part of this chapter is written from a mostly American perspective.

It's a common misperception that "national security" is enshrined in the US Constitution. This is understandable because courts routinely dismiss cases about constitutional rights when government officials raise the specters of "national security" and "state secrets." The Fourth

Amendment to the US Constitution has the clearest expression of national security when it says, "The right of the people to be secure in their persons, houses, papers, and effects against unreasonable searches and seizures, shall not be violated." Unfortunately, *unreasonable* wasn't defined, probably because reasonable people understood it at the time. Note that this amendment confers security on the people, not the state—that whole "by the people, for the people" thing.

The heart of the issue is whether or not the government's duty to protect people is stronger than the rights of those people.

Most people would like to be able to relax knowing that someone else was keeping them safe. One could consider it a social contract. Unfortunately, that social contract has been undermined by violations of trust.

There's a bias, completely unsupported by fact, that people in government are "better" or "more honest" than everyone else. At best, they're like people everywhere; some are good, some are bad. There's more than enough documented evidence of law enforcement personnel committing crimes. An aggravating factor is secrecy; positions lacking oversight and accountability tend to accumulate bad people, which is exactly why the notions of transparency and openness are the foundation of a good trust model. For example, as part of mind-control experiments in the 1960s, the CIA illegally dosed men with LSD and observed their reactions. Known as MKUltra, this program had no oversight and led to at least one known death of an unwitting test subject. After MKUltra was shut down, agent George White said, "Where else could a red-blooded American boy lie, kill, cheat, steal, rape, and pillage with the sanction and blessing of the All-Highest?" And the FBI under J. Edgar Hoover had quite the history of political abuse—not just spying for political purposes but actively sabotaging perceived enemies.

In case you've been sleeping under a rock, more and more trust abuses have recently come to light, and these are likely only a small fraction of actual abuses, given the secrecy and lack of oversight. Most relevant to this chapter are Edward Snowden's revelations about illegal government surveillance.

Without oversight, it's difficult to tell whether government secrecy is covering up illegal activities or just incompetence. Back in 1998, the US government encouraged the use of an encryption scheme called the Data Encryption Standard (DES). The Electronic Frontier Foundation (EFF) built a machine called Deep Crack for about $250,000 (which was *way* less than the NSA budget) that broke the DES code. Part of the reason they did so was to be able to point out that either agency experts were incompetent or they were lying about the security of the algorithm. The EFF was trying to expose the disingenuous violation of trust perpetrated for the convenience of American spies. And it worked somewhat—while it didn't change the behavior of the agency experts, it did spur the development of the Advanced Encryption Standard that replaced DES.

It's easy to argue that "it's a dangerous world." But if lots of bad folks were being caught by these secret programs, we'd be hearing about it. Instead, what we hear about is the entrapment of "clueless and broke" people who weren't actual threats. Another thing people often say is, "I don't care if the government looks at my stuff; I have nothing to hide." That may be true, but it's a reasonable guess that people saying that *do* want to hide their bank account password. It often seems like those raising the scariest arguments are actually the ones behaving badly.

Trust violations have international implications. There's a reluctance to purchase products whose security might be compromised. Outsourcing poses threats too. There may be laws in your country protecting your information, but someone elsewhere might have access to that data. There have been cases of outsourced data being sold. There are recent indications that personal data acquired by outside actors has been used to meddle in political processes, possibly spelling the end of "Westphalian sovereignty."

Trust violations also impact freedom. A "chilling effect" results when people engage in self-censorship or become afraid of being tracked when meeting or communicating with others online. There's plenty of historical evidence showing the impact of chilling effects on political movements.

Modern cell phones have several different unlocking options: passcode or pattern, fingerprint reader, facial recognition. Which should you use? At least in America, I recommend using a passcode or pattern, even though they're slightly less convenient. There are three reasons for this. First, some courts have interpreted the portion of the Fifth Amendment that states "No person . . . shall be compelled in any criminal case to be a witness against himself" to mean that you can't be ordered to give "testimonial" information that's in your head. In other words, you can't be forced to divulge passwords, passcodes, patterns, and so on. But some courts have ruled that you *can* be compelled to provide your fingerprint or face. Second, there is a trust issue. Even if you don't mind unlocking your phone on request, how do you know what your phone is doing with your fingerprint or facial data? Is it just unlocking your phone, or is it uploading it to databases for some future undisclosed uses? Will you start getting targeted ads when walking in front of stores that recognize your face? Third, plastic fingerprints and fake retinas, long staples of cheesy movies, have actually been demonstrated in real life. Biometric data is easier to fake than a password.

Authentication and Authorization

I've mentioned authentication and authorization. *Authentication* is proving that someone or something is what it claims to be. *Authorization* is limiting access to something unless proper "credentials" are presented.

Authorization is arguably the easier of the two; it requires properly designed and implemented hardware and software. Authentication is much trickier. How can a piece of software tell whether it was you who entered a password or someone else?

Two-factor authentication (2FA) is now available on many systems. A *factor* is an independent means of verification. Factors include things hopefully unique to you (such as a fingerprint), things in your possession (for example, a cell phone), and things that you know (for example, passwords or PINs). Two-factor authentication therefore uses two of these. For example, using a bank card with a PIN or entering a password that sends a message to your phone to supply a one-time code. Some of these systems work better than others; obviously, sending a message to a cell phone that others can access isn't secure. Parts of the cell phone infrastructure make relying on 2FA dangerous. Attackers can use your email address and other easily available information to port your phone number to a SIM card in a phone that they control. This not only gives them access to your data but locks you out.

Cryptography

As I mentioned earlier, cryptography allows a sender to scramble a communication so that only the designated recipients can decode it. It's pretty important when you're taking money out of your bank account; you don't want someone else to be able to do it too.

Cryptography isn't important just for privacy and security, however. Cryptographic signatures allow one to attest to the veracity of data. It used to be that physical originals could be consulted if there was some question as to the source of information. Those don't often exist for documents, audio, video, and so on because the originals were created on computers and never reduced to physical form. Cryptographic techniques can be used to prevent and detect forgeries.

Cryptography alone doesn't turn your castle into a mighty fortress, though. It's part of a security system, and all parts matter.

Steganography

Hiding one thing within another is called *steganography*. It's a great way to communicate secrets because there's no traceable connection between the sender and the recipient. This used to be done through newspaper classified ads, but it's now much easier to do online since there's a near-infinite number of places to post.

Steganography is not technically cryptography, but it's close enough for our purposes. Take a look at Figure 13-1. On the left is a photo of Mister Duck and Tony Cat. In the center is that same photo that includes a hidden secret message. Can you tell the two photos apart? On the right is the secret message.

Help!!! Space aliens have invaded Mister Duck and are sucking out Tony Cat's brains while he's sleeping.

Figure 13-1: Secret message hidden in image

How was this accomplished? On the left is an 8-bit grayscale image. The center image was made by replacing the least significant bit on each pixel of the image with the corresponding least significant bit from the secret message on the right. Recovering the secret message, then, is just a matter of stripping away the seven most significant bits from the center image.

This isn't the best way to hide a message. It would be much less obvious if the secret message were given in ASCII character codes instead of images of the characters. And it would be pretty much impossible to discover if the secret message bits were scattered throughout the image or encrypted. Another approach, recently published by researchers Chang Xiao, Cheng Zhang, and Changxi Zheng at Columbia University, encodes messages by slightly altering the shape of text characters. This isn't a completely novel idea; "America's first female cryptanalyst," Elizabeth Smith Friedman (1892–1980), used a similar technique to include a secret message on her husband's tombstone.

Steganograpy is used by advertisers to track web pages that you visit because they don't get that "no means no" when you block ads. Many websites include a single-pixel image hidden on web pages linked to an identifying URL. This isn't always innocuous; this type of tracking software was abused to accuse thousands of treason in Turkey in 2016.

This technique isn't limited to images. Secret messages could even be encoded as the number of blank lines in a blog posting or web page comment. Messages can be scattered among frames in a video or hidden in digital audio in a similar manner to the previous one-pixel example. One crazy-sounding example of the latter is *dog-whistle marketing*, in which web pages and ads play ultrasonic sounds, which are above the human audio range. These sounds can be picked up by the microphone on your cell phone, allowing advertisers to make connections between your various computing devices and determine what ads you have seen.

Steganography has other uses, too. For example, a studio might embed unique identifying marks in unreleased movies that it sends to reviewers. This would allow them to track down the source if the movie gets leaked. This use is akin to the practice of using a watermark on paper.

Steganography is used in almost every computer printer. The EFF received a document in response to a Freedom of Information Act request that suggests the existence of a secret agreement between governments and manufacturers to make sure that all printed documents are traceable. Color printers, for example, add small yellow dots to each page that encode the printer's serial number. EFF distributed special LED flashlights that one could use to find them. This could be considered an invasion of privacy.

Substitution Ciphers

If you ever had a secret decoder ring, it probably implemented a substitution *cipher*. The idea is pretty simple: you build a table that maps each character to another, such as that shown in Figure 13-2. You *encrypt* a message by replacing each original character with its counterpart from the table and *decrypt* by doing the reverse. The original message is called *cleartext*, and the encrypted version is called *ciphertext*.

a	b	c	d	e	f	g	h	i	j	k	l	m	n	o	p	q	r	s	t	u	v	w	x	y	z
q	s	a	o	z	w	e	n	y	d	p	f	c	x	k	g	u	t	m	v	l	b	r	h	j	i

Figure 13-2: Substitution cipher

This cipher maps *c* to *a*, *r* to *t*, *y* to *j*, and so on, so the word *cryptography* would be enciphered as *atjgvketqgnj*. The reverse mapping (*a* to *c*, *t* to *r*, and so on) deciphers the ciphertext. This is called a *symmetric* code, since the same cipher is used to both encode and decode a message.

Why isn't this a good idea? Substitution ciphers are easy to break using statistics. People have analyzed how often letters are used in various languages. For example, in English the most common five letters are *e, t, a, o, n*, in that order—or at least they were when Herbert Zim (1909–1994) published *Codes & Secret Writing* in 1948. Breaking a substitution cipher involves looking for the most common letter in the ciphertext and guessing that it's an *e*, and so on. Once a few letters are guessed correctly, it's easy to figure out some words, which makes figuring out other letters easy. Let's use the plaintext paragraph in Listing 13-1 as an example. We'll make it all lowercase and remove the punctuation to keep it simple.

```
theyre going to open the gate at azone at any moment
amazing deep untracked powder meet me at the top of the lift
```

Listing 13-1: Plaintext example

Here's the same paragraph as ciphertext using the code from Figure 13-2:

```
vnzjtz ekyxe vk kgzx vnz eqvz qv qikxz qv qxj ckczxv
qcqiyxe ozzg lxvtqapzo gkrozt czzv cz qv vnz vkg kw vnz fywv
```

Listing 13-2 shows the distribution of letters in the enciphered version of the paragraph. It's sorted by letter frequency, with the most commonly occurring letter at the top.

```
zzzzzzzzzzzzzzzz
vvvvvvvvvvvvvv
qqqqqqqqq
kkkkkkkk
xxxxxxx
ccccc
eeee
gggg
nnnn
ooo
ttt
yyy
ii
jj
ww
a
f
l
p
r
```

Listing 13-2: Letter frequency analysis

A code breaker could use this analysis to guess that the letter z in the ciphertext corresponds to the letter e in the plaintext, since there are more of them in the ciphertext than any other letter. Continuing along those lines, we can also guess that v means t, q means a, k means o, and x means n. Let's make those substitutions using uppercase letters so that we can tell them apart.

```
TnEjtE eOyNe TO OgEN TnE eATE AT AiONE AT ANj cOcENT
AcAiyNe oEEg lNTtAapEo gOroEt cEET cE AT TnE TOg Ow TnE fywT
```

From here we can do some simple guessing based on general knowledge of English. There are very few three-letter words that begin with *t* and end with *e*, and *the* is the most common, so let's guess that n means h. This is easy to check on my Linux system, as it has a dictionary of words and a pattern-matching utility; grep '^t.e$' /usr/share/dict/words finds all three-letter words beginning with a t and ending with an e. Also, there is only one grammatically correct choice for the c in cEET cE, which is m.

```
THEjtE eOyNe TO OgEN THE eATE AT AiONE AT ANj MOMENT
AMAiyNe oEEg lNTtAapEo gOroEt  MEET ME AT THE TOg Ow THE fywT
```

There are only four words that match o□en: omen, open, oven, and oxen; only open makes sense, so g must be p. Likewise, the only word that makes sense in to open the □ate is gate, so e must be g. There's only one two-letter word that begins with o, so ow must be of, making the w an f. The j must be a y because the words and and ant don't work.

```
THEYtE GOyNG TO OPEN THE GATE AT AiONE AT ANY MOMENT
AMAiyNG oEEP lNTtAapEo POroEt MEET ME AT THE TOP OF THE fyFT
```

We don't need to completely decode the message to see that statistics and knowledge of the language will let us do so. And so far we've used only simple methods. We can also use knowledge of common letter pairs, such as th, er, on, and an, called *digraphs*. There are statistics for most commonly doubled letters, such as ss, and many more tricks.

As you can see, simple substitution ciphers are fun but not very secure.

Transposition Ciphers

Another way to encode messages is to scramble the positions of the characters. An ancient transposition cipher system supposedly used by the Greeks is the *scytale*, which sounds impressive but is just a round stick. A ribbon of parchment was wound around the stick. The message was written out in a row along the stick. Extra dummy messages were written out in other rows. As a result, the strip contained a random-looking set of characters. Decoding the message required that the recipient wrap the ribbon around a stick with the same diameter as the one used for encoding.

We can easily generate a transposition cipher by writing a message out of a grid of a particular size, the size being the key. For example, let's write out the plaintext from Listing 13-1 on an 11-column grid with the spaces removed, as shown in Figure 13-3. We'll fill in the gaps in the bottom row with some random letters shown in italics. To generate the ciphertext shown at the bottom, we read down the columns instead of across the rows.

t	h	e	y	r	e	g	o	i	n	g
t	o	o	p	e	n	t	h	e	g	a
t	e	a	t	a	z	o	n	e	a	t
a	n	y	m	o	m	e	n	t	a	m
a	z	i	n	g	d	e	e	p	u	n
t	r	a	c	k	e	d	p	o	w	d
e	r	m	e	e	t	m	e	a	t	t
h	e	t	o	p	o	f	t	h	e	l
i	f	t	a	s	d	f	g	h	i	j
tttaatehihoenzrrefeoayiamttyptmnceoareaogkepsenzmdetodgtoeedmffohnnepetgieetpoahhngaauwteigatmndtlj										

Figure 13-3: Transposition cipher grid

The letter frequency in a transposition cipher is the same as that of the plaintext, but that doesn't help as much since the order of the letters in the words is also scrambled. However, ciphers like this are still pretty easy to solve, especially now that computers can try different grid sizes.

More Complex Ciphers

There's an infinite variety of more complex ciphers that are substitution ciphers, transposition ciphers, or combinations of the two. It's common to convert letters to their numeric values and then convert the numbers back to letters after performing some mathematical operations on the numbers. Some codes include extra tables of numbers added in to inhibit letter-frequency analysis.

The history of code breaking during World War II makes fascinating reading. One of the methods used to break codes was to listen to messages that were transmitted by radio. These *intercepts* were subjected to exhaustive statistical analysis and were eventually broken. The human mind's ability to recognize patterns was also a key factor, as was some clever subterfuge.

Clues were also gleaned from messages that were sent about known events. The Americans won a major victory at the Battle of Midway because they knew that the Japanese were going to attack, but didn't know where. They had broken the code, but the Japanese used code names for targets, in this case AF. The Americans arranged to have a message sent from Midway that they knew could be intercepted, saying that the island was short on fresh water. Shortly, the Japanese re-sent this message in code, confirming that AF was Midway.

The complexity of ciphers was limited by human speed. Although the Americans had some punch-card tabulating machines available to help with code breaking, this was before the computer age. Codes had to be simple so that messages could be encoded and decoded quickly enough to be useful.

One-Time Pads

The most secure method of encryption, called a *one-time pad*, harkens back to the work of American cryptographer Frank Miller (1842–1925) in 1882. A one-time pad is a set of unique substitution ciphers, each of which is only used once. The name comes from the way in which the ciphers were printed on pads of paper so that the one on top could be removed once it was used.

Suppose we want to encode our earlier message. We grab a page from our pad that looks something like Listing 13-3.

```
FGDDXEFEZOUZGBQJTKVAZGNYYYSMWGRBKRATDSMKMKAHBFGRYHUPNAFJQDOJ
IPTVWQWZKHJLDUWITRQGJYGMZNVIFDHOLAFEREOZKBYAMCXCVNOUROWPBFNA
```

Listing 13-3: One-time pad

The way it works is that each letter in the original message is converted to a number between 1 and 26, as is each corresponding letter in the one-time pad. The values are added together using base-26 arithmetic. For example, the first letter in the message is T, which has a value of 20. It's paired with the first letter in the one-time pad, which is F with a value of 6. They're added together, giving a value of 26, so the encoded letter is Z. Likewise, the second letter H has a value of 8 and is paired with G, which has a value of 7, so the encoded letter would be O. The fourth letter in the message is Y with a value of 24, which when paired with a D with a value of 4 results in 28. Then, 26 is subtracted, leaving 2, making the encoded letter B. Decryption is performed with subtraction instead of addition.

One-time pads are perfectly secure provided they're used properly, but there are a couple of problems. First, both parties to a communication must have the same pad. Second, they must be in sync; somehow they need to both be using the same cipher. Communication becomes impossible if someone forgets to tear off a page or accidentally tears off more than one. Third, the pad must be at least as long as the message to prevent any repeating patterns.

An interesting application of one-time pads was the World War II–era SIGSALY voice encryption system that went into service in 1943. It scrambled and unscrambled audio using one-time pads stored on phonograph records. These were not portable devices; each one weighed over 50 tons!

The Key Exchange Problem

One of the problems with symmetric encryption systems is the need for both ends of a communication to be using the same key. You can mail a one-time pad to somebody or use a hopefully trusted courier, but you won't know if it was intercepted along the way and a copy made. And it's useless if it gets lost or damaged. It's just like mailing a house key to a friend; you have no way to know whether or not someone made a copy along the way. In other words, it's vulnerable to a man-in-the-middle attack.

Public Key Cryptography

Public key cryptography solves many of the problems we've discussed so far. It uses a pair of *related* keys. It's like a house with a mail slot in the front door. The first key, called the *public key*, can be given to anybody and allows them to put mail in the slot. But only you, who can unlock the front door using the second or *private key*, can *read* that mail.

Public key cryptography is an *asymmetric* system in that the encoding and decoding keys are different. This solves the key exchange problem because it doesn't matter if people have your public key since that can't be used to decode messages.

Public key cryptography relies on *trapdoor functions*, mathematical functions that are easy to compute in one direction but not in the other without some piece of secret information. The term originates from the fact that it's easy to fall through a trapdoor, but climbing back out is difficult without a ladder. As a really simple example, suppose we have a function $y = x^2$. Pretty easy to compute y from x. But computing x from y using $x = \sqrt{y}$ is harder. Not a lot harder, because this is a simple example, but you've probably discovered that multiplication is easier than finding a square root. There is no mathematical secret for this function, but you could consider having a calculator to be the secret because that makes solving for x as easy as solving for y.

The idea is that the public and private keys are related by some complicated mathematical function, with the public key as the trapdoor and the private key as the ladder, making messages easy to encrypt but hard to decrypt. A high-level view of this is to have the keys be factors of a really large random number.

Asymmetric encryption is computationally expensive. As a result, it's often used only to secretly generate a symmetric *session key* that's used for the actual message content. A common way to do this is with the *Diffie–Hellman Key Exchange*, named after American cryptographers Whitfield Diffie and Martin Hellman.

Diffie and Hellman published a paper about public key cryptography in 1976. But it wasn't until 1977 that an implementation became available because, although the concept of a trapdoor function is relatively simple, it turns out to be very difficult to invent one. It was solved by cryptographer Ronald Rivest in 1977, reportedly after a Manischewitz drinking binge, thus proving that mathematical prowess is unrelated to taste buds. Together with Israeli cryptographer Adi Shamir and American scientist Leonard Adleman, Rivest produced the *RSA* algorithm, whose name derives from the first letter of each contributor's last name. Unfortunately, in a trust violation exposed by government contractor-leaker Edward Snowden, it turns out their company, RSA Security, took money from the NSA to install a kleptographic backdoor in their default random-number generator. This made it easier for the NSA, and anyone else who knew about it, to crack RSA-encoded messages.

Forward Secrecy

One of the problems with using a symmetric cipher session key for actual communications is that all messages can be read if that key is discovered. We know that many governments have the technical capability to record and store communications. If, for example, you're a human rights activist whose safety depends on the security of your communications, you don't want to take a chance that your key could be discovered and all your messages decoded.

The way to avoid this is with *forward secrecy*, wherein a new session key is created for each message. That way, discovering a single key is useful only for decoding a single message.

Cryptographic Hash Functions

We touched on hash functions back in Chapter 7 as a technique for fast searching. Hash functions are also used in cryptography, but only functions with certain properties are suitable. Just like with regular hash functions, cryptographic hash functions map arbitrary inputs into fixed-size numbers. Hash functions for searching map their input into a much smaller range of outputs than their cryptographic cousins, as the former are used as memory locations and the latter are just used as numbers.

A key property of cryptographic hash functions is that they're *one-way* functions. That means that although it's easy to generate the hash from the input, it's not practical to generate the input from the hash.

Another important property is that small changes to the input data generate hashes that aren't correlated. Back in Chapter 7, we used a hash function that summed the character values modulo some prime number. With such a function, the string b would have a hash value 1 greater than that of the string a. That's too predictable for cryptographic purposes. Table 13-1 shows the SHA-1 (Secure Hash Algorithm #1) hashes for three strings that differ in only one letter. As you can see, there's no discernible relationship between the input and the hash value.

Table 13-1: Corned Beef Hash

Input	SHA-1 Hash Value
Corned Beef	005f5a5954e7eadabbbf3189ccc65af6b8035320
Corned Beeg	527a7b63eb7b92f0ecf91a770aa12b1a88557ab8
Corned Beeh	34bc20e4c7b9ca8c3069b4e23e5086fba9118e6c

Cryptographic hash functions must be hard to spoof; given a hash value, it should be very difficult to come up with input that generates it. In other words, it should be difficult to produce collisions. Using the hash algorithm in Chapter 7 with prime number of 13, we'd get a hash value of 4 for an input of Corned Beef. But we'd get the same hash value for an input of Tofu Jerky Tastes Weird.

For a long time, the MD5 hash function was the most widely used algorithm. But in the late 1990s, a way was found to produce *collisions*, which you saw back in "Making a Hash of Things." At the time of writing, MD5 has been replaced by variants of the SHA algorithm. Unfortunately, the SHA-0 and SHA-1 variations of this algorithm were developed by the NSA, which makes them untrustworthy.

Digital Signatures

Cryptography can help to verify the authenticity of data though *digital signatures*, which provide integrity, nonrepudiation, and authentication.

Integrity verification means we can determine whether or not a message was altered. For example, in ancient times, report cards were actual printed paper cards that listed classes and grades, which students brought home to their parents. I remember a poorly performing classmate in fourth grade adding vertical lines to the right side of his *F*s to turn them into *A*s. His parents couldn't tell that the message was altered.

Integrity verification is accomplished by attaching a cryptographic hash of the data. But, of course, anybody can attach a hash to a message. To prevent this, the sender encrypts the hash using their private key, which the recipient can decrypt using the corresponding public key. Note that for signatures, the roles of the public and private keys are reversed.

The use of the private key provides both nonrepudiation and authentication. *Nonrepudiation* means it would be hard for a sender to claim that they didn't sign a message that's signed with their private key. *Authentication* means that that the recipient knows who signed the message since their public key is paired with the signer's private key.

Public Key Infrastructure

There's a big gaping hole in public key encryption. Suppose you use your web browser to connect to your bank using a secure (HTTPS) connection. The bank sends its public key to your browser so that your browser can encrypt your data, such that the bank can decrypt it using its private key. But how do you know that that public key came from your bank instead of some third party tapping into your communications? How does your browser authenticate that key? Who can it trust if it can't trust the key?

Though unfortunately not a great solution, what's used today is a *public key infrastructure (PKI)*. Part of such an infrastructure is a trusted third party called a *certificate authority (CA)* to vouch for the authenticity of keys. In theory, a CA makes sure that a party is who they say they are and issues a cryptographically signed document called a *certificate* that one can use to validate their key. These certificates are in a format called X.509, a standard defined by the International Telecommunications Union (ITU).

While PKI generally works, it comes back to the trust problem. CAs have been hacked. Sloppy mistakes at CAs have caused their private keys to be accidentally published, making it possible for anyone to sign bogus certificates (fortunately, there's a mechanism to *revoke* certificates). Some CAs have been found to be insecure in that they didn't authenticate parties requesting certificates. And one can reasonably assume that governments believe that they have the right to force CAs to generate bogus certificates.

Blockchain

Blockchain is another application of cryptography. It's a pretty simple idea backed by a lot of complicated math. Much of the media discussion of blockchain in connection to Bitcoin and other cryptocurrencies is about its applications, not about how it works.

You can think of blockchain as a mechanism for managing a ledger, similar to your bank account statement. A problem with ledgers is that they're easy to alter on paper, and even easier to alter electronically since computers don't leave eraser smudges.

A ledger usually consists of a set of records, each on subsequent lines. The blockchain equivalent of a ledger line is a *block*. Blockchain adds a cryptographic hash of the previous block (line) and a block creation timestamp to the next block. This makes a chain of blocks (hence the name) linked by the hashes and timestamps, as shown in Figure 13-4.

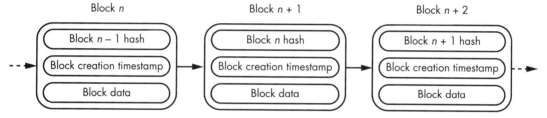

Figure 13-4: Simplified blockchain

As you can see, if the contents of block *n* were modified, it would change its hash so that it wouldn't match the one stored in block *n* + 1. The properties of cryptographic hashes make it unlikely that a block could be modified in any useful way and still have the same hash. Each block effectively includes a digital signature of the prior block.

The only effective way to attack a blockchain is to compromise the software that manages it, an approach that can be somewhat mitigated by having the blockchain data be both public and duplicated on multiple systems. Attacking such a distributed system would require collusion among a number of people.

Password Management

Another application of cryptography is *password management*. In the good old days, computers maintained a file of passwords as *cleartext*. When someone logged in, the password they entered would be compared to the one stored in the file.

This is a bad approach primarily because anyone with access to the file knows everybody's passwords. Keep in mind that this doesn't have to be the result of an attack on the computer. Many organizations send their backups to third parties for storage (it's a good idea to have at least three backups geographically far from each other, preferably on different tectonic plates). We're back to trust again because someone could access the password file or any other data on these backups. You can encrypt your backups, but that's a bit more fragile, as small-storage medium defects (such as a bad disk drive block) can render the entire backup unrecoverable. There's a trade-off between protecting your data and being able to recover it.

A simple solution to this problem is to store the passwords in an encrypted format such as a cryptographic hash. When a user tries to log in, their password is converted to the cryptographic hash, which is then compared to the one on file. The properties of cryptographic hashes make it very unlikely that a password could be guessed. As an additional precaution, most systems prevent the password file from being accessible by normal users.

Passwords are problematic even with these practices, though. In the early days of shared computing, you might have needed passwords for a handful of systems. But now, you need countless passwords for bank accounts, school websites, many different online stores, and so on. Many people navigate this situation by using the same password everywhere; it turns out that the most common password is `password`, followed by `password123` for sites that require numbers in the password. Reusing a password is equivalent to not using forward secrecy; if one site is compromised, your password can be used on every other site. You can have a different password for each site, but then you have to remember them all. You can use a *password manager* that stores all of your various passwords in one place protected by a single password, but if that password or the password manager itself is compromised, so are all of your other passwords. Probably the most effective but problematic approach is two-factor authentication, mentioned earlier. But that often relies on something like a cell phone and prevents you from accessing your accounts when you're somewhere without cell service. Also, it's cumbersome, which causes people to stay logged in to many sites.

Software Hygiene

Now that you know a little about security and cryptography, what can you do about it as a programmer? You don't need to be a cryptography expert or security wizard to be able to avoid many common pitfalls. The vast majority of security flaws in the wild result from easily avoidable situations, many of which can be found in Henry Spencer's *The Ten Commandments for C Programmers*. We'll look at some of these in this section.

Protect the Right Stuff

When designing a system that keeps things secure, it's tempting to make it keep everything secure. But that's not always a good idea. If, for example, you make users log in to view things that don't need to be secure, it makes users log in and stay logged in. Since logged-in users can access the "secure" content, that increases the chances that someone else can get access—for example, if the user walks away from their computer for a short time.

This is illustrated by the way in which many cell phones work. For the most part, everything is locked up, except possibly the camera. There are things that *should* be locked up; you don't necessarily want someone to be able to send messages in your name if you lose your phone. But suppose you and your friends are listening to music. You have to hand your unlocked phone to someone else if they're picking the tunes, giving them access to everything. Texting a code to your phone is a common second factor in two-factor authentication, and handing that factor to a third party defeats the purpose.

Triple-Check Your Logic

It's pretty easy to write a program that you *think* does something when in fact it doesn't. Errors in logic can be exploited, especially when an attacker has access to the source code and can find bugs that you didn't. One method that helps is to walk through your code with someone else out loud. Reading aloud forces you to go through things more slowly than when reading silently, and it's always amazing what you find.

Check for Errors

Code that you write will use system calls and call library functions. Most of these calls return error codes if something goes wrong. Don't ignore them! For example, if you try to allocate memory and the allocation fails, don't use the memory. If a read of user input fails, don't assume valid input. There are many of these cases, and handling every error can be tedious, but do it anyway.

Avoid library functions that can silently fail or overflow bounds. Make sure that error and warning reporting is enabled on your language tools. Treat memory allocation errors as fatal because many library functions rely on allocated memory and they may fail in mysterious ways after an allocation failure elsewhere.

Minimize Attack Surfaces

This section paraphrases some of the April 19, 2016, testimony by cryptography researcher Matt Blaze to a US House of Representatives subcommittee following the San Bernardino shootings. It's worth reading the whole thing.

We have to assume that all software has bugs because it's so complex. Researchers have tried to produce "formal methods," akin to mathematical proofs, that could be used to demonstrate that computer programs are "correct." Unfortunately, to date this is an unsolved problem.

It follows that every feature added to a piece of software presents a new attack surface. We can't even prove that one attack surface is 100 percent secure. But we know that each new attack surface adds new vulnerabilities and that they add up.

This is the fundamental reason that actual security professionals, as opposed to politicians, are against the notion of installing backdoors for law enforcement. Not only does it make the software more complicated by adding another attack surface, but just like the locker example earlier in this chapter, there's a pretty good chance that unauthorized parties will figure out how to access such a backdoor.

It turns out that Matt Blaze really knows what he's talking about here. The NSA announced its development of the Clipper chip in 1993. The NSA's intent was to mandate that it be used for encryption. It contained a government-access backdoor. This was a difficult political sell because people in other countries would be reluctant to use American products that could spy on them. The Clipper sank both because of political opposition and because Blaze published a paper titled "Protocol Failure in the Escrowed Encryption Standard" in 1994 that showed how easy it was to exploit the backdoor. As an aside, Blaze found himself completely unprepared to be hauled in front of Congress to testify but is now very good at it. It was a part of the universe that he didn't understand at the time. Consider learning to speak in public, as it might come in handy someday.

Good security practice is to keep your code as simple as possible, thus minimizing the number of attack surfaces.

Stay in Bounds

Chapter 10 introduced the concept of buffer overflows. They're one example of a class of bugs attackers can exploit that can remain undetected in programs for a long time.

To recap, a buffer overflow occurs when software doesn't check for boundaries and can end up overwriting other data. For example, if a "you're authorized" variable exists past the end of a password buffer, a long password can result in authorization even if it's not correct. Buffer overflows on the stack can be especially troublesome because they can allow an attacker to change the return address from a function call, allowing other parts of the program to be executed in an unintended manner.

Buffer overflows aren't just limited to strings. You also must ensure that array indices are in bounds.

Another bounds problem is the size of variables. Don't just assume, for example, that an integer is 32 bits. It might be 16, and setting the 17th bit might do something unexpected. Watch out for user input, and make sure to check that any user-supplied numbers fit into your variables. Most systems include definitions files that your code can use to ensure that you're using the correct sizes for things. In the worst case, you should use these to prevent your code from building when the sizes are wrong. In the best case, you can use these definitions to automatically choose the correct sizes. Definitions exist for the sizes of numbers and even the number of bits in a byte. Don't make assumptions!

It's also important to stay in memory bounds. If you're using dynamically allocated memory and allocate n bytes, make sure that your accesses are in the range of 0 to $n - 1$. I've had to debug code in which memory was allocated and then the address of memory was incremented because it was convenient for the algorithm to reference `memory[-1]`. The code then freed `memory` instead of `memory[-1]`, causing problems.

Many microcomputers designed for embedded use include much more memory than is needed by a program. Avoid dynamic allocation in these cases and just use static data; it avoids a lot of potential problems. Of course, make sure that your code respects the bounds of the data storage.

Another bounds area is timing. Make sure your program can handle cases where input comes in faster than your interrupt handlers can respond. Avoid allowing your interrupt handlers to be interrupted so that you don't blow off of the end of the stack.

There's a testing technique called *fuzzing* for which tools are available that can help catch these types of bugs. But it's a statistical technique and not a substitute for writing good code. Fuzzing involves hitting your code with a large number of variations on legal input.

Generating Good Random Numbers Is Hard

Good random numbers are important for cryptography. How do you get them?

The most common random-number generators actually generate *pseudorandom* numbers. That's because logic circuits can't generate true random numbers. They'll always generate the same sequence of numbers if they start at the same place. A simple circuit called a *linear feedback shift register* (*LFSR*), such as that shown in Figure 13-5, can be used as a pseudorandom-number generator (PRNG).

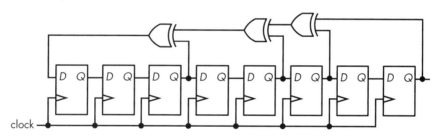

Figure 13-5: Linear feedback shift register

You can see that as the number is shifted right, a new bit comes in from the left that is generated from some of the other bits. The version in the figure generates only 8-bit numbers, but larger versions can be constructed. There are two problems here. The first is that the numbers repeat cyclically. The second is that if you know the most recent random number, you always know the next one; if it just generated 0xa4, the next is always 0x52. Note that although this is a problem for cryptography, it's useful when debugging programs.

The initial value in the register is called the *seed*. Many software implementations allow the seed to be set. There have been many improvements on the LFSR, such as the Mersenne Twister, but in the end they all have the same two problems I mentioned. There's no true randomness.

Modern software addresses this problem by harvesting entropy from a variety of sources. The term *entropy* was co-opted from thermodynamics, where it refers to the universal tendency toward randomness.

One of the first entropy sources, called LavaRand, was invented at SGI in 1997. It worked by pointing a webcam at a couple of lava lamps. It could generate almost 200Kb of random data per second. The performance of entropy sources is important; if you're a website generating lots of session identifiers for lots of clients, you need lots of good random numbers quickly.

It's not practical to ship a pair of lava lamps with every computer, even though it would be groovy. Some chip manufacturers have added random-number generators to their hardware. Intel added an on-chip thermal noise generator random-number generator in 2012 that produced 500MB of random numbers per second. But people refused to use it because it was released right after the Snowden revelations and couldn't be trusted.

There's another factor in trusting on-chip random-number generators. A manufacturer could publish its design so that it could be reviewed. You could even *decap*, or remove the lid from, a chip and examine it using an electron microscope to verify that it matches the design. But it's possible to undetectably change it during manufacturing. This is the hardware equivalent of a doping scandal. Chapter 2 mentioned doping in our discussion of transistors; *dopants* are the nasty chemicals that are used to create *p* and *n* regions. The behavior of the circuit can be altered by subtly adjusting the dopant levels. The result would be undetectable even through a microscope.

Security professionals have realized that they can't trust hardware random-number generators. Entropy is harvested from random occurrences that are independent of computer programs, such as mouse movements, time between keyboard clicks, disk access speeds, and so on. This approach works pretty well, but quickly producing large quantities of random numbers is difficult.

Entropy harvesting has run afoul of some major dumb bugs, especially in the Linux-based Android operating system. It turns out that Android phones don't generate entropy quickly, so random numbers used shortly after booting up aren't so random. And it turns out that some of the early implementations copied code that harvested entropy from disk access times. Of course, cell phones don't have disks; they have flash memory with predictable access times, making for predictable entropy.

If your security depends on good random numbers, make sure you understand the system that's generating them.

Know Thy Code

Large projects often include *third-party code*, code not written by members of the project team. In many cases, your team doesn't even have access to the source code; you have to take the vendor's word that their code works and is secure. What could possibly go wrong?

First of all, how do you know that that code really works and is secure? How do you know that someone working on that code didn't install a secret backdoor? This isn't a hypothetical question; a secret backdoor was found in a major networking vendor's products in 2015. An extra account with a hardcoded password was found in another vendor's products in 2016. The list goes on, and will continue to grow as long as bad practices are tolerated. Plan for future abuses that are worse than the ones already known.

Ken Thompson's 1984 Turing Award Lecture entitled "Reflections on Trusting Trust" gives an idea of how much damage a malicious actor can do.

Using third-party code causes another, subtler problem, which shows up with terrifying frequency in physical infrastructure software—the stuff that makes power plants and such work. You would think that critical software like this would be designed by engineers, but that's the rare case. Engineers may specify the software, but it's usually constructed by "system integrators." These are people whose training is similar to what you're getting under the auspices of "learning to code"; system integration pretty much boils down to importing code that others have written and gluing function calls together. The result is that product code ends up looking like Figure 13-6.

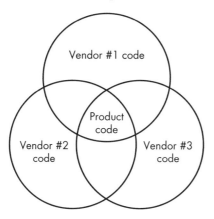

Figure 13-6: Unused vendor code and product code

This means a lot of unused code is included in products; in the figure, there's more nonproduct code than product code. I once gave a series of talks about this where I labeled it "digital herpes," because there's all this code coiled around the central nervous system of your product, waiting for an external stimulus in order to break out, just like the human version of the virus.

This puts a coder into a difficult situation. How do you decide what third-party code is safe to use? Not everybody working on a power plant is an expert in cryptography or networking protocols.

First, this is an area in which open source code has an advantage. You can actually look at open source code and, because you can, there's a good chance that others are looking at it too. This "more eyeballs" principle means that there's at least a better chance of bugs being found than in closed source code that is seen by only a few. Of course, this isn't a panacea. A major bug was discovered in the popular OpenSSL cryptography library in 2014. On the bright side, the discovery of this bug caused a large number of people to eyeball that code plus other security-critical packages.

Another good practice is to keep an eye on the ratio of code that you're actually using in a third-party package to the overall size of the package. I once worked on a medical instrument project where management said, "Let's use this cool operating system that we can get for a good price." But that operating system included all sorts of functionality we weren't going to use. I pushed back, and we just wrote our own code for the stuff that we needed. This was a couple of decades ago, and bugs have just been found in some deployments of this operating system.

One more area to watch is debugging code. It's common to include extra code for debugging during product development. Make sure it gets removed before it's shipped! That includes passwords. If you included default passwords or other shortcuts to make your code easier to debug, make sure that they're gone.

Extreme Cleverness Is Your Enemy

If you're using third-party code, avoid using obscure, clever facilities. That's because vendors often discontinue support for features that aren't widely used by their customers. When that happens, you're often locked out of the upgrade path. Vendors often provide fixes only for the latest version of their products, so if your code depends on a no-longer-supported feature, you may not be able to install critical security fixes.

Understand What's Visible

Think about the ways in which sensitive data can be accessed by programs other than yours—and not just data but metadata too. Who else can see your program's data? This is an important part of defining a threat model. What could be compromised if someone absconds with your otherwise perfectly secure system? Can an attacker bypass protections by pulling the memory chips out of your device and accessing them directly?

Apart from making your code secure, you need to watch out for *side-channel attacks*—exploits based on metadata, or side effects, of the implementation. For example, say you have code that checks a password. If it takes longer to run on a password that's close to correct than it does on one that isn't, that gives clues to an attacker. This sort of thing is called a *timing attack*.

A camera pointed at the keypad on an ATM is a side-channel attack.

Attacks based on electromagnetic emissions have been documented. A cool one is called *van Eck phreaking*, which uses an antenna to pick up the radiation from a monitor to generate a remote copy of the displayed image. It has been demonstrated that ballot secrecy in some electronic voting systems can be compromised in this manner.

Side-channel attacks are really insidious and take serious systems thinking to ameliorate; just knowing how to write code isn't enough. Examples abound, especially from the World War II era, which was the beginning of modern cryptography. The Germans were able to determine that Los Alamos National Laboratory existed because several hundred Sears catalogs were all being mailed to the same PO box. And British chemical plant locations were determined from the scores of the plant soccer team games published in local newspapers.

In general, make sure that your critical security code's externally visible behavior is independent of what it's actually doing. Avoid exposing information via side channels.

Don't Overcollect

This is so obvious that I shouldn't need to say anything, but experience demonstrates that few people get this. The best way to keep things secure is not to keep them at all. Don't collect sensitive information unless you really need to.

A classic example is found on a lot of medical forms. I'm always perplexed when the forms ask for both my birthdate and my age. Do I really want a doctor who can't figure out one from the other? If you collect them both, you have to protect them both, so collect only the one that you need.

Don't Hoard

Just because you've collected sensitive information doesn't mean you should keep it around forever. Get rid of it as soon as possible. For example, you may need somebody's password to log them in to some system. Once you're done checking the password, it's no longer needed. Clean it up. The longer you leave it around, the better the chances of someone discovering it.

Cleaning up is becoming more legally important as the world struggles to understand the European Union's General Data Protection Regulation (GDPR), which adds consequences for leaking personal information.

Dynamic Memory Allocation Isn't Your Friend

Chapter 7 talked about dynamic memory allocation using the heap. In this section, we'll look at the C standard library functions `malloc`, `realloc`, and `free`, which can cause a number of different problems.

Let's start by looking at what happens when dynamically allocated memory is freed; see Figure 13-7.

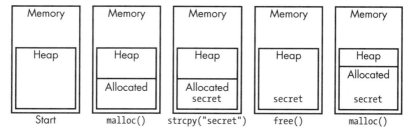

Figure 13-7: Freeing memory

On the left side of Figure 13-8, you can see the heap sitting in memory. Moving to the right, a piece of memory from the heap is allocated for use by the program. Continuing toward the right, a piece of secret information is copied into the allocated memory. At some point later, that memory is no longer needed, so it's freed and goes back onto the heap. Finally, on the far right, memory is allocated from the heap for some other purpose. But the secret is still in that piece of memory where it can be read. Rule #1 of using dynamic memory is to make sure you erase any sensitive information in memory before freeing.

The realloc function lets you grow or shrink the size of allocated memory. Look at the shrink case in Figure 13-8.

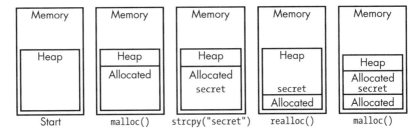

Figure 13-8: Memory shrink

The first steps are the same as in the previous example. But then the amount of allocated memory is shrunk. The secret was in the excess memory, so it goes back onto the heap. Then a later allocation of memory gets a block that contains the secret. Rule #2 of using dynamic memory is to make sure that any memory that's going back on the heap due to a shrink is erased. This is similar to Rule #1.

There are two cases to consider when using realloc to grow the size of an allocated memory block. The first case is easy and isn't a security problem. As shown in Figure 13-9, if there's room above the already allocated block on the heap, the size of the block is increased.

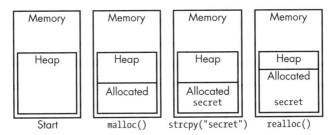

Figure 13-9: Good memory grow

Figure 13-10 shows the case that can cause security problems.

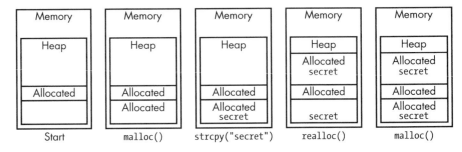

Figure 13-10: Bad memory grow

In this example, there's another piece of memory that has already been allocated for some other purpose. When we try to increase the size of our allocated memory block, there's not enough space because of the other block, so the heap is searched for a large enough contiguous block of memory. The memory is allocated, the data from the old block is copied in, and the old block is freed. Now there are two copies of the secret in memory, and one is in unallocated memory that could be allocated. The big problem here is that the realloc caller has no visibility into what's happening. The only way to tell whether or not the memory block was moved is to compare its address to the original address. But even if it moved, you've found out too late because the old block is no longer under your control. This leads to rule #3: Don't use realloc when security is critical. Use malloc to allocate new memory, copy the old to the new, erase the old, and then call free. Not as efficient, but much more secure.

Garbage Collection Is Not Your Friend Either

I've talked about erasing critical data once it's no longer needed. The preceding section showed that this isn't as easy to do as it sounds with explicit memory management. Garbage-collected systems have their own set of unique problems. Let's say we have a program in C that contains something "sensitive," as shown in Figure 13-11.

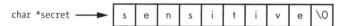

Figure 13-11: C string of sensitive data

How do we clean this up once we're done with it? Because C strings are NUL terminated, we can make it an empty string by setting the first character to NUL, as in Figure 13-12.

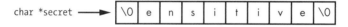

Figure 13-12: Poorly erased C string of sensitive data

It wouldn't be hard for a nefarious individual to guess the contents. We really need to overwrite the entire string.

This string could be in a memory array, or it could be in memory dynamically obtained using malloc. Make sure the string is set to NULs or some recognizable value that's easy to spot when debugging, erasing every character before calling free; otherwise, the sensitive data just ends up back on the heap and might be given out on a later malloc call.

What if we're using a language that uses garbage collection instead of explicit memory management? Something like secret = "xxxxxxxxxxxxxx" doesn't do what you think in languages like JavaScript, PHP, and Java. Rather than overwrite the sensitive data, these languages might just make a new string for you and add the sensitive data string to the list of things to be garbage-collected. The sensitive data isn't erased, and you have no ability to force it to be erased.

It would be nice if these sorts of issues were limited to programming languages and environments, but that's not the case. Flash memory is used in more and more places. One of those places is in solid-state disk drives (SSDs). Because flash memories wear out, these drives use *load leveling* to equalize the usage among the various flash memory chips. That means that writing something to one of these devices doesn't guarantee that the old version was erased. It's just like freeing allocated memory and having it end up on the heap.

As you can see, even the act of erasing something securely is more complex than anything you're being taught while "learning to code." You need a thorough understanding of all aspects of an environment in order to do the job well, which is of course why you're reading this book.

Data as Code

You should be aware by now that "code" is just data in a particular format that's understood by a computer. That originally meant computer hardware, but now many programs, such as web browsers, execute data including in the form of JavaScript programs. And JavaScript can also execute data; its eval statement treats any string as if it's a program and runs it.

In Chapter 5, we looked at some of the hardware that prevents computers from treating arbitrary data as code. Memory management units or Harvard architecture machines keep code and data separate, preventing data from being executed. Programs that can execute data don't have that sort of protection, so you have to provide it yourself.

A classic example is *SQL injection*. SQL, short for Structured Query Language, is the interface to many database systems. The *structured* part allows data to be organized into, for example, personnel records. The *query* part allows that data to be accessed. And, of course, the *language* is how it's done.

SQL databases organize data as a set of *tables*, which are rectangular arrays of rows and columns. Programmers can create tables and specify the columns. Queries insert, remove, modify, or return rows in tables.

You don't need to know all the details of SQL to understand the following example. What you do need to know is that SQL statements are terminated with semicolons (;) and that comments begin with the number or hash sign (#).

Your school probably has a website you can use to check your grades. Our example uses a SQL database that includes a table called students, as shown in Table 13-2.

Table 13-2: Students Table in Database

student	class	grade
David Lightman	Biology 2	F
David Lightman	English 11B	D
David Lightman	World History 11B	C
David Lightman	Trig 2	B
Jennifer Mack	Biology 2	F
Jennifer Mack	English 11B	A
Jennifer Mack	World History 11B	B
Jennifer Mack	Geometry 2	D

The website offers an HTML text field in which a student can enter the name of a class. A bit of JavaScript and jQuery sends the class name to the web server and displays the returned grade. The web server has some PHP code that looks up the grade in the database and sends it back to the web page. When a student logs in, the $student variable is set to their name so that they can access only their own grades. Listing 13-4 shows the code.

HTML
```
<input type="text" id="class"></input>
```

JavaScript
```
$('#class').change(function() {
 $.post('school.php', { class: $('#class').val() }, function(data) {
  // show grades
 });
});
```

PHP
```
$grade = $db->queryAll("SELECT * FROM students
 WHERE class='{$_REQUEST['class']}' && student='$student'");

header('Content-Type: application/json');
echo json_encode($grade);
```

Listing 13-4: Student website code fragments

The database query is straightforward. It selects all (*) columns from all rows in the students table where the class column matches the class field from the web page and the student column matches the variable containing the logged-in student name. What could possibly go wrong?

Well, David may not be paying much attention to Biology, but he's good with computers. He logs in to his account. Instead of entering Biology 2 for a class, he enters Biology 2' || 1=1 || '; #. This turns the select statement into what's shown in Listing 13-5.

```
SELECT * FROM students WHERE class='Biology 2' || 1=1 || ''; # && student='David Lightman'
```

Listing 13-5: SQL injection

This reads as "select all columns from students where class is `Biology 2` or 1 equals 1 or an empty string." The semicolon ends the query early, and the rest of the line is turned into a comment. Because 1 always equals 1, David has just gained access to the entire set of student grades. I could go on to show you how David impresses Jennifer by changing her Biology grade, but you can just watch the 1983 movie *WarGames*. As a teaser, he could enter something in the field with a semicolon, then follow that with a database update command.

These aren't just theoretical science fiction movie scenarios; see xkcd cartoon #327. As recently as 2017, a major SQL injection bug was found in the popular WordPress website software, which was used by a very large number of websites. This should further demonstrate the problems that can occur when you rely on third-party code.

As another example, many websites allow users to submit comments. You must be careful to sanitize every comment to make sure it doesn't contain JavaScript code. Otherwise, a user viewing those comments would inadvertently run that code. And if you don't prevent users from submitting comments in HTML, you'll likely find the comments filled with advertisements and links to other websites. Make sure user input can never be interpreted as code.

Summary

In this chapter, you've gained a basic understanding of security principles. You learned a bit about cryptography, a key computer security technology. You also learned about a number of things that you can do to make your code more secure.

In addition, hopefully you've learned that security is very difficult and not for amateurs. Consult experts until you've become one. Don't go it alone.

Just like security, machine intelligence is another advanced topic that's worth knowing a bit about. We'll turn our attention to it in the next chapter.

14

MACHINE INTELLIGENCE

How many times a day do you submit something like "cats and meetloafs" to a search engine only to have it come back with, "Did you mean *cats and meatloaves*?" You probably take this for granted, without pausing to consider how the search engine knew not only that there was an error in your input, but also how to fix it. It's not very likely that someone wrote a program to match all possible errors with corrections. Instead, some sort of *machine intelligence* must be at work.

Machine intelligence is an advanced topic that includes the related fields of *machine learning*, *artificial intelligence*, and *big data*. These are all concepts you'll likely encounter as a programmer, so this chapter gives you a high-level overview.

Artificial intelligence was first out of the gate when the term was coined at a Dartmouth College workshop in 1956. *Machine learning* was a close second with the *perceptron* in 1957, which we'll discuss shortly. Today, machine learning has a huge lead, thanks in part to two trends. First, technological progress has dramatically increased storage size while reducing the price of it, and it has also led to faster processors and networking. Second, the internet has facilitated the collection of large amounts of data, and people can't resist poking at all of it. For example, data from one large company's book-scanning and translation project was used to dramatically improve a separate language translation project. Another example is a mapping project that fed into the development of self-driving cars. The results from these and other projects were so compelling that machine learning now is being applied to a large number of applications. More recently, people have also realized that these same two trends—cheaper storage and more computing power, and the collection of large amounts of data—support revitalizing artificial intelligence, resulting in a lot of new work in that area as well.

The rush to employ machine intelligence, however, mimics the "What can possibly go wrong?" philosophy that already pervades the computer security world. We don't yet know enough to avoid producing psychotic systems such as HAL from the 1968 movie *2001: A Space Odyssey*.

Overview

You should know by now that programming is the grunt work needed to implement solutions to problems. Defining the problems and their solutions is the interesting and harder part. Many would rather devote their entire careers trying to get computers to do this work instead of doing it themselves (another example of the "peculiar engineering laziness" mentioned in Chapter 5).

As noted earlier, it all started with artificial intelligence; machine learning and big data came later. Though the term wasn't coined until the 1956 Dartmouth workshop, the notion of artificial intelligence goes all the way back to Greek myths. Many philosophers and mathematicians since have worked to develop formal systems that codify human thought. While this hasn't yet led to true artificial intelligence, it has laid a lot of groundwork. For example, George Boole, who gave us our algebra in Chapter 1, published *An Investigation of the Laws of Thought on Which Are Founded the Mathematical Theories of Logic and Probabilities* in 1854.

We've accumulated a lot of information about human decision making but still don't really know how humans think. For example, you and your friends can probably distinguish a cat from a meatloaf. But you might be taking different paths to reach that distinction. Just because the same data yields the same result doesn't mean that we all processed it the same way. We know the inputs and outputs, we understand parts of the "hardware," but we don't know much about the "programming" that transforms one into the other. It follows that the path that a computer uses to recognize cats and meatloaves would also be different.

One thing that we do think we know about human thought processing is that we're really good at statistics unconsciously—not the same thing as consciously suffering through "sadistics" class. For example, linguists have studied how humans acquire language. Infants perform a massive amount of statistical analysis as part of learning to tease important sounds out of the environment, separate them into phonemes, and then group them into words and sentences. It's an ongoing debate as to whether humans have specialized machinery for this sort of thing or whether we're just using general-purpose processing for it.

Infant learning via statistical analysis is made possible, at least in part, by the existence of a large amount of data to analyze. Barring exceptional circumstances, infants are constantly exposed to sound. Likewise, there is a constant barrage of visual information and other sensory input. Infants learn by processing a big amount of data, or just *big data*.

The massive growth in compute power, storage capacity, and various types of network-connected sensors (including cell phones) has led to the collection of huge amounts of data, and not just by the bad guys from the last chapter. Some of this data is organized and some isn't. Organized data might be sets of wave height measurements from offshore buoys. Unorganized data might be ambient sound. What do we do with all of it?

Well, statistics is one of those well-defined branches of mathematics, which means that we can write programs that perform statistical analysis. We can also write programs that can be trained using data. For example, one way to implement spam filters (which we'll look at in more detail shortly) is to feed lots of collected spam and nonspam into a statistical analyzer while telling the analyzer what is spam and what isn't. In other words, we're feeding organized *training data* into a program and telling the program what that data means (that is, what's spam and what's not). We call this *machine learning (ML)*. Kind of like Huckleberry Finn, we're "gonna learn that machine" instead of "teaching" it.

In many respects, machine learning systems are analogous to human autonomic nervous system functions. In humans, the brain isn't actively involved in a lot of low-level processes, such as breathing; it's reserved for higher-level functions, such as figuring out what's for dinner. The low-level functions are handled by the autonomic nervous system, which only bothers the brain when something needs attention. Machine learning is currently good for recognizing, but that's not the same thing as taking action.

Unorganized data is a different beast. We're talking big data, meaning that it's not something that humans can comprehend without assistance. In this case, various statistical techniques are used to find patterns and relationships. For example, this approach—sometimes known as *data mining*—could be used to extract music from ambient sound (after all, as French composer Edgard Varèse said, music is organized sound).

All of this is essentially finding ways to transform complex data into something simpler. For example, one could train a machine learning system to recognize cats and meatloaves. It would transform very complex image data into simple cat and meatloaf bits. It's a *classification* process.

Back in Chapter 5, we discussed the separation of instructions and data. In Chapter 13, I cautioned against allowing data to be treated as instructions for reasons of security. But there are times when it makes sense, because data-driven classification can only get us so far.

One can't, for example, create a self-driving car based on classification alone. A set of complicated programs that acts on classifier outputs must be written to implement behavior such as "Don't hit cats, but it's okay and possibly beneficial to society to drive over a meatloaf." There are many ways in which this behavior could be implemented, including combinations of swerving and changing speed. There are large numbers of variables to consider, such as other traffic, the relative position of obstacles, and so on.

People don't learn to drive from complex and detailed instructions such as "Turn the wheel one degree to the left and put one gram of pressure on the brake pedal for three seconds to avoid the cat," or "Turn three degrees to the right and floor it to hit the meatloaf dead on." Instead, they work from goals such as "Don't hit cats." People "program" themselves, and, as mentioned earlier, we have no way yet to examine that programming to determine how they choose to accomplish goals. If you observe traffic, you'll see a lot of variation in how people accomplish the same basic tasks.

People are not just refining their classifiers in cases like this; they're writing new programs. When computers do this, we call it *artificial intelligence (AI)*. AI systems write their own programs to accomplish goals. One way to achieve this without damaging any actual cats is to provide an AI system with simulated input. Of course, philosophical thermostellar devices such as Bomb 20 from the 1974 movie *Dark Star* show that this doesn't always work out well.

A big difference between machine learning and artificial intelligence is the ability to examine a system and "understand" the "thought processes." This is currently impossible in machine learning systems but is possible with AI. It's not clear if that will continue when AI systems get huge, especially as it's unlikely that the processes will resemble human thought.

Machine Learning

Let's see if we can come up with a way to distinguish a photograph of a cat from a photograph of a meatloaf. This is a lot less information than a human has available with real cats and meatloaves. For example, humans have discovered that cats typically run away when chased, which is not common meatloaf behavior. We'll try to create a process that, when presented with a photograph, will tell us whether "it sees" a cat, a meatloaf, or neither. Figure 14-1 shows the original images of a meatloaf-looking Tony Cat on the left and an actual meatloaf on the right.

Figure 14-1: Original Tony Cat and meatloaf

There's a high probability that you'll encounter statistics at all levels of machine intelligence, so we'll start by reviewing some of the basics.

Bayes

English minister Thomas Bayes (1701–1761) must have been concerned about the chances of his flock getting into heaven because he thought a lot about probability. In particular, Bayes was interested in how the probabilities of different events combined. For example, if you're a backgammon player, you're probably well aware of the probability distribution of numbers that result from rolling a pair of six-sided dice. He's responsible for the eponymous *Bayes'* theorem.

The part of his work that's relevant here is what's called a *naive Bayes classifier*. Leaving our meatloaf with the cat for a while, let's try to separate out messages that are spam from messages that aren't. Messages are collections of words. Certain words are more likely to occur in spam, from which we can infer that messages without those words might not be spam.

We'll start by collecting some simple statistics. Let's assume that we have a representative sample of messages, 100 that are spam and another 100 that aren't. We'll break the messages up into words and count the number of messages in which each word occurs. Since we're using 100 messages, that magically gives us the percentage. Partial results are shown in Table 14-1.

Table 14-1: Words in Messages Statistics

Word	Spam percentage	Nonspam percentage
meatloaf	80	0
hamburger	75	5
catnip	0	70
onion	68	0
mousies	1	67
the	99	98
and	97	99

You can see that some words are common to both spam and nonspam. Let's apply this table to an unknown message that contains "hamburger and onion:" respectively, the spam percentages are 75, 97, and 68, and the nonspam percentages are 5, 97, and 0. What's the probability that this message is or isn't spam?

Bayes' theorem tells us how to combine probabilities (p) where p_0 is the probability that a message containing the word *meatloaf* is spam, p_1 is the probability that a message containing the word *hamburger* is spam, and so on:

$$p_{\text{combined}} = \frac{p_0 p_1 p_2 \cdots p_n}{p_0 p_1 p_2 \cdots p_n + (1 - p_0)(1 - p_1)(1 - p_2) \cdots (1 - p_n)}$$

This can be visualized as shown in Figure 14-2. Events and probabilities such as those from Table 14-1 are fed into the classifier, which yields the probability that the events describe what we want.

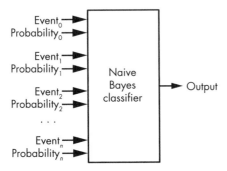

Figure 14-2: Naive Bayes classifier

We can build a pair of classifiers, one for spam and one for non-spam. Plugging in the numbers from the above example, this gives us a 99.64 percent chance that the message is spam and a 0 percent chance that it's not.

You can see that this technique works pretty well. Statistics rules! There are, of course, a lot of other tricks needed to make a decent spam filter. For example, understanding what's meant by "naive." It doesn't mean that Bayes didn't know what he was doing. It means that just like rolling dice, all of the events are unrelated. We could improve our spam filtering by looking at the relationship between words, such as the fact that "and and" appears only in messages about Boolean algebra. Many spammers try to evade filters by including a large amount of "word salad" in their messages, which is rarely grammatically correct.

Gauss

German mathematician Johann Carl Friedrich Gauss (1777–1855) is another statistically important person. You can blame him for the *bell curve*, also called a *normal distribution* or *Gaussian distribution*. It looks like Figure 14-3.

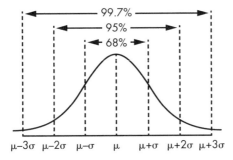

Figure 14-3: Bell curve

The bell curve is interesting because samples of observed phenomena fit the curve. For example, if we measure the height of basketball players at a park and determine the mean height μ, some players will be taller and some will be shorter. (By the way, μ is pronounced "mew," making it the preferred Greek letter for cats.) Of the players, 68 percent will be within one *standard deviation* or σ, 95 percent within two standard deviations, and so on. It's more accurate to say that the height distribution converges on the bell curve as the number of samples increases, because the height of a single player isn't going to tell us much. Carefully sampled data from a well-defined population can be used to make assumptions about larger populations.

While that's all very interesting, there are plenty of other applications of the bell curve, some of which we can apply to our cat and meatloaf problem. American cartoonist Bernard Kliban (1935–1990) teaches us that a cat is essentially a meatloaf with ears and a tail. It follows that if we could extract features such as ears, tails, and meatloaves from photographs, we could feed them into a classifier that could identify the subject matter for us.

We can make object features more recognizable by tracing their outlines. Of course, we can't do this unless we can find their edges. This is difficult because both cats and a fair number of meatloaves are fuzzy. Cats in particular have a lot of distinct hairs that are edges unto themselves, but not the ones we want. While it might seem counterintuitive, our first step is to blur the images slightly to eliminate some of these unwanted aspects. Blurring an image means applying a low-pass filter, like we saw for audio in Chapter 6. Fine details in an image are "high frequencies." It's intuitive if you think about the fine details changing faster as you scan across the image.

Let's see what Gauss can do for us. Let's take the curve from Figure 14-3 and spin it around μ to make a three-dimensional version, as shown in Figure 14-4.

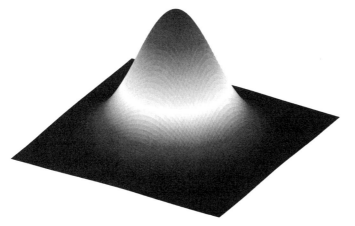

Figure 14-4: Three-dimensional Gaussian distribution

We'll drag this across the image, centering μ over each pixel in turn. You can imagine that parts of the curve cover other pixels surrounding the center pixel. We're going to generate a new value for each pixel by multiplying the values of the pixels under the curve by the value of the curve and then adding the results together. This is called a *Gaussian blur*. You can see how it works in Figure 14-5. The image in the middle is a magnified copy of what's in the square in the image on the left. In the right-hand image, you can see how the Gaussian blur weights a set of pixels from the center image.

Figure 14-5: Gaussian blur

The process of combining the value of a pixel with the values of its neighbors might seem convoluted to you, and in fact it's mathematically known as *convolution*. The array of weights is called a *kernel* or *convolution kernel*. Let's look at some examples.

Figure 14-6 shows a 3×3 and a 5×5 kernel. Note that the weights all add up to 1 to preserve brightness.

3×3				**5×5**			
$\frac{1}{16}$	$\frac{2}{16}$	$\frac{1}{16}$	$\frac{1}{256}$	$\frac{4}{256}$	$\frac{6}{256}$	$\frac{4}{256}$	$\frac{1}{256}$
$\frac{2}{16}$	$\frac{4}{16}$	$\frac{2}{16}$	$\frac{4}{256}$	$\frac{16}{256}$	$\frac{24}{256}$	$\frac{16}{256}$	$\frac{4}{256}$
$\frac{1}{16}$	$\frac{2}{16}$	$\frac{1}{16}$	$\frac{6}{256}$	$\frac{24}{256}$	$\frac{36}{256}$	$\frac{24}{256}$	$\frac{6}{256}$
			$\frac{4}{256}$	$\frac{16}{256}$	$\frac{24}{256}$	$\frac{16}{256}$	$\frac{4}{256}$
			$\frac{1}{256}$	$\frac{4}{256}$	$\frac{6}{256}$	$\frac{4}{256}$	$\frac{1}{256}$

Figure 14-6: Gaussian convolution kernels

Figure 14-7 shows an original image on the left. Your eye can trace the outline of the tree trunks even though there are many gaps. The center image shows the results of a 3×3 kernel. While it's fuzzier, the edges are easier to discern. The right image shows the results of a 5×5 kernel.

You can think of the image as if it's a mathematical function of the form $brightness = f(x, y)$. The value of this function is the pixel brightness at each coordinate location. Note that this is a *discrete* function; the values for x and y must be integers. And, of course, they have to be inside the image boundaries. In a similar fashion, you can think of a convolution kernel as a small image whose value is $weight = g(x, y)$. Thus, the process of performing the convolution involves iterating through the neighboring pixels covered by the kernel, multiplying the pixel values by the weights, and adding them together.

Figure 14-7: Gaussian blur examples

Figure 14-8 shows our original images blurred using a 5×5 Gaussian kernel.

Figure 14-8: Blurred cat and meatloaf

Note that because the convolution kernels are bigger than 1 pixel, they hang off the edges of the image. There are many approaches to dealing with this, such as not going too close to the edge (making the result smaller) and making the image larger by drawing a border around it.

Sobel

There's a lot of information in Figure 14-1 that isn't really necessary for us to identify the subject matter, such as color. For example, in his book *Understanding Comics: The Invisible Art* (Tundra), Scott McCloud shows that we can recognize a face from just a circle, two dots, and a line; the rest of the details are unnecessary and can be ignored. Accordingly, we're going to simplify our images.

Let's try to find the edges now that we've made them easier to see by blurring. There are many definitions of *edge*. Our eyes are most sensitive to changes in brightness, so we'll use that. The change in brightness is just the difference in brightness between a pixel and its neighbor.

About half of calculus is about change, so we can apply that here. A *derivative* of a function is just the slope of the curve generated by the function. If we want the change in brightness from one pixel to the next, then the formula is just *brightness* = $f(x + 1, y) - f(x, y)$.

Take a look at the horizontal row of pixels in Figure 14-9. The brightness level is plotted underneath, and beneath that is plotted the change in brightness. You can see that it looks spiky. That's because it only has a nonzero value during a change.

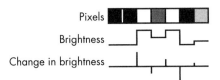

Figure 14-9: Edges are changes in brightness

There's a problem with measuring brightness changes this way—the changes happen in the cracks between the pixels. We want the changes to be in the middle of the pixels. Let's see if Gauss can help us out here. When we were blurring, we centered μ on a pixel. We'll take the same approach, but instead of using the bell curve, we'll use its first derivative, shown in Figure 14-10, which plots the slope of the curve from Figure 14-3.

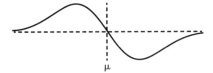

Figure 14-10: Slope of the Gaussian curve from Figure 14-3

If we call the positive and negative peaks of the curve +1 and –1 and center those over the neighboring pixels, the change of brightness for a pixel is $\Delta\text{brightness}_n = 1 \times \text{pixel}_{n-1} - 1 \times \text{pixel}_{n+1}$. You can see how this plays out in Figure 14-11.

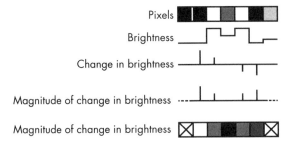

Figure 14-11: Brightness change centered on pixels

Of course, this has the same image edge problem that we saw in the last section, so we don't have values for the end pixels. At the moment, we don't care about the direction of change, just the amount, so we calculate the *magnitude* by taking the absolute value.

Detecting edges this way works pretty well, but many people have tried to improve on it. One of the winning approaches, the *Sobel operator*, was announced by American scientist Irwin Sobel along with Gary Feldman in a 1968 paper.

Similar to what we did with our Gaussian blur kernel, we generate a Sobel edge detection kernel using values from the slope of the Gaussian curve. We saw the two-dimensional version in Figure 14-10, and Figure 14-12 shows the three-dimensional version.

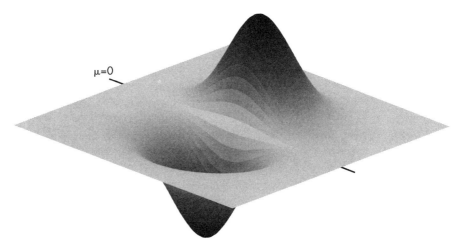

Figure 14-12: Three-dimensional slope of Gaussian curve from Figure 14-10

Since this isn't symmetrical around both axes, Sobel used two versions—one for the horizontal direction and another for the vertical. Figure 14-13 shows both kernels.

Sobel$_x$			Sobel$_y$		
+1	0	−1	+1	+2	+1
+2	0	−2	0	0	0
+1	0	−1	−1	−2	−1

Figure 14-13: Sobel kernels

Applying these kernels produces a pair of *gradients*, G_x and G_y, for each pixel; you can think of a gradient as a slope. Since we have a gradient in each Cartesian direction, we can use trigonometry to convert them into polar coordinates, yielding a *magnitude G* and a *direction* θ, as shown in Figure 14-14.

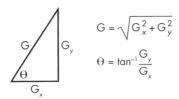

$$G = \sqrt{G_x^2 + G_y^2}$$

$$\Theta = \tan^{-1}\frac{G_y}{G_x}$$

Figure 14-14: Gradient magnitude and direction

The gradient magnitude tells us how "strong" an edge we have, and the direction gives us its orientation. Keep in mind that direction is perpendicular to the object; a horizontal edge has a vertical gradient.

You might have noticed that the magnitude and direction calculation is really just the transformation from Cartesian to polar coordinates that we saw in Chapter 11. Changing coordinate systems is a handy trick. In this case, once we're in polar coordinates, we don't have to worry about division by zero or huge numbers when denominators get small. Most math libraries have a function of the form atan2(y, x) that calculates the arctangent without division.

Figure 14-15 shows the gradient magnitudes for both images.

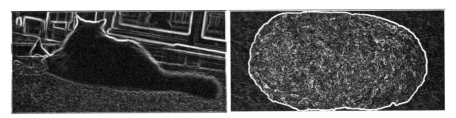

Figure 14-15: Sobel magnitudes for blurred cat and meatloaf

There's an additional issue with the direction, which is that it has more information than we can use. Take a look at Figure 14-16.

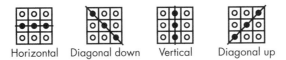

Figure 14-16: Pixel neighbors

As you can see, because a pixel has only eight neighbors, there are really only four directions we care about. Figure 14-17 shows how the direction is quantized into the four "bins."

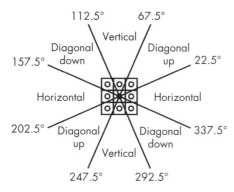

Figure 14-17: Gradient direction bins

Figure 14-18 shows the binned Sobel directions for the blurred images. You can see the correspondence between the directions and the magnitudes. The top row is the horizontal bin followed by the diagonally up bin, the vertical bin, and the diagonally down bin.

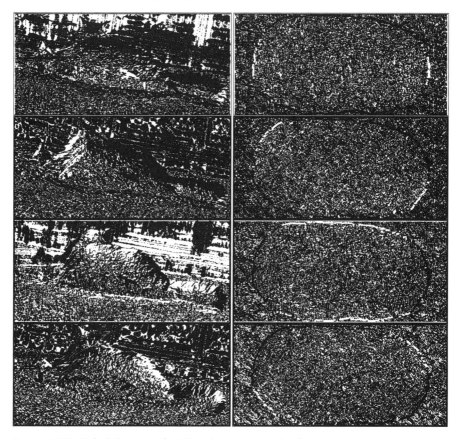

Figure 14-18: Sobel directions for blurred cat and meatloaf

As you can see, the Sobel operator is finding edges, but they're not great edges. They're fat, which makes it possible to mistake them for object features. Skinny edges would eliminate this problem, and we can use the Sobel directions to help find them.

Canny

Australian computer scientist John Canny improved on edge detection in 1986 by adding some additional steps to the Sobel result. The first is *nonmaximum suppression*. Looking back at Figure 14-15, you can see that some of the edges are fat and fuzzy; it'll be easier later to figure out the features in our image if the edges are skinny. Nonmaximum suppression is a technique for *edge thinning*.

Here's the plan. We compare the gradient magnitude of each pixel with that of its neighbors in the direction of the gradient. If its magnitude is greater than that of the neighbors, the value is preserved; otherwise, it's suppressed by being set to 0 (see Figure 14-19).

Keep   Suppress

Figure 14-19: Nonmaximum suppression

You can see in Figure 14-19 that the center pixel on the left is kept, as it has a greater magnitude (that is, it's lighter) than its neighbors, while the center pixel on the right is suppressed because its neighbors have greater magnitude.

Figure 14-20 shows how nonmaximum suppression thins the edges produced by the Sobel operator.

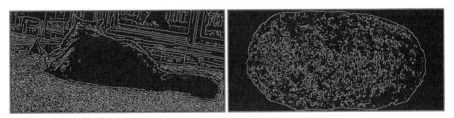

Figure 14-20: Nonmaximum suppression cat and meatloaf results

This is looking pretty good, although it makes a good case for meatloaf avoidance. Nonmaximum suppression found a lot of edges in the images. If you look back at Figure 14-15, you'll see that many of these edges have low gradient magnitudes. The final step in Canny processing is *edge tracking with hysteresis*, which removes "weak edges," leaving only "strong edges."

Back in Chapter 2, you learned that hysteresis involves comparison against a pair of thresholds. We're going to scan the nonmaximum suppression results looking for edge pixels (white in Figure 14-20) whose gradient magnitude is greater than a high threshold. When we find one, we'll make it a final edge pixel. We'll then look at its neighbors. Any neighbor whose gradient magnitude is greater than a low threshold is also marked as a final edge pixel. We follow each of these paths using recursion until we hit a gradient magnitude that's less than the low threshold. You can think of this as starting on a clear edge and tracing its connections until they peter out. You can see the results in Figure 14-21. The strong edges are white; the rejected weak edges are gray.

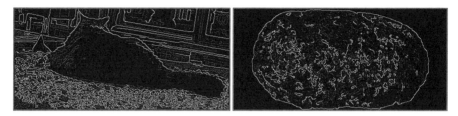

Figure 14-21: Edge tracking with hysteresis

You can see that a lot of the edges from nonmaximum suppression are gone and the object edges are fairly visible.

There is a great open source library for computer vision called *OpenCV* that you can use to play with all sorts of image processing, including what we've covered in this chapter.

Feature Extraction

The next step is easy for people but difficult for computers. We want to extract features from the images in Figure 14-21. I'm not going to cover feature extraction in detail because it involves a lot of math that you probably haven't yet encountered, but we'll touch on the basics.

There are a large number of feature extraction algorithms. Some, like the *Hough transform*, are good for extracting geometric shapes such as lines and circles. That's not very useful for our problem because we're not looking for geometric shapes. Let's do something simple. We'll scan our image for edges and follow them to extract objects. We'll take the shortest path if we find edges that cross.

This gives us blobs, ears, cat toys, and squigglies, as shown in Figure 14-22. Only a representative sample is shown.

Figure 14-22: Extracted features

Now that we have these features, we can do just what we did with our earlier spam detection example: feed them into classifiers (as shown in Figure 14-23). The classifier inputs marked + indicate that there's some chance that the feature is indicative of our desired result, while – means that it's counterindicative and 0 means that it has no contribution.

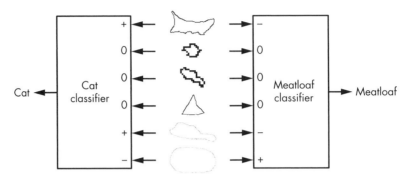

Figure 14-23: Feature classification

Notice that there's information in our images that can be used to improve on naive classification, such as the cat toys. They're commonly found near cats but rarely associated with meatloaves.

This example isn't good for much other than showing the steps of feature classification, which are summarized in Figure 14-24.

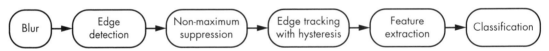

Figure 14-24: Image recognition pipeline

While meatloaves are mostly sedentary, cats move around a lot and have a plethora of cute poses. Our example will work only for the objects in our sample images; it's not going to recognize the image in Figure 11-44 on page 323 as a cat. And because of context issues, it has little chance of recognizing that the cat in Figure 14-25 *is* Meat Loaf.

Figure 14-25: Cat or Meat Loaf?

Neural Networks

At a certain level, it doesn't really matter what data we use to represent objects. We need to be able to deal with the huge amount of variation in the world. Just like people, computers can't change the inputs. We need better classifiers to deal with the variety.

One of the approaches used in artificial intelligence is to mimic human behavior. We're pretty sure that *neurons* play a big part. Humans have about 86 billion neurons, although they're not all in the "brain"—nerve cells are also neurons, which is possibly why some people think with their gut.

You can think of a neuron as a cross between logic gates from Chapter 2 and analog comparators from Chapter 6. A simplified diagram of a neuron is shown in Figure 14-26.

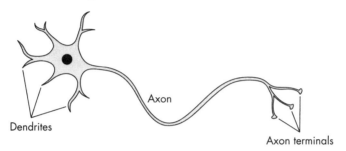

Figure 14-26: Neuron

The *dendrites* are the inputs, and the *axon* is the output. The *axon terminals* are just connections from the axon to other neurons; neurons only have a single output. Neurons differ from something like an AND gate in that not all inputs are treated equally. Take a look at Figure 14-27.

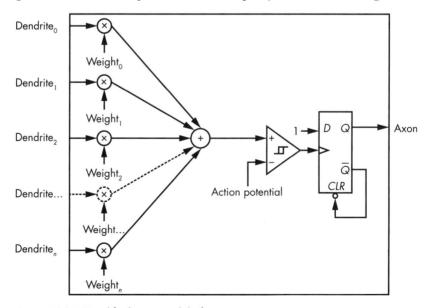

Figure 14-27: Simplified gate model of a neuron

The value of each dendrite input is multiplied by some *weight*, and then all of the weighted values are added together. This is similar to a Bayes classifier. If these values are less than the *action potential*, the comparator output is false; otherwise, it's true, causing the neuron to *fire* by setting the flip-flop output to true. The axon output is a *pulse*; as soon as it goes to true, the flip-flop is reset and goes back to false. Or, if you learned neuroscience from Mr. Miyagi: ax-on, ax-off. Neuroscientists might quibble with the depiction of the comparator as having hysteresis; real neurons do, but it's time-dependent, which this model isn't.

Neurons are like gates in that they're "simple" but can be connected together to make complicated "circuits," or *neural networks*. The key takeaway from neurons is that they fire based on their weighted inputs. Multiple combinations of inputs can cause a neuron to fire.

The first attempt at an artificial neuron was the *perceptron* invented by American psychologist Frank Rosenblatt (1928–1971). A diagram is shown in Figure 14-28. An important aspect of perceptrons is that the inputs and outputs are binary; they can only have values of 0 or 1. The weights and threshold are real numbers.

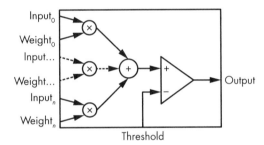

Figure 14-28: Perceptron

Perceptrons created a lot of excitement in the AI world. But then it was discovered that they didn't work for certain classes of problems. This, among other factors, led to what was called the "AI winter" during which funding dried up.

It turns out that the problem was in the way that the perceptrons were being used. They were organized as a single "layer," as shown in Figure 14-29, where each circle is a perceptron.

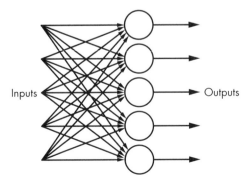

Figure 14-29: Single-layer neural network

Inputs can go to multiple perceptrons, each of which makes one decision and produces an output. Many of the issues with perceptrons were solved by the invention of the multilayer neural network, as shown in Figure 14-30.

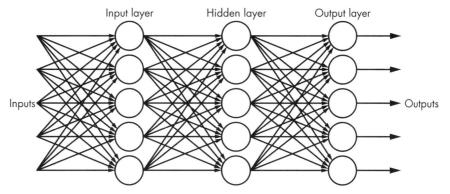

Figure 14-30: Multilayer neural network

This is also known as a *feedforward network* since the outputs produced from each layer are fed forward into the next layer. There can be an arbitrary number of *hidden layers*, so named because they're not connected to either the inputs or outputs. Although Figure 14-30 shows the same number of neurons in each layer, that's not a requirement. Determining the number of layers and number of neurons per layer for a particular problem is a black art outside the scope of this book. Neural networks like this are much more capable than simple classifiers.

Neuroscientists don't yet know how dendrite weights are determined. Computer scientists had to come up with something because otherwise artificial neurons would be useless. The digital nature of perceptrons makes this difficult because small changes in weights don't result in proportional changes in the output; it's an all-or-nothing thing. A different neuron design, the *sigmoid neuron*, addresses this problem by replacing the perceptron comparator with a *sigmoid function*, which is just a fancy name for a function with an S-shaped curve. Figure 14-31 shows both the perceptron transfer function and the sigmoid function. Sure looks a lot like our discussion of analog and digital back in Chapter 2, doesn't it?

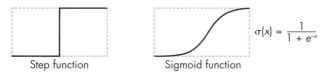

$$\sigma(x) = \frac{1}{1 + e^{-x}}$$

Step function   Sigmoid function

Figure 14-31: Artificial neuron transfer functions

The guts of a sigmoid neuron are shown in Figure 14-32.

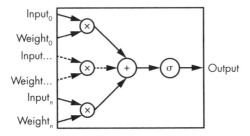

Figure 14-32: Sigmoid neuron

One thing that's not obvious here is that the sigmoid neuron inputs and outputs are "analog" floating-point numbers. Just for accuracy, there's also a bias used in a sigmoid neuron, but it's not essential for our understanding here.

The weights for neural networks built from sigmoid neurons can be determined using a technique called *backpropagation* that's regularly lost and rediscovered, the latter most recently in a 1986 paper by David Rumelhart (1942–2011), Geoffrey Hinton, and Roland Williams. Backpropagation uses wads of linear algebra, so we're going to gloss over the details. You've probably learned how to solve simultaneous equations in algebra; linear algebra comes into play when there are large numbers of equations with large numbers of variables.

The general idea behind backpropagation is that we provide inputs for something known, such as cat features. The output is examined, and if we know that the inputs represent a cat, we'd expect the output to be 1 or pretty close to it. We can calculate an *error function*, which is the actual output subtracted from the desired output. The weights are then adjusted to make the error function value as close to 0 as possible.

This is commonly done using an algorithm called *gradient descent*, which is a lot like Dante's descent into hell if you don't like math. Let's get a handle on it using a simple example. Remember that "gradient" is just another word for "slope." We'll try different values for the weights and plot the value of the error function. It might look something like Figure 14-33, which resembles one of those relief maps that shows mountains, valleys, and so on.

All that's involved in gradient descent is to roll a ball around on the map until it lands in the deepest valley. That's where the value of the error function is at its minimum. We set the weights to the values that represent the ball's position. The reason that this algorithm gets a fancy name is that we're doing this for very large numbers of weights, not just the two in our example. And it's even more complicated when there are weights in multiple layers, such as we saw in Figure 14-30.

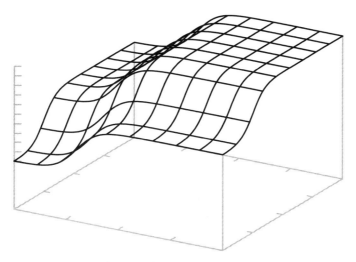

Figure 14-33: Gradient topology

You might have noticed the mysterious disappearance of the output pulsing mechanism that we saw in Figure 14-27. The neural networks that we've seen so far are essentially combinatorial logic, not sequential logic, and are effectively DAGs. There is a sequential logic variation called a *recurrent neural network*. It's not a DAG, which means that outputs from neurons in a layer can connect back to the inputs of neurons in an earlier layer. The storing of outputs and clocking of the whole mess is what keeps it from exploding. These types of networks perform well for processing sequences of inputs, such as those found in handwriting and speech recognition.

There's yet another neural network variation that's especially good for image processing: the *convolutional neural network*. You can visualize it as having inputs that are an array of pixel values similar to the convolution kernels that we saw earlier.

One big problem with neural networks is that they can be "poisoned" by bad training data. We can't tell what sort of unusual behavior might occur in adults who watched too much television as kids, and the same is true with machine learning systems. There might be a need for machine psychotherapists in the future, although it's hard to imagine sitting down next to a machine and saying, "So tell me how you really feel about pictures of cats."

The bottom line on neural networks is that they're very capable classifiers. They can be trained to convert a large amount of input data into a smaller amount of outputs that describe the inputs in a way that we desire. Sophisticates might call this *reducing dimensionality*. Now we have to figure out what to do with that information.

Using Machine Learning Data

How would we build something like a self-driving ketchup bottle using classifier outputs? We'll use the test scenario shown in Figure 14-34. We'll move the ketchup bottle one square at a time as if it's a king on a chessboard with the goal of hitting the meatloaf while avoiding the cat.

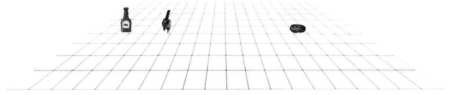

Figure 14-34: Test scenario

In this "textbook example," the classifiers give us the positions of the cat and meatloaf. Since the shortest distance between two points is a straight line, and since we're on an integer grid, the most efficient way to reach the meatloaf is to use the Bresenham line-drawing algorithm from "Straight Lines" on page 292. Of course, it'll have to be modified as shown in Figure 14-35, because cats and condiments don't go well together.

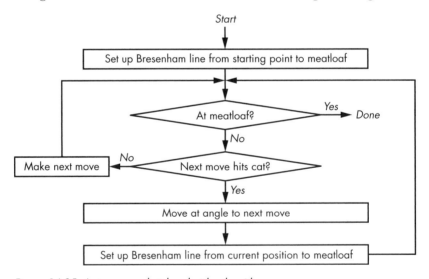

Figure 14-35: Autonomous ketchup bottle algorithm

As you can see, it's pretty simple. We make a beeline for the meatloaf, and if the cat's in the way, we jog and make another beeline for the meatloaf. Of course, this gets much more complicated in the real world, where the cat can move and there may be other obstacles.

Now let's look at one of the other machine intelligence subfields to see a different way to approach this problem.

Artificial Intelligence

Early artificial intelligence results, such as learning to play checkers and solve various logic problems, were exciting and produced a lot of funding. Unfortunately, these early successes didn't scale to harder problems, and funding dried up.

One of the attendees at the 1956 Dartmouth workshop where the term was coined was American scientist John McCarthy (1927–2011), who designed the LISP programming language while at the Massachusetts Institute of Technology. This language was used for much of the early AI work, and LISP officially stands for *List Processor*—but anybody familiar with the language syntax knows it as *Lots of Insipid Parentheses.*

LISP introduced several new concepts to high-level programming languages. Of course, that wasn't hard back in 1958, since only one other high-level language existed at the time (FORTRAN). In particular, LISP included singly linked lists (see Chapter 7) as a data type with programs as lists of instructions. This meant that programs could modify themselves, which is an important distinction with machine learning systems. A neural network can adjust weights but can't change its algorithm. Because LISP can generate code, it can modify or create new algorithms. While it's not quite as clean, JavaScript also supports *self-modifying code*, although it's dangerous to do in the minimally constrained environment of the web.

Early AI systems quickly became constrained by the available hardware technology. One of the most common machines used for research at the time was the DEC PDP-10, whose address space was initially limited to 256K 36-bit words, and eventually expanded to 4M. This isn't enough to run the machine learning examples in this chapter. American programmer Richard Greenblatt and computer engineer Tom Knight began work in the early 1970s at MIT to develop *Lisp machines*, which were computers optimized to run LISP. However, even in their heyday, only a few thousand of these machines were ever built, possibly because general-purpose computers were advancing at a faster pace.

Artificial intelligence started making a comeback in the 1980s with the introduction of *expert systems*. These systems assist users, such as medical professionals, by asking questions and guiding them through a knowledge database. This should sound familiar to you; it's a serious application of our "Guess the Animal" game from Chapter 10. Unfortunately, expert systems seem to have matured into annoying phone menus.

We're going to attack our self-driving ketchup bottle problem with a *genetic algorithm*, which is a technique that mimics evolution (see Figure 14-36).

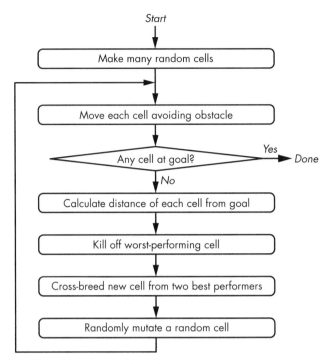

Start

Make many random cells

Move each cell avoiding obstacle

Any cell at goal? — Yes → Done

No

Calculate distance of each cell from goal

Kill off worst-performing cell

Cross-breed new cell from two best performers

Randomly mutate a random cell

Figure 14-36: Genetic algorithm

We randomly create a set of car *cells* that each have a position and a direction of movement. Each cell is moved one step, and then a "goodness" score is calculated, in this case using the distance formula. We breed the two best-performing cells to create a new one, and we kill off the worst-performing cell. Because it's evolution, we also randomly mutate one of the cells. We keep stepping until one of the cells reaches the goal. The steps that the cell took to reach the goal are the generated program.

Let's look at the results from running the algorithm with 20 cells. We got lucky and found the solution shown in Figure 14-37 in only 36 iterations.

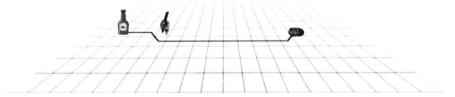

Figure 14-37: Good genetic algorithm results

Our algorithm created the simple program in Listing 14-1 to accomplish the goal. The important point is that a programmer didn't write this program; our AI did it for us. The variables x and y are the position of the ketchup bottle.

```
x++;
x++;
x++; y++;
x++;
x++;
x++;
x++;
x++;
x++;
x++;
x++;
x++;
x++; y--;
```

Listing 14-1: Generated code

Of course, being genetics, it's random and doesn't always work out so cleanly. Another run of the program took 82 iterations to find the solution in Figure 14-38. Might make the case for "intelligent design."

Figure 14-38: Strange genetic algorithm results

You can see that AI programs can generate surprising results. But they're not all that different from what children come up with when exploring the world; it's just that people are now paying more attention. In fact, many AI results that surprise some people were predicted long ago. For example, there was a lot of press when a company's AI systems created their own private language to communicate with each other. That's not a new idea to anybody who has seen the 1970 science fiction film *Colossus: The Forbin Project.*

Big Data

If it's not obvious from the examples so far, we're processing a lot of data. An HD (1920×1080) video camera produces around a third of a gigabyte of data every second. The Large Hadron Collider generates about 25 GiB/second. It's estimated that network-connected devices generate about 50 GiB/second, up from about 1 MiB/second a quarter-century ago. Most of this information is garbage; the challenge is to mine the useful parts.

Big data is a moving target; it refers to data that is too big and complex to process using brute-force techniques in the technology of the day. The amount of data created 25 years ago is fairly trivial to process using current technology, but it wasn't back then. Data collection is likely to always exceed data analysis capabilities, so cleverness is required.

The term *big data* refers not only to analysis but also to the collection, storage, and management of the data. For our purposes, we're concerned with the analysis portion.

A lot of the data that's collected is personal in nature. It's not a great idea to share your bank account information or medical history with strangers. And data that is collected for one purpose is often used for another. The Nazis used census data to identify and locate Jews for persecution, for example, and American census data was used to locate and round up Japanese Americans for internment, despite a provision in the law keeping personally identifiable portions of that data confidential for 75 years.

A lot of data is released for research purposes in "anonymized" form, which means that any personally identifying information has been removed. But it's not that simple. Big data techniques can often reidentify individuals from anonymized data. And many policies designed to make reidentification difficult have actually made it easier.

In America, the Social Security number (SSN) is regularly misused as a personal identifier. It was never designed for this use. In fact, a Social Security card contains the phrase "not for identification purposes," which was part of the original law—one that's rarely enforced and now has a huge number of exceptions.

An SSN has three fields: a three-digit area number (AN), a two-digit group number (GN), and a four-digit serial number (SN). The area number is assigned based on the postal code of the mailing address on the application form. Group numbers are assigned in a defined but nonconsecutive order. Serial numbers are assigned consecutively.

A group of Carnegie Mellon researchers published a paper in 2009 that demonstrated a method for successfully guessing SSNs. Two things made it easy. First is the existence of the Death Master File. (That's "Death" "Master File," not "Death Master" "File.") It's a list of deceased people made available by the Social Security Administration ostensibly for fraud prevention. It conveniently includes names, birth dates, death dates, SSNs, and postal codes. How does a list of dead people help us guess the SSNs of the living?

Well, it's not the only data out there. Voter registration lists include birth data, as do many online profiles.

Statistical analysis of the ANs and postal codes in the Death Master File can be used to link ANs to geographic areas. The rules for assigning GNs and SNs are straightforward. As a result, the Death Master File information can be used to map ANs to postal codes. Separately obtained birth data can also be linked to postal codes. These two sources of information can be interleaved, sorting by birth date. Any gap in the Death Master SSN sequence is a living person whose SSN is between the preceding and following Death Master entries. An example is shown in Table 14-2.

Table 14-2: Combining Data from Postal Code 89044

Death Master File			Guessed SSN	Birth records	
Name	**DOB**	**SSN**		**DOB**	**Name**
John Many Jars	1984-01-10	051-51-1234			
John Fish	1984-02-01	051-51-1235			
John Two Horns	1984-02-12	051-51-1236			
			051-51-1237	1984-02-14	Jon Steinhart
John Worfin	1984-02-20	051-51-1238			
John Bigboote	1984-03-15	051-51-1239			
John Ya Ya	1984-04-19	051-51-1240			
			051-51-1241	1984-04-20	John Gilmore
John Fledgling	1984-05-21	051-51-1242			
			051-51-1243	1984-05-22	John Perry Barlow
John Grim	1984-06-02	051-51-1244			
John Littlejohn	1984-06-03	051-51-1245			
John Chief Crier	1984-06-12	051-51-1246			
			051-51-1247	1984-07-05	John Jacob Jingleheimer Schmidt
John Small Berries	1984-08-03	051-51-1250			

Of course, it's not quite as straightforward as this example, but it's not much more difficult either. For example, we only know the range for SSN SNs if there's a gap in the Death Master data, such as the one shown between John Chief Crier and John Small Berries. Many organizations often ask you for the last four digits of your SSN for identification. As you can see from the example, those are the hardest ones to guess, so don't make it easy by giving these out when asked. Push for some other means of identification.

Here's another example. The Massachusetts Group Insurance Commission (GIC) released anonymized hospital data for the purpose of improving health care and controlling costs. Massachusetts governor William Weld assured the public that patient privacy was protected. You can probably see where this is going, with the moral being that he should have kept his mouth shut.

Governor Weld collapsed during a ceremony on May 18, 1996, and was admitted to the hospital. MIT graduate student Latanya Sweeney knew that the governor resided in Cambridge, and she spent $20 to purchase the complete voter rolls for that city. She combined the GIC data with the voter data, much as we did in Table 14-2, and easily deanonymized the governor's data. She sent his health records, including prescriptions and diagnoses, to his office.

While this was a fairly easy case since the governor was a public figure, your phone probably has more compute power than was available to Sweeney in 1996. Computing resources today make it possible to tackle much harder cases.

Summary

We've covered a lot of really complicated material in this chapter. You learned that machine learning, big data, and artificial intelligence are interrelated. You've also learned that many more math classes are in store if you want to go into this field. No cats were harmed in the creation of this chapter.

15

REAL-WORLD CONSIDERATIONS

Since this book is intended as a companion for someone learning to code, you hopefully know something about software at this point and about the hardware on which it runs as well. You might think that you're ready to be a programmer. But programming involves more than knowing about hardware and writing code. How do you know what code to write, and how do you go about writing it? How do you know that it works?

Those aren't the only important questions you face. Can others figure out how to use your code? How easy is it for others to add features or find and fix bugs? How hard is it to make your code run on hardware other than that for which it was originally written?

This chapter covers various topics related to the creation of software. While you can do small projects yourself sitting in a dark room with a sufficient quantity of junk food, most projects are a team sport that involves dealing with people. That's harder than you might think—the hardware/software systems that we call people are way buggier than even the most terrifying internet-of-things abomination. And forget about documentation; even if you could find any, it would be out-of-date.

That's why this chapter also covers some of the philosophical and practical issues around being a programmer. Yup, this is where the old curmudgeon tries to pass on some hard-earned wisdom.

The Value Proposition

There's an overarching question that you should keep in mind when working on a project: "Am I adding value?" I'm not talking about the intrinsic value of accomplishing some task here; I'm talking about increasing productivity.

If you're programming for a living, you need to meet whatever goals your employer has set. But, of course, there's more than one way to meet those goals. You could just do what you need to do to get by. Or, you could put a little thought into things that might not have occurred to management. For example, you might realize that your code would be useful in another project and structure it so it's easily reusable. Or, you might sense that you were tasked to implement a special case of a more general problem and solve that general problem instead, paving the way for future enhancements. Of course, you should talk about this with management so that they're not surprised.

You can add value to yourself by making sure that you're proficient in a variety of technologies. Side projects are a common way to get experience; it's equivalent to doing homework but more fun.

One classic way in which people attempt to add value is by creating tools. This is trickier than it seems because sometimes adding value for yourself reduces value for others. People often create new tools because some feature that they think they need is missing from existing ones. A good example is the make utility (invented by Stuart Feldman at Bell Labs in 1976), which is used to build large software packages. As time went on, new features were needed. Some of these were added to make, but in many other cases, people created well-intentioned but incompatible new utilities that performed similar functions. (For example, I consulted for a company once that wrote their own solely because they didn't bother to completely read the make documentation and were unaware that it would do exactly what they needed.) Now there's make, cmake, dmake, imake, pick-a-letter-make, and other programs that all do similar things in incompatible ways. The result is that practitioners like you need to learn multiple tools in each category. It makes everyone's life harder, not easier. It doesn't add value—it detracts. Figure 15-1 sums up the situation nicely.

Figure 15-1: Not adding value (courtesy of Randall Munroe, xkcd.com)

Creating burdens for others doesn't add value. Experienced programmers know that doing something that's already been done in a way that they personally prefer rarely adds value. Instead, it shows off one's immaturity as a programmer. Improve existing tools wherever possible because more people will be able to use the result. Save making new tools for new things. Make sure that you fully understand existing tools because they might be more capable than you realized at first glance.

Mucking up the ecosystem into which you release code does not add value. Many developers behave as if they're stereotypical Americans vacationing in another country, or for that matter my father-in-law visiting—the "I just came to your place, so do things my way" attitude.

For example, UNIX systems have a command that displays manual pages for programs. You can type `man foo` and it'll show you the page for the `foo` command. There's also a convention that really complex commands, such as yacc, have both a manual page and a longer, more in-depth document that describes the program in more detail. When the GNU project (which I'll discuss shortly) added commands to UNIX, it used its own `texinfo` system for manuals, which wasn't compatible with the `man` system. The result was that users would have to try both the `man` and `info` commands to find documentation. Even if, as some believe, the GNU approach was superior, any possible benefits were outweighed by the UNIX community's huge loss of productivity that resulted from the fragmented ecosystem.

There are many other examples, such as the replacement of the `init` system with `systemd`. A big part of the UNIX philosophy, as discussed later in this chapter, is modular design, but `systemd` replaced the modular `init` system with a huge monolithic beast. There was no attempt to retrofit new features into the existing system. The entire user base lost productivity because they had to learn a new system that mostly did just what the old one did. It would have added more value to add multithreading and other new features to the existing system.

Yet another example is the jar utility, which is part of the Java programming environment. The tar utility was created in the 1970s to pack multiple files into a single one. This solved a problem caused by using magnetic tape for storage. Mag tape is a block device, and packing files together allowed full blocks to be used thereby increasing efficiency. ZIP files, which first made their appearance on Windows, are similar. Rather than using either of these existing formats, though, Java made its own. The result was that users now needed to learn yet another command for no particularly good reason.

So don't be the programmer equivalent of an "ugly American." Work with the ecosystem, not against it. Use the rule of "least astonishment" as a guide. You've added value if your work seems a natural extension of the existing environment.

How We Got Here

Before we get going on more practical issues, let's look at how we got here. Much more has happened in the field than we can cover here, so we'll just touch on some important historical highlights and a few more recent developments.

A Short History

A long time ago, people made money selling computers, which were really expensive. Software was written and given away in order to help sell computers. There was a culture of sharing and working together to improve software. More and more people wrote and shared software as computers became more accessible.

The *Multics* operating system, which ran on the huge GE645 mainframe computer, was collaboratively developed in the 1960s by Bell Telephone Laboratories, General Electric, and the Massachusetts Institute of Technology. Bell pulled out of the project, and some of the people there who had worked on it—most notably, Ken Thompson and Dennis Ritchie—went off to experiment with some filesystem ideas they'd had when working on Multics using the smaller computers produced by the Digital Equipment Corporation (DEC). Their work resulted in an innovative new operating system called UNIX, which embodied a new minimalist and modular philosophy for software. While not planned at the outset, it became the first *portable* operating system, meaning it could run on more than one type of computer. The term *UNIX* in this book refers to all similar systems including Linux, FreeBSD, NetBSD, OpenBSD, and the modern macOS. Microsoft Windows is the only major outlier, but even it is incorporating more and more UNIX features—for example, the socket model for networking.

Bell wasn't the only Multics participant to go their own way. The Incompatible Timesharing System (ITS) was developed over at MIT. While ITS included a number of groundbreaking features, its most influential contribution is arguably the Emacs (Editor MACroS) text editor, which began as a set of macros for the DEC TECO (Text Editor and Corrector) text editor. The user interface for ITS and Emacs influenced the GNU project, also started at MIT.

Ken Thompson brought a copy of UNIX with him in 1975 when he took a sabbatical year to teach at the University of California, Berkeley. This had a huge effect that still reverberates today. Students had access to a real working system. They could examine the code to see how things worked, and they could make changes. Not only that, but they were exposed to the philosophy as well. Berkeley produced its own version of UNIX, called *BSD* for Berkeley Software Distribution.

Students added many new important features to the system. BBN's networking stack, which is the foundation of the internet, was integrated into UNIX at Berkeley, where the now-ubiquitous socket interface was born. University graduates started to use the BSD version of UNIX and formed companies such as Sun Microsystems, which made commercial UNIX-based systems.

Personal computers changed this. All of a sudden the people writing software weren't the people selling computers, so they needed to charge for it. But there was still an attitude of "it's great that we make a living doing this cool stuff." This changed dramatically when Bill Gates (one of the founders of Microsoft) came on the scene. As is evident from numerous court depositions, his focus was on making money. If he had to do something cool to make money, he would, but his priorities were opposite those of others in the industry. How did this change things?

Software development began to be driven more by politics, lawyers, and sometimes-underhanded behavior than by superior engineering. This approach frequently focused on suppressing innovation that competed with existing products. For example, Microsoft started with MS-DOS, a program that they bought from its developer, American computer programmer Tim Paterson. Microsoft let the program languish, as they were making plenty of money from it. A company called Digital Research came out with an improved version called DR-DOS. When Microsoft released Windows, the original version of which ran on top of DOS, they included a hidden, encrypted piece of code that checked to see whether the system was running MS-DOS or DR-DOS and generated phony errors if it found DR-DOS. This made DR-DOS unsuccessful in the marketplace even though it was arguably a better product for the money.

It wasn't just Microsoft, however. Apple also sued Digital Research for "copying" their user interface in a product called GEM. Digital Research would probably have prevailed eventually, but would have gone bankrupt in the process because Apple had much deeper pockets. It's somewhat ironic when you realize that the Apple user interface was substantially copied from the Xerox Alto.

Unfortunately, this mindset continues today with threatened big players resorting to the courts instead of innovating their way out of their difficulties. Examples abound, such as SCO versus IBM, Oracle versus Google, Apple versus Samsung, Samsung versus Apple, Intellectual Ventures shell companies versus the world, and so on.

Personal computers started becoming popular in the mid-1980s. It wasn't practical to run UNIX on them because the hardware lacked a memory management unit (see Chapter 5), although there was a variant called Xenix that did run on the original IBM PC hardware.

Colleges started using personal computers running Microsoft Windows to teach computer science because they were cheaper. However, unlike the UNIX-era graduates from UC Berkeley and other schools, these students weren't able to look at the source code of the system they were using. And the system with which they became familiar was considerably less advanced than UNIX. As a result, graduates from this era are often not of the same quality as their earlier counterparts.

In part as a reaction to the closed nature of the source code, Richard Stallman started the GNU (Gnu's Not Unix) project in 1983. Among other things, the goal was to create a freely available and legally unencumbered version of UNIX. Today we call this "free and open source software," or *FOSS. Open source* means that the source code is available for others to see, and more importantly, modify and improve. Stallman, working with his lawyer, created the *copyleft*, a variant of the copyright used by others to protect their software. The copyleft essentially said that others were free to use and modify the code as long as they made their modifications available under the same terms. In other words, "we'll share our code with you if you share yours with everyone else." The GNU project did a great job of re-creating the UNIX utilities such as cp and, possibly most important, the gcc C compiler. But the project team was slow to create an operating system itself.

Linus Torvalds began work on what is now known as the *Linux* operating system in 1991, partly because there was no GNU operating system. To a large degree, this work was made possible by both the existence of the GNU tools such as the C compiler and the nascent internet, which enabled collaboration. Linux has become extremely popular. It's used heavily in data centers (the cloud), it's the underlying software in Android devices, and it's used in many appliances. This book was written on a Linux system.

Large companies were originally skeptical about using open source software. Who would fix the bugs? This is somewhat ludicrous; if you've ever reported a bug to Microsoft, Apple, or any other large company, you know how much attention it gets. In 1989, John Gilmore, DV Henkel-Wallace (a.k.a. Gumby), and Michael Tiemann founded *Cygnus Support* to provide commercial support for open source software. Its existence greatly increased the willingness of companies to use open source software.

In many ways, Linux and GNU have brought us a new golden era similar to the Berkeley UNIX days. It's not *quite* as shiny, though, because some of the people from the PC era are making changes without really understanding the philosophy. In particular, some programmers who didn't grow up with UNIX are reducing the value of the ecosystem by replacing small modular components with huge monolithic programs.

Open Source Software

Open source software is widely successful despite alarmist propaganda by some established closed source companies. For example, senior Microsoft personnel claimed, "Open source is an intellectual property destroyer. I can't imagine something that could be worse than this for the software business and the intellectual property business," despite the fact that they were secretly using open source tools in-house. A main advantage of open source software is that many more eyeballs are available to look at the code, which translates into benefits such as greater security and reliability. Another is that it allows programmers to build on work that others have done instead of having to reinvent everything. Even if you use a closed source computer system, there's a pretty good chance that you're still using some open source components. Even Microsoft recently appears to have seen the light and makes many UNIX tools available on their systems.

The development of open source software was greatly enhanced by the internet and cloud services. It's trivial to find open source projects or to start your own. But—and this is a big but—the majority of open source projects out there are garbage just like their closed source counterparts.

A lot of open source software comes from student projects. Since they're often first projects, the authors haven't yet mastered the art of writing good code. And much of this software is unfinished, as the student programmers completed their class, graduated, or just moved on. It's often easier to rewrite something than it is to decipher someone else's poorly written and documented code. This is a vicious cycle because the rewrite often doesn't get done, so there are multiple versions that don't work in different ways. For example, I recently needed to extract tags from MP3 files and tried six different open source programs, each of which failed in a different way. It's often difficult to determine whether or not there is a good working version of something because there is so much litter.

When Richard Stallman started the GNU project, he assumed that the world was filled with programmers of similar quality to him and his peers. That assumption didn't turn out to be valid. There is still a belief that one of the advantages of open source software is that you can add features and fix bugs that you find. Unfortunately, much of this software is poorly written and completely undocumented, making the amount of effort too great for a casual user or even an experienced programmer.

Just because something is open source doesn't mean that it's a great example of the craft. But you can learn what not to do just as well as you can learn what to do from looking at other people's code.

Here are two indicators, one positive and one negative, that you can use to help determine the quality of a piece of code.

The positive indicator is whether or not a project is under active development with more than one contributor. This doesn't apply to projects that have been around for a long time and are actually "done." It often helps if a project is supported by some organization. Many of the major open source projects originated at companies that still support their development. However, you must be wary of open source projects created at companies that are later acquired by other companies with different philosophies. For example, Sun Microsystems was a prodigious developer of open source software, including OpenOffice, Java, and VirtualBox. However, Sun was acquired by Oracle, which ended support for some of these projects and tried to find ways to control and monetize others; see the Oracle versus Google lawsuit for details. Other projects have been donated by companies to foundations that support their development. This often yields a consistent vision that keeps the project on track. This indicator is not completely reliable, so take it with a grain of salt. For example, the code base for the Firefox web browser is a poorly documented mess.

The negative indicator is the type and quantity of dialog that you'll see at various programmer "self-help" websites. If you see lots of "I can't figure out how to make this work" and "Where do I start to make this change?" questions, then it's probably not a great piece of code. Furthermore, if the responses are mostly useless nonanswers or are snarky and unhelpful, then the project probably lacks good developers. Developers who blame the questioner for their own lack of quality work are not good role models. Of course, it's also a bad sign if there are no comments or questions at all, as it means that the code is probably not used.

Cautionary tales aside, open source is a great thing. Make your code open source when it makes sense to do so. But first, learn how to do a good job so that your code becomes a good example to others.

Creative Commons

The copyleft worked well for software, but software isn't the only area in which society benefits from the ability to build on the past. When the copyleft was first created, most computer applications were text based; graphics, images, audio, and video were too expensive for the average consumer. Today, the sounds and visuals that are part of programs are arguably as important as the programs themselves.

American lawyer and academic Lawrence Lessig recognized the importance of artistic works and created a set of licenses for them similar to the copyleft called *Creative Commons*. There are many variants of these licenses, just like there are a variety of open source licenses for software. These range from "you can do anything you want" to "you have to give the creator credit" to "you have to share all of your changes" to "noncommercial use only" to "no derivative works allowed."

The Creative Commons legal framework has greatly enhanced our ability to build on the work of others.

The Rise of Portability

The term *portability* has a specific meaning for software. Code that is portable can run in a different environment than the one for which it was developed. That may be a different software environment, different hardware, or both. Portability wasn't an issue in the early days of computing when there were just a handful of computer vendors, although standard languages like COBOL and FORTRAN allowed programs to be run on different machines. It became more important in the 1980s when the EDA industry (see "Hardware vs. Software" on page 90) and the availability of UNIX enabled the formation of a much larger number of computer companies.

These new computer vendors ported UNIX to their products; their customers didn't have to worry about it. But another change happened at about the same time, which is that these less-expensive UNIX systems made inroads into the commercial market instead of being limited to academia. Source code was not shipped with many of these systems since the end users would never be building programs themselves. And, in an effort to increase profits, some companies started charging extra for certain UNIX tools, such as the C compiler. People who needed these tools started turning to the GNU tools since they were free, and often at least as good—and in many cases better than—the original UNIX tools.

But now, users had to port these tools to different systems themselves, which quickly became a huge pain point. Different systems had header files and libraries in different places, and many of the library functions had subtle differences in their behavior. This was addressed in two different ways. First, standards such as POSIX (portable operating system interface) were created to bring some consistency to the APIs and user environments. Second, the GNU project created a set of *build tools*, such as automake, autoconf, and libtool, to automate some of the system dependency checking. Unfortunately, these tools are incredibly cryptic and hard to use. Plus, they have their own dependencies, so code built with a particular version often can't be built with another.

This is the state of the world today. Modern systems are more similar than they used to be because the world is pretty much UNIX based. And, while they're clunky, the GNU build tools get the job done most of the time.

Package Management

Open source software, especially Linux, exacerbated the problem of distributing software. While people refer to Linux as if it's a single system, there are many different configurations—from what's used in data centers to desktops to the base for Android phones and tablets. Even if all systems had the same configuration, there are many different versions of each system. While source code is available, a lot of code is now distributed in precompiled, ready-to-run form.

We talked about shared libraries back in "Running Programs" on page 137. A precompiled program won't work unless the system includes the right versions of the libraries on which it depends. Some large programs use huge numbers of libraries, and all of them need to be present and of the versions that the programs expect.

While there were some earlier attempts, *package management* really took off with Linux. Package management tools allow programs to be bundled into *packages* that include a list of dependencies. Package management tools such as apt, yum, and dnf not only download and install software but also check the target system for dependencies, downloading and installing them as necessary.

These tools work a good part of the time. But they tend to run into problems when different programs need different versions of the same dependencies. And, since package managers aren't compatible, it's a lot of work to get software ready to be installed on different systems.

Containers

Containers are a more recent, different approach to the package management problems. The idea is that an application and all of its dependencies are bundled up into a container. The container is then run in an environment where all of its pieces, such as data files, are kept isolated from the rest of the system.

Containers simplify software deployment because they bundle up all of the dependencies (libraries and other programs) required by an application into a single package. This means that, provided your type of container is supported, you can just install a containerized application without having to worry about other things that it needs. A downside of this approach is that it effectively eliminates shared libraries (see "Running Programs" on page 137), resulting in less efficient memory utilization. Containers are also larger than applications by themselves.

Security is touted as a benefit of containers. The idea is that running multiple applications on the same operating system allows applications to interfere with each other by leveraging OS bugs. While that may be true, it just means that a different class of bugs needs to be exploited.

Containerized applications called *snaps* are an option on many Linux systems. *CoreOS*, now *Container Linux*, is one of the major Linux container efforts. One of the developers was among the first people to suffer through the course notes that were the foundation of this book, so you're in good company.

Java

The Java programming language was created by a team at Sun Microsystems led by James Gosling starting in 1991. Gosling has a track record of recognizing when technology has changed to the point where a different approach becomes practical. In this case, he realized that machines were fast enough that interpreters were a practical alternative to compiled code in many circumstances. The Java language looks a lot like C and C++.

One of the ideas behind Java was that rather than recompiling your code for every target machine, someone would do that for the Java interpreter and then your code would just run. You would only have to write your code once and run it anywhere. This wasn't a completely original concept, as Java wasn't the first interpreted language.

Java was originally designed for television set–top boxes (back when it was called Oak). It was repurposed as a way to run code in browsers that was independent of the machine on which the browser was running. It has been somewhat eclipsed by JavaScript in that environment, although it's still used. JavaScript is unrelated to Java, and is not quite as nice a language, but it's much easier to write since it doesn't require any special tools.

Java is important because it has become a popular teaching language. This is partly due to the fact that it uses garbage collection, which frees beginners from the complexity of explicit memory management. It's a great place to start as long as you don't stop there.

Java has become much more than a language; there is a whole ecosystem of software that surrounds it. That ecosystem includes a lot of custom tools and file formats, making life more difficult for programmers. The ecosystem is so complicated and fragmented that it's not uncommon to hear programmers grumble that while they only have to write code once, getting the ecosystem installed and functional so that they can actually run that code is often pretty difficult.

Another downside to Java is the programming culture that has grown up around it. Java programmers tend to use hundreds of lines of code where one would suffice. When looking at someone else's Java code, you often wonder where to find the line that actually does something. Some of this stems from Java being a good object-oriented language. Fanatics obsess over having a beautiful class hierarchy and often prioritize that over getting a job done.

A good example is a Java database tool called *Hibernate*, which, as far as I can tell, tries to solve two "problems." The first is that Java classes and subclasses do a great job of *data hiding*, or limiting the visibility of internal variables. But, despite the data hiding, code at the bottom of the class hierarchy accesses a global database, which causes some people to freak out philosophically. Hibernate uses special comments in Java to provide database manipulation, hiding reality from the programmer. Of course, this is all well and good until something breaks, at which time reality must be faced.

The second thing that Hibernate does is to provide an abstraction called HQL (Hibernate Query Language) on top of the underlying database API, which is usually SQL (Structured Query Language). In theory, this allows programmers to perform database operations without having to worry about the differences between database systems.

Back before the C programming language was formally standardized, there were a number of incompatibilities between compilers. Rather than invent a "meta-C," people came up with programming guidelines like "don't use this feature." By following these guidelines, code would work on any compiler.

The differences between SQL implementations can be handled in a similar way without introducing yet another mechanism. It's also worth noting that most serious SQL projects include something called *stored procedures* for which there is no compatibility among implementations. And HQL doesn't provide support for them, so it missed out on the one place where it could have been really useful.

The feel-good value of hiding the underlying database system is not balanced out by having to learn a new language that doesn't do everything you need.

Node.js

As you've seen in this book, JavaScript began life as a scripting language for browsers. *Node.js* is the latest environment that allows JavaScript to be run outside of a browser. One of its primary attractions is that it allows both the client and server sides of an application to be written in the same programming language.

While the idea is good, the results vary. I avoid Node.js for a couple of reasons. First, Node.js invented its own package manager. Just what everyone needed—another incompatible method making it harder to maintain systems. As a contrast, even though Perl has its own package manager, it avoids decreasing value by making its packages available via system package managers such as apt and dnf.

Second, there are hundreds of thousands of Node.js packages with twisty interdependencies. The vast majority are not suitable for serious work. For some reason, Node.js attracts bad code.

Cloud Computing

Cloud computing means using someone else's computers over a network. It's not really a new concept; it's an updated version of the 1960s invention of time sharing. Two factors make cloud computing interesting:

- Networks have become more ubiquitous and speeds have increased dramatically. This makes functionality like streaming audio and video possible, not to mention offloading storage for things like email.

- Hardware prices have come down to the point where an incredible amount of computing power and storage is available. This has led to new algorithms and ways to solve problems that were previously not practical. Of course, the same can be said for desktop computers. My current machine has eight processor cores, 64GB of RAM, and 28TiB of disk. This was neither practical nor economical when I started programming. Another way of looking at it is that the machine on which I'm writing this book has more RAM than the total amount of disk storage on the machine that I used 20 years ago.

There's nothing really magical about cloud computing; it's just hardware and software. It has created new business models for renting computing resources.

Cloud computing has sparked a lot of innovation in hardware packaging. Data centers have completely different economies of scale, and reliability is important. Cramming huge numbers of machines into a space means paying a lot of attention to power and cooling. One creative scheme pioneered by Sun Microsystems involves building data centers in shipping containers instead of buildings.

Virtual Machines

It used to be that one program would run on one computer at a time. Operating systems made it possible to run multiple programs via time sharing. But not all application programs that users wanted were available on all operating systems, especially when closed source systems became the norm. Many users had to resort to using multiple computers running different operating systems, or having to reboot their machine to run different operating systems.

Hardware is now fast enough that entire operating systems can be considered applications, making time sharing between multiple operating systems practical. Keep in mind that this might require interpreting an instruction set that is different than that of the underlying physical machine. Also, it's not enough just to be able to run the instruction set—the expected hardware environment must be present as well.

Since these operating systems aren't necessarily running directly on the physical machine hardware, they're called *virtual machines*. Virtual machines provide many advantages other than eliminating the proprietary operating system lockout. They're really useful for development, especially for operating system development. That's because when the system under development crashes, it doesn't also crash your development system.

Virtual machines are a mainstay of the cloud-computing world. You can rent space in the cloud and run whatever mix of operating systems you desire.

The operating system that supports the virtual machines is often called a *hypervisor*.

Portable Devices

Just as with cloud computing, improvements in communication technology and hardware price/performance have made it possible to build portable devices with great power and functionality. A single modern cell phone has more computing power and storage than all of the computers in the world combined a few decades ago. Other than the portability, there's nothing new or magical about these devices. Each has its own ecosystem and tools.

The big challenge with portable device programming is power management. Because portable devices are battery powered, great care must be taken to minimize operations such as memory accesses, as they consume power and run down the battery.

The Programming Environment

Programming for a living is not the same thing as working on personal or school projects. Working as a programmer means taking direction from, giving direction to, and working with others. Little if anything is taught about this aspect of the field in school. It's often learned through a series of weird on-the-job experiences.

Are You Experienced?

So here you are, a new programmer with little or no experience. What is experience and how do you acquire it?

Employers are always looking for "experienced professionals." What does that mean? The simplest definition is that a candidate has exactly the sought-after skills. But that's not really a very good definition, and it's often impractical. For example, I received a call in 1995 from a recruiter looking for someone with five years of Java programming experience. I had to explain that even the authors of Java didn't have that level of experience because it hadn't been around that long.

One of the satisfying things about programming is that you get to do things that have never been done before. So how can you start with the skills that you won't have until you're done? What's a good definition of experience?

First of all, you need to be grounded in the fundamentals. If all you know is how to build a website, you're unlikely to be able to successfully contribute to a surgical robot project. But more importantly, experience is knowing what you can do and what you can't do. How do you know what you can do when you haven't done it yet? You need to learn to estimate. It's not just guesswork; it's heuristics.

Learning to Estimate

One of the most damaging things you can do as a member of a project team is to fail to deliver your work on time without warning. The key here is *without warning*; nobody delivers everything on time, but when being late is a surprise, it's difficult for other team members to work around.

How do you learn to estimate? With practice. Start with this: before you do a task, such as a homework assignment, jot down your estimate of how long it will take. Then keep track of how long the task actually took. After a while, you might discover that you're getting better at estimating. This is good practice because with homework, just like with programming, you're always doing something that you haven't done before.

An oft-abused but worthwhile management technique is status reporting: you regularly generate a short list of what you accomplished since the last report, what problems arose, and what your plans are for the next reporting period. This is just a more formal method of tracking your homework predictions. When a status report shows that the plans were not achieved but no problems were encountered, that's a red flag. Status reporting gives you a way to adjust your estimates by comparing them to actual results.

Scheduling Projects

Programming projects are generally more complex than your homework (with the possible exception of your programming class homework). How do you estimate a more complex project?

A fairly simple method is to make a list of all of the pieces in the project. Put them into three appropriately sized bins, such as 1 hour, 1 day, and 1 week. Add up the results. You will probably be wrong about most of your guesses, but on average the total estimate will be pretty close. Status reporting is key here, because it shows that some things take more time than expected while others take less time, making it possible to track the original estimate.

Approaches like this are an important trade-off, because generating a complete and accurate schedule for a complex project often takes longer than just doing the project. And it still wouldn't account for things like snow days.

Related to this is how projects actually get planned in the industry, which I explained when answering a question from the audience at an ACM lecture in 2004 at Oregon State University. It's not really possible to convey the slack-jawed silence that followed. Goes to show, you don't learn everything you need to know in class. What happens is that you'll distinguish yourself by doing a great job on some project. Your manager will take you aside and say, "Hey, nice job. We're thinking about doing this new thing. Can you tell me how long it will take and how much it'll cost?" You'll feel so honored that you'll give up your social life for a while to figure it all out in detail. You'll do this without knowing (except you will, because you've read this) that before your manager talked to you, they already had some numbers in mind, possibly given to them by their manager. You'll show your results to your manager, who will respond with, "Oh. Well, you know, if it's going to take this long and cost this much, we just won't do it." A light will go on in your head and you'll ask yourself, "Do I want to have a job next week?" You'll say, "Well, this was conservative, I can pull it in here and there." Now, a very interesting thing is taking place. You're lying to your manager, who knows that you're lying. Your manager also knows that your original numbers are correct, and that the project would come in on time and on budget if you were allowed to use them. Furthermore, they know that forcing you to use the more aggressive numbers will make the project late and over budget. But sadly, that's the way it's often done.

While this scenario may be hard to believe, keep in mind the popularity of *Dilbert* comics.

As this example indicates, a common challenge in scheduling is management that refuses to accept schedules and true costs. Nonengineers often view schedules as something that can be negotiated; managers often feel that engineers are too conservative in scheduling and try to negotiate down the estimated time. This almost always leads to bigger problems down the road. The only legitimate way in which to decrease the time is to remove features.

Decision Making

There are many possible ways to do most projects. There are choices of programming languages, data structures, and more. Engineers are famous for having heated debates over the "right" way to do something. Sometimes projects don't happen and people lose their jobs because they can never stop arguing and get down to work. Heated discussions often make management uncomfortable.

An otherwise unexceptional manager taught me something very useful about resolving these sorts of problems. At the beginning of a project, he took all of us into a conference room and told us how he worked. He said that decisions were going to be made first and foremost on technical grounds. But, he said, many times there is no technical reason for doing things one way or another. He said that in those cases, it was perfectly okay to say, "I want to do it this way because I like it." He explained that as long as nobody else preferred a different way, then he'd go along. He didn't want to hear complicated pseudotechnical arguments that in reality were just someone justifying their particular preference but not saying so. In that case, not only would that person not get their way, but they'd probably also lose their job. The moral of this story is to keep technical necessities separate from personal preferences.

You've already gotten a taste of this sort of behavior in Chapter 12, where you learned that the actual rationale for and benefits of JavaScript promises are obfuscated by a fear of pyramid-of-doom rationalization.

Working with Different Personalities

I mentioned earlier in this chapter that programming usually involves working with other people.

Numerous "learn to code" boosters emphasize that "programming is fun." I don't agree; my sympathies are more in line with those expressed by Italian researcher Walter Vannini in his article "Coding Is Not 'Fun', It's Technically and Ethically Complex." Recall the two-step programming process from the book's introduction. The second step, explain it to a three-year-old (that is, doing the actual programming), requires meticulous attention to detail. You're probably at a stage where you have trouble keeping your room clean; that doesn't translate to programming. I would say that programming is *satisfying*. The fun comes in the first step, understanding the problem. But even that's not a barrel of laughs.

People in any profession have a wide range of personalities, not all of which would be described as "well adjusted." Programmers are no exception. While many programmers have balanced personalities, some favor technical prowess over social skills. There is a wide spectrum between Richard Stallman and Dennis Ritchie, with Linus Torvalds somewhere in between. This can be a source of problems, especially in this age where people are highly sensitive to word choices.

There's a lot of discussion in the media these days about abusive behavior in the workplace. Let me be clear: workplace abuse is never acceptable, so don't be an abuser and don't allow yourself to be abused. But it can often be difficult to determine what is abuse and what isn't. That's because people don't have the same worldviews, and something that might be fine for one person might not be for another. The classic example is Apple founder Steve Jobs.

You might think that this issue could be addressed with some simple rules. And it can, but there are trade-offs. Many years ago, I worked with a manager who expressed it pretty well. He said that while he could force the people in his group into "good behavior," such as being less argumentative, the result would be losing much of the creative manic energy for which he hired those people. He felt that a large part of his job was to smooth over personality differences so that people would be productive.

A big source of problems is that programmers who are passionate about their work may be intensely critical of someone else's. A hard lesson to learn is that it's not personal. I once had an employee who—as I eventually learned—if I pointed out a bug in his code, he would interpret that as me telling him he was a bad person. As a contrast, when that same employee took delight at pointing out bugs in my code, my reaction was, "Let's fix it because we want this to succeed." At the core, this is about people having confidence in themselves. Try to build the confidence of your team members, as confident people are less likely to take things personally.

Related to this, I once worked for someone who regularly told me that what I was doing was stupid. Eventually, I figured out what was happening and said the following: "You know, I finally realized that when you tell me that what I'm doing is stupid, you're really saying that you don't understand what I'm doing. Now that I know that, I'll ignore you as best I can. But I'm human, so every time you say 'stupid,' I get less work done for the next few days. So if you want to get your money's worth, you might try to just tell me that you don't understand things."

Communication is important. A characteristic of insecure people is that they try to make others feel inferior either by talking way above their level or by being condescending. The job of a secure person is to figure out how to speak to others at their level of understanding. As an example, I was at a party at the 1989 SIGGRAPH (Special Interest Group on Computer Graphics) conference and overheard someone there ask another person for help in understanding a paper written by Loren Carpenter, the first geek to win an Academy Award. This other person patiently explained the paper. Afterward, the first person said, "Hey, thanks. That really helped. My name is Joe, what's yours?" to which the other person replied, "I'm Loren." Be like Loren.

One more thing to keep in mind if you do end up in a difficult situation at work: Human Resources is not your friend. Their job is not to protect you; it's to protect the company from liability.

Navigating Workplace Culture

Each workplace has its own unique culture. Finding one that matches your personality is key to having a successful and enjoyable career. Results-based and personality-based cultures are opposite ends of the spectrum.

Amy Wrzesniewski, Clark McCauley, Paul Rozin, and Barry Schwartz's 1997 article "Jobs, Careers, and Callings: People's Relations to Their Work" partitions people's work into the three categories in the article's title. In short, people get financial rewards from jobs, advancement from careers, and enjoyment from callings. Matching your category and personality to your workplace is a key component of success.

Jobs and careers work better in personality-based cultures. These cultures reward drama-free personal interactions. People treat each other well, at least face-to-face.

Callings and results-based cultures go together. Getting the best job done is the reward even if doing so involves heated arguments and intense discussions.

As an example, this book's technical editor and I spent a month having an intense argument about a paragraph in Chapter 7. We were both happy that we reached a great solution, and that happiness made up for all of the arguing. We were both annoyed that it took so long to find a solution, but that's the way it is; sometimes solutions are not obvious. If that sort of process and outcome makes you happy, you want to find a workplace that values such behavior.

It's worth taking a step back to reframe the problem when a solution is elusive. However, it's difficult to remember to do this in the middle of a passionate discussion.

Making Informed Choices

You may have noticed that I haven't exactly had glowing things to say about certain parts of the technology spectrum, such as the web. This may have you wondering why you'd want to work in this field. A lot depends on what you want to get out of your work, as per the previous section. Keep in mind that all endeavors have their good and bad aspects. Choose your work situations with your eyes open.

There's often a trade-off between interesting work and making lots of money. People with callings prefer interesting work and would do it for free if necessary. People with jobs or careers often get paid handsomely for working with cumbersome or broken technology. A good example is the large number of people who remembered how to program in COBOL, who found and fixed Y2K bugs. These were bugs in antiquated code that involved dates and kept only the last two digits of the year. The transition from 1999 to 2000 would have broken this code, which was in use for lots of critical infrastructure.

Development Methodologies

It seems like every field of endeavor spawns "methodology experts." Programming is no different, except possibly that there is such zeal that *ideology* is a more appropriate term than *methodology*. And every methodology seems to come with its own uniform, hairstyle, terminology, and secret handshakes. To a large degree, this just makes it easier for adherents to exclude the non-believers, the opposite of the Loren Carpenter example earlier. And it can become ridiculous: I was discussing methodology with a client who finally blurted out, "As long as we have a completely Agile pivoting scrum, things should be okay."

My expert advice is to not take any ideology too seriously. None of them work in pure form; you need to cherry-pick the ideas and use those that make sense for your project. How do you decide what works for your project? Let's look at the various stages of development (Figure 15-2).

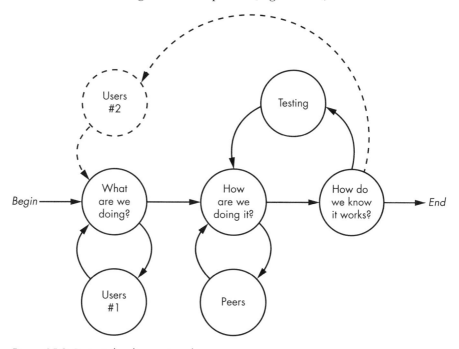

Figure 15-2: Project development cycle

We have the three questions with which we began this chapter. A big distinction between ideologies is the role of the user.

Contrary to what you might believe from observing the world around you, software is written for things other than entertainment. An ideology that works for a website or video game is probably not appropriate for a satellite, power plant, pacemaker, or car.

It's important to know exactly what you're doing for projects in which the cost of failure is high, so the users (#1) are involved early on in order to come up with a clear definition. Once you have a definition, you can begin coding, which is usually—and should be—reviewed by peers. The result is tested against the definition.

When the cost of failure is low, there's less incentive to come up with a clear definition in advance. It's common to take more of a "We'll know it when we see it" attitude. Users (#2) play a more important role in looking at results and deciding whether or not the right thing has been done. Testing to determine whether or not the code actually works is often confused with testing to determine whether or not users like the current definition.

Laziness and incompetence are not good development methodologies. Many people don't write specifications because they don't know how. Choose a methodology that's right for the project first and the people second.

Project Design

A project starts with an idea. It might be your idea, or it might come from someone else. How does that turn into code?

You can, of course, just start coding. And that's just fine for small personal projects. But for anything significant, there are some processes that you can follow that lead to better results.

Writing It Down

Start by writing the idea down. You'll be surprised by how that gets you to fill in a lot of missing details.

It's important for your documentation to be at the correct level. Talk about what you're going to do, not how you're going to do it.

As an example of how not to go about it, I was once asked to help out on a project to design a new blood pressure monitor. The client sent me about 5,000 pages of documentation and asked me to estimate the cost, which I was unable to do. It turns out that, due to prior problems, company management had issued an edict that no code would be written without documentation. Sounds good, but they ignored the fact that none of their people knew how to write documentation, and they didn't provide any training. So the engineers wrote code without telling management and then described their code in longhand English. Nowhere did their documents even mention that the product was a blood pressure monitor.

Another example is the Apache web server. Good piece of software. Tons of documentation on how to set this or that configuration parameter. Never says that it's a web server or describes how the pieces relate.

Fast Prototyping

One development methodology that deserves a mention is *fast prototyping*. This involves whipping out a partially working version of your project. Just like writing things down, prototyping helps you to understand your idea in more depth. A prototype can also be a useful tool to help explain your idea to others.

Watch out for these pitfalls:

- Don't mistake your prototype for production code. Throw it out and write new code using what you learned from doing the prototype.
- Don't allow yourself to be forced into coming up with a hard schedule for the prototype. After all, a big reason for prototyping is that you don't know enough to be able to generate a realistic schedule.
- Most difficult, don't let your management mistake your prototype for a shippable product.

One of the hallmarks of prototype code that got shipped is a lack of coherency. In his book *The Stuff of Thought* (Penguin), Steven Pinker discusses the difference between working with blocks and working with the principles that govern the behavior of those blocks. You're mainly working with blocks during prototyping. It's important to take a step back after the prototype is functional to observe those governing principles and then reimplement the code to use those principles consistently.

Interface Design

Your project will occupy some place in a *software stack*; you saw an overview of this in Figure 1 on page xxxiii. Software is the filling in a sandwich that communicates with things above and below it. The interfaces that your application uses make up the bottom piece of bread. You need to define the top piece.

System programming occupies the space between the hardware and the applications. System programs communicate with hardware using whatever combination of registers and bits are detailed in the device manufacturer's datasheets. But system programs also have to communicate with applications. The line between them is called the *application program interface (API)*. An API is called a *user interface (UI)* if it's used by people instead of by other programs. There are numerous APIs since programs are built in layers; there may be an operating system at the bottom with an API that is used by libraries, which in turn are used by applications. How is an API designed? What makes a good one?

A good way to start is to document the *use cases*, situations in which the API is used to accomplish some task or set of tasks. You can collect use cases by querying the eventual users of a program. But keep in mind that users often give shortsighted answers because they're already using something. A lot of their feedback tends to be of the "make it like this with that change" variety. And a pile of discrete requirements doesn't make for a clean result.

Now, you could just do what the users request, and it might work out for a while. But for an API to have legs, you need to abstract the user requirements and synthesize an elegant solution. Let's look at a few examples.

The original Apple Macintosh API was published in 1985 in a three-volume set of books called *Inside Macintosh* (Addison-Wesley). The set was over 1,200 pages long. It's completely obsolete; modern (UNIX-based) Macs don't use any of it. Why didn't this API design last?

The Mac API could be described as very wide and shallow. It had a huge number of functions, each of which did one particular thing. An argument could be made that this interface didn't last because it was too specific; the lack of abstractions, or generalizations, made it impossible to extend as new use cases arose. Of course, more functions could have been added, making it even wider, but that's not a very practical approach.

By contrast, version 6 of the UNIX operating system was released 10 years earlier in 1975, with a 321-page manual. It embodied a completely different approach that sported a narrow and deep API. The narrowness and depth were made possible by a good set of abstractions. What's an abstraction? It's a broad category of things; for example, rather than talking individually about cats, dogs, horses, cows, and so on, you could use the abstraction "animals." These abstractions were evident not just in the system calls (see "System and User Space" on page 133) but also in the applications.

For example, you're probably familiar with the concept of a file as a place to store data. Many operating systems had different system calls for each type of file. UNIX had a single type of file with a handful of system calls. For example, the creat system call could create any type of file. (When asked if he would do anything different if he were redesigning the UNIX system, Ken Thompson replied, "I'd spell creat with an e.") As part of the file abstraction, even I/O devices were treated as files, as you saw in Chapter 10.

Compare this abstraction to the pip (Peripheral Interchange Program) utility on contemporary DEC systems. It was a hugely complicated and ungainly tool that had special commands that allowed users to copy files. There were specific commands to copy files to tapes, printers, and more. By contrast, UNIX had a single cp (copy) command that users could use to copy files independent of their type and where they lived. You could copy a file to an I/O port connected to a printer as easily as you could copy a file from one place to another.

The UNIX abstractions supported a novel programming philosophy:

- Each program should do one thing and do it well. Make another program to do something new instead of adding complication to old ones.

- Build programs to work together; the output of programs should be usable as input to other programs. Do complicated things by hooking simple programs together instead of writing huge monolithic programs.

Both the UNIX API and a large number of the original applications are still in widespread use today, more than 40 years later, which is a testament to the quality of the design. Not only that, but a large number of the libraries are still in use and essentially unchanged, though their functionality has been copied into many other systems. And the book *The UNIX Programming Environment* (Prentice Hall) by Brian Kernighan and Rob Pike is still worth a read even though it's decades old.

A more subtle advantage of this modular approach is that new programs not only have intrinsic value but also add to the value of the ecosystem as a whole.

Switching gears slightly, I mentioned earlier that a UI is an API for users instead of other programs. In his 2004 book *The Art of Unix Usability*, Eric Raymond supplies an interesting case study of the Common Unix Printing System (CUPS), which gives numerous insights on how not to design user interfaces.

Designing a great interface is hard. Here are a few points to keep in mind:

- An API should not expose implementation internals. It should not depend on a particular implementation.

- APIs should exhibit *conceptual heaviness*, which is another way of saying that there should be good abstractions.

- APIs should be *extensible*, or adaptable to future needs. Good abstractions help here.

- APIs should be *minimal*, meaning that they shouldn't be larded with multiple ways to do the same thing.

- *Modularity* is good; if an API provides related sets of functionality, make them as independent as possible. This also makes it easier to break a project into pieces so that multiple people can work on it simultaneously.

- Functionality should be *composable*; that is, it should be easy to combine the pieces in useful ways. (Don't misread this as *compostable*. The world already has too many poorly designed interfaces rotting away.) For example, if you had an interface that returned sorted search results, it might make sense to separate out the searching and sorting so that they could be used both independently and in combination.

Unless you've been asleep, you've noticed that I'm a fan of the UNIX philosophy. This is because it works, not because it's flashy and trendy. And it illuminates the previous points.

As we discussed earlier, one UNIX feature that is now also available on many other systems is the file abstraction. Most operations on files are not performed using the filename; instead, the filename is converted into a handle called a *file descriptor*, which is used instead. This abstraction allows users to perform file operations on things that are not technically files, such as connecting to something over a network.

As we saw in Chapter 10, when a program is started on UNIX, it is passed a pair of file handles called *standard input* and *standard output*. You can think of a program as a water filter in a pipe; unfiltered water flows into standard input, and filtered water pours from standard output. One of the clever things about UNIX is that the standard output of one program can be hooked to the standard input of another via something called a *pipe*. For example, if you had a water filter program and a water heater program, you could hook them together to get heated, filtered water without having to write a special program to do that. You can think of UNIX as a crate full of random tools and parts from which things can be built.

An amusing illustration of this philosophy occurred in 1986, when Don Knuth (professor emeritus of computer science at Stanford University and author of *The Art of Computer Programming* series, which you should own a copy of) wrote an article for *Communications of the ACM* that included more than 10 pages of code to cleverly solve a particular problem. This was followed by a critique from Doug McIlroy (Ken Thompson and Dennis Ritchie's boss at Bell Laboratories) showing how the entire solution could be written as a single line of six pipelined UNIX commands. The moral of the story is that good general-purpose tools that can be interconnected beat one-off special solutions.

One of the things that made pipelining work was that programs mostly worked on text and thus had a common format. Programs didn't rely on much structure in the data other than a line of text or fields separated by some character. Some claim that this approach only worked because in "simpler times," text could be a common format. But again, the API has legs. Program suites such as ImageMagick provide complex image-processing pipelines. Programs also exist to handle data with a more complex structure, such as XML and JSON.

Reusing Code or Writing Your Own

While defining the top-slice-of-bread interface is critical to a project, you'll also face difficult decisions in selecting the bottom slice of bread. On what code that you didn't write are you going to rely?

Your program will likely use libraries (see "Running Programs" on page 137) other people have written that include functions you can use instead of writing your own. How do you know when to use a library function and when to write something yourself?

At one level, this is the same problem as finding good open source software, as we discussed earlier in "Open Source Software" on page 419. If a library doesn't have a stable API, then it's likely that future releases will break your code. Multiply this by the number of libraries, and it's clear that all of your time will go into fixing things instead of writing your own code. Too many libraries can make your code fragile. For example, a package on which many other packages depended was broken in Node.js recently, affecting a large number of programs.

Sometimes you need to use libraries because they implement something that takes really specialized knowledge that you don't have. A good example of this is the OpenSSL cryptography libraries.

Some argue that using libraries is better than writing your own code because libraries in wide use have been debugged. Unfortunately, that's not always true; the OpenSSL library is a notable example.

Normally I would say that you shouldn't use a library when the number of lines of code to include the library exceeds the number of lines of code needed to write it yourself—for example, using glibc to implement singly linked lists. However, you also need to think about the environment in which the library is used; glibc is used by so many programs that it likely resides in memory as a shared library, so it effectively gets you code without using any memory space.

It's often very difficult to find useful libraries. A recent article mentioned that there are over 350,000 Node.js packages. It's probably faster to write your own code than it is to find the right needle in such a gargantuan haystack.

Project Development

At this point, you can hopefully create a specification for a project and a schedule for implementation. How do you turn this into reality?

Consider using Linux or some other UNIX derivative for your programming. There are many ways to do this. If you have a Mac, you're all set because there's a variant of UNIX underneath. You can install Linux on your PC. If that's not practical, you can run a *live image*, which means running from a DVD and not changing anything on your PC's hard drive. A better option is to run Linux in a *virtual machine*, which is a piece of software that lets you run a different operating system within a window on your computer. For example, you can install *VirtualBox* on a Windows machine and then run Linux there.

The Talk

Okay, it's time for the talk. Maybe your parents were too embarrassed; maybe they thought that you'd hear about it at school. Or maybe they think that you'll find out what you need on the internet. That's all pretty lame. If you're going to be a serious code slinger, you need to have an adult relationship with computers. You need to put down the mouse and learn to use a text editor.

Adult Relationships with Computers

Your relationship with computers has been pretty childlike so far. You've been pointing, clicking, poking, and otherwise tickling the computer and watching it giggle in response. That doesn't cut it for programming.

Programming involves a pretty intense relationship with a computer. You'll be doing a lot more than just typing up a paper or watching a video—so much more that you're going to need to be much more productive. That means that it's time to learn how to use power tools.

Many of these tools are cryptic and a bit difficult to learn. Too bad. Once you get the hang of them, you'll never go back because you can get so much more accomplished with much less effort. So, grit your teeth and put in the up-front work; it'll pay off big-time later!

Terminals and Shells

Remember all that stuff about terminals in Chapter 6? Well, guess what? Real programmers still use 'em. Terminals don't make a racket or do the green flash anymore. And they're not a separate machine; they're a piece of software that runs on the computer.

All desktop computer systems have terminals, even if they make them hard to find. By default, terminals run *command interpreters*. You'll be presented with a command *prompt*. As you might expect, you enter commands at a command prompt. Systems rooted in UNIX—such as Apple products, Linux, and FreeBSD—have a command interpreter or *shell* named *bash*. Of course, Windows does its own thing, but it's possible to install bash on Windows systems.

Many of the commands have cryptic names, such as grep (global regular expression printer). It's a lot like anatomy, where many body parts are named after something else they resemble or after the person who first discovered them. For example, the awk command was named after its authors: Alfred Aho, Peter Weinberger, and Brian Kernigan. It all makes a compelling case for evolution. It's hard to distinguish people talking about these commands from grunting cavemen.

A big reason to learn these cryptic commands is automation. A powerful shell feature is that you can put commands into a file, creating a program that runs those commands. If you find yourself doing something a lot, you can just make a command to do it for you. This is way more productive than sitting at a fancy graphical program clicking buttons and waiting for results.

Text Editors

Text editors are programs that let you create and modify vanilla ASCII data, which is the stuff of which programs are made (I am completely unqualified to comment on programming languages that use non-ASCII characters such as Chinese). A main advantage of text editors is that they operate using commands, which is way more efficient than cutting and pasting stuff with a mouse—at least, once you learn them.

There are two popular text editors: *vi* and *Emacs*. Learn to use one (or both). Each has its fanatical following (Figure 15-3).

Figure 15-3: vi vs. Emacs

Eclipse and Visual Studio are examples of fancy programming tools known as *integrated development environments,* or *IDEs.* (Check their release date: beware the IDEs of March.) While IDEs are great for untangling someone else's poorly written code, you're already lost if you need them. Going way back to the book's introduction, learn the fundamentals before losing sight of them in fancy tools. Also, you'll find that such tools are pretty slow and you can be much more effective with simple but powerful alternatives. For example, you can edit a program with a text editor and rebuild it faster than you can start one of these tools.

Portable Code

While you may never intend to use a piece of software elsewhere, it's surprising how often it happens. And if your code is open source, others may want to use it (or pieces of it) elsewhere. How do we write code so that it's not overly difficult to port? The short answer is to avoid hardwiring where possible.

As you learned earlier in this book, there's a wide variety of ways in which hardware can differ, such as the bit and byte ordering and word size. Separate from the hardware, there are differences in how programming languages present the hardware to the programmer. For example, a trouble spot in C and C++ is that the language standards don't define whether or not a char is signed or unsigned. The workaround is to be explicit in your code.

You can use the sizeof operator in C to determine the number of bytes in a data type. Unfortunately, you need to write small programs to determine the bit and byte order. Many languages include ways to find out, for example, the largest and smallest numbers that can be stored in a particular data type.

Character sets are another troublesome area. Using UTF-8 avoids many problems.

Many programs use external libraries and other facilities. How do you insulate something like string comparison from system differences? One way is to stick to standard functionality. For example, standards such as POSIX define the behavior of library functions.

There will be differences between target environments that can't be dealt with easily. Put as many of these dependencies as possible in a single place instead of scattering them throughout your code. That makes it easy for someone else to make the needed changes.

Just because code can be built for another system doesn't mean that it's a good idea. A classic example is the X Window System. In the early 1980s, Stanford graduate student Andy Bechtolsheim designed a special workstation-like personal terminal to run on the Stanford University Network. Stanford licensed the hardware design, which became the foundation of SUN Microsystems' line of Sun Workstation products. Stanford professors David Cheriton and Keith Lantz developed the V operating system, which ran on the SUN. It featured a very fast synchronous interprocess communication mechanism, which meant that programs could communicate with each other very quickly. Paul Asente and Brian Reed developed the W window system, which ran on the V system. This code eventually made it to MIT, where it was ported to UNIX and renamed X. But UNIX didn't have the fast synchronous IPC; it had a slower asynchronous IPC designed for the embryonic internet. X's performance was worse than awful, and it took a major redesign to get it up to terrible.

Source Control

Programs change: you add to them, you modify them to fix bugs, and so on. How do you keep track of all of your old versions? It's important to be able to go back in time, because you may introduce a bug in a new version and need to see what changed.

Time to flog more UNIXisms. Doug McIlroy created a program called *diff* in the early 1970s that compared two files and generated a list of differences. This program could optionally produce output in a form that could be piped into a text editor so that users could take a file and a list of differences and produce a changed file, leveraging composability. Mark Rochkind built on this idea to create the *Source Code Control System (SCCS)*. Rather than storing a complete copy of every changed file, SCCS stored the original and a list of changes for each version. This allowed users to request any version of the file, which would get constructed on the fly.

SCCS had an awkward user interface, and it was slow because as revisions piled up, more sets of changes had to be applied to reconstruct a version. Walter Tichy released *Revision Control System (RCS)* in 1982. RCS had a better user interface and used backward differencing instead of SCCS's forward differencing, meaning that RCS kept the most recent version and the changes needed to generate older versions. Since the current version was mostly what users wanted, it was much faster.

SCCS and RCS only worked well on a single computer. Dick Grune developed the *Concurrent Versioning System (CVS)*, which essentially provided network access to RCS-like functionality in addition to being the first system to use merges instead of locks.

The original SCCS and RCS tools didn't scale well because they relied on file locking; users would "check out" a file, edit it, and then "check in." A checked-out file couldn't be edited by others. This was especially problematic if someone locked a file and went on vacation. In response to this limitation, *distributed* systems such as Subversion, Bitkeeper, and Git were created. These tools replace the lock problem with the merge problem. Anyone can edit files, but they must reconcile their changes with changes made by others when checking back in.

Use one of these programs to track your code. RCS is very simple and easy to use if you're just working on a project by yourself on your own system. Right now, Git is the most popular for distributed projects. Learn it.

Testing

You can't really know if a program is working unless you test it. Develop a set of tests along with your program. (Some methodologies espouse starting with the tests.) Keep the tests under source control. Again, one of the great things about UNIX automation is that you can craft a single command that fires off a complete batch of tests. It's often useful to do a nightly build, where the program build is started at a particular time every day and tests are run. *Regression testing* is a term used to describe the process of verifying that code changes didn't break anything that used to work. *Regress* in this context means "to go backward"; regression testing helps to make sure that fixed bugs aren't reintroduced.

Several programs are available to help you do testing. While it's complicated, there are frameworks that allow you to test user interfaces by programmatically typing and clicking.

Where possible, have someone else also generate tests for your code. It's natural for the person writing the code to be subconsciously blind to known problems and to avoid writing tests for them.

Bug Reporting and Tracking

Users will find bugs in your code independent from your own testing. You need some way for them to report bugs and some way to track how and whether those bugs were fixed.

Again, there are many tools available to support this.

Refactoring

Refactoring is the process of rewriting code without changing the behavior or interfaces. It's sort of like fast prototyping slowly. Why would you do this? Primarily because when the code was fully fleshed out, it became a mess and you think you know how to do it better. Refactoring can reduce maintenance costs. However, you need a good set of tests to make sure that the refactored code works like it's supposed to. Also, any time things are being rewritten, there's a temptation to add new features—don't give in to it. Refactoring is a good time to reexamine the principles behind what's already been done as mentioned earlier in "Fast Prototyping" on page 432.

Maintenance

One programming fact that's not obvious is that for any serious piece of code, the cost of maintenance greatly exceeds the cost of development. Keep this in mind. Avoid doing cute twisty things that might impress your peers. Remember that if people doing maintenance were as smart as you, they'd be doing design, not maintenance.

In Chapter 12, you saw several different ways to write asynchronous JavaScript code. Some of these ways keep everything in one place, while others separate setup from execution. It takes longer for maintainers to find and fix bugs when they have to track down all of the pieces.

Some programmers believe that a program is a work of art that must be understood in its fullness before being touched. This is a great-sounding philosophy. But in reality, it's more important that someone be able to look at any part of the code and quickly understand what it does. Writing beautiful code that can't be maintained often leads to failure. Find the beauty in making code that's easy to understand.

Something that really helps maintainers if your code talks to hardware is to include references to the hardware datasheets in your code. If you're poking at some register, include the datasheet page number(s) where that register is described.

Be Stylish

People often learn about programming without understanding the environment in which it exists. There are a few things to keep in mind here.

You may not have thought too much about the educational system. Right now it's spewing knowledge at you, some of which you'll actually absorb. Where did this knowledge come from? Other people discovered it. At some point, especially if you pursue an advanced degree, it'll be your turn to discover things that other people will learn. One of the great things about open source software projects is that you can contribute to them. Even if you're not ready to code, many of these projects need help with documentation, so if there's some program that you use or that interests you, get involved. It's a great way to meet people, and it also looks good on college and job applications. Be cautious, as many programmers are not particularly adept socially. Have a thick skin.

When you write software, write it clearly and document it well. Make sure that others can understand what's going on, or nobody will be able to help you. Get your "job security" by garnering a reputation for doing good work instead of by making sure that nobody but you can work on your code. Again, bear in mind that, as I said before, the cost of maintaining software greatly exceeds the cost of development.

Where possible, make your software open source. Give back to the body of work on which you rely.

Learn to write coherent, correctly spelled English (or the human language of your choice). Write real documentation for your code. Avoid documentation-generating tools such as Doxygen. You may have noticed that those are wonderful tools for generating large volumes of worthless documentation.

Documentation needs to describe what the code is doing. It should illuminate the structure of the data and how it is manipulated by the code. My first job writing code was at Bell Telephone Laboratories when I was in high school. Lucky me! My boss told me that every line of code should be commented. Not being very smart at the time, I did things like this:

```
lda foo ; load foo into the accumulator
add 1   ; add 1
sta foo ; store the result back in foo
```

As you can probably see, these comments were completely worthless. It would have been better to say something like:

```
; foo contains the number of gremlins hiding in the corner.
; Bump the count because we just found another.
lda foo
add 1
sta foo
```

Way back in 1985, I had the idea that it would be cool to be able to extract documentation from source code files, especially because you could change the documentation in the same place where you were changing the code. I wrote a tool called *xman* (extract manual) that generated troff-format typeset manuals from the source code. It used a special C comment that began with /** to introduce documentation. On a different world-track, my proposal to teach a course at the 1986 SIGGRAPH conference was accepted. I needed some additional speakers and contacted James Gosling, later an inventor of Java. I demonstrated xman for him. A short time later, we abandoned xman because it became clear that, while it could produce lots of pretty documentation, it was the wrong type of documentation. While correlation does not demonstrate causation (and Gosling doesn't remember), Java included *Javadoc*, a way to include documentation in source files, and documentation was introduced by /** comments. This technique was copied by many other tools. So maybe I'm responsible for this mess.

When you look at automatically generated documentation, it tends to be of the "add 1" variety. There are volumes of documentation that contain only function names, plus the names and types of the arguments. If you can't figure this out just by glancing at the code, you shouldn't be programming! Little of this documentation says what the function does, how it does it, and how it relates to the rest of the system. The moral is, don't be fooled into thinking that fancy tools are the same thing as good documentation. Write good documentation.

One last comment on documentation: include things that are obvious to you, the things that you don't think about at all. People reading your documentation don't know the things that are obvious to you. There is a famous comment in UNIX version 6—which had few comments—that said, "You are not expected to understand this." Not the most helpful!

Fix, Don't Re-create

The software universe, especially the open source part, is littered with partially working programs and programs that do many but not all of the same things. Avoid this type of behavior.

Try to finish both your own projects and those started by others. If you don't finish yours, at least leave them in good enough shape that someone else can easily take over the development. Remember, it's about adding value.

Summary

Now you've learned that programming involves more than just knowing about hardware and software. It's a complex and rewarding endeavor that requires a lot of disparate knowledge. We've covered a lot of ground together. You've seen how to represent and operate on complex information using bits. You've learned why we use bits and how we build them in hardware. We've explored fundamental hardware building blocks and how to assemble those blocks into computers. We looked at the additional functionality needed to make computers more usable and various technologies for connecting computers to the outside world. This was followed by a discussion of how to organize data to take advantage of memory architectures. We looked at the process for converting computer languages into instructions that the hardware can understand. You learned about web browsers and how they organize data and process languages. High-level applications were compared to lower-level system programs. A number of interesting tricks for solving problems were examined, along with a lot of cat pictures. Some of the issues resulting from multitasking were discussed. We looked at the advanced topics of security and machine intelligence, which involved even more cats. Hopefully you noticed that the fundamental building blocks and tricks are used again and again in different combinations. Finally, you learned that the task of programming involves people in addition to hardware and software.

This is all just the beginning. It puts what you've learned or are learning about programming into perspective and gives you a foundation. Don't stop here; there is much, much more to learn.

You might recall that way back in the book's introduction I mentioned the need to understand the universe. It's not possible for any one person to understand everything about the universe. One of the parts that I've never been able to figure out is how to nicely end a book. So that's it. We're done. The end.

INDEX

asynchronous functions and promises, 346–353

Asynchronous JavaScript and XML (AJAX), 252

AT&T, 155

atomic operations, 339, 342, 343

attack surfaces, 355, 373–374

audio

    amplifier transfer function, 39–40

    differential signaling applications, 57

    digital representation, 165–173

    frame layout, 210

audio filters, 168–169

authentication, 356, 358–359, 361–362, 370

authorization, 361

autodialers, 355

autoincrement/autodecrement modes, 114

axon terminals, 401

B

B-trees, 205

Babbage, Charles, 35

back-EMF effect, 48

backdoors and security, 356, 368, 373–374

backpropagation, 404

Backus, John, 222

Backus-Naur form (BNF), 222–223

    examples, 226–227

bandpass filters, 168

bandwidth, 156

Barlow, John Perry, 357

barrel shifters, 100

base-2 system, 6

Base64 encoding, 26–27

bash shell, 437–438

BASIC, 219–220

batch processing, 176

Battle of Midway code breaking, 366–367

Baud rate, 154

Baudot, Émile, 154

Bayer, Bryce, 325

Bayer matrix, 325–326

Bayer, Rudolf, 205

Bayes' theorem, 389–390

Bayes, Thomas, 389

BCD (binary-coded decimal) system, 18

Bechtolsheim, Andy, 439

Bell, Alexander Graham, 56

bell curve, 390–391

Bell Telephone Laboratories, 150, 179, 209, 220, 225, 416, 442

Bentley, Jon, 228

Berners-Lee, Sir Tim, 159, 239–240

Berryman, Jeff, 134

big data, 387, 409–412

binary-coded decimal (BCD) system, 18

binary, defined, 3

binary numbers

    addition with, 8–10

    coded as decimals, 18

    context notation, 20

    as integers, 6–8

    as negative numbers, 10–14

    octal and hexadecimal forms, 18–20

    as real numbers, 14–18

binary thresholds, 41

binary trees, 199–203

binning, 71

bipolar junction transistors (BJTs), 51

bison program, 226

bit density, 87

bitmaps, 187–188, 204, 312

bits

    as binary numbers, 6, 8

    defined, 3

    groupings, 20–22

    overflow, 10

    page table control, 131

    as right choice for technology, 33–34, 40–41

BJTs (bipolar junction transistors), 51

Blaze, Matt, 373–374

blits (terminals), 209

block storage devices

    addressing, 203–204

    hardware, 85–88

blockchain, 371

blocking mode, 341

Bluetooth, 158, 352–353

Boole, George, 4, 386

Boolean algebra, 4–5

booting, 218

bootstrap, defined, 218

Bourne, Stephen, 438

branch prediction, 135

branching instructions, 105–106

Bray, John, 29

breadth-first traversal, 123

break statement (C), 195, 196

Bresenham, Jack, 294–295
browsers. *See* web browsers
buffer overflows, 275, 374–375
buffers
    in logic gates, 53
    program, 270–273, 274
    raster frame, 311
bugs. *See also* errors
    buffer overflow, 275
    likelihood of, 282
    reporting and tracking, 441
    term origin, 50
build tools, 421
Burks, Arthur, 125
buses, 80, 94–95, 96–97
Bush, Vannevar, 159
button circuits, 144–146, 147–148
bytes, defined, 21

C

C programming language
    brief overview, 114, 220
    compiler, 268
    input and output, 274–275
    optimized code examples, 235
    primitive data types, 184–189
    runtime libraries, 275–276
    sorting functions, 213
    unions, 190
C++ language concepts, 211–212
CA (certificate authorities), 370–371
cache management, 134–135
calculator program examples, 226–227,
        229–230
Canny, John, 398
canvas, 255, 290–291
card reader technologies, 84, 85
career success
    decision-making, 427–428
    estimating and scheduling,
        426–427
    job/career vs. calling, 430
    and open source projects, 442–443
    working with people, 428–429
    and workplace culture, 429–430
Carpenter, Loren, 322–323, 429
carrier waves, 155–156
Cartesian coordinate mapping, 291, 301
Cascading Style Sheets (CSS),
        244–248, 267

cat vs. meatloaf image example, 388,
        391–393, 396–400
cathode ray tube (CRT) terminals,
        177–179
cathodes, 50
CDs, 87–88, 170
cel animation, 29–30
cell phone programs, 425
cell phone systems
    security exposures, 361–362,
        373, 376
    surveillance, 359
central processing unit (CPU), 97–102,
        118–119
certificate authorities (CAs), 370–371
chaining code, 348–349
Chang Xiao, 363
Changxi Zheng, 363
characters
    classification, 288–290
    control, 23–24
    defined, 22
    graphics display, 311–312
    and language variations, 439
    numbers as, 25–27
    sorting, 213
    and steganography, 362–363
checksum method, 89
chem (language), 228
Cheng Zhang, 363
Cheriton, David, 439
child nodes, 243
chips. *See also* specific types
    design, 90, 119, 127, 376
    economics, 154
    invention of, 52
chord construction, 166–167, 168
ciphers
    complex, 366–367
    one-time pads, 367
    substitution, 363–365
    transposition, 365–366
ciphertext and cleartext messages, 363
circuit-switched networks, 157
circuits, 44, 47
circular buffers, 272–273
CISC. *See* complicated instruction set
        computers (CISC)
class attribute (CSS), 267

index register, 129
indices
    array, 185
    database, 206
    hash table, 214–215
indirect address registers, 110
indirect addressing
    and linked lists, 193–194
    mode, 104
indirect blocks, 204
infix notation, 125, 227
inline styles, 267
inodes, 203–204
input and output
    computer access to, 96–97
    device drivers, 268–269, 270–273
    in UNIX file abstraction, 435
inputs. *See also* noise
    error-checking, 373, 374
    and transfer functions, 39–40
Institute of Electrical and Electronic
        Engineers (IEEE), 17
instruction register, 109
instructions. *See also* code
    addressing modes, 104–105
    as bit patterns, 101
    branching, 105–106
    condition codes, 105
    data as, 382–384, 387–388
    layouts, 102–104, 106–107
insulators, 43
integer methods
    in CORDIC algorithm, 313–318
    drawing curves, 298–300
    drawing gradients, 296–297
    drawing straight lines, 295–296
    and performance, 290
    with polynomials, 301
integer representations, 6–8
integrated circuits. *See also* chips; logic
        gates, 52, 53, 100
integrated development environments
        (IDEs), 439
integrated peripherals, 127
integrity verification, 370
Intel, 90, 113
interface design, 433–436
interference, 37–38
interior node, 243
International Standards Organization
        (ISO) characters, 24

internet
    accessing, 158–160
    as attack surface, 357–359
interpreters
    vs. compilers, 228–229
    execution, 231–232
    web browsers as, 237
interrupt handlers, 129–130, 375
interrupts, 125–128, 341
inverters, 49, 53–54, 70, 72
IP addresses, 159
isochronous transfers, 156

J

Japanese Industrial Standard (JIS)
        characters, 24
Java programming language, 198, 416,
        422–423
Javadoc, 443
JavaScript language
    and asynchronous issues, 343–346
    function example, 120
    and garbage collection, 198,
        381–382
    "Guess the animal" game,
        264–266, 276
    and jQuery, 254
    and JSON, 255–256
    promise construct, 346–350
    as self-modifying code, 407
    and web browser, 251–253
JavaScript Object Notation (JSON),
        255–256
Johnson, Stephen C., 226
Jordan, Frank, 76
JPEG compression, 122–124, 174
jQuery, 253–254, 345–346
JSON (JavaScript Object Notation),
        255–256

K

Kernighan, Brian, 228, 434, 438
ketchup bottle AI example, 406,
        408–409
key exchanges, 367–369
keyboards, 181
keyframes, 176
Kilby, Jack, 52
kilobytes, defined, 21
Kleene, Stephen Cole, 224

maintenance, 441–442

malloc function (C), 195–196, 197, 379–381

man-in-the-middle attacks, 357, 368

Mandelbrot, Benoit, 319

mantissa, 15–16, 17–18

MapReduce, 216

mark-space signaling, 153–154, 155–156

markup languages, 238–239, 248–251

mask-programmable ROM, 85

masking. *See* shifting and masking

masks
    bitmap, 187
    defined, 85
    interrupt controls, 128
    in raster graphics, 311–312

mass storage, 85–87

Massachusetts Institute of Technology, 407, 416

MD5 hash function, 370

Mead, Carver, 90

Media Access Control (MAC) addresses, 158

medium-scale integration (MSI) parts, 60

megabytes, defined, 21

memory. *See also* storage technologies
    arranging data in, 136–137
    computer access to, 94–96
    error detection and correction, 88–89
    hierarchy and performance, 133–135, 138
    organization and addressing, 79–81
    random access, 82
    read-only, 83–85
    relative addressing, 129–130
    as shared resource, 337

memory chips, 81

memory controller, 134

memory management. *See also* buffer overflows
    bug prevention, 373, 374–375
    in C programming, 276–280
    dynamic allocation, 195–197, 379–381
    garbage collection, 197–198, 381–382

memory management units (MMUs)
    design and operations, 130–132, 133
    and libraries, 138, 195

Men in Black (film), 356

messages, command and control, 358

metadata and security exposure, 359

metal-oxide semiconductor field effect transistors (MOSFETs), 52

Metcalfe, Bob, 158

methodology vs. ideology, 430–431

methods, C++, 211–212

microcode, 112–113

microcomputers, 119, 137, 375

microprocessors, 119, 141–142

Microsoft, 339, 355, 358, 417

Miller, Frank, 367

MIP mapping, 285–288

MIT. *See* Massachusetts Institute of Technology

MKUltra government program, 360

ML. *See* machine learning (ML)

MMUs *See* memory management unit (MMUs)

modems, 156

modulation/demodulation, 155–156

moiré artifacts, 328

MOSFETs (metal-oxide semiconductor field effect transistors), 52

most significant bit (MSB), 8

motion compression, 176

mouse technology, 151, 181

MP3 frame layout, 210

MSB (most significant bit), 8

multicore processors, 119

multiplexers (mux), 65–66

multiplexing, examples, 81, 147

multiplication, 100

multiprocessor systems, 118–119, 216

multitasking, 118, 133, 177, 335–336

The Mythical Man-Month: Essays on Software Engineering (Brooks), 219

N

naive Bayes classifier, 389–390

namespaces, 249

NaN (not a number), 18

NAND gates, 53–54

Napier, John, 34

National Security Agency (NSA), 355, 368, 374

Naur, Peter, 222

negative logic, 5–6

negative number representation, 10–14

Nelson, Nils Peter, 288
networking, 156–160
neural networks, 401–406
new operator, 198
nixie tubes, 63
no-execute bit, 131
Node.js, 424
nodes. *See also* trees
    adding new, 280–281
    in C programming, 276
    coalescing, 307
    leaf, 123
    lexicon, 243
noise
    and differential signaling, 55–57
    immunity, 38, 54–55
nonaligned access, 95
nonblocking mode, 341
nonmaximum suppression, 398
nonrepudiation, 370
NOR gates, 53–54, 72
normalization, of numbers, 17
NOT
    operation, 4–5, 5–6, 11
    with relays, 49
notch filters, 168
Noyce, Robert, 52
NUL terminator, 188, 189
numbers as characters, 25–27
nuxi syndrome, 96
Nyquist, Harry, 169

O

object code, 219
object-oriented programming
            concepts, 211–212
octal representation, 18–19, 20
octets, 24–25
octrees, 310–311
Ohm, Georg Simon, 44
Ohm's law, 44
one-time pads, 367
one's complement representation, 11–13
opcodes, 97, 98
open-collector (or open-drain)
            outputs, 58–59, 148
open source software, 377, 418,
            419–420, 436, 442, 443
OpenCV library, 399
OpenGL graphics language, 181
OpenSSL cryptography library, 377, 436

operands, 97, 221
operating systems (OS)
    context switching, 269–270
    and files, 271–272
    and I/O devices, 259–260, 268–269
    locking functionality, in, 341
    operations, 118, 128–129
    with programs vs. browsers, 273–274
    threads, 337–339
    time-sharing, 177
optical disks, 87–88
optimizers, 234–236
OR
    logic gates, 53–54
    operation, 4–5, 5–6
    in plumbing example, 43
    with relays, 49
Ørsted, Hans Christian, 47
OS. *See* operating systems (OS)
oscillators, 70–71
Ossanna, Joseph, 274
out-of-order execution, 135
outputs
    in differential signaling, 56
    of gates, 58–60
    and transfer functions, 39–40
overclocking, 71
overflow condition, 10

P

package management, 421–422
packet-switched networks, 157
packets (USB), 156
padding, 190
page fault exception, 131
page swapping, 132
page tables, 130–131
pages, 82, 130–131
The Paging Game (Berryman), 134
parallel communications, 152, 154
parallel connections, 43
parallel processing, 119
PARC. *See* Xerox Palo Alto Research
            Center (PARC)
parent node, 243
parity checking, 89
parse trees
    construction and evaluation,
            229–230, 231
    examples, 242–243
    optimizing, 234

Pascal (programming language), 220
passive pull-ups, 59
password exposures, 353, 354, 378
password management, 371–372
path (URL), 240
pattern matching, 224–225
Patterson, David, 113
PCs. *See* personal computers (PCs)
PDF (Portable Document Format),
    254–255
Peano, Giuseppe, 319
perceptrons, 402–403
periodic signals, 70
peripherals, 96, 127
personal computers (PCs), 417, 418
personal data
    privacy, 352, 359–361, 410–412
    and trust, 353–355, 361
phase difference, 170
phone security, 359, 361, 362, 373
phones. *See* cell phone programs; cell
        phone systems
photolithograpy, 51
physical security, 355–356
piezoelectric effect, 70
Pike, Robert, 24, 209, 434
pins, defined, 127
pip (Peripheral Interchange Program,
        DEC), 434
pixels
    in Gaussian blur, 392–393
    as image representation, 27, 173
    and MIP mapping, 286
    unions, 190–191
    in video, 175
    voxels, 310
PKI (public key infrastructure),
        370–371
pointers, 114, 184–185, 212
polar coordinates, 301–304
Polish notation, 125
polling, 127
pop and push, 124
portable device programming, 425
Portable Document Format (PDF),
        254–255
portable operating system interface
        (POSIX), 421
portable software, 416, 420–421,
        439–440
Porter, Thomas, 30

ports
    I/O, 97, 142–144
    IEEE 1284 parallel, 152
    RS-232 serial, 154
positive logic, 5–6
positive number representation, 6–8
POSIX (portable operating system
        interface), 421, 439
post function (jQuery), 345–346
postfix notation, 125, 227
PostScript language, 124, 254
power consumption vs. performance, 138
power series approximations, 313
power wall, 119
prefetching, 135
prefix notation, 125
prepress technologies, 29
primitive data types
    arrays, 185–187
    bitmaps, 187–188
    overview, 184–185
    strings, 188–189
Principles of Compiler Design (Aho and
        Ullman), 228
print servers, 337–338
printers
    color system, 173
    and steganography, 363
printf (print formatted) function
        (C), 277
priority interrupts, 128
privacy. *See also* personal data
    and data visibility, 378–379
    as security, 352
privileged instructions, 133
privileges, and security, 356
PRNGs (pseudorandom number
        generators), 375
procedures. *See* functions
processes, 337–338
processor cores, 119, 135
processor interrupt handling, 341
production grammars, 320–322
program counter, 101–102
programmable read-only memory
        (PROM), 85
programmers. *See also* career success
    adding value, 414–416, 442, 443
    finishing projects, 419
    productive environment for,
        437–439
    training, 418, 426

surveillance, 359
SVG (Scalable Vector Graphics), 254–255
switches
    electrical, 44–47
    networking, 157
    in plumbing example, 43
symbols, 2, 3, 221
symmetric encryption, 364, 367–368
synchronous counters, 77–78
syntactic sugar, 189, 346, 347
system calls, 133, 269–271, 343
system integrators, 377
system on a chip (SoC), 119
system programming vs. application
        programming, 259, 282
system space, 133

T

table lookups
    character classification, 288–290
    conversion tables, 284
    texture mapping, 285–288
tags, 241–242, 248
Talbot, Henry, 325
tape technologies, 84, 85, 87
Taylor series, 313
TCP/IP (Transmission Control
        Protocol/Internet
        Protocol), 158–159
Tektronix storage tubes, 179
telephone networks, 157
telephone technologies, 155
teletype technology, 153–154, 176–177
The Ten Commandments for C Programmers
        (Spencer), 372
terabytes, defined, 21
terminal node, 243
terminals
    blit, 209
    and buffering, 270–271
    as coding interface, 437
    hardcopy output, 176–177
    screen based, 177–178
    software implemented, 268–269
test and set instruction, 342
testing, 440–441
Texas Instruments, 53
text editors, 438–439
text. *See* characters
texture mapping, 285–288
third-party code, 376–378, 436

This Is Spinal Tap (film), 39
Thompson, Ken, 24, 224, 377, 416,
        417, 434
thrashing, 177
threads, 338–339
threat model, 352–353, 378
thresholds
    binary vs. decimal, 41
    in graphics, 324
    in hyperesis, 55
    negative- and positive-going, 55–56
    and transfer functions, 49
Tiemann, Michael, 418
time and date structure, 189–190
time division multiplexing, 154, 157
time references, 70–71
time-sharing systems, 177
timers, 128, 133
timing attacks, 378
tokens, 221, 225–226
Torvalds, Linus, 418
totem-pole outputs, 58
touch devices, 181
traffic control unit, 110–113
transactions, 340–341
transfer functions, 38–40, 49, 54–55, 168
transformations (graphic), 291
transistors, 51–52
translations (graphic), 291
Transmission Control Protocol/
        Internet Protocol (TCP/IP),
        158–159, 211
transparency
    color, 29–30
    open source code, 376–378
    and security, 355
transposition ciphers, 365–366
trapdoor functions, 368
tree balancing, 202–203
tree lexicon, 243
tree of knowledge, 260, 262
tree traversal, 123, 244, 280–281
trees. *See also* nodes; octrees; quadtrees
    B-tree, 205
    binary, 199–203
    defined, 123
    examples, 229–230, 242–243
tri-state outputs, 60
trigonometric functions, 301, 313–318
triodes, 50–51
troff (typesetting language), 228, 239,
        274–275